Lecture Notes in Compute

Commenced Publication in 1973
Founding and Former Series Editors:
Gerhard Goos, Juris Hartmanis, and Jan van Leeuwen

Adrian-Horia Dediu Carlos Martín-Vide
Bianca Truthe (Eds.)

Theory and Practice of Natural Computing

First International Conference, TPNC 2012
Tarragona, Spain, October 2-4, 2012
Proceedings

Springer

Volume Editors

Adrian-Horia Dediu
Universitat Rovira i Virgili
Research Group on Mathematical Linguistics
Avinguda Catalunya, 35
43002 Tarragona, Spain
E-mail: adrian.dediu@urv.cat

Carlos Martín-Vide
Universitat Rovira i Virgili
Research Group on Mathematical Linguistics
Avinguda Catalunya, 35
43002 Tarragona, Spain
E-mail: carlos.martin@urv.cat

Bianca Truthe
Otto-von-Guericke-Universität Magdeburg
Fakultät für Informatik
Universitätsplatz 2
39106 Magdeburg, Germany
E-mail: truthe@iws.cs.uni-magdeburg.de

ISSN 0302-9743   e-ISSN 1611-3349
ISBN 978-3-642-33859-5   e-ISBN 978-3-642-33860-1
DOI 10.1007/978-3-642-33860-1
Springer Heidelberg Dordrecht London New York

Library of Congress Control Number: 2012947810

CR Subject Classification (1998): F.1, I.2, C.2, F.2, I.4, H.4, J.3

LNCS Sublibrary: SL 1 – Theoretical Computer Science and General Issues

Typesetting: Camera-ready by author, data conversion by Scientific Publishing Services, Chennai, India

Printed on acid-free paper

Springer is part of Springer Science+Business Media (www.springer.com)

Preface

These proceedings contain the papers that were presented at the First International Conference on the Theory and Practice of Natural Computing (TPNC 2012), held in Tarragona, Spain, during October 2–4, 2012.

The scope of TPNC is rather broad, containing topics of either theoretical, experimental, or applied interest. The topics include but are not limited to:

Nature-inspired models of computation
- amorphous computing
- cellular automata
- chaos and dynamical systems based computing
- evolutionary computing
- membrane computing
- neural computing
- optical computing
- swarm intelligence

Synthesizing nature by means of computation
- artificial chemistry
- artificial immune systems
- artificial life

Nature-inspired materials
- computing with DNA
- nanocomputing
- physarum computing
- quantum computing and quantum information
- reaction-diffusion computing

Information processing in nature
- developmental systems
- fractal geometry
- gene assembly in unicellular organisms
- rough/fuzzy computing in nature
- synthetic biology
- systems biology

Applications of natural computing to algorithms, bioinformatics, control, cryptography, design, economics, graphics, hardware, learning, logistics, optimization, pattern recognition, programming, robotics, telecommunications, etc.

TPNC 2012 received 34 submissions. Each one was reviewed by three Program Committee members and there were also several external referees. After a thorough and vivid discussion phase, the committee decided to accept 12 papers (which represents an acceptance rate of 35.29%). The conference program also included six invited talks and one invited tutorial.

Part of the success in the management of the submissions and reviews is due to the excellent facilities provided by the EasyChair conference management system.

We would like to thank all invited speakers and authors for their contributions, the Program Committee and the reviewers for their cooperation, and Springer for its very professional publishing work.

July 2012

Adrian-Horia Dediu
Carlos Martín-Vide
Bianca Truthe

Organization

TPNC 2012 was organized by the Research Group on Mathematical Linguistics, GRLMC, from the University Rovira i Virgili, Tarragona, Spain.

Program Committee

Ajith Abraham	Auburn, USA
Selim G. Akl	Kingston, Canada
Enrique Alba	Málaga, Spain
Artiom Alhazov	Chişinău, Moldova
Peter J. Bentley	London, UK
Mauro Birattari	Brussels, Belgium
Christian Blum	Barcelona, Spain
Óscar Castillo	Tijuana, Mexico
Weng-Long Chang	Kaohsiung, Taiwan
Parimal Pal Chaudhuri	Calcutta, India
Carlos A. Coello Coello	Mexico City, Mexico
Kalyanmoy Deb	Kanpur, India
Peter Dittrich	Jena, Germany
Andries Petrus Engelbrecht	Pretoria, South Africa
Toshio Fukuda	Nagoya, Japan
Enrique Herrera-Viedma	Granada, Spain
César Hervás-Martínez	Córdoba, Spain
Julia Kempe	Tel Aviv, Israel and Paris, France
Elmar Wolfgang Lang	Regensburg, Germany
Pier Luca Lanzi	Milan, Italy
Vincenzo Manca	Verona, Italy
Maurice Margenstern	Metz, France
Carlos Martín-Vide	Tarragona, Spain (Chair)
Kaisa Miettinen	Jyväskylä, Finland
Michael O'Neill	Dublin, Ireland
Ferdinand Peper	Kobe, Japan
Ion Petre	Turku, Finland
Carla Piazza	Udine, Italy
A.C. Cem Say	Istanbul, Turkey
Jürgen Schmidhuber	Lugano, Switzerland
Moshe Sipper	Beer-Sheva, Israel
El-Ghazali Talbi	Lille, France

Kay Chen Tan	Singapore
Jirí Wiedermann	Prague, Czech Republic
Takashi Yokomori	Tokyo, Japan
Ivan Zelinka	Ostrava, Czech Republic

External Reviewers

Casagrande, Alberto
Czeizler, Elena
Czeizler, Eugen
Dediu, Adrian-Horia
Kobayashi, Satoshi

Organizing Committee

Adrian-Horia Dediu, Tarragona
Peter Leupold, Tarragona
Carlos Martín-Vide, Tarragona (Chair)
Bianca Truthe, Magdeburg
Florentina-Lilica Voicu, Tarragona

Table of Contents

Hybrid Metaheuristics in Combinatorial Optimization: A Tutorial

Christian Blum

ALBCOM Research Group, Universitat Politécnica de Catalunya
c/ Jordi Girona 1-3, Barcelona, Spain
cblum@lsi.upc.edu

Abstract. This article is about a tutorial on hybrid metaheuristics which was given at the first edition of the conference *Theory and Practice of Natural Computing*, held in October 2012 in Tarragona, Spain. Hybrid metaheuristics are techniques for (combinatorial) optimization that result from a combination of algorithmic components originating from different optimization methods. The tutorial covers five representative examples: (1) the extension of iterated local search towards population-based optimization, (2) the introduction of elements from constraint programming into ant colony optimization, (3) the integration of branch & bound into variable neighborhood search, (4) the use of problem relaxation for guiding tabu search, and (5) the combination of dynamic programming with evolutionary algorithms.

Keywords: hybrid metaheuristics, combinatorial optimization.

1 Introduction

The research activity in the area of metaheuristics for combinatorial optimization problems [21,10,6] has lately witnessed a noteworthy shift towards the combination of metaheuristics with other techniques for optimization. Moreover, the research focus has changed from being mostly algorithm-oriented to being more problem-oriented. In other words, in contrast to promoting a certain metaheuristic, researchers nowadays rather aim at solving the problem at hand in the best way possible. This requires, inevitably, that researchers not only focus on their preferred technique for optimization, but also study other research lines in optimization. This has led to a fruitful cross-fertilization of different optimization lines, which is documented by a multitude of powerful hybrid algorithms that were developed as combinations of two (or more) different optimization techniques. Hereby, hybridization is not restricted to the combination of different metaheuristics but includes, for example, the combination of metaheuristics with exact algorithms.

This tutorial provides an overview of the research field of hybrid metaheuristics for combinatorial optimization problems. This is done by illustrating prominent and paradigmatic examples, which range from the integration of

A.-H. Dediu, C. Martín-Vide, and B. Truthe (Eds.): TPNC 2012, LNCS 7505, pp. 1–10, 2012.

Algorithm 1. Iterated Local Search

1: $s \leftarrow$ GenerateInitialSolution()
2: $\hat{s} \leftarrow$ LocalSearch(s)
3: **while** termination conditions not met **do**
4:     $s' \leftarrow$ Perturbation($\hat{s}, history$)
5:     $\hat{s}' \leftarrow$ LocalSearch(s')
6:     $\hat{s} \leftarrow$ ApplyAcceptanceCriterion($\hat{s}', \hat{s}, history$)
7: **end while**

---

metaheuristic techniques among themselves, to the combination of metaheuristics with exact methods such as dynamic programming. Each of the following five sections is devoted to one such example. In addition, the interested reader may consult [7,9,19,4,20,12,14,5] for obtaining more information on hybrid metaheuristics.

2   Population-Based Iterated Local Search

The example presented in this section deals with the combination of algorithmic components originating from different metaheuristics. A prime example for this type of hybridization is the use of local search within population-based techniques such as evolutionary algorithms and ant colony optimization. In contrast, the example presented in the following deals with the enhancement of a metaheuristic based on local search—namely, iterated local search—with concepts from population-based approaches. The resulting algorithm, which was applied to the quadratic assignment problem (QAP), was labelled *population-based iterated local search* [25].

Iterated local search (ILS) [24,13] is an extension of simple local search, which works as follows (see also Algorithm 1). First, an initial solution s is generated either randomly or by some heuristic. Then, local search is applied to improve this initial solution. At each iteration, the algorithm first generates a perturbation s' of the current solution s. Afterwards, local search is applied to s', which hopefully results in a local optimum $\hat{s}'$ that is different to s. Finally, the last action of each iteration consists in choosing between s and $\hat{s}'$ as the incumbent solution for the next iteration. This action is called the *acceptance criterion*, which may—or may not— be based on search history. The most basic acceptance criterion simply chooses the better solution between s and $\hat{s}'$. The method for generating the perturbation is generally non-deterministic. Moreover, the degree of the perturbation is crucial for the working of the algorithm. In case the perturbation is too weak, the perturbed solution s' may still be in the basin of attraction of solution s. On the other side, if the perturbation is too strong the algorithm resembles a random-restart local search method.

The extension of ILS to work in a population-based way (as proposed in [25]) is rather simple. Instead of being restricted to maintain one single incumbent solution at all times, population-based ILS maintains a whole population P of size n. At each iteration, the three main steps of ILS—that is, perturbation,

---

Algorithm 2. Population-Based Iterated Local Search

1: $P \leftarrow$ GenerateInitialPopulation(n)
2: Apply LocalSearch() to all $s \in P$
3: **while** termination conditions not met **do**
4:     $P' \leftarrow P$
5:     **for** all $s \in P$ **do**
6:         $s' \leftarrow$ Perturbation($s, history$)
7:         $\hat{s}' \leftarrow$ LocalSearch(s')
8:         $P' \leftarrow P' \cup \{\hat{s}'\}$
9:     **end for**
10:    $P \leftarrow$ Best n solutions from P'
11: **end while**

---

local search, and the acceptance criterion—are applied to each of the n solutions in P. The resulting solutions are added to P and, finally, the worst n solutions are deleted from P. The pseudo-code of this procedure is shown in Algorithm 2.

3   Combining Ant Colony Optimization with Constraint Programming

Ant colony optimization (ACO) is a metaheuristic inspired by the foraging behavior of ants [8]. In general, the ACO approach attempts to solve an optimization problem by iterating the following two steps: (1) candidate solutions are constructed using a pheromone model, that is, a parameterized probability distribution over the search space, and (2) the candidate solutions are used to modify the pheromone values in a way that is aimed at biasing future sampling toward areas in the search space containing high quality solutions. In particular, the reinforcement of solution components depending on the solution quality is an important aspect of ACO algorithms. It implicitly assumes that good solutions consist of good solution components. To learn which components contribute to good solutions can help assembling them into better solutions.

In constraint programming (CP) [15], constrained optimization problems are modelled by means of variables together with their domains, and constraints. Each constraint is associated to a *filtering* algorithm whose purpose is to delete values from variable domains which do not contribute to feasible solutions. The solution process of CP is characterized by an alternation of a so-called *propagation* phase—in which values are removed from domains by means of the filtering algorithm— and a *labelling* phase, in which an unassigned variable is chosen and assigned a value from its domain. In case of an empty domain, backtracking is performed. When an optimization problem is tackled, a bound constraint on the cost function is posted every time a new improving solution is found. This way, non-improving assignments are considered infeasible.

Both ACO and CP are based on the construction of solutions. Moreover, the following complementary strengths can be identified: ACO is characterized by a learning capability, while CP is efficient in handling constraints. The core idea

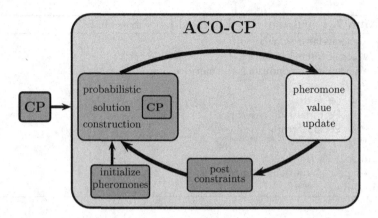

Fig. 1. A possible integration of CP into ACO. First, CP may be applied for reducing the variable domains before the ACO algorithm is even started. Second, CP may be used to filter the variable domains during each solution construction. Moreover, whenever a new best solution is found, a global constraint may be posted in order to enforce that all constructed solutions should be better.

of the hybridization of ACO and CP proposed by Meyer in [16] is illustrated in Figure 1. Moreover, a general framework for combining ACO and CP, along with insights on the possible ways for integrating both methods, is the subject of a book by Solnon [23].

As shown in Figure 1, the combination of ACO and CP adopts the main algorithmic framework of ACO and makes use of CP as a tool employed by the ants while constructing a solution. The usual approach for constraint handling in ACO—and any metaheuristics, for that matter—is to relax some (or all) of the problem constraints and penalize complete solutions that violate these constraints. This procedure may not be very useful, especially in case of highly constrained problems. Therefore, the fact that ants make use of CP for finding feasible solutions concentrates the search on good-quality solutions that are feasible. Experimental practice shows that a large amount of computational effort—in comparison to the pure ACO approach—can be saved in this way. At this point it is important to observe that, in the algorithmic scheme as presented in Figure 1, the choice of solution components during the construction of solutions comes into play in the context of variable and value selection. In other words, while CP provides filtering mechanisms, ACO is used for labelling.

4   Variable Neighborhood Search Hybridized with Large Neighborhood Search

The most crucial decision when applying local search (or neighborhood search) generally concerns the choice of an appropriate neighborhood structure for generating the set of neighboring solutions—that is, the neighborhood—of any feasible

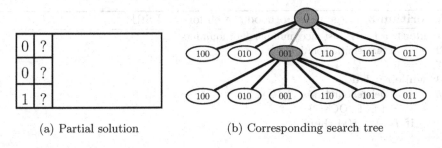

(a) Partial solution   (b) Corresponding search tree

Fig. 2. (a) shows a partial solution for the FSRP (where $k = 3$) with the first column already filled. (b) shows the corresponding (partial) search tree of the B&B-method RECBLOCK.

solution. In those cases in which the neighborhoods are rather small, the search for an improving neighbor will be rather fast. However, the average quality of the local minima will be low. On the other side, when neighborhoods are rather large, the search for improving neighbors make take a considerable amount of computation time, but the average quality of the local minima will be rather high. Therefore, depending on the way in which local search is to be utilized, an appropriate neighborhood structure must be found such that the computational cost is not too high and the average quality of the local minima is acceptable.

Rather recent research has shown that, in some cases, it is possible to define large neighborhoods that can efficiently be explored by a complete method such as constraint programming, mixed-integer programming, and dynamic programming. In many of these cases, finding the best solution within a neighborhood is itself an NP-hard problem. This field of research is nowadays known as *large neighborhood search*. The interested reader may find further information on large neighborhood search in [18,17].

In the following we shortly describe an example application of large neighborhood search in the context of a problem from computational biology, the founder sequence reconstruction problem (FSRP) [22]. For the subsequent description it is sufficient to know that solutions to the FSRP are binary matrices of size $k \times n$, where k is the number of rows and n is the number of columns. Note that k is also referred to as the number of *founders*. When n, and especially k, are small the literature offers an efficient branch & bound (B&B) method, called RECBLOCK, for solving the problem to optimality [28]. This algorithm works by filling the columns of the solution matrix one-by-one, starting at the left-hand side; see Figure 2. Unfortunately, due to excessive computation time requirements RECBLOCK can not be used when k and n grow large.

Therefore, Roli et al. [22] developed a large neighborhood search technique which makes use of RECBLOCK as a subordinate method, embedded in the framework of a metaheuristic known as variable neighborhood search (VNS) [11]. Generally, VNS works on a set of neighborhood structures $\mathcal{N}_1, \ldots, \mathcal{N}_l$. Given a current solution s and a current neighborhood structure with index r, VNS randomly chooses a solution from $\mathcal{N}_r(s)$. Then, local search is applied to this

---

Algorithm 3. Large neighborhood search for the FSRP

1: INPUT: a FSRP instance, number k of founders
2: $s :=$ GenerateInitialSolution()
3: $r := 1$
4: **while** $r \leq k$ **do**
5:     $\hat{s} :=$ DeleteFounders(s, r)
6:     $s' :=$ RECBLOCK($\hat{s}$)
7:     **if** $f(s') < f(s)$ **then**
8:         $s := s'$
9:         $r := 1$
10:    **else**
11:        **if** maximal number of trials reached **then** $r := r + 1$
12:    **end if**
13: **end while**
14: OUTPUT: best solution (s) generated

---

solution on the basis of a neighborhood structure $\mathcal{N}$ which is different to the other l neighborhood structures. If the resulting solution ($\hat{s}$) is better than s, $\hat{s}$ is adopted as the new current solution and r is set to 1. Otherwise, a random solution from $\mathcal{N}_{r+1}(s)$ is chosen and local search is applied. This scheme is repeated until the stopping criterion is met.

In the context of the FSRP, the neighborhood $\mathcal{N}_r$ of a solution s is generated as follows. First, r rows are randomly deleted from the binary matrix corresponding to s. The neighborhood consists of all feasible solutions that contain the resulting partial solution. The main idea of the LNS approach for the FSRP is the fact that when r is rather small, RECBLOCK can be used to generate the best neighbor in an efficient way. In other words, given a partial solution with r deleted rows, RECBLOCK is used to generate the best filling for these rows. As shown in Algorithm 3, this mechanism is embedded in the framework of (a slightly modified) VNS.

5   Combining Tabu Search with Problem Relaxation

Relaxations of difficult combinatorial optimization problems may be obtained in several different ways. Examples concern the simplification of certain problem constraints, the dropping of constraints such as, for example, integrality constraints, or the moving of constraints to form part of an augmented objective function. A well-known example for this last methodology is Lagrangian relaxation. Such relaxations may assist in different ways for solving the original optimization problems. Branch & bound algorithms, for example, heavily rely on tight bounds, which may be obtained by means of problem relaxations. Another example concerns the dropping of integrality constraints. The optimal solution to such a relaxation may be rounded to be an integer solution. Finally, information obtained from relaxations may also be used as a type of greedy information for the construction of solutions.

The example of a hybrid between a metaheuristic and problem relaxation which is presented in this section concerns the combination of tabu search with problem relaxation in the context of the multi-dimensional 0–1 knapsack problem (MKP) [26,27]. The main idea of the proposed algorithm consists in solving (to optimality) a number of relaxed problems obtained by dropping the integrality constraints. A first algorithmic phase is used for this purpose. In a second phase, tabu search is applied to search around the optimal solutions to the relaxed problems. Hereby, tabu search is obliged to stay within a sphere around the non-integral solutions. This approach is described in more detail in the following.

The MKP may be stated as follows. Given are n objects, each object i having a profit c_i. Moreover, given are m resources, each resource j having a capacity b_j. Moreover, each object i has a requirement a_{ij} of each resource j. A binary decision variable $x_i \in \{0, 1\}$ for each object i indicates if an object is chosen or not. The goal is choose a set of objects that fulfills the problem constraints and that maximizes the total profit. The MKP can be expressed in terms of the following integer program:

$$\mathbf{max} \sum_{i=1}^{n} c_i \cdot x_i \tag{1}$$

subject to

$$\sum_{i=1}^{n} a_{ij} \cdot x_i \leq b_j \qquad j = 1, \ldots, m \tag{2}$$

$$x_i \in \{0, 1\} \qquad i = 1, \ldots, n \tag{3}$$

Note that the LP relaxation obtained by replacing (3) by inequalities $\{0 \leq x_i \leq 1 \mid i = 1, \ldots, n\}$ may not be very helpful. This is because it is known that the structure of an optimal solution to this relaxation may not have much in common with the structure of an optimal solution to the original MKP. Therefore, the main idea by Vasquez and Hao was to add a constraint that fixes the number of selected items to a certain value k, i.e.

$$\sum_{i=1}^{n} x_i = k \ , \tag{4}$$

where $k \in I\!\!N$. In addition, the integrality constraints are dropped. In this way the optimal solutions to the relaxed problems are generally closer in structure to good (or optimal) solutions to the original MKP. The relaxed problems are then solved to optimality for all k between a lower bound $k_{\min}$ and an upper bound $k_{\max}$, where $0 \leq k_{\min} \leq k_{\max} \leq n$. These bounds are computed by solving a linear program for each of them. We refer to [26] for more details.

The second phase of the algorithm applies tabu search to search around the non-integral solutions obtained during the first algorithm phase. For each k, tabu search is restricted to solutions where exactly k objects are selected. Moreover, tabu search is restricted to search in the vicinity of the non-integral solutions. The algorithm presented in [27] is further enhanced by various variable fixing strategies.

6 Utilizing Dynamic Programming within Metaheuristics

The last hybridization example which is presented in this tutorial concerns the use of dynamic programming (DP) within two different metaheuristics. Just like branch & bound, DP is another example of an optimization method from operations research and control theory that can be successfully integrated with metaheuristics. The nature of DP is as follows. It provides a method for defining an optimal strategy that leads from an initial state to the final goal state. DP has been successfully applied to many optimization and control problems. The interested reader may find many examples in [1].

In [3], Blum and Blesa present the use of a DP algorithm within two different metaheuristics for the so-called k-cardinality tree (KCT) problem. The general idea of their approaches may also be interesting for the solution of optimization problems other than the KCT problem. In particular, it may be useful in the context of other subset selection problems. The basic idea of the algorithms proposed in [3] is to let the metaheuristic generate objects that are larger than solutions. In general, these objects may contain an exponential number of solutions to the problem under consideration. DP is then used to extract from each of these objects the best solution it contains. The implementation of this idea for the KCT problem is described in more detail in the following.

The KCT problem can technically be formalized as follows. Let $G(V, E)$ be an undirected graph. Each edge $e \in E$ has a weight $w_e \geq 0$, and each node $v \in V$ has a weight $w_v \geq 0$. Furthermore, $\mathcal{T}_k$ denotes the set of all k-cardinality trees in G, that is, the set of all trees with exactly k edges. The problem consists in finding a k-cardinality tree $T_k \in \mathcal{T}_k$ that minimizes the following objective function:

$$f(T_k) = \left(\sum_{e \in E_{T_k}} w_e \right) + \left(\sum_{v \in V_{T_k}} w_v \right) \tag{5}$$

Hereby, E_{T_k} denotes the set of edges and V_{T_k} the set of nodes of T_k. In those cases in which G is itself a tree, the KCT problem can efficiently be solved by DP [2]. This DP algorithm was beneficially used within the ACO approach and the EC approach presented in [3].

The main idea of the ACO approach can be stated as follows. At each iteration, a number of n_a artificial ants construct solutions in a step-by-step manner. However, instead of concluding the solution construction once a k-cardinality tree is obtained, the construction process is continued until the corresponding tree has $k < l \leq |V| - 1$ edges. Afterwards, DP is applied to each of the constructed l-cardinality trees in order to find the best k-cardinality trees in each of them. The resulting k-cardinality trees are then used for updating the pheromone values. In the context of the EC approach presented in [3], DP is used within the crossover operator. This operator works on the basis of two different k-cardinality input trees. These two trees are merged, resulting in a tree that contains more than k edges. Finally, DP is applied to this larger tree in order to obtain the best k-cardinality tree it contains. This resulting tree serves as the output of the crossover operator.

Both algorithms that were shortly sketched above obtain better solutions faster than their *standard* counterparts. This holds especially for rather large input graphs.

7　Conclusions

This tutorial has covered five representative examples for the combination of a metaheuristic with another technique for solving combinatorial optimization problems. In general, the last years have shown a growing interest of the research community in such hybrid algorithms. Specialized workshops and conferences such as **CPAIOR** (Constraint Programming, Artificial Intelligence, Operations Research), **HM** (Hybrid Metaheuristics), and **Matheuristics** are indicators of this trend. In the opinion of the author, the field of hybrid metaheuristics still offers sufficient room for new developments and research lines. Especially useful could be the development of guidelines for the use of certain types of (hybrid) metaheuristics when facing different optimization problems.

Acknowledgements. This work was supported by grant TIN2007-66523 (FOR-MALISM) of the Spanish government.

References

1. Bertsekas, D.P.: Dynamic Programming and Optimal Control, 3rd edn. Athena Scientific, Nashua (2007)
2. Blum, C.: Revisiting dynamic programming for finding optimal subtrees in trees. European Journal of Operational Research 177(1), 102–115 (2007)
3. Blum, C., Blesa, M.J.: Solving the KCT problem: Large-scale neighborhood search and solution merging. In: Alba, E., Blum, C., Isasi, P., León, C., Gómez, J.A. (eds.) Optimization Techniques for Solving Complex Problems, pp. 407–421. Wiley & Sons, Hoboken (2009)
4. Blum, C., Blesa Aguilera, M.J., Roli, A., Sampels, M. (eds.): Hybrid Metaheuristics – An Emerging Approach to Optimization. SCI, vol. 114. Springer, Berlin (2008)
5. Blum, C., Puchinger, J., Raidl, G., Roli, A.: Hybrid metaheuristics in combinatorial optimization: A survey. Applied Soft Computing 11(6), 4135–4151 (2011)
6. Blum, C., Roli, A.: Metaheuristics in combinatorial optimization: Overview and conceptual comparison. ACM Computing Surveys 35(3), 268–308 (2003)
7. Cotta, C.: A study of hybridisation techniques and their application to the design of evolutionary algorithms. AI Communications 11(3-4), 223–224 (1998)
8. Dorigo, M., Stützle, T.: Ant Colony Optimization. MIT Press, Cambridge (2004)
9. Dumitrescu, I., Stützle, T.: Combinations of Local Search and Exact Algorithms. In: Raidl, G.R., Cagnoni, S., Cardalda, J.J.R., Corne, D.W., Gottlieb, J., Guillot, A., Hart, E., Johnson, C.G., Marchiori, E., Meyer, J.-A., Middendorf, M. (eds.) EvoWorkshops 2003. LNCS, vol. 2611, pp. 211–223. Springer, Heidelberg (2003)
10. Glover, F., Kochenberger, G. (eds.): Handbook of Metaheuristics. International Series in Operations Research & Management Science, vol. 57. Kluwer Academic Publishers (2003)

11. Hansen, P., Mladenovic, N., Brimberg, J., Moreno Pérez, J.A.: Variable neighborhood search. In: Gendreau, M., Potvin, J.Y. (eds.) Handbook of Metaheuristics, 2nd edn. International Series in Operations Research & Management Science, vol. 146, pp. 61–86. Springer, Berlin (2010)
12. Jourdan, L., Basseur, M., Talbi, E.: Hybridizing exact methods and metaheuristics: A taxonomy. European Journal of Operational Research 199(3), 620–629 (2009)
13. Lourenço, H.R., Martin, O., Stützle, T.: Iterated local search. In: Glover, F., Kochenberger, G. (eds.) Handbook of Metaheuristics. International Series in Operations Research & Management Science, vol. 57, pp. 321–353. Kluwer Academic Publishers, Norwell (2002)
14. Maniezzo, V., Stützle, T., Voß, S. (eds.): Matheuristics. Annals of Information Systems, vol. 10. Springer, Berlin (2010)
15. Marriott, K., Stuckey, P.J.: Introduction to Constraint Logic Programming. MIT Press, Cambridge (1998)
16. Meyer, B.: Hybrids of constructive meta-heuristics and constraint programming: A case study with ACO. In: Blum, et al. [4], vol. 114, ch. 6, pp. 151–183 (2008)
17. Pesant, G., Gendreau, M.: A Constraint Programming Framework for Local Search Methods. Journal of Heuristics 5, 255–279 (1999)
18. Pisinger, D., Ropke, S.: Large neighborhood search. In: Gendreau, M., Potvin, J.Y. (eds.) Handbook of Metaheuristics, 2nd edn. International Series in Operations Research & Management Science, vol. 146, pp. 399–419. Springer, Berlin (2010)
19. Raidl, G.R.: A Unified View on Hybrid Metaheuristics. In: Almeida, F., Blesa Aguilera, M.J., Blum, C., Moreno Vega, J.M., Pérez Pérez, M., Roli, A., Sampels, M. (eds.) HM 2006. LNCS, vol. 4030, pp. 1–12. Springer, Heidelberg (2006)
20. Raidl, G.R., Puchinger, J., Blum, C.: Metaheuristic hybrids. In: Gendreau, M., Potvin, J.Y. (eds.) Handbook of Metaheuristics, 2nd edn. International Series in Operations Research & Management Science, vol. 146, pp. 469–496. Springer, Berlin (2010)
21. Reeves, C.R. (ed.): Modern heuristic techniques for combinatorial problems. John Wiley & Sons, New York (1993)
22. Roli, A., Benedettini, S., Stützle, T., Blum, C.: Large neighbourhood search algorithms for the founder sequence reconstruction problem. Computers & Operations Research 39(2), 213–224 (2012)
23. Solnon, C.: Ant Colony Optimization and Constraint Programming. Wiley-ISTE (2010)
24. Stützle, T.: Local Search Algorithms for Combinatorial Problems - Analysis, Algorithms and New Applications. DISKI - Dissertationen zur Künstlichen Intelligenz, Infix, Sankt Augustin, Germany (1999)
25. Stützle, T.: Iterated local search for the quadratic assignment problem. European Journal of Operational Research 174(3), 1519–1539 (2006)
26. Vasquez, M., Hao, J.K.: A hybrid approach for the 0–1 multidimensional knapsack problem. In: Nebel, B. (ed.) Proceedings of the 17th International Joint Conference on Artificial Intelligence, IJCAI 2001, pp. 328–333. Morgan Kaufman, Seattle (2001)
27. Vasquez, M., Vimont, Y.: Improved results on the 0–1 multidimensional knapsack problem. European Journal of Operational Research 165(1), 70–81 (2005)
28. Wu, Y., Gusfield, D.: Improved Algorithms for Inferring the Minimum Mosaic of a Set of Recombinants. In: Ma, B., Zhang, K. (eds.) CPM 2007. LNCS, vol. 4580, pp. 150–161. Springer, Heidelberg (2007)

Theory and Applications
of DNA Codeword Design

Max H. Garzon

Computer Science, The University of Memphis, TN 38152, USA
mgarzon@memphis.edu

Abstract. We survey the origin, current progress and applications on
one major roadblock to the development of analytic models for DNA computing and self-assembly, namely the so-called *Codeword Design* problem.
The problem calls for finding large sets of single DNA strands that do not
crosshybridize to themselves or to their complements (so-called *domains*
in the language of chemical reaction networks) and has been recognized
as an important problem in DNA computing, self-assembly, DNA memories and phylogenetic analyses because of their error correction and
prevention properties. Major recent advances include the development
of experimental techniques to search for such codes, as well as a theoretical framework to analyze this problem, despite the fact that it has been
proven to be **NP**-complete using any single concrete *metric* space to
model the Gibbs energy. In this framework, codeword design is reduced
to finding large sets of strands maximally separated in DNA spaces and,
therefore, the key to finding such sets would lie in knowledge of the geometry of these spaces. A new general technique has been recently found
to embed them in Euclidean spaces in a hybridization-affinity-preserving
manner, i.e., in such a way that oligos with high/low hybridization affinity are mapped to neighboring/remote points in a geometric lattice, respectively. This isometric embedding materializes long-held mataphors
about codeword design in terms of sphere packing and leads to designs
that are in some cases known to be provable nearly optimal for some
oligo sizes. It also leads to upper and lower bounds on estimates of the
size of optimal codes of size up to 32−mers, as well as to infinite families
of DNA strand lengths, based on estimates of the kissing (or contact)
number for sphere packings in Euclidean spaces. Conversely, this reduction suggests interesting new algorithms to find dense sphere packing
solutons in high dimensional spheres using prior results for codeword design priorly obtained by experimental or theoretical molecular means, as
well as to a proof that finding these bounds exactly is **NP**-complete in
general. Finally, some applications and research problems arising from
these results are described that might be of interest for further research.

Keywords: Gibbs energy, DNA space, molecular chip design, noncrosshybridizing oligonucleotide bases, spherical codes, DNA memories, phylogenetic analysis.

A.-H. Dediu, C. Martín-Vide, and B. Truthe (Eds.): TPNC 2012, LNCS 7505, pp. 11–26, 2012.
© Springer-Verlag Berlin Heidelberg 2012

1   DNA CodeWord Design: Origins and State-of-the-Art

The discovery of the role and structure of DNA (Watson and Crick, 1953) ush-
ered in a new era for the biological sciences that continues unabated despite
enormous progress for well over half a century now. The success of the human
genome project of the 1990s marked a transformation in the theory and practice
of experimental biology. While sequencing has continued to be in itself an ongoing challenge, enormous progress has brought genome sequencing to the verge
of a commodity that humans can have for well under $1,000 in the near future
(http://www.genome.gov/sequencingcosts/). These developments not withstand-
ing, DNA has simultaneously demonstrated great potential as a substrate for
molecular computers (Adleman, 1994) and "intelligent" self-assembly of complex
materials, both in terms of the relative simplicity of their manufacture (Seeman,
2003; Seeman, 1982) and of the complexity of the resulting structures (Qian and
Sinfree, 2011; Winfree et al., 1998). More recent applications include natural
language processing (Garzon et al., 2009; Neel at al., 2008; Bobba et al., 2006),
DNA-based memories (Garzon et al., 2010; Neel & Garzon, 2008) and, more
recently, biological phylogenies based purely on whole-genomic DNA (Garzon &
Wong, 2011).

A common and fundamental "magic" underpins these attributes of the double helix, namely the formation of DNA complexes through the characteristic
properties of DNA (sometimes referred to as "intelligent glue"), including strand
hybridization, ligation, and their dynamic relaxation to lower Gibbs energy states
from fairly arbitrary initial configurations, in contrast to the formation of the
better known covalent bonds. While unveiling the basic biochemistry of these
nanoscopic interactions has long been achieved in thermodynamics and biochemistry, the analogous and important problem of developing some understanding
of their implications and potential at a more intuitive global (microscopic, meso-
scopic and ordinary) scales has emerged as an important problem. What structures (DNA complexes) can and cannot be self-assembled out of primitive building blocks (such as oligonucleotides or so-called DNA tiles)? What is the nature
of the *dynamical* system/process (some would say kinetics) characterizing self-
assembly that leads to optimal or efficient self-assembly protocols? Although
promising beginnings of theories that might provide some answers to these questions are budding off in the horizon (e.g. Tkachenko, 2010; Doty et al., 2009; Sahu
et al., 2005; Winfree, 1998), a theory of self-assembly powerful enough to enable
analysis of the capabilities, limitations and fidelity of biomolecular assembling
appears to be a difficult challenge, among other things because these processes
are much more akin to how nature and biology build things (bottom-up), rather
than the top-down approaches of standard man-made manufacturing processes
typically found hitherto in human activity.

In this article, we therefore focus on a single roadblock to these problems,
namely the so-called *Codeword Design* problem. The problem calls for the identification of and search methods for small DNA molecules that may serve as
building blocks for the self-assembly process in order to guarantee that the desirable reactions take place as intended, amidst the tendency of DNA molecules

to form other structures due to the uncertainty and variability inherent in hybridization affinity and chemical reactions due to multiple factors, as discussed below. This is a meaningful first step because the largest complexity of feasible computational solutions or self-assembled nanostructures attainable through oligonucleotides of a given size n is usually directly related to the largest ensemble of DNA oligonucleotides that satisfy a given set of cross-hybridization and noncrosshybrization constraints. DNA Codeword Design has seen some progress in the last decade mainly in two subareas. First, methods to find large such sets of short oligonucleotides with noncrosshybridizing (nxh) properties have been produced by several groups (Garzon et al., 2009; Deaton et al., 2006; Tulpan et al., 2005; particularly the PCR Selection (PCRS) protocol (Chen et al., 2006). This problem has also recently shown to be amenable to analytic models of hybridization, such as the mathematical $h-$distance metric (Phan & Garzon, 2009) that can be used as a theoretical framework to conceptualize this type of problems, find solutions, and organize the knowledge about the subject in a systematic manner. In this framework, codeword design is reduced to finding large sets of strands maximally separated in the DNA space of all oligos of a given size. The size of such sets is thus essentially linked on the geometry of these metric DNA spaces. However, it is shown therein that Codeword Design is **NP**-complete using any single concrete measure that approximates the Gibbs energy by any reasonable metric that would provide such a nice geometry to analyze DNA spaces, thus practically excluding the possibility of finding any general procedure to find truly maximal sets exactly and efficiently through such an approach.

Nevertheless, (Garzon & Bobba) succeeded in finding a general technique to bring the problem into the more geometric context of ordinary Euclidean spaces, where ordinary intuition may provide better insights into the nature and characteristics of DNA spaces. Section 3 brielfy describes this method to embed DNA spaces in Euclidean spaces and thus reduce the word design problem to the long and well known sphere packing problem in ordinary geometry. The embedding not only sheds some insights into the geometry of DNA spaces via the $h-$distance , which is briefly described in Section 2.1, but it has also shown to afford information relevant to the *dynamics* of hybridization kinetics (Garzon & Bobba, 2012). In Section 2.2, a normalization of this metric is described that yields a provably close approximation of the Gibbs energies of duplex formation, while preserving the metric property. From this embedding, one can obtain nearly optimal codeword sets for short oligomer spaces (up to 12-mers or so), as sketched in Section 3 (see (Garzon & Bobba, 2012) for full details.) The quality of these sets has been evaluated against the only general purpose method to produce maximal codes experimentally, the PCR Selection protocol, using a well accepted model of the Gibbs energy of duplex formation, namely the nearest neighbor model (NN). Section 4 sketches three other applications of these DNA code design for DNA memories and philogenetic analysis. Full descriptions can be found in (Garzon & Wong, 2011; Garzon et al., 2010; Neel & Garzon, 2008). In the conclusion in section 5, other interesting applications and research problems are discussed towards further understanding of the nature and dynamics of DNA Gibbs energy landscapes.

2   Gibbs Energies, DNA Spaces and Optimal DNA Codes

DNA codes for given parameters and bounds therefore have been previously established only for simple models based on the Hamming distance and classical coding theory -see (Garzon & Deaton, 2004) for a review, but were largely unknown under more realistic measures of hybridization. Attempts to construct non-crosshybridizing sets *in silico* using various methods such as templates (Arita et al. 2002) or heuristic search (Marathe et al., 2001) tended to produce relatively small sets. Experimental methods to create non-crosshybridizing sets (Chen et al., 2006) in vitro are attractive for being able to physically produce a maximal set, but suffer from the challenge of identifying precisely its size and, more importantly, the composition of the sequences. More recently, nearly optimal codes have explicitly obtained by simulations of the PCR Selection (PCRS) protocol (Garzon et al., 2005; Garzon et al., 2004) for short length oligonculetoides (up to 13−mers) and for longer lengths by a so-called shuffle operation to generate longer codes from smaller ones (Garzon et al., 2009). General, scalable, analytic and efficient methods capable of producing the explicit sequences in DNA codeword sets are hard to find due to the sheer enormity of the search space and the heuristic nature of known Gibbs energy approximations. One such method has been produced recently using a models introduced earlier on by (Garzon et al., 1997) and later proved to have the properties of a metric space by (Phan & Garzon, 2009; Garzon et al., 1997).

2.1   Gibbs Energies

DNA duplex formation from two single strands is determined by the familiar Gibbs energy in thermodynamics, which generally depends on physical parameters such as the internal energy (U), pressure (p), volume (V), temperature (T), and entropy (S) of the environment in which the duplex is formed. The Gibbs energy is the chemical equivalent of the potential energy in physics. The more negative the Gibbs energy, the more stable the duplex formed. Unfortunately, biochemical models are inherently approximations and so no gold standard exists to assess Gibbs energies (Wetmur, 1997), although it is known that the energy depends not only on the nucleotide composition of the strands but also on their arrangement, in addition to other thermodynamical factors (temperature, pressure, acidity of the solvent, etc.).

On the other hand, knowledge of the corresponding Gibbs energy landscapes would appear critical in an analysis of the codeword design problem. The most popular method to approximate the Gibbs energy is the so-called nearest-neighbor (NN hereafter) method, which postulates that the free energy for duplex formation basically depends on three factors: the initial free energy given by the unfavorable entropy due to the loss of translational freedom, the sum of the complementary pair-wise terms between the nucleotides sequences being stacked to form the duplex, and the entropic penalty of the maintenance of the symmetry in a double strand. The NN model gives the Gibbs energy as a summation of all values for the stacked pairs in a running window over all pairs in a given frameshift of the given strands. To date, several different experimental thermodynamic parameters for the 10 'nearest-neighbor' di-nucleotide sequences, namely dAA/dTT, dAT/dTA, dTA/dAT, dCA/dGT, dGT/dCA, dCT/dGA, dGA/dCT, dCG/dGC, dGC/dCG, dGG/dCC, have been measured experimentally (Huguet et al., 2010; SantaLucia, 1998). A full use of even the NN model to analyze the codeword design problem forces the examination of exponentially many configurations in the minimization of the energy and thus it is computationally intractable, where we need to deal in principle with 2^{4^n} possible subsets of the entire DNA space to search for the code set of the largest size.

2.2   A Combinatorial Approximation to the Gibbs Energy

A different method, the so-called $h-$distance was introduced in (Garzon et al., 1997) as a rougher but also more tractable and close approximation of the Gibbs energy. Briefly, the relevant chemistry is abstracted as two operations of interest for our purpose, a unary operation of Watson-Crick complementation and a binary operation of hybridization. The Watson-Crick complement y' of strand y is obtained by reversing it and swapping nucleotides within the pairs a, t and c, g. Hybridization is modeled as a binary operation between two single strands x, y that forms a double-stranded molecule in which pairs of nucleotides are joined in a duplex molecule by two or three hydrogen bonds, for an $a - t$ or a $c - g$ pair, respectively. The likelihood of hybridization is defined in terms of the h-measure between two single strands x, y given by

$$h(x, y) := \min_{-n < k < n} \left\{ |k| + H(x, \sigma^k(y')) \right\} \tag{1}$$

where $\sigma^k(y)$ is the shift of y by k positions (right-shift if $k > 0$; left-shift if $k < 0$) with respect to x, y' is the Watson-Crick complement of y, and the Hamming distance H measures the number of different bases in the overlap of x and y' in the specified frameshift $\sigma^k(y')$. In words, the h-measure finds *the optimal alignment in which x and y have the maximum number of complementary pairs, thus forming the most stable duplex.* A measure of $h(x, y) = 0$ means $x = y'$. A large distance indicates that even when x finds itself in the proximity of y, they contain few complementary base pairs regardless of the position they find themselves in, and thus are unlikely to form a stable duplex, i.e. no hybridization will take place. For example, if $x = agc$, $y = tgg$ (and $y' = cca$), at shift $k = -2$, there are 2 base pair mismatches and one identity match, so $2 + H(a, a) = 2$; at shift $k = -1$, there are 3 pair mismatches $1 + H(ag, ca) = 3$; At shift 0 (perfect alignment) there are 3 mismatches $H(agc, cca) = 3$; at shift 1, the number of mismatches is $1 + H(gc, cc) = 2$; and at shift 2, the distance is $2 + H(c, c) = 2$. Therefore, $h(agc, ttg) = 2$. Note that h is invariant under

Watson-Crick complementation, as well as under both reversal and pointwise complementation of each nucleotide, i.e., for every pair of strands $x, y \in \mathbf{D}_n$,

$$h(x, y) = h(x', y') = h(x^r, y^r) = h(x^c, y^c)$$

From an analytic point of view, it is desirable to have a measure of hybridization that satisfies rather conflicting constraints. On the othe hand, it should be a good approximation of the chemical Gibbs energy, while on the other, is should reflect some structural constratins about the space of all possible DNA strands, $\mathbf{D}_n$. Some of the most amenable such spaces are so-called *metric spaces*, which are intuitively analogous to the ordinary distance in Euclidean spaces. Unfortunately, the h-measure does not possess the requisite properties to make $\mathbf{D}_n$ a metric space because it misses the triangle inequality (since x can be chosen so that $0 < h(x, x)$ but $0 = h(x, x') + h(x', x)$.) This measure becomes a true distance function, however, if we bundle together complementary strands into so-called *poligos* $X = \{x, x'\}$ and measure the distance between them as

$$h(X, Y) = \min_{x \in X, y \in Y} h(x, y). \tag{2}$$

It has been established in (Phan & Garzon, 2009) that this function truly defines a metric in $\mathbf{D}_n$. This metric model reduces codeword design to a well known problem that has been researched for over half a century, namely the design of communication codes in information theory (Roman, 1995). Although the analogy has proved useful in using error-correcting codes in information theory to produce DNA codes (Arita et al., 2003), the fact that the $h-$distance is very different in nature from the Hamming distance (as can be seen by perusing eq. (1) and other properties below) makes the analogy only a metaphor. By constrast, the h-distance quantifies hybridization afinity more closely while preserving the advantages of a metric space structure in $\mathbf{D}_n$.

The reduction of the problem has been carried further into more familiar territory in (Garzon & Bobba, 2012) by normalizing the distance onto the unit inteval and comparing it with the Gibbs energy as approximated by an equally normalized version of the NN model. The normalization of the $h-$distance is obtained by fitting a set of weights (shown in Table 1) to the multiplicity counts of mismatches in the optimal alignment that produced the standard $h-$distance $h(x, y)$ between strands x and y. Normalization of the $h-$distance is calculated as a ratio of the sum of the weights for all the mismatches in the best alignment in computing the $h-$distance to the sum over the maximum possible number of mismacthes,. i.e., $2n-1$, where n is the size of the words in the code set. Now, the proof in (Phan & Garzon, 2009) is easily seen to carry over to this modification of the $h-$distance so that the normalized $h-$distance remains a metric. On the other hand, the normalization of the Gibbs energy was obtained by a piecewise linear function so that the minimum Gibbs energy of the set maps to 0, -6.0 Kcal/mole maps to 0.5 and the maximum Gibbs energy of the set maps to 1.

As shown in Fig 1, two independent fitnesses show that over 80% of the two agree across all oligo sets tested for the purpose of deciding whether or not a hybridization event occurs (Gibbs energies were computed at 20°C.) Further, the uniformity of the results shown in Table 1 show that this result is likely to scale for larger oligos as far as the NN model holds, albeit with decreasing values and slightly lower performance. Further evidence of the apropriateness of the h−distance as an approximation can be obtained by comparison of results in optimal code sets obtained independently by both methods. These results can be constrated in columns 3 and 4 of Table 2, although a more complete set of results up to 20−mers is not yet available. A more principled argument can be given from the definitions of the Gibbs energy in the NN model and the h−distance since both are minimizing over all possible frameshifts, under the hypothesis of stiffness mentioned below, but the argument is too long for the space allowed and will be reported elsewhere.

Table 1. Weights for the corresponding counts of mismatches in the optimal alignment that normalizes the h−distance into the interval $[0, 1]$ so that hybridization between strands occurs when $h(x, y) < 0.5$ (equivalent to $\Delta G < -6.0$ Kcal/mole.) The weights were obtained by search through a genetic algorithm that minimizes the RMSE difference between a linear combination (with the weights) of the number of occurrences of the di-nucleotides mismatches in optimal alignments for the h−distance and the (normalized) NN Gibbs energies (at 20°C) across a representative sample of all strands. Naturally, the weights depend on the temperature at which the NN Gibbs energy is computed, but analogous weights can be similarly obtained for other temperatures (Garzon & Bobba, 2012).

Mismatches	6−mers (100%)	6−mers (40%)	7−mers (1%)	8−mers (1%)
AA	2.651	2.620	2.616	2.443
AC/CA	2.631	2.605	2.485	2.417
AG/GA	2.602	2.631	2.560	2.516
A-/-A	1.328	1.307	1.257	1.011
CC	2.636	2.562	2.532	2.347
CT/TC	2.647	2.629	2.558	2.476
C-/-C	1.334	1.317	1.280	1.040
TT	2.642	2.636	2.586	2.672
TG/GT	2.639	2.633	2.545	2.458
T-/-T	1.258	1.335	1.274	1.226
GG	2.560	2.632	2.535	2.321
G-/-G	1.315	1.316	1.268	1.437

That *these two metrics can be regarded as nearly equivalent* can be gathered from an analysis of the comparison shown in Fig 1 based on two fitness functions: accuracy and RMSE (statistical root mean square error) over all n−mers for code sets in the column headers in Table 1. The *accuracy* is defined as the ratio of the weighted h−distance that are within a certain range of their Gibbs energy (as given by the NN model) to the total number of possible Gibbs energies for that set. The range that was used for deciding whether the weighted

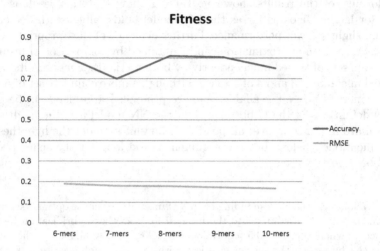

Fig. 1. Accuracy of the normalized $h-$distance in predicting hybridization events, as compared to a Gibbs energy model of duplex formation (nearest neighbor model.) The accuracy is measured by the percentage of hits ($h(x,y) < 0.5$ exactly when $\Delta G(x,y) < -6.0$ Kcal/mole) and the Root Mean Square Error (RMSE) of the difference of the two, in both cases over the entire DNA space (Garzon & Bobba, 2012).

$h-$distance was close to Gibbs energy or not was calculated with a parabolic function that will make sure that difference should be minimal in the critical region about -6.0 Kcal/mole. A function of $\epsilon + (\Delta G - 0.5)^2$ was the threshold for the difference between the normalized weighted $h-$distance and Gibbs energy ΔG. The *RMSE* fitness is defined as $1 - RMSE$ of the differences over the same distribution. The $h-$distance thus provides a more computationally efficient approximation of the Gibbs energy based solely on composition and sequence. Although the $h-$distance makes the assumption that DNA oligos are stiff and do not form bulges or hairpins, this is a mild assumption for short oligos up to $16-$mers or so because pre-processing can filter out in polynomial time strands not satisfying this condition (such as Watson-Crick palindromes.) On the other hand, the $h-$distance allows a fine control of hybridization stringency, considers hybridization in all possible frameshifts, and is therefore in some sense more realistic than the simpler models mentioned above.

3   Optimal Codes and Geometric Packings

A second phase in the study of the structure of Gibbs energy landscapes is to gain some insights into the nature of the metric DNA spaces with the $h-$distance. Somewhat surprisingly, it turns out that this metric is very much akin to the familiar Euclidean spaces, but in higher dimensions. Precisely, DNA spaces are mapped into ordinary Euclidean spaces so that their Gibbs energy landscapes are basically converted into more intuitive and analyzable geometric objects. As a result, the codeword design problem can be reduced to an age-old problem in geometry, originated in Newton's problem of the 12 spheres (Conway & Sloane, 1999, p. 21). While one might argue that such problems are therefore historically proven to be very difficult, much more is known about them and they have been studied for a long time and a number of solutions to this problem do provide answers that are nearly optimal given the state of the art of the geometric problem. For space reasons, in this section we will be illustrate with a particular case, the so-called h_0-distance defined as above but without considering frameshifts, i.e.,

$$h_0(x, y) := \min \{H(x, y), H(x, y')\} \tag{3}$$

The technique scales to the full normalized $h-$distance (Phan & Garzon, 2009), but the technical details are more involved to explain than the space allowed here -see (Phan & Garzon, 2009) for more details.

For the first stage in the reduction, we find a representation of DNA strands $x \in \mathbf{D}_n$ as vectors in the Euclidean space $\mathbf{R}^{4n}$ of dimension $4n$ by coarse coding them as follows. Given a basis $b \in \{a, c, g, t\}$, let $\Psi_b(x) \in \mathbf{R}^{4n}$ be the vector given by $\Psi_b(x)_i = \psi(b, x_i) = 1$ if $b = x_i$ and 0 otherwise, i.e., $\Psi_b(x)_i = 1$ indicates the presence or absence of nucleotide b in position i in x. The representation Ψ of a strand x is given by the concatenation of these vectors in the following order

$$\Psi(x) = \Psi_a(x)\Psi_c(x)\Psi_g(x)\Psi_t(x). \tag{4}$$

The following properties of Ψ are easy to verify for every pair of strands x, y, where $||\Psi(x)||$ is the standard Euclidean norm of a vector, "$\cdot$" denotes the standard dot (scalar) product between two vectors in $\mathbf{R}^{4n}$, and $|x|$ denotes the length of strand x:

1. Strands of length n are represented as points on a sphere of radius $\sqrt{n}$, i.e.

$$||\Psi(x)||^2 = |x| = n \quad \text{and} \quad ||\Psi(x)|| = \sqrt{n};$$

2. The number of Watson-Crick complementary matches between x and y in perfect alignment is $m(x, y) = \Psi(x) \cdot \Psi(y)$. Therefore

$$H(x, y) = n - \Psi(x) \cdot \Psi(y);$$

3. The Hamming distance can be normalized as

$$\frac{1}{n} H(x, y) = 1 - \frac{1}{\sqrt{n}} \Psi(x) \cdot \frac{1}{\sqrt{n}} \Psi(y) \tag{5}$$

$$= 1 - \cos \theta(\Psi(x), \Psi(y)) = 2 \sin^2(\theta/2). \tag{6}$$

where θ is the angle between the two $4n$D vectors $\Psi(x), \Psi(y)$. This metric essentially is equivalent to H and has the advantage that it represents DNA strands as points on the unit sphere in the Euclidean space of dimension $4n$. From now on, we will identify a DNA oligo x with its representation $\Psi(x)$.

4. Complementation is reduced to a reversal operation, i.e.,

$$\Psi(y') = \Psi(y)^r = R(\Psi(y)) \,,$$

where R is a linear transformation reversing the coordinates of a vector in $\mathbf{R}^{4n}$. This operation can in fact be shown to be a *reflection* about a subspace of dimension $2n$. For example, when $n = 1$, the bases $a \equiv 1000, c \equiv 0100$ can be obtained by reversal of the vectors for the bases $t \equiv 0001, g \equiv 0010$, respectively, in 4D-space. This linear transformation has two eigenvalues ± 1, each of multiplicity 2, with eigenvectors $1001, 0110$ (left invariant for being palindromes) and $\bar{1}001, 0\bar{1}10$, respectively ($\bar{1} \equiv -1$.) The complement of strand x is thus obtained by image reflection about the fixed 2D plane generated by the first two eigenvalues (hereforth called the *mirror*) and amounts to a change in sign of the other two components in the orthogonal coordinate system consisting of these eigenvalues. Longer strands can then be represented by adding sets of 4-tuples for the additional bases without changing these procedures to find the complementary strands by reflection (about a higher dimensional subspace of dimension $2n$, of course.)

5. The normalized h_0−distance is then computed by just the simple normalized Hamming distance *provided* we ensure that the two vectors x, y lie on the "same side" of the mirror (the invariant subspace), i.e.,

$$\frac{1}{n} h_0(x, y) = 2 \sin^2(\theta/2) \,. \tag{7}$$

Therefore, maximal DNA codeword sets of n−mers with a noncrosshybridizing quality given by a minimum separating h_0−distance of τ (now normalized after division by $\sqrt{n}$) is reduced to an age-old problem in packing problem in ordinary geometry going back to Newton and Gauss in the 1600-1800s. This is the so-called **spherical packing problem**, analogous to but essentially different from the ordinary sphere packing problem in geometry and classical coding theory (Conway & Sloane, 1999, p.24). This problem is challenging and far from resolved, but a wealth of knowledge has been gathered over the centuries, which can now be used to help answer critical questions about the DNA codeword design problem. For example, the well-known *kissing number* problem in nD-Euclidean space asks for the maximum number of congruent spheres that can be arranged to touch a given one. We are actually concerned here with the analogous kissing number on the surface of the unit sphere Ω_{4n} in the same 4nD space, denoted $A^*(n, \phi)$, where $2 \sin^2(\phi/2) \geq \tau$ and $\tau > 0$ is the parameter coding for quality in the codeword set (fault-tolerance to reaction conditions, etc.). Resolving this inequality gives a minimum angle $\phi = 2 \arcsin(\sqrt{\tau/2})$ for the minimum separation between DNA points on Ω_{4n} for $\tau < 1$. As a second example, known solutions to the spherical code problem (usually called *spherical codes*, i.e., a set of points $\mathcal{C} \subseteq \Omega_{4n}$ satisfying a minimal separation distance as measured by the angle $\phi = x \cdot y$ between two points/vectors x, y) can be used to obtain sets of noncrosshybridizing DNA codeword of nearly the same quality as the centers of the kissing spheres in Ω_{4n} by selecting vectors representing n−mers that come close enough to points in $\mathcal{C}$.

The optimality and/or quality of the solutions to the kissing spheres problem is usually inversely related to the simplicity in generating them. The best known solutions are afforded by so-called *lattice packings*, obtained by diophantine (integer coefficients) combinations of n linearly independent vectors (usually assumed to be diophantine as well.) We illustrate the third stage in our method to obtain a DNA codeword set with the optimal solution for lattice packings in 24D-space (i.e., for 6−mers), the *Leech lattice*, which can be generated from Golay's [24,12] 3-error correcting code in 24D Hamming space and is known to have a separation angle of $\arccos(1/3) \approx 70°$ (Conway & Sloane, 1999, p. 27). The basic idea is to decompose the lattice points in 4nD-space into nearly concentric layers (usually referred to as *shells*) around one of its points located as origin (perhaps after a translation.) The points in this shell are then projected onto Ω_{4n} by dividing by their norm. They provide an approximate solution to the sphere kissing problem on Ω_{4n} because their angle separation does not change due to the projection. Finally, the DNA codeword sets to be guaranteed to be at a minimum distance τ will be obtained by filtering from this kissing set those 4n-dimensional points coding for DNA strands that are within a suitable angle ϵ/k (usually $k = 2$ or 3 will do) of a (normalized) shell point, for a suitable value of k. Here $\epsilon = |\phi - Arccos(1/3)|$ is the difference between the angle separation of two lattice points and the desired angle separation between DNA codewords. Table 2 shows the results for the corresponding set of 6−mers obtained from the Leech lattice. It is clear from this construction that the codeword sets thus obtained are nearly optimal in the DNA space with respect to the h_0−distance IF the spherical code is (nearly) optimal.

Thus, well established solutions to sphere packing problems can be used to obtain DNA codeword designs that are in some cases known to be nearly optimal

Table 2. Size of DNA (nearly optimal) codeword sets obtained from (nearly) optimal spherical codes and packings in comparison to best known sets obtained by exhaustive computational searches (Garzon et al., 2009) or other means. The second/last column shows the best (or best known) *proven* theoretical lower/upper bounds, respectively, on $A^*(n, \phi)$, the kissing numbers for h−distance spheres in the DNA space of all n−mers, as derived from the respective bounds for $A(4n, \phi)$ for 4nD-spaces (Conway & Sloane, 1999, p. 24-27). Footnotes † indicate a result for metric h_0 only (hence the $<$), and * a result from PCRS *in vitro*; c is a constant independent of n and $\phi < \phi_0 \approx 70°$. (Blank cells either follow the general bounds or precise values are still being computed) (Garzon & Bobba, 2012).

D_n, n−mers	$? \leq A^*(n, \phi)$	Spherical codes†	Best Known	$A^*(n, \phi) \leq ?$
6		$< 1,268$	620	$196,560$
8		$< 4,096$	4,549	$261,120$
10			15,600	(N/A)
16			$>> 58,500$	$9,694,080$
20		$< 100,000^*$		(N/A)
n	$2^{-4n \log_2(c\sin\phi)}$	(N/A)	(N/A)	$2^{7608(1-\cos\phi)^{-4n}}$

(through difficult and elaborate proofs.) They include upper and lower bounds on estimates of the size of optimal codes for dimensions up to 128–mers as well as infinite families of DNA strand lengths, based on estimates of the kissing (or contact) number for sphere packings in Euclidean spaces, as shown in Table 2.

4   Some Applications of DNA Codeword Designs

Solutions to the Codeword Design problem have proven to be of use in areas outside DNA computing and molecular programming as well. Three applications are particularly noteworthy.

First, codeword designs are important in bioinformatics, particularly in the areas of **microarray design**. Microarrays has been the technique of choice for genomic and metabolomic analyses for about 10 years now. Originally, entire genes (represented by complementary cDNA strands, so called *probes*) were fixed to a solid substrate and target mRNAs allowed to hybridize to them at various times during gene expression in order to ascertain the genomic activity of genes of interest in biological cells (e.g., under various conditions for different patients, normal and having a disease, for example.) It is thus usually considered that the more genes and nucleotides on the chip, the more information the microarray will capture. However, an analysis of the noise involved on "cross-talking" of the genes due to cross-hybridization revealed that that is not necesssarily the case and that, in fact, pre-processing of the genes through the normalizaiton process to extract a noncrosshybridizing set will produce a smaller set of genes where the cross-talk has been virtually eliminated. By choosing a subset of a solution to Codeword design problem covering the hybridization of the original probes, the microarray can be re-designed to increase the sensitivity and signal-to-noise ratio. This technique makes possible discrimination between genomic data impossible with current designs because of the noise inherent in crosshybridization with the maximum number of genes normally packed on the chip. A more detailed presentation of these results can be found in (Garzon et al., 2009; Garzon et al., 2006).

Second, DNA codeword designs are critical in a general implementation of DNA indexing, akin to the well known Latent Semantic Indexing (LSA or LSI). LSA is a technique used to produce *semantic* models of text corpora that capture a significant fraction of the semantic meaning that humans would normally associate with ordinary text in natural language. (Garzon et al., 2010) demonstrated that it is feasible to develop representations of symbolic strings (text in natural language) so that semantic similarity between texts is captured by hybridization affinity as represented by Euclidean distances between the corresponding DNA signatures on a DNA chip (such as Euclidean distances, or angles between the corresponding vectors.) Preliminary validations demonstrate that the quality of these encoding are competitive with that of the well established and accepted LSA in natural language processing. A more detailed presentation of these results can be found in (Garzon et al., 2010; Neel & Garzon, 2008; Neel & Garzon, 2006).

A further application of DNA indexing led to the development of an associative memory for phylogenies in important bacteria that produces results comparable to those produced by solidly established and well accepted in biology.

The new technique also demonstrated that DNA indexing does provide novel and principled insights into the phylogenesis of organisms hitherto inaccessible by current methods, such as a prediction of the origin of the Salmonella plasmid 50 as being acquired horizontally, likely from some bacteria somewhat related to Yersinia. DNA indexing thus offers the promise of a universal DNA chip (say, a full nxh of 16−mers or 20−mers) that can be used as a universal coordinate system in DNA spaces to characterize very large groups (families, genera, and even phylla) of organisms on a uniform biomarker reference system, a veritable and comprehensive "Atlas of Life", as it is or as it could be on earth. A more detailed presentation of these results can be found in (Garzon & Wang, 2011).

5 Conclusions and Future Work

DNA Codeword design addresses the issue of *capacity* of fixed size olignucleotides for fault-tolerant self-assembly and computing and therefore is an important and challenging problem for molecular programming and bioinforamtics and other fields. A theoretical framework has been described in (Garzon & Bobba, 2012; Phan & Garzon, 2009; Garzon et al., 1997) to address this problem in a principled and analytic fashion. Codeword Design problem of selecting noncrosshybrizing DNA oligonucleotides for DNA computing can be approximated through a geo-metric approach, despite its established **NP**-complete status. In this framework, Codeword Design is reduced to finding large sets of strands maximally sepa-rated in DNA spaces endowed with a mathematical metric directly related to the Gibbs energy of duplex formation (or rather its nearest neighbor model.) Although the geometry of these spaces is still difficult to discern, a linear time reduction can be made to sphere packing problems in Euclidean spaces (e.g., the so-called spherical code design problem (Conway & Sloan, 1999, p. 24)), which are still difficult to optimize but are much better understood.

There remains the question of whether these codes will be appropriate for use *in vitro*. This paper also presented a validation of the h−distance using the nearest neighbor model of the Gibbs energy, which is a standard model in ex-perimental applications. Thus there is a good degree of confidence that these codes will increase the error-preventing/-correcting capability of codeword de-signs close to the extent possible. Moreover, the visualization of Gibbs energy landscapes for a given size of n−mers enabled by this embedding affords a more analytic and accessible tool to understanding biomolecular programming. For example, it appears now plausible that this new metric approximation of Gibbs energies may allow other applications in shedding light on the structure of Gibbs energy landscapes for DNA spaces, particularly for designing long sequences of strands to form cascades descending towards stable equilibria along trajecto-ries in Gibbs energy landscapes. For example, the embedding of DNA space of n−mers onto a hypersphere maps oligos with high (low) hybridization affinity (a *domain* in the language of chemical reaction networks) to neighboring (re-mote, respectively) points in a geometric lattice. Given an initial strand x in a domain and a target strand y in another, a shortest path connecting x to y in the spherical embedding (which can be easily found using Dijkstra's algorithm) suggests an optimal cascade of chemical reactions through intermediate strands to effect the transformation through minimal energy changes in going from one neighbor to the next. Moreover, this cascade would be fully fault-tolerant in the sense that nowhere along the cascade will the strands ever have a chance to "switch domains", i.e., to myshybridize with other strands in the mixture. (A more detailed description can be found in the analogy with planetary motion described in the Appendix on "Planetary Perturbations" in (Conway & Sloan, 1999, p. 29).) This is an intriguing possibility that may lead to a procedure for optimizing molecular DNA protocols.

These results have important applications in molecular programming as well as other areas. For example, upper and lower bounds on the size of optimal codeword designs for dimensions up to 128−mers as well as infinite families of DNA strand lengths have been obtained. A full optimal solution to the problem of codeword design via this reduction, however, remains difficult despite their familiarity, because sphere packings are age-old difficult geometric problems. For example, their computational complexity and even specific solutions for a fixed dimension (including 3) are still unknown. Conversely, solutions to codeword design obtained by experimental or other means also enable solutions to spherical packing problems via our embedding. Prior results for optimal codes by exhaustive search (Garzon et al., 2009) can be used to obtain packing lattices of reasonable quality for various applications (such as microarray design, crystallography, error-correcting codes in communication theory, and numeric integration.) As another example, the **NP**-completeness of finding optimal codeword sets for the h−distance implies the **NP-completeness of computing the kissing number** $A(n, \phi)$ **for** Ω_n, a problem that to the best of our knowledge has been open for some time. DNA codeword designs in general have demonstrated to have important applications to bioinformatics (such as microarray design), phylogenetic analyses, design of DNA memories for associative retrieval and for natural language processing.

References

1. Adleman, L.: Molecular computation of solutions of combinatorial problems. Science 266, 1021–1024 (1994)
2. Arita, M., Kobayashi, S.: DNA Sequence Design Using Templates. New Generation Computing 20(3), 263–277 (2002)
3. Bobba, K.C., Neel, A.J., Phan, V., Garzon, M.H.: "Reasoning" and "Talking" DNA: Can DNA Understand English? In: Mao, C., Yokomori, T. (eds.) DNA12. LNCS, vol. 4287, pp. 337–349. Springer, Heidelberg (2006)
4. Chen, J., Deaton, R., Garzon, M., Wood, D.H., Bi, H., Carpenter, D., Wang, Y.Z.: Characterization of Non-Crosshybridizing DNA Oligonucleotides Manufactured in vitro. J. of Natural Computing 5(2), 165–181 (2006)
5. Deaton, J., Chen, J., Garzon, M., Wood, D.H.: Test Tube Selection of Large Independent Sets of DNA Oligonucleotides, pp. 152–166. World Publishing Co., Singapore (2006) (Volume dedicated to Ned Seeman on occasion of his 60th birthday)

6. Doty, D., Patitz, M.J., Summers, S.M.: Limitations of Self-assembly at Temperature One. In: Deaton, R., Suyama, A. (eds.) DNA 15. LNCS, vol. 5877, pp. 35–44. Springer, Heidelberg (2009)
7. Garzon, M.H., Bobba, K.: A Geometric Approach to Gibbs Energy Landscapes and Optimal DNA Codeword Design. In: Stefanovic, D., Turberfield, A. (eds.) DNA 18. LNCS, vol. 7433, pp. 73–85. Springer, Heidelberg (2012)
8. Garzon, M.H., Bobba, K.C., Neel, A.J., Phan, V.: DNA-Based Indexing. Int. J. of Nanotechnology and Molecular Computing 2(3), 25–45 (2010)
9. Garzon, M.H., Wong, T.Y.: DNA Chips for Species identification and Biological Phylogenies. J. Natural Computing 10, 375–389 (2011)
10. Garzon, M.H., Phan, V., Neel, A.: Optimal Codes for Computing and Self-Assembly. Int. J. of Nanotechnology and Molecular Computing 1, 1–17 (2009)
11. Garzon, M.H., Yan, H. (eds.): DNA 2007. LNCS, vol. 4848. Springer, Heidelberg (2008)
12. Garzon, M.H., Phan, V., Bobba, K.C., Kontham, R.: Sensitivity and Capacity of Microarray Encodings. In: Carbone, A., Pierce, N.A. (eds.) DNA 2005. LNCS, vol. 3892, pp. 81–95. Springer, Heidelberg (2006)
13. Garzon, M.H., Deaton, R.: Codeword Design and Information Encoding in DNA Ensembles. J. of Natural Computing 3(3), 253–292 (2004)
14. Garzon, M.H., Blain, D., Neel, A.J.: Virtual Test Tubes for Biomolecular Computing. J. of Natural Computing 3(4), 461–477 (2004)
15. Garzon, M.H., Neathery, P.I., Deaton, R., Murphy, R.C., Franceschetti, D.R., Stevens Jr., S.E.: A New Metric for DNA Computing. In: Koza, J.R., et al. (eds.) Proc. 2nd Annual Genetic Programming Conference, pp. 230–237. Morgan Kaufmann (1997)
16. Marathe, A., Condon, A.E., Corn, R.M.: On combinatorial DNA word design. J. Computational Biology 8(3), 201–219 (2001)
17. Neel, A.J., Garzon, M.H.: DNA-based Memories: A Survey. SCI, vol. 113, pp. 259–275. Springer (2008)
18. Neel, A., Garzon, M.H.: Semantic Retrieval in DNA-Based Memories with Gibbs Energy Models. Biotechnology Progress 22(1), 86–90 (2006)
19. Phan, V., Garzon, M.H.: On Codeword Design in Metric DNA Spaces. J. Natural Computing 8(3), 571–588 (2009)
20. Roman, J.: The Theory of Error-Correcting Codes. Springer, Berlin (1995)
21. Sahu, S., Yin, P., Reif, J.H.: A Self-assembly Model of Time-Dependent Glue Strength. In: Carbone, A., Pierce, N.A. (eds.) DNA 11. LNCS, vol. 3892, pp. 290–304. Springer, Heidelberg (2006)
22. SantaLucia, J.: A unified view of polymer, dumbbell, and oligonucleotide DNA nearest-neighbor thermodynamics. Proc. Natl. Acad. Sci. 95(4), 1460–1465 (1998)
23. Seeman, N.: Nuclei-Acid Junctions and Lattices. J. Theoretical Biology 99, 237–247 (1982)
24. Seeman, N.: DNA in a material world. Nature 421, 427–431 (2003)
25. Tkachenko, A.V.: Theory of Programmable Hierarchic Self-Assembly. Phys. Rev. Lett. 106, 255501 (2011)

26. Tulpan, D., Andronescu, M., Chang, S.B., Shortreed, M.R., Condon, A., Hoos, H.H., Smith, L.M.: Thermodynamically based DNA strand design. Nucleic Acids Res. 33(15), 4951–4964 (2005)
27. Qian, L., Winfree, E.: Scaling Up Digital Circuit Computation with DNA Strand Displacement Cascades. Science 332, 1196–1201 (2011)
28. Winfree, E., Liu, F., Wenzler, L.A., Seeman, N.C.: Design and self-assembly of two-dimensional DNA crystals. Nature 394, 539–544 (1998)
29. Winfree, E.: Algorithmic self-assembly of DNA. Ph.D. Thesis, California Institute of Technology (1998)

Scalable Neuroevolution
for Reinforcement Learning

Faustino Gomez

IDSIA
USI-SUPSI
Galleria 2, Manno-Lugano
6928, Switzerland
tino@idsia.ch

Abstract. The idea of using evolutionary computation to train artificial neural networks, or *neuroevolution* (NE), has now been around for over 20 years. The main appeal of this approach is that, because it does not rely on gradient information (e.g. backpropagation), it can potentially harness the universal function approximation capability of neural networks to solve reinforcement learning (RL) tasks, where there is no "teacher" (i.e. no targets or examples of correct behavior). Instead of incrementally adjusting the synaptic weights of a single network, the space of network parameters is searched directly according to principles inspired by natural selection: (1) encode a population of networks as strings, or *genomes*, (2) transform them into networks, (3) evaluate them on the task, (4) generate new, hopefully better, nets by recombining those that are most "fit", (5) goto step 2 until a solution is found. By evolving neural networks, NE can cope naturally with tasks that have continuous inputs and outputs, and, by evolving networks with feedback connections (recurrent networks), it can tackle more general tasks that require memory.

Early work in the field focused on evolving rather small networks (hundreds of weights) for RL benchmarks, and control problems with relatively few inputs/outputs. However, as RL tasks become more challenging, the networks required become larger, as do their genomes. The result is that scaling NE to large nets (i.e. tens of thousands of weights) is infeasible using a straightforward, direct encoding where genes map one-to-one to network components. Therefore, recent efforts have focused on *indirect* encodings [3,7,8,11,12,14] where the genome is translated into a network by a more complex mapping that allows small genomes to represent nets of potentially arbitrary size.

At IDSIA, in addition to state of the art direct methods [1,4,6,15,16], we have developed a novel indirect encoding scheme where networks are encoded by a set of Fourier coefficients which are converted into network weight matrices via an inverse Fourier-type transform [5,9,10,13]. Since there often exist network solutions whose weight matrices contain regularity (i.e. adjacent weights are correlated), the number of coefficients required to represent these networks in the frequency domain is much smaller than the number of weights (in the same way that natural images can be compressed by ignore high-frequency components). This

A.-H. Dediu, C. Martín-Vide, and B. Truthe (Eds.): TPNC 2012, LNCS 7505, pp. 27–29, 2012.
© Springer-Verlag Berlin Heidelberg 2012

"compressed" encoding can reduce the search-space dimensionality by as much as two orders of magnitude, both accelerating convergence and yielding more general solutions.

We have also explored an entirely different approach where, instead of trying to efficiently search the space of compactly-encoded, large networks, NE is scaled by combining it with unsupervised learning (UL) [2]. Here, the standard NE architecture is augmented by a UL module that learns to transform high-dimensional inputs (e.g. video) generated by the controllers being evaluated, into a low-dimensional code that they use instead of the raw input. Because the number of inputs becomes small after the UL dimensionality reduction, the controllers can be small as well. Research is currently underway combining these two approaches (compressed nets fed by a small number UL features), to discover controllers for real robot manipulation using stereo vision input.

References

1. Cuccu, G., Gomez, F.: Block Diagonal Natural Evolution Strategies. In: Coello, C.A.C., Cutello, V., Deb, K., Forrest, S., Nicosia, G., Pavone, M. (eds.) PPSN XII, Part II. LNCS, vol. 7492, pp. 488–497. Springer, Heidelberg (2012)
2. Cuccu, G., Luciw, M., Schmidhuber, J., Gomez, F.: Intrinsically motivated evolutionary search for vision-based reinforcement learning. In: Proceedings of the IEEE Conference on Development and Learning, and Epigenetic Robotics (2011)
3. Dürr, P., Mattiussi, C., Floreano, D.: Neuroevolution with Analog Genetic Encoding. In: Runarsson, T.P., Beyer, H.-G., Burke, E.K., Merelo-Guervós, J.J., Whitley, L.D., Yao, X. (eds.) PPSN IX. LNCS, vol. 4193, pp. 671–680. Springer, Heidelberg (2006)
4. Glasmachers, T., Schaul, T., Sun, Y., Wierstra, D., Schmidhuber, J.: Exponential Natural Evolution Strategies. In: Genetic and Evolutionary Computation Conference (GECCO), Portland, OR (2010)
5. Gomez, F., Koutník, J., Schmidhuber, J.: Compressed Network Complexity Search. In: Coello, C.A.C., Cutello, V., Deb, K., Forrest, S., Nicosia, G., Pavone, M. (eds.) PPSN XII, Part I. LNCS, vol. 7491, pp. 316–326. Springer, Heidelberg (2012)
6. Gomez, F., Schmidhuber, J., Miikkulainen, R.: Accelerated neural evolution through cooperatively coevolved synapses. Journal of Machine Learning Research 9, 937–965 (2008)
7. Gruau, F.: Cellular encoding of genetic neural networks. Tech. Rep. RR-92-21, Ecole Normale Superieure de Lyon, Institut IMAG, Lyon, France (1992)
8. Kitano, H.: Designing neural networks using genetic algorithms with graph generation system. Complex Systems 4, 461–476 (1990)
9. Koutník, J., Gomez, F., Schmidhuber, J.: Evolving neural networks in compressed weight space. In: Proceedings of the Conference on Genetic and Evolutionary Computation, GECCO 2010 (2010)
10. Koutník, J., Gomez, F., Schmidhuber, J.: Searching for minimal neural networks in fourier space. In: Proceedings of the 4th Annual Conference on Artificial General Intelligence, pp. 61–66 (2010)
11. Risi, S., Lehman, J., Stanley, K.O.: Evolving the placement and density of neurons in the hyperneat substrate. In: Proceedings of the 13th Annual Conference on Genetic and Evolutionary Computation, GECCO 2010, pp. 563–570 (2010)

12. Schmidhuber, J.: Discovering neural nets with low Kolmogorov complexity and high generalization capability. Neural Networks 10(5), 857–873 (1997)
13. Srivastava, R.K., Schmidhuber, J., Gomez, F.: Generalized Compressed Network Search. In: Coello, C.A.C., Cutello, V., Deb, K., Forrest, S., Nicosia, G., Pavone, M. (eds.) PPSN XII, Part I. LNCS, vol. 7491, pp. 337–346. Springer, Heidelberg (2012)
14. Stanley, K.O., Miikkulainen, R.: A taxonomy for artificial embryogeny. Artificial Life 9(2), 93–130 (2003)
15. Sun, Y., Wierstra, D., Schaul, T., Schmidhuber, J.: Efficient Natural Evolution Strategies. In: Genetic and Evolutionary Computation Conference, GECCO (2009)
16. Wierstra, D., Schaul, T., Peters, J., Schmidhuber, J.: Natural Evolution Strategies. In: Proceedings of the Congress on Evolutionary Computation (CEC 2008), Hongkong. IEEE Press (2008)

Differential Evolution Algorithm: Recent Advances

Ponnuthurai Nagaratnam Suganthan

School of Electrical and Electronic Engineering,
Nanyang Technological University, Singapore 639798
epnsugan@ntu.edu.sg

Abstract. Differential Evolution (DE) has been a competitive stochastic real-parameter optimization algorithm since it was introduced in 1995. DE possesses computational steps similar to a standard Evolutionary Algorithm (EA). DE perturbs the population members with the scaled differences of distinct population members. Hence, a step-size parameter used in algorithms such as evolutionary programming and evolution strategy is not required to be specified. Due to its consistent robust performance, DE has drawn the attention of many researchers all over the world. This article presents a brief review of the recent DE-variants for bound constrained single objective, multi-objective and multimodal optimization problems. It also suggests potential applications of DE in remanufacturing.

Keywords: Differential evolution, differential mutation, linearly scalable exponential crossover, ensemble differential evolution, multimodal, multiobjective, evolutionary algorithms.

1 Introduction

The Differential Evolution (DE) algorithm was introduced as a technical report by Rainer Storn and Kenneth V. Price in 1995 [1-2]. DE demonstrated its robust performance at the 1st International Contest on Numerical Optimization at the 1996 IEEE International Conference on Evolutionary Computation (CEC) by securing the third spot. In 2005 CEC competition on real parameter optimization [3], on 10-dimensional problems classical DE secured 2nd rank and a self-adaptive DE variant called SaDE [4] secured 3rd rank. Although a powerful variant of evolution strategy (ES), called restart CMA-ES (Covariance Matrix Adaptation ES) [5], yielded better results than DE, later on many improved DE variants [6-8] were proposed which are competitive against the restart CMA-ES. In fact, variants of DE continued to secure top ranks in the subsequent CEC competitions[1]. Hence, it is obvious that no other single search paradigm was able to secure competitive rankings in all CEC competitions.

DE operates through the similar computational steps employed by other evolutionary algorithms (EAs). However, DE employs difference of the parameter vectors to explore the objective space. Since late 1990s, DE has found several applications to optimization problems from diverse domains of engineering and science. Next, we

---

[1] http://www3.ntu.edu.sg/home/epnsugan/

A.-H. Dediu, C. Martín-Vide, and B. Truthe (Eds.): TPNC 2012, LNCS 7505, pp. 30–46, 2012.
© Springer-Verlag Berlin Heidelberg 2012

highlight some reasons for the popularity of DE as an attractive optimization tool: (a) The standard DE is much more simple and straightforward to implement. Main body of the algorithm requires 4-5 lines in any programming language; (b) As evidenced by the recent studies on DE [6], DE exhibits much better performance in comparison with several other EAs; (c) DE requires only a very few control parameters to be tuned (*Cr*, *F* and *NP* in classical DE); (d) The space complexity of DE is also low as compared to some of the most competitive real parameter optimizers like CMA-ES [5]. Hence, DE is able to handle large scale and expensive optimization problems more effectively [9-12]. Apparently, these issues triggered the popularity of DE among researchers all around the globe in recent years [6,13]. This paper commences with the standard DE and then provides a survey of recent DE algorithms for solving bound constrained, multi-objective, and multimodal optimization problems. The rest of this paper is arranged as follows. Section 2 presents the basic concepts of the classical DE. Section 3 presents prominent variants of the DE for solving single objective problems. Section 4 describes a multiobjective realization of DE. A multimodal implementation of DE is presented in Section 5. Finally the paper is concluded in Section 6.

2   The Standard DE Algorithm

Usually the parameters governing the optimization problem are represented as a vector: $\vec{X} = [x_1, x_2, x_3, ..., x_D]^T$. In real parameter optimization, each parameter x_i is a real number. To measure the quality of each solution, an objective function or fitness function is used for single objective optimization. The task of optimization is to search for the parameter vector $\vec{X}^*$ to minimize the objective function $f(\vec{X})$ ($f : \Omega \subseteq \Re^D \rightarrow \Re$), that is $f(\vec{X}^*) < f(\vec{X})$ for all $\vec{X} \in \Omega$, where Ω is a non-empty large finite set serving as the domain of the search. For unconstrained optimization problems $\Omega = \Re^D$. Important stages of DE are explained in the following subsections.

2.1   Initialization of the Population

DE begins with a randomly initialized population of *NP* *D* dimensional real-valued vectors. Each vector is a candidate solution to the optimization problem. We denote generations in DE by $G = 0,1..., G_{max}$. Since the parameter vectors may change with generations, the ith vector in the population at the current generation:

$$\vec{X}_{i,G} = [x_{1,i,G}, x_{2,i,G}, x_{3,i,G}, ..., x_{D,i,G}] \tag{1}$$

For each parameter of the problem, there may be a range within which the value of the parameter should be confined because parameters are usually related to physical entities that have natural bounds. The initial population should ideally cover this range as much as possible by uniformly randomizing initial solution candidates within the search space:

$$x_{j,i,0} = x_{j,\min} + rand_{i,j}[0,1] \cdot (x_{j,\max} - x_{j,\min})$$ (2)

where $\vec{X}_{\min} = \{x_{1,\min}, x_{2,\min}, ..., x_{D,\min}\}$ and $\vec{X}_{\max} = \{x_{1,\max}, x_{2,\max}, ..., x_{D,\max}\}$. $rand_{i,j}[0,1]$ is a uniformly distributed random variable lying between 0 and 1. It is instantiated independently for each component of ith vector.

2.2   Mutation with Difference Vectors

In DE-literature, a parent vector in the current generation is called the target vector. A mutant vector is obtained through the differential mutation operation and is known as the donor vector. Finally, an offspring, called the trial vector, is formed by recombining the donor with the target vector. The simplest of DE-mutation creates the donor vector $\vec{V}_{i,G}$ for each i-th target vector from the current population by using three other distinct parameter vectors $\vec{X}_{r_1^i}, \vec{X}_{r_2^i}$ and $\vec{X}_{r_3^i}$ which are sampled randomly from the current population. The indices r_1^i, r_2^i and r_3^i are mutually exclusive integers randomly chosen from the range [1, NP], which are also different from the target vector's index i. These indices are randomly generated independently for each mutant vector. The difference of any two of these three vectors is scaled by a scale factor F (that is usually in the interval [0.2, 1]) and the scaled difference is added to the third vector to obtain the donor vector $\vec{V}_{i,G}$ as:

$$\vec{V}_{i,G} = \vec{X}_{r_1^i,G} + F \cdot (\vec{X}_{r_2^i,G} - \vec{X}_{r_3^i,G}).$$ (3)

2.3   Crossover

To increase the diversity of the population, a crossover operation is usually used after generating the donor vector through mutation. The donor (*i.e.* mutant) vector exchanges its components with the target (*i.e.* parent) vector $\vec{X}_{i,G}$ to form the trial vector $\vec{U}_{i,G} = [u_{1,i,G}, u_{2,i,G}, u_{3,i,G}, ..., u_{D,i,G}]$. The DE family of algorithms can use one of the two kinds of crossover methods - exponential (*i.e.* two-point modulo) and binomial (*i.e.* uniform) [6]. In exponential crossover, we must first choose an integer n randomly among the numbers $[1, D]$. This integer is the starting point in the target vector, from where the crossover or exchange of components with the donor vector commences. We need to choose another integer L from the interval $[1, D]$. L represents the number of components the donor vector contributes to the target vector. After selecting n and L the trial vector is:

$$u_{j,i,G} = \begin{cases} v_{j,i,G}, & \text{for } j = \langle n \rangle_D, \langle n+1 \rangle_D, ..., \langle n+L-1 \rangle_D \\ x_{j,i,G}, & \text{for all other } j \in [1, D] \end{cases}$$ (4)

where the angular brackets $\langle \rangle_D$ denote the modulo operation with modulus D. The integer L is drawn from $[1, D]$ as follows:

$$L = 0; \ DO \ \{ \ L = L+1; \ \} \ WHILE \ ((rand(0,1) \leq Cr) \ AND \ (L \leq D \ ));$$

Cr is called the crossover rate and is a control parameter of DE. For each donor vector, a new set of n and L values must be chosen randomly as shown above.

On the other hand, the binomial crossover is performed on each of the D variables if a randomly generated number between 0 and 1 is less than or equal to the Cr value. The number of parameters inherited from the donor obeys approximately a binomial distribution:

$$u_{j,i,G} = \begin{cases} v_{j,i,G}, & \text{if } (rand_{i,j}[0,1] \leq C_r \text{ or } j = j_{rand}) \\ x_{j,i,G}, & \text{otherwise,} \end{cases} \qquad (5)$$

where $rand_{i,j}[0,1]$ is a uniform random number, that is regenerated for each j-th component of the i-th parameter vector. $j_{rand} \in [1,2,....,D]$ is a randomly chosen index to make sure that $\vec{U}_{i,G}$ has at least one component from $\vec{V}_{i,G}$. Due to this additional requirement, Cr is only approximating the probability of crossover p_{Cr} of the event that a component of the trial vector is inherited from the donor.

2.4   Selection

To keep the population size fixed over subsequent generations, the next step of the algorithm employs a selection process to determine whether the target or the trial vector survives to the next generation $G = G+1$:

$$\vec{X}_{i,G+1} = \vec{U}_{i,G}, \qquad \text{if } f(\vec{U}_{i,G}) \leq f(\vec{X}_{i,G})$$

$$= \vec{X}_{i,G}, \qquad \text{if } f(\vec{U}_{i,G}) > f(\vec{X}_{i,G}) \qquad (6)$$

where $f(\vec{X})$ is the objective function to be minimized. Therefore, if the new trial vector yields an equal or lower value, it replaces the corresponding target vector in the next generation. Otherwise, the target remains in the population while the trial vector is discarded. Hence, the population can either become better (with respect to the minimization of the objective function) or remain the same with respect to fitness, but can never deteriorate. Note that in (6) the target vector is replaced by the trial vector even if both have the same value of the objective function thereby enabling the DE-vectors to move over flat fitness landscapes over generations. DE is presented in pseudo-code format in [6].

3   DE Variants for Bound Constrained Single Objectives

Several DE variants have been proposed. In this section, a few of the significant variants are briefly described.

3.1   jDE: Self-adaptive DE

Brest et al. proposed a self-adaptation scheme (jDE) for the DE's control parameters [14] F and Cr by encoding them into the individual and adjusting them by introducing two new parameters τ_1 and τ_2. A set of F and Cr values was assigned to each individual in the population, increasing the dimensionality of each vector. The better values of these encoded control parameters are likely to generate better individuals that are more likely to survive and produce better offspring thereby propagating the superior parameter values. The new control parameters for the next generation are adapted as follows:

$$\left.\begin{aligned} F_{i,G+1} &= F_l + rand_1 * F_u \text{ with probability } \tau_1 \\ &= F_{i,G} \text{ else} \end{aligned}\right\} \tag{7a}$$

and

$$\left.\begin{aligned} Cr_{i,G+1} &= rand_3 \text{ with probability } \tau_2 \\ &= F_{i,G} \text{ else} \end{aligned}\right\} \tag{7b}$$

where F_l and F_u are the lower and upper limits of F and both lie in [0, 1]. In [14], Brest et al. used $\tau_1 = \tau_2 = 0.1$. As $F_l = 0.1$ and $F_u = 0.9$, the new F takes a value from [0.1, 0.9] while the new Cr takes a value from [0, 1]. As $F_{i,G+1}$ and $CR_{i,G+1}$ values are obtained before the mutation is performed, they influence the mutation, crossover, and selection operations for the new vector $\vec{X}_{i,G+1}$.

3.2   SaDE: Self-adaptive DE

Qin et al. [15] proposed the Self-adaptive DE (SaDE) algorithm with self-adaptation of both the trial vector generation strategies and their associated control parameters F and Cr by learning from the past experiences of generating solutions as good as or better than its parent. The parameter F is approximated by a normal distribution with mean value 0.5 and a standard deviation 0.3 denoted by $N(0.5, 0.3)$. A set of F values are randomly generated from the normal distribution and applied to each target vector. Hence, SaDE is able to perform both exploitation with small F values and exploration with large F values throughout the evolution process. SaDE progressively adjusts the range of Cr values according to mean value of previous Cr values that have generated trial vectors successfully entering the next generation. Specifically, it is assumed that Cr can be effectively learned and adapted by using a normal distribution with mean value Cr_m and a standard deviation Std =0.1, denoted by $N(Cr_m, Std)$, where Cr_m is initialized as 0.5. The Std should be set as a small value to guarantee that most Cr values generated by $N(Cr_m, Std)$ are between [0, 1] and very close to Cr_m. Hence, the value of Std is set as 0.1. Note that adaptive schemes like SaDE often themselves have additional parameters to be adjusted like the standard deviation in the normal distributions. However, self-adaptive DE performs better than the standard DE because sensitive parameters in DE are replaced by less sensitive parameters in SaDE.

3.3   DEGL: DE with Global and Local Neighborhoods

Das et al. [16] proposed two kinds of topological neighborhood models for DE in order to achieve superior balance between exploration and exploitation. The resulting algorithm was called DEGL (DE with Global and Local neighborhoods). Suppose we have a DE population $P_G = [\vec{X}_{1,G}, \vec{X}_{2,G}, ..., \vec{X}_{NP,G}]$ at generation G. For every vector $\vec{X}_{i,G}$, we define a neighborhood of radius k (where k is an integer from 0 to $(NP-1)/2$ as the neighborhood size must be smaller than the population size *i.e.* $2k+1 \leq NP$), consisting of vectors $\vec{X}_{i-k,G}, ..., \vec{X}_{i,G}, ..., \vec{X}_{i+k,G}$. We consider the ring topology with respect to their indices, such that vectors $\vec{X}_{NP,G}$ and $\vec{X}_{2,G}$ are the two immediate neighbors of vector $\vec{X}_{1,G}$. For each member of the population, a local do-nor vector is created by employing the best vector in the neighborhood of that member and any two other vectors chosen from the same neighborhood. The model can be expressed as:

$$\vec{L}_{i,G} = \vec{X}_{i,G} + \alpha \cdot (\vec{X}_{n\_best_i,G} - \vec{X}_{i,G}) + \beta \cdot (\vec{X}_{p,G} - \vec{X}_{q,G}) \qquad (8)$$

where the subscript n_best_i represents the best vector in the neighborhood of $\vec{X}_{i,G}$ and $p, q \in [i-k, i+k]$ with $p \neq q \neq i$. Likewise, the global donor vector is generated as:

$$\vec{g}_{i,G} = \vec{X}_{i,G} + \alpha \cdot (\vec{X}_{g\_best,G} - \vec{X}_{i,G}) + \beta \cdot (\vec{X}_{r_1,G} - \vec{X}_{r_2,G}) \qquad (9)$$

where the subscript g_best represents the best vector in the entire population at itera-tion G and $r_1, r_2 \in [1, NP]$ with $r_1 \neq r_2 \neq i$. α and β are the scaling factors. Next, we combine the local and global donor vectors by using a scalar weight $w \in (0,1)$ to form the actual donor vector:

$$\vec{V}_{i,G} = w.\vec{g}_{i,G} + (1-w).\vec{L}_{i,G} \qquad (10)$$

Apparently, if $w = 1$ and $\alpha = \beta = F$, the donor vector generation procedure in eq-uation (10) reduces to DE/target-to-best/1. Hence, the latter is a special case of this more general strategy involving both global and local neighborhood of each vector synergistically. We can observe that DE/target-to-best/1 favors exploitation only, since all vectors are attracted to the same best position found so far by the whole pop-ulation, thereby converging faster to the same neighborhood.

3.4   JADE: DE with pbest Mutation

In order to improve the convergence characteristics of DE, an adaptive DE-variant, called JADE, was recently proposed [17]. The algorithm implements a new mutation strategy, named as DE/current-to-pbest. The algorithm may also use an optional external archive to store the history of pbest solutions. It updates the control parameters adaptively. The DE/current-to-pbest strategy is a less greedy variant of the DE/current-to-best/ strategy. Instead of using only the best individual in the DE/current-to-best/1 strategy, the current-to-pbest/1 strategy benefits from the information in other good solutions too. Moreover, the recent pbest solutions are also incorporated in this strategy. The DE/current-to-pbest/1 without external archive generates the donor vector as:

$$\vec{V}_{i,G} = \vec{X}_{i,G} + F_i \cdot (\vec{X}_{best,G}^p - \vec{X}_{i,G}) + F_i \cdot (\vec{X}_{r_1^i,G} - \vec{X}_{r_2^i,G}), \tag{11}$$

where $\vec{X}_{best,G}^p$ is a randomly chosen one of the top $100p\%$ individuals of the current population with $p \in (0,1]$. F_i is the scale factor associated with the i-th individual and it is updated each generation. JADE can optionally use an external archive, which stores the recently discarded parents from the population. Let A denote the archive of solutions replaced by offspring and P denote the current population. Then DE/current-to-pbest/1 with external archive generates the mutant vector as:

$$\vec{V}_{i,G} = \vec{X}_{i,G} + F_i \cdot (\vec{X}_{best,G}^p - \vec{X}_{i,G}) + F_i \cdot (\vec{X}_{r_1^i,G} - \vec{X}'_{r_2^i,G}), \tag{12}$$

where $\vec{X}_{i,G}$, $\vec{X}_{best,G}^p$, and $\vec{X}_{r_1^i,G}$ are selected from P as before in (11), but $\vec{X}'_{r_2^i,G}$ is selected randomly from the union of the current population and archive, $P \cup A$. The archive is initially empty. After each generation, the parent solutions that fail in the selection process are stored in the archive. If the size of the archive exceeds a pre-specified threshold, some solutions are randomly removed from the archive to maintain the archive size fixed.

3.5 MDE_pBX: Modified DE with p-best Crossover

Islam et al. [7] proposed three algorithmic components, one or more of which can be integrated with the DE-family of algorithms to improve their performances. They are:

(1) A less greedy and more explorative variant of the DE/current-to-best/1 mutation strategy called DE/current-to-gr_best/1 (gr stands for group) was proposed. Unlike DE/current-to-best/1 that always uses the best member of the current population to perturb a parent vector, DE/current-to-gr_best/1 forms a group, corresponding to each target vector, by randomly selecting population members to form a group made of $q\%$ of the total population size. The best member of this group is used to perturb the parent vector:

$$\vec{V}_{i,G} = \vec{X}_{i,G} + F_i \cdot \left(\vec{X}_{gr\_best,G} - \vec{X}_{i,G} + \vec{X}_{r_1^i,G} - \vec{X}_{r_2^i,G} \right) \tag{13}$$

where $\vec{X}_{gr\_best,G}$ is the best of out of $q\%$ vectors randomly chosen from the current population whereas $\vec{X}_{r_1^i,G}$ and $\vec{X}_{r_2^i,G}$ are two distinct vectors picked up randomly from the current population and none of them is equal to the $\vec{X}_{gr\_best,G}$ or the target vector to ensure that none of the vectors is identical to each other in eqn (13). Under this scheme, the target solutions are not always attracted to the same best position found so far by the whole population and this property is helpful in avoiding premature convergence to a local optimum. It is seen that keeping the group size equal to 15% of the population yields good results overall.

(2) An exploitative crossover scheme, named as "p-best crossover" is developed. This crossover scheme allows a mutant vector to exchange its components not just with the parent at the same index, but with a randomly selected member from the p top-ranked individuals from the current generation. The parameter p is linearly reduced with generations in the following way:

$$p = ceil\left[\frac{Np}{2} \cdot \left(1 - \frac{G-1}{G_{max}}\right)\right]$$

(14)

where G is the current generation number, G_{max} is the maximum number of generations, $G=[1,2,\ldots,G_{max}]$, and ceil(y) is the 'ceiling' function returning the lowest integer greater than its argument y. The reduction routine of p favors exploration at the beginning of the search and exploitation during the later stages.

(3) Efficient schemes are developed to update the values of F and Cr in each generation based on their successful values that were able to generate better offspring in the previous generations. The details are presented in [7]. A stand-alone DE-variant called MDE_pBX (Modified DE with p-best Crossover) is developed by including the above-mentioned three components in DE.

3.6   EPSDE: Ensemble of Parameters and Strategies DE

The effectiveness of the original DE in solving a particular numerical optimization problem depends on the selected mutation and crossover strategies and their associated parameter values. Obviously, different optimization problems may require different mutation strategies with different parameter values depending on the nature of problems and available computation resources. Further, to solve a specific problem, different mutation strategies with different parameter settings may be beneficial during different stages of the evolution than a single mutation strategy with fixed parameter settings. Motivated by these observations, we proposed an ensemble of mutation and crossover strategies and parameter values for DE (EPSDE) in which a pool of mutation strategies and a pool of values corresponding to each associated parameter compete to produce offspring population. The candidate pool of mutation and mutation strategies and parameters should be restricted to avoid the unfavorable influences of highly greedy mutation strategies and parameters [8,18]. The mutation-crossover strategies and the parameter values present in a pool should possess diverse characteristics, so that they can perform distinctively during different stages of the evolution.

EPSDE consists of a pool of mutation and crossover strategies along with a pool of values for each of the control parameters. Each member in the initial population is randomly assigned with a mutation strategy, crossover strategy and associated parameter values chosen from the respective pools. The population members produce offspring using these assigned mutation strategy, crossover strategy and parameter values. If the offspring is better than the parent vector, the mutation strategy, crossover strategy and parameter values are retained with offspring which becomes the parent (target vector) in the next generation. The combination of the mutation strategy, crossover strategy and the parameter values that produced a better offspring than the parent are stored. If the parent is better than the offspring, then the parent is randomly reinitialized with a new mutation strategy, crossover strategy and associated parameter values from the respective pools or from the successful combinations stored in an archive with equal probability. This leads to an increased probability of producing offspring by using a better combination of strategies and the associated control parameters in the next generations.

In [8], the EPSDE formed used the following mutation and crossover strategies and parameter values:

1) Mutation strategies: JADE [17] and DE/current-to-rand/1 [6]
2) Crossover strategies: Binomial crossover and exponential crossover [6]

In this particular EPSDE implementation, the population size ($NP = 50$) is maintained constant throughout the evolution process. The following parameter values are used in the ensemble: $CR \in \{0.1, 0.5, 0.9\}$ and $F \in \{0.5, 0.9\}$. Our experimental results demonstrated statistically [19] superior performance of the ensemble approach.

3.7   S-EXP: Linearly Scalable EXP Crossover

Even though binomial (*i.e.* uniform) and exponential (*i.e.* modular two-point) crossover operators were proposed simultaneously, binomial crossover has been more frequently used. Recently, the exponential crossover operator outperformed the binomial operator when solving large dimensional problems. We point out that the commonly used definition of exponential crossover operator does not scale linearly with the dimensionality of the problem being solved. Motivated by these observations, we investigated the performance of the currently used exponential crossover operator (EXP) and demonstrated its deficiencies. Subsequently, a linearly scalable exponential crossover operator (S-EXP) based on a number of consecutive dimensions to crossover is defined. Experimental results obtained on the most recent benchmark suite [9] with dimensions ranging from 50 to 1000 showed superior performance of the S-EXP [20] over the standard exponential crossover operator, EXP.

Binomial crossover operator is uniform. In other words, irrespective of the location of each parameter in the mutant vector, each parameter has the same probability approximately, crossover rate CR, to contribute its value to the trial vector. The probability for a component to be replaced with a mutated one (denoted as ProbM) for each component is $CR = $ ProbM. For the exponential crossover operator in the original paper [1-2], which suggested to choose $L \in \{1, \ldots, D\}$ such that approximately Prob(L) ~= CR^L [21]. It is easy to observe that this is independent of D, the dimensionality of the problem. Hence, the number of dimensions L copied from the mutant vector is independent of D, the dimensionality of the problem. Hence, ProbM=CR in the binomial crossover while there is a nonlinear relationship between ProbM and CR for the exponential crossover operation. The ProbM of the exponential crossover is rapidly decreasing when L increases. Hence, non-linear scaling of exponential crossover operator adversely affects when solving high dimensional problems since only a relatively small segment of mutant vector can be extracted to contribute to the target vector by the commonly used CR value of 0.9. Hence, it is obvious that choosing an appropriate value for CR in the original exponential crossover operator is neither intuitive nor easy.

These results suggested that the proper range of values for L of scalable exponential crossover is within [1, 10] for these test problems with dimensions scaling from 50D to 1000D. Further, the best choice of L is approximately linearly related to the dimensionality of the problems, which can be approximated by L = ceil (Dim/100), where Dim is the dimensionality of the problem being solved. This observation can also be verified by the boxplot in Fig. 3 in [20]. In the figure, for each dimensionality of the problems, the best choice of L is presented as a boxplot. Each boxplot shows the distribution of best choices of L for all 19 test problems.

4   DE for Multiobjective Optimization

A multiobjective optimization problem (MOP) can be defined as follows [22-23]:

$$minimize \qquad F(x) = (f_1(x),..., f_m(x))^T \qquad (15)$$

$$subject\ to: \qquad x \in \Omega$$

where Ω is the decision variable space, $F : \Omega \rightarrow R^m$ consists of m real-valued objective functions and R^m is the objective space. In many real-world applications, since the objectives in equation (15) may conflict with each other, no solution in Ω can minimize all objectives simultaneously.

Let $u, v \in R^m$. u dominates v if and only if $u_i \leq v_i$ for every $i \in \{1,...,m\}$ and $u_j < v_j$ for at least one index $j \in \{1,...,m\}$. A solution $x^* \in \Omega$ is Pareto optimal if there is no other solution $x \in \Omega$ such that $F(\mathbf{x})$ dominates $F(\mathbf{x}^*)$. $F(\mathbf{x}^*)$ is then called a Pareto optimal objective vector. In other words, an improvement to a Pareto optimal solution with respect to one objective must lead to a deterioration of at least one other objective. The set of all Pareto optimal objective vectors is known as the Pareto front (PF) [22].

Many multi-objective evolutionary algorithms (MOEAs) have been developed to find a set of approximated Pareto optimal solutions in a single run. Vast majority of them are Pareto dominance based. Guided mainly by dominance-based fitness measures of individual solutions, all these algorithms push the whole population to the PF. NSGA-II, MOPSO, SPEA-II and PAES [22] are the most popular Pareto-dominance based MOEAs.

Multi-objective evolutionary algorithm based on decomposition (MOEA/D) [22] uses conventional aggregation approaches by decomposing the approximation of the PF into a number of single objective optimization sub-problems. The objective of each sub-problem is a weighted aggregation of all the objectives in the MOP being solved. Neighborhood relations among these sub-problems are defined based on the Euclidean distances among their aggregation weight vectors. Each sub-problem is optimized by using information from its neighboring sub-problems.

There are many MOEA/D variants. We employed MOEA/D with dynamic resource allocation [24], which won the CEC2009 multiobjective algorithm competition. To decompose equation (15), MOEA/D needs N evenly distributed weight vectors $\lambda^1,...,\lambda^N$. Each $\lambda^j = (\lambda_1^j,...,\lambda_m^j)^T$ satisfies $\sum_{k=1}^{m} \lambda_k^j = 1$ and $\lambda_k^j \geq 0$ for all k and m. Let $z^* = (z_1^*,...,z_m^*)^T$ where $z_i^* = \min\{f_i(x) \mid x \in \Omega\}$. Then, the problem of approximating the PF of equation (15) can be decomposed into N scalar optimization sub-problems and the objective function of the j-th minimization sub-problem is:

$$g^{te}(x \mid \lambda, z^*) = \max_{1 \leq i \leq m}\{\lambda_i \mid f_i(x) - z_i^* \mid\} \tag{16}$$

z^* is often unknown before the search, the algorithm uses the lowest f_i-value found during the search to substitute z_i^* [22, 24]. During the search, MOEA/D maintains: (a) a population of N points $x^1,...,x^N \in \Omega$, where x^i is the current best solution to i-th sub-problem, (b) $FV^1,...,FV^N$, where FV^i is the F-value of x^i, i.e., $FV^i = F(x^i)$ for each $i = 1,...,N$, and (c) $z = (z_1,...,z_m)^T$, where z_i is the best value found so far for objective f_i.

For every weight vector, its neighborhood is the set of NS closest weight vectors to it. Correspondingly, every solution and every sub-problem has its neighborhood of size NS. At each generation, a set of the current solutions is selected. For every selected solution x^i, MOEA/D does the following:

1. Set the mating and update range P to be the T-neighborhood of x^i with a large probability, and the whole population otherwise.

2. Randomly select three current solutions from P.

3. Apply genetic operations on the above selected solutions to generate an offspring y, repair y if necessary. Compute $F(y)$.

4. Replace one or a few solutions in P by y if y is better than them for their sub-problems.

No solution will be replaced in Step 4 if y is not better than any solution in P for its sub-problem. In this scenario, update fails. Otherwise, update is successful.

The neighborhood size (NS) plays an important role in MOEA/D [22,24]. Apparently, different multiobjective problems require different neighborhood sizes. Even for a problem, using different neighborhood sizes at different search stages can be beneficial. When some solutions are trapped in a locally optimal region, a large NS is required to increase diversity by helping these solutions to escape from the trapped region. On the other hand, if the globally optimal area has been found, a small NS will be beneficial for local exploitation. However, for diverse problems, a trial-and-error approach [25] can be too demanding for tuning fixed neighborhood sizes. Hence, motivated by these observations, we employ an ensemble of neighborhood sizes which are selected according to their past performances of generating improved solutions. The method is called ENS-MOEA/D [26].

In ENS-MOEA/D, K fixed neighborhood sizes (NSs) were employed as a pool of candidates. During the evolution, a neighborhood size would be selected for each sub-problem from the pool based on the candidates' past performances of generating improved solutions. In ENS-MOEA/D, the certain fixed number of past generations used to compute the success probability is called as the Learning Period (LP). At the generation $G>LP-1$, the probability of choosing the k-th ($k = 1, 2, ..., K$) NS is computed by:

$$p_{k,G} = \frac{R_{k,G}}{\sum_{k=1}^{K} R_{k,G}} \tag{17}$$

where

$$R_{k,G} = \frac{\sum_{g=G-LP}^{G-1} FEs\_success_{k,g}}{\sum_{g=G-LP}^{G-1} FEs_{k,g}} + \varepsilon \quad (k=1, 2,.., K; G > LP) \tag{18}$$

$R_{k,G}$ denotes the proportion of improved solutions generated with the k-th NS within the last LP generations. Improved solutions represent the offspring successfully entering the next generation. $FEs_{k,g}$ is the total number of solutions generated with the k-th NS within the last LP generations, $FEs\_success_{k,g}$ is the number of improved solutions generated with the k-th NS within the last LP generations. A small value $\varepsilon = 0.05$ was used to avoid zero selection probabilities. To make sure that the probabilities of choosing strategies are always summed to 1, we further normalize $R_{k,G}$ by $\sum_{k=1}^{K} R_k$ when calculating $p_{k,G}$. The ENS-MOEA/D is presented in detail in [26]. ENS-MOEA/D was compared with MOEA/D variant [24] that won the CEC 2009 MOEA contest [27] to demonstrate statistically superior performance of the ENS-MOEA/D over [24].

5   DE for Multimodal Optimization

When a single objective optimization problem requires more than one optimal solution, it is known as a multimodal optimization problem [28]. The requirement of locating different optima in a single run makes multimodal optimization more challenging than locating a single global optimal solution. Several niching methods have been introduced to enable EAs to maintain a diverse population and locate multiple solutions in a single run. The concept of niching was inspired by the way organisms evolve in nature. When integrated with EAs, niching involves the formation of many sub-populations within a single population. Each sub-population aims to locate one good solution and together the whole population is expected to locate multiple global or local optimal solutions in a single run. Various niching methods have been proposed in the past. In general, the niching methods may be divided into two major categories namely sequential niching and parallel niching. Sequential niching general-ly runs an algorithm iteratively to obtain multiple optima. As sequential niching me-thods are time-consuming and their performance is relatively inferior, parallel niching methods are keenly investigated in the literature.

5.1   Niching Methods

Clearing [28-29] is a widely used niching method. Clearing removes the bad individ-uals and keeps only the best individual (or a few top individuals) within each niche. The clearing algorithm first sorts the population in descending order of the fitness values. Then it picks one individual at a time from the top with best fitness and removes all the individuals falling within the pre-specified clearing radius. This oper-ation is repeated until all the individuals in the population are either selected or re-moved. Clearing eliminates similar individuals, retains best solutions and maintains the diversity among the selected individuals. Clearing requires a user specified para-meter σ_{clear} called clearing radius. This parameter is used as a dissimilarity thre-shold.

The fitness sharing was introduced by Holland and extended by Goldberg and Richardson [28]. This method divides the population into different subgroups accord-ing to the similarity of the individuals. An individual must share its fitness with other individuals within the same niche. The shared fitness of i-th individual is defined as:

$$f_{shared}(i) = \frac{f_{original}(i)}{\sum_{j=1}^{N} sh(d_{ij})} \tag{19}$$

where the sharing function is defined as

$$sh(d_{ij}) = \begin{cases} 1-(\dfrac{d_{ij}}{\sigma_{share}})^{\alpha}, & \text{if } d_{ij} < \sigma_{share} \\ 0, & \text{otherwise} \end{cases}.$$

d_{ij} is the distance between individuals i and j, σ_{share} is the sharing radius, N is the population size and α is a constant called sharing level.

Speciation is also used in multimodal optimization [28]. This method uses a radius parameter r_s, which measures Euclidean distance from the center of a species to its boundary. The center of a species is called species seed. Each of the species is devel-oped around the dominating species' seed. All solutions falling within the radius of the species seed are identified as the same species. In this way, the whole population is divided into several groups according to their similarity.

Several DE-based niching algorithms have also been proposed to solve multimodal problems [28,30]. Thomsen incorporated the fitness sharing concept within DE to form the sharing DE. Thomsen also extended DE with a crowding Scheme called Crowding DE (CDE) to allow it to solve multimodal optimization problems. CDE which has a crowding factor equal to the population size has outperformed the sharing DE.

In CDE, when an offspring is generated, it only competes with the most similar (as determined by Euclidean distance) individual in the current population. The offspring replaces this individual if it has a better fitness value. Species-based DE (SDE) [28,30] is also a commonly used DE niching algorithm. The concept is the same as speciation described above. Different niches are formed around the species seed. The DE mutation is carried out within each species.

5.2   Neighborhood Mutation Based DE for Niching

In DE, the differential mutation is performed between randomly picked individuals form the entire population. This will allow any two members to generate the difference vector in DE/rand/1, even if they are far apart from each other in the search space. This mutation is efficient when searching for a single global solution. It prevents premature local convergence as all individuals evolve to one optimal point. However, when solving a multimodal optimization problem, multiple optima need to be located simultaneously. If the global mutation is used, it will not be efficient for multiple local convergences at the final search stage as required by the multimodal optimization. At final search stage, the whole population should be distributed around different optimal regions when solving multimodal optimization problems. If the parameter space distances between different optima are large, efficient convergence to any of the optima will become impossible as the difference vectors can be generated using individuals from different optimal regions with relatively large magnitudes. Although some of the niching techniques can limit the mutation within each niche (SDE), they all require specification of certain niching parameters such as the species radius. Choosing a proper niching parameter itself is almost impossible for different problems and the algorithm is greatly affected by the niching parameter.

In [13], Neri et al. stated that DE needed some special moves to improve the performance and the lack of these search moves can cause stagnation. In [31], Brest and Maucec also indicated the importance of reducing population size in order to improve the performance of DE. Inspired by these observations, a neighborhood based mutation is proposed and integrated with three different DE based niching algorithms namely CDE, SDE and sharing DE. Our proposed neighborhood concept allows a higher exploitation of the areas around each niche thereby facilitating multiple convergences. In neighborhood mutation, differential vector generation is limited to a number (parameter m) of similar individuals as measured by Euclidean distance. For example, if $m=6$, for every parent 6 nearest individuals in the population is identified. The differential vectors are generated using these 6 individuals and an offspring is generated using a distinct member of these 6 as the base vector. In this way, each individual is evolved towards its nearest optimal point and the possibility of between niche difference vector generation is reduced. The neighborhood based CDE, neighborhood based SDE and neighborhood based sharing DE are presented in [30]. These neighborhood based DE-niching methods outperformed the state-of-the-art methods on a challenging test suite [32].

6   Conclusions and Further Work

This paper presented an introduction to the original differential evolution (DE) algorithm. Subsequently, important DE variants for solving single objective bound constrained problems are described. Recently developed DE variants for solving multi-objective optimization and multimodal optimization are also presented. Our current research applies these DE variants for solving important problems in remanufacturing [33-35].

References

1. Storn, R., Price, K.V.: Differential Evolution—A Simple and Efficient Adaptive Scheme for Global Optimization over Continuous Spaces. International Computer Science Institute, Berkeley, TR-95-012 (1995)
2. Storn, R., Price, K.V.: Differential Evolution – A simple and Efficient Heuristic for Global Optimization over Continuous Spaces. J. of Global Optimization 11(4), 341–359 (1997)
3. Suganthan, P.N., Hansen, N., Liang, J.J., Deb, K., Chen, Y.-P., Auger, A., Tiwari, S.: Problem Definitions and Evaluation Criteria for the CEC 2005 Special Session on Real-Parameter Optimization. Technical Report, Nanyang Technological University, Singapore AND KanGAL Report #2005005, IIT Kanpur, India (2005)
4. Qin, A.K., Suganthan, P.N.: Self-adaptive Differential Evolution Algorithm for Numerical Optimization. In: IEEE Congress on Evolutionary Computation, Edinburgh, UK, pp. 1785–1791 (2005)
5. Auger, A., Kern, S., Hansen, N.: A Restart CMA Evolution Strategy with Increasing Population Size. In: IEEE Congress on Evolutionary Computation, Edinburgh, UK, pp. 1769–1776 (2005)
6. Das, S., Suganthan, P.N.: Differential Evolution: A Survey of the State of the Art. IEEE Trans. on Evolutionary Computation 15(1), 4–31 (2011)
7. Islam, S.M., Das, S., Ghosh, S., Roy, S., Suganthan, P.N.: An Adaptive Differential Evolution Algorithm with Novel Mutation and Crossover Strategies for Global Numerical Optimization. IEEE Trans. on Systems, Man, and Cybernetics, Part B: Cybernetics 42(2), 482–500 (2012)
8. Mallipeddi, R., Suganthan, P.N.: Differential Evolution Algorithm with Ensemble of Parameters and Mutation and Crossover Strategies. In: Panigrahi, B.K., Das, S., Suganthan, P.N., Dash, S.S. (eds.) SEMCCO 2010. LNCS, vol. 6466, pp. 71–78. Springer, Heidelberg (2010)
9. Herrera, F., Lozano, M., Molina, D.: Test Suite for the Special Issue of Soft Computing on Scalability of Evolutionary Algorithms and Other Metaheuristics for Large Scale Continuous Optimization Problems (2010), http://sci2s.ugr.es/eamhco/CFP.php
10. LaTorre, A., Muelas, S., Peña, J.-M.: A MOS-Based Dynamic Memetic Differential Evolution Algorithm for Continuous Optimization: A Scalability Test. Soft Computing 15(11), 2187–2199 (2011)
11. Zhao, S.Z., Suganthan, P.N., Das, S.: Self-adaptive Differential Evolution with Multi-Trajectory Search for Large Scale Optimization. Soft Computing 15(11), 2175–2185 (2011)
12. Brest, J., Maucec, M.S.: Self-adaptive Differential Evolution Algorithm Using Population Size Reduction and Three Strategies. Soft Computing 15(11), 2157–2174 (2011)

13. Neri, F., Tirronen, V.: Recent Advances in Differential Evolution: A Review and Experimental Analysis. Artificial Intelligence Review 33(1), 61–106 (2010)
14. Brest, J., Greiner, S., Bošković, B., Mernik, M., Žumer, V.: Self-Adapting Control Parameters in Differential Evolution: A Comparative Study on Numerical Benchmark Problems. IEEE Trans. on Evolutionary Computation 10(6), 646–657 (2006)
15. Qin, A.K., Huang, V.L., Suganthan, P.N.: Differential Evolution Algorithm with Strategy Adaptation for Global Numerical Optimization. IEEE Trans. on Evolutionary Computation 13(2), 398–417 (2009)
16. Das, S., Abraham, A., Chakraborty, U.K., Konar, A.: Differential Evolution Using a Neighborhood Based Mutation Operator. IEEE Trans. on Evolutionary Computation 13(3), 526–553 (2009)
17. Zhang, J., Sanderson, A.C.: JADE: Adaptive Differential Evolution with Optional External Archive. IEEE Trans. on Evolutionary Computation 13(5), 945–958 (2009)
18. Mallipeddi, R., Suganthan, P.N., Pan, Q.K., Tasgetiren, M.F.: Differential Evolution Algorithm with Ensemble of Parameters and Mutation Strategies. Applied Soft Computing 11(2), 1679–1696 (2011)
19. Derrac, J., García, S., Molina, D., Herrera, F.: A Practical Tutorial on the Use of Nonparametric Statistical Tests as a Methodology for Comparing Evolutionary and Swarm Intelligence Algorithms. Swarm and Evolutionary Computation 1(1), 3–18 (2011)
20. Zhao, S.Z., Suganthan, P.N.: Empirical Investigations into the Exponential Crossover of Differential Evolution. Revised and Resubmitted to Swarm and Evolutionary Computation
21. Zaharie, D.: Influence of Crossover on the Behavior of Differential Evolution Algorithms. Applied Soft Computing 9(3), 1126–1138 (2009)
22. Zhou, A., Qu, B.-Y., Li, H., Zhao, S.-Z., Suganthan, P.N., Zhang, Q.: Multiobjective Evolutionary Algorithms: A Survey of the State-of-the-Art. Swarm and Evolutionary Computation 1(1), 32–49 (2011)
23. Qu, B.-Y., Suganthan, P.N.: Multi-Objective Evolutionary Algorithms Based on the Summation of Normalized Objectives and Diversified Selection. Information Sciences 180(17), 3170–3181 (2010)
24. Zhang, Q., Liu, W., Li, H.: The Performance of a New Version of MOEA/D on CEC09 Unconstrained MOP Test Instances. In: IEEE Congress on Evolutionary Computation, Norway, pp. 203–208 (2009)
25. Eiben, A.E., Smit, S.K.: Parameter Tuning for Configuring and Analyzing Evolutionary Algorithms. Swarm and Evolutionary Computation 1(1), 19–31 (2011)
26. Zhao, S.Z., Suganthan, P.N., Zhang, Q.: Decomposition Based Multiobjective Evolutionary Algorithm with an Ensemble of Neighborhood Sizes. IEEE Trans. on Evolutionary Computation 16(3), 442–446 (2012)
27. Zhang, Q., Zhou, A., Zhao, S.-Z., Suganthan, P.N., Liu, W., Tiwari, S.: Multiobjective Optimization Test Instances for the CEC 2009 Special Session and Competition. Technical Report CES-887, University of Essex and Nanyang Technological University (2008)
28. Das, S., Maity, Qu, B.-Y., Suganthan, P.N.: Real-Parameter Evolutionary Multimodal Optimization — A Survey of the State-of-the-Art. Swarm and Evolutionary Computation 1(2), 71–88 (2011)
29. Yu, E.L., Suganthan, P.N.: Ensemble of Niching Algorithms. Information Sciences 180(15), 2815–2833 (2010)
30. Qu, B.-Y., Suganthan, P.N., Liang, J.J.: Differential Evolution with Neighborhood Mutation for Multimodal Optimization. IEEE Trans. on Evolutionary Computation (2012), doi:10.1109/TEVC.2011.2161873

31. Brest, J., Maučec, M.S.: Population Size Reduction for the Differential Evolution Algorithm. Applied Intelligence 29(3), 228–247 (2008)
32. Qu, B.-Y., Suganthan, P.N.: Novel Multimodal Problems and Differential Evolution with Ensemble of Restricted Tournament Selection. In: IEEE Congress on Evolutionary Computation, Barcelona, Spain, pp. 1–7 (July 2010)
33. Ganguly, S., Chowdhury, A., Mukherjee, S., Suganthan, P.N., Das, S., Chua, T.J.: A Hybrid Discrete Differential Evolution Algorithm for Economic Lot Scheduling Problem with Time Variant Lot Sizing. In: Snasel, V., Abraham, A., Corchado, E.S. (eds.) SOCO 2012. AISC, vol. 188, pp. 1–12. Springer, Heidelberg (2012)
34. Tasgetiren, M.F., Bulut, O., Fadiloglu, M.M.: A Discrete Artificial Bee Colony for the Economic Lot Scheduling Problem. In: IEEE Congress on Evolutionary Computing (CEC), New Orleans, USA, pp. 347–353 (2011)
35. Zhang, R., Wu, C.: A Hybrid Differential Evolution and Tree Search Algorithm for the Job Shop Scheduling Problem. Mathematical Problems in Engineering 2011, Article ID 390593 (2011), doi:10.1155/2011/390593

The Fragility of Quantum Information?

Barbara M. Terhal

Institute for Quantum Information, RWTH Aachen University
52056 Aachen, Germany
terhal@physik.rwth-aachen.de

Abstract. We address the question whether there is a fundamental reason why quantum information is more fragile than classical information. We show that some answers can be found by considering the existence of quantum memories and their dimensional dependence.

1 Classical Information

To store a bit of information robustly, redundancy is needed. The bits of information recorded in Egyptian hieroglyphs, written on the walls of Egyptian temples, have been preserved for over 5000 years. The characters can still be recognized and deciphered as they are captured by a macroscopic displacement of hard stone, a carving. Microscopic details, the particular placement of the sandstone particles, the particular quantum states of the SiO_2 molecules and their binding together in a crystal, have been thoroughly altered by the weather over centuries. However the microscopic details do not affect the macroscopic message as long as the variations of the microscopic details are small, random and do not accumulate over time to lead to macroscopic changes. In this sense, the encoded information is a phenomenon which robustly *emerges* from an underlying statistical reality [3]. And when we decypher such glyphs, we error-correct: a carving of an owl with an obliterated head is still sufficiently different from a feather hieropglyph, as what makes the owl an owl is redundantly present in the hieroglyph. What this one example teaches us, is that (1) classical information can be stored for incredibly long times in the presence of a steadily-acting physical environment, that (2) we need to error-correct upon read-out, i.e. ignore the small fluctuations and (3) there will always be events which can destroy the information, easily and decisively, e.g. hacking into the stone by iconoclasts or the demolition of the entire temple, but these events can be assumed to be rare and non-random.

Of course, this principle of robust storage still underlies our modern computer technology, for example in the form of the hard-disk drive. The jump from hieroglyphs to hard-disk drives is a huge jump in storage density, from, say, 5 bits per square inch to almost 10^{12} bits per square inch. This jump is only possible, because even in an area of $10^{-8} \times 10^{-8} \, m^2$, a macrosopic number of degrees of freedom, namely electrons and their spins, are swimming around to provide redundancy. The encoding of a single bit "0" or "1" is done using tens of magnetic grains in a ferromagnetic material (for example, gamma ferric oxide γ-Fe_2O_3).

A.-H. Dediu, C. Martín-Vide, and B. Truthe (Eds.): TPNC 2012, LNCS 7505, pp. 47–56, 2012.

The bit "1" is represented by a domain wall in the ensemble of grains at which the sign of the magnetization changes whereas the "0" bit is repesented by a uniform magnetization of the underlying grains. The stability of the magnetization of a single grain is due to the phenomenon of ferromagnetism: even in the absence of a magnetic field the electron spins and their angular momenta in the crystalline atomic structure give rise to a nonzero magnetization. Ferromagnetism is temperature-dependent, the capability to spontaneously magnetize is lost above the Curie temperature T_c ($T_c = 600°C$ for γ-Fe$_2$O$_3$). For small magnetic grains the stability also depends on the size of the grain as the *energy barrier* to switch the overall magnetization depends on the volume of the grain. Smaller magnetic grains thus have an increased susceptibility to thermal fluctuations, –an effect which is called superparamagnetism–, which sets limits to miniaturization of hard-drive technology.

We see that the root cause of robustness is redundancy at the physical level of many electrons mutually aligning their magnetic moments in magnetic domains. Why do the electrons do this? This turns out to be largely due to a quantum mechanical effect. Electrons in unfilled iron shells interact via the ferromagnetic Heisenberg exchange interaction, i.e. the interaction between two spins i and j is $-J(X_iX_j + Y_iY_j + Z_iZ_j)$ where X, Y, Z are the three Pauli matrices [1] and J is a coupling constant larger than zero. A simple model which could allow us to understand the origin of stability is that of a lattice of spin-1/2 particles, qubits, locally interacting with their neighbors by this Heisenberg exchange interaction. If the geometry of the lattice is two-dimensional, the Mermin-Wagner theorem states that there can be no spontaneous symmetry breaking, –no low-temperature phase characterized by a nonzero magnetization is possible–. This is in contrast with the situation for a three-dimensional lattice where spontaneous magnetization does occur for temperatures below the critical temperature. Even though the magnetic recording film is thin, it is still many atoms thick and the three-dimensional picture applies. Naturally, –as a curious child which keeps on asking–, we are led to ask why the Mermin-Wagner theorem holds in one and two dimensions and not in three dimensions. In all dimensions, at any temperature, excitations above the ferromagnetic ground-state in the form of spin waves contribute negatively to the magnetization. Whether they overwhelm the ferromagnetic order in the ground-state depends on the energy spectrum of these excitations and the number of excitations at any given energy (i.e. the free energy) which in turn depends on the dimension of the system [4].

That the interplay between entropy and energy cost of the excitations can be dimensionally-dependent was first understood for an even simpler model of ferromagnetism, namely the Ising model, by Peierls [19]. In the one-dimensional (1D) Ising model the Hamiltonian on n qubits is $H = -J \sum_{i=1}^{n-1} Z_iZ_{i+1}$ so that the two degenerate ground-states are $|00\ldots0\rangle$ and $|11\ldots1\rangle$. A single bit can be redundantly encoded in these two ground-states. The encoding of such bit is robust if thermal excitations do not wipe out the average magnetization $M = \frac{1}{n}\sum_i\langle Z_i\rangle$,

---

[1] $X = \begin{pmatrix} 0 & 1 \\ 1 & 0 \end{pmatrix}, Y = \begin{pmatrix} 0 & -i \\ i & 0 \end{pmatrix}, Z = \begin{pmatrix} 1 & 0 \\ 0 & -1 \end{pmatrix}.$

in other words, if the system would exhibit spontaneous magnetization at non-zero temperature. In 1D this is not the case and a quick way of understanding this is to realize that there are no energy barriers for creating large domains of spins with opposite magnetization. In the language of errors and coding, one can say that there are no energy mechanisms which prevent errors from accumulating and thus error accumulation eventually leads to a reversal of the magnetization which represents a *logical* error on the encoded bit. We error-correct upon read-out as we consider, not the individual expectation of each operator Z_i, but the average magnetization M which, when $M < 0$ is interpreted as signaling the bit "1", and when $M > 0$ the bit "0". The two-dimensional (2D) version of the Ising model has a different phase-diagram with a critical temperature T_c separating a ferromagnetic phase where robust storage of a bit is possible from a higher-temperature paramagnetic phase. The reason for the discrepancy is dimensional. In any dimensions an excitation consisting of a domain of spins of opposite magnetization costs an energy proportional to its boundary. In two dimensions this boundary grows as the domain grows, providing a mechanism to energetically suppress the growth of excitations. The energy barrier, defined as the minimum energy cost of a spin configuration through which one necessarily has to pass to get from $|00\ldots0\rangle$ to $|11\ldots1\rangle$ (or vice versa), is L for a two-dimensional $L \times L$ lattice. For a 1D chain of spins, the energy of an excited domain is $O(1)$ as the boundary is 0-dimensional, and thus the energy barrier is $O(1)$ for a one-dimensional chain of spins. For the 2D Ising model the energy barrier grows with system-size, providing more robustness the larger the system. Studies of mixing times of Markov chains mimicking the interaction with a thermal environment have confirmed this basic picture, see e.g. [11].

Now that we have perhaps sketched the ideas underlying the robust storage of classical information, is it time to turn to quantum bits [18]. Wouldn't it be nice to preserve a quantum bit for 5000 years? Is there a fundamental principle at play that prevents us from doing this?

2   Quantum Information, Anyone?

At first sight the idea to encode information in the states of a single atoms, electrons or a single bosonic mode, is terribly, incredibly, naive. In hindsight it could only have come about in a time as prosperous and full of hubris as the past 30 years and by people who were unburdened by their knowledge of physics. By and large in order to understand macroscopic phenomena, whether something conducts electricity or heat, whether it shines or is dull, whether it is a magnet or not, whether it superconducts, we have recourse to the quantum mechanical properties of electrons and atoms in materials. We use quantum theory to obtain a description of the emergent phenomena which are intrinsically classical; but emergent phenomena which are quantum in themselves, this is something that we may even have a hard time conceptualizing. As we argued above, robust are those phenomena which emerge from such statistical microscopic reality due to their redundancy. States of single electron spins decohere in microseconds, electronic states in trapped-ion or nuclear spin qubits may survive for seconds. Without any back-up redundancy these qubits are bound to such smallish coherence times, whereas with redundancy, i.e. statistical ensembles, lattices, arrays of such coupled qubits we expect to be back in the world of classical phenomena. But perhaps not quite.

The best demonstration of an emergent quantum phenonemon is superconductivity: the complex order parameter ψ of the condensate is a macrosopic degree of freedom emerging from the interactions of many electrons. A superconducting flux or persistent current qubit in the state $|0\rangle$ is realized as superconducting loop with current going clock-wise, while current going counter clock-wise can represent the orthogonal state $|1\rangle$. The magnetic flux in the loop is quantized in units of $\frac{hc}{2e}$. Upon application of half of such unit of flux, it is energetically most favorable for the loop to carry currents, clockwise or, energetically-equivalent, counterclockwise, so that these currents make the magnetic flux an integer flux unit. The transition from $|0\rangle$ to $|1\rangle$ can be prohibited as it would require a macrosopic change of the state of the condensate through processes which are energetically unfavorable.

This flux qubit could be operated as a classical bit in which only the states $|0\rangle$ or $|1\rangle$ are used, or as a qubit which we wish to keep in a coherent superposition $\alpha|0\rangle + \beta|1\rangle$ [17]. In its first incarnation it has been proposed as the developing RSFQ (rapid-single-flux-quantum) technology [16] and such flux quantum bit can be preserved for, in all likelihood, many years. If we wish to use it as a qubit then more protection from noise is required, as qubits can dephase while classical bits cannot. If a qubit is defined as two degenerate (or nondegenerate) eigenstates of a Hamiltonian, dephasing occurs whenever the energies of these two eigenstates randomly fluctuate in time. The eigenenergies are susceptible typically to any coupling of the selected two-level system with the environment: charges, spins, phonons, stray magnetic or electric fields, even though these couplings may be relatively weak.

One may thus be led to ask: are there systems in which additional weak terms in the Hamiltonian do not affect the eigenenergies of, say, a degenerate ground-space in which one stores a qubit? It was the important insight of Alexei Kitaev to address this question and relate it to the concept of topology and topological order [14]. Kitaev envisioned using a two-dimensional, topologically-ordered material supporting anyonic excitations. By braiding of these excitations (i.e. moving them around) one would be able to perform universal logic on the qubits encoded in a degenerate eigenspace of the Hamiltonian of the material. The quest to realize this topological quantum computation scheme in a fractional quantum Hall system is ongoing.

Kitaev also introduces a toy model Hamiltonian related to a quantum error-correcting code, the toric code [14], which although extremely simple, captures the essential features of how may be able to store a qubit robustly in a 2D macroscopic system. The features of this model are most easily explained by considering the variant of this model which is called the surface code. We imagine elementary qubits laid out on the edges of a 2D lattice, see Fig. 1. The surface

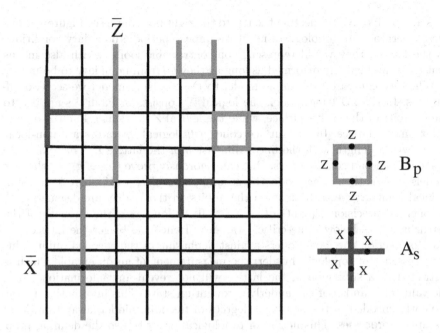

Fig. 1. Surface Code Model on a $L \times L$ lattice. A qubit lives on every *edge* of the black lattice, in total there are $L^2 + (L-1)^2$ qubits. Two types of local parity check operators, A_s and B_p, each act on four qubits (except at the boundary). The subspace of states which satisfy the parity checks, i.e. for which $A_s = +1$ and $B_p = +1$, is two-dimensional and hence represents a qubit. The logical $\overline{Z}$ and $\overline{X}$ operator of this qubit is any string of Z operators connecting the top- to bottom (realizing $\overline{Z}$) or any string of X operators connecting the left- to right boundary of the lattice (realizing $\overline{X}$).

code Hamiltonian reads $H = -\Delta(\sum_s A_s + \sum_p B_p)$ where $\sum_p$ is the sum over all plaquettes on the lattice and $\sum_s$ is the sum over stars and $\Delta > 0$. The plaquette term B_p equals the product of four Pauli Z operators around a plaquette on the lattice. One can view this operator as a parity check on the qubits, $B_p = +1$ for even parity and $B_p = -1$ for odd parity. The star operator A_s is similarly a 4-qubit parity check, but on the dual lattice, i.e. it applies to the 4 qubits on edges emanating from a vertex, and the check occurs in the Hadamard-rotated basis so that it is a product of Pauli Xs (the Hadamard transformation $H : X \leftrightarrow Z$). At the boundaries the parity checks become 3-qubit checks, see the Figure. This Hamiltonian, like the 2D Ising model, has a two-dimensional degenerate ground-space. One can take two orthogonal states in this space and call them the logical "0" denoted as $|\overline{0}\rangle$ and "1" denoted as $|\overline{1}\rangle$.

Can we understand how one can store a qubit as $\alpha|\overline{0}\rangle + \beta|\overline{1}\rangle$ robustly? The qubit is characterized by the logical operations $\overline{X} : |\overline{0}\rangle \leftrightarrow |\overline{1}\rangle$ and $\overline{Z} : |\overline{0}\rangle + |\overline{1}\rangle \leftrightarrow |\overline{0}\rangle - |\overline{1}\rangle$. The logical operator $\overline{Z}$ can be chosen to be a product of Pauli Zs connecting the top boundary to the bottom boundary, and the logical operator

$\overline{X}$ is any path of Xs connecting the left to the right boundary, see Figure 1. Both these operators are topological, i.e. if we impose periodic boundary conditions on the lattice, they would represent non-contractible loops, which also means that they can be freely deformed as long as they go from boundary to boundary.

When we compare this simple model to the 2D Ising model we see two differences. In the 2D Ising model, the logical $\overline{X}$ consists of Pauli Xs applied to the (qu)bits of the entire surface, while the logical $\overline{Z}$ is a single Pauli Z on any qubit on the lattice. In the surface code, *both* logical operators are non-local, i.e. growth in length with the linear dimension of the lattice L. This difference has good and bad consequences. One can rigorously prove (see e. g. [8]) that for models such as the surface code, the ground-states of $H + \epsilon V$ where V is a sum of local arbitrary perturbations on the qubits on the lattice, are degenerate to exponential precision $O(\exp(-cL^{\alpha}))$ ($\alpha > 0$) as long as ϵ, the strength of the perturbation, is below some critical value ϵ_c. Hence the bigger the lattice, the more protection the model offers against dephasing of the encoded qubit. This is the essence of topological order: the measurement of an observable which is restricted to a subregion of the lattice will not reveal any information about the value of α and β of the underlying quantum state. This information is conveniently encoded in the non-local degrees of freedom, hidden away from local disruptive processes. This notion of topological order is also the defining property of the surface code as a quantum error correcting code for which the code distance, defined as the minimum weight of any logical operator, is L.

But there is bad news too, which has a dimensional dependence. The two logical operators are both strings and not surfaces as in the 2D Ising model and this directly impacts the protection of our qubit against thermal excitations, as was first noted in [12]. A thermal excitation or an error corresponds to a change in the parity check values: for a X error on a certain edge, the plaquette operators B_p next to this edge will flip sign from $+1$ to -1. A string of X errors similarly terminates at two sites where the plaquette operator has flipped signs; these can be called defects or particles which can diffuse (the string of X errors gets longer) or be annihilated (the X error disappears). As in the 1D Ising model, a long connected string of X errors has the same energy as a short string, because the price for the excitation is paid at the 0-dimensional boundary. Phrased differently, the energy barrier for thermal excitations that destroy the stored quantum information, is a constant, independent of lattice size L. This finding has been corroborated in [1] by showing that the storage time of such a qubit at finite temperature T is $O(e^{-c\Delta/T})$ (with some constant c), independent of system size. This means that the possibility of robustly storing a qubit is restricted to the realm of sufficiently low temperatures $T \ll \Delta$.

It is natural to ask what can then be achieved in three or higher dimensions. It was Franz Wegner in 1971 who considered this question in the setting of Z_2-gauge theories [22,15]. The surface code or toric model can be alternatively represented as a doubled version of a Z_2-gauge theory. The gauge theory has the Hamiltonian $H = -\Delta \sum_p B_p$, and the commuting star operators A_s are the local gauge symmetries of the Hamiltonian that flip the spins surrounding a vertex of the lattice. Wegner defined a 3D version of this model on a cubic lattice with 4-qubit plaquette terms B_p^z, B_p^x, B_p^y orthogonal to the z, x and y axis respectively. He observed that this 3D model has a finite-temperature phase transition but no spontaneous symmetry breaking of a local order parameter such as the magnetization in the Ising model. In modern days this 3D Wegner model can be viewed as a three-dimensional version of the toric code. This 3D toric code was analyzed in detail in [10]. The 3D toric code has an energy barrier scaling with lattice dimension L for the logical $\overline{X}$ operator. What this means is that at sufficiently low temperature, below the critical temperature, a qubit initially encoded in $|\overline{0}\rangle$, will remain in the state $|\overline{0}\rangle$ modulo small fluctuations, i.e. small local X errors. The candidate for the nonlocal order *operator* would then be $\overline{Z}$, whose expectation however depends on microscopic detail, the presence of small X errors, and is therefore not expected to be stable. One can define an *error-corrected* order operator $\overline{Z}_{ec}$ [2] in which the process of correction against X errors is taken into account, similar as the magnetization is robust against small sets of spin flips. Below the phase transition, the expectation of this operator $\overline{Z}_{ec}$ is expected to be stable [2].

The crucial departure from gauge theories comes from realizing that this is only half the story. We get the 3D toric code by adding the gauge symmetries to the 3D gauge theory so that $H = -\Delta(\sum_p \sum_{i=x,y,z} B_p^i + \sum_s A_s)$ where the star operators A_s are now X-parity checks on the 6 qubits on edges emanating from a vertex in the 3D cubic lattice. In order to be thermally protected *against both* $\overline{X}$ and $\overline{Z}$ errors, we demand that in *both* gauge theories there is "spontaneous-symmetry breaking characterized by a non-local order parameter" below a critical temperature. This means that below the phase transition, both $\overline{X}_{ec}$ and $\overline{Z}_{ec}$ should have stable expectations. To understand this, imagine that we prepare the quantum memory initially in the state $\frac{1}{\sqrt{2}}(|\overline{0}\rangle + |\overline{1}\rangle)$. Dephasing of this state would of course not affect the expectation of $\overline{Z}_{ec}$ (which for this state is $\langle \overline{Z}_{ec} \rangle = 0$). But complete dephasing to the mixed state $\frac{1}{2}(|\overline{0}\rangle\langle\overline{0}| + |\overline{1}\rangle\langle\overline{1}|)$ lets $\overline{X}_{ec}$ go from an initial value of $+1$ to 0.

Alas, in the 3D model, the star A_s operators detect, similar as in the 2D surface code model, the end-points of strings of Z-errors. Such Z-error strings can grow and merge without energy expenditure leading to an $O(1)$ energy barrier for a logical $\overline{Z}$ error. In this sense the 3D toric code can be viewed as a model of robust storage of a classical bit which is protected against bit-flip errors $\overline{X}$ but not phase-flip errors $\overline{Z}$.

That there are dimensional obstructions to realizing thermally-stable topological order, or finite-temperature robust storage of quantum information, or self-correcting quantum memories [5] was also confirmed in [9]. These results

---

[2] Most of the discussion on determining a nonlocal order parameter has been focused on finding a single parameter which distinguishes the low-temperature topological phase from the high-temperature phase. Characterizing the topological phase by a set of stable nonlocal order operators $(\overline{Z}_{ec}, \overline{X}_{ec})$ whose expectations both vanish in the high-temperature phase, seems a proper quantum generalization of magnetization in classical memories.

prove the existence of an $O(1)$ energy barrier for any 2D stabilizer quantum code. A 4D version of the toric code model does exhibit all desired features and it has been shown that contact with a heat-bath would allow for a storage time τ growing exponentially with system-size below the critical temperature [2], a true demonstration of macroscopic quantum coherence, however in four spatial dimensions...

So, is this an answer to the question formulated in the article? Quantum information is intrinsically less robust than classical information as we live only in three spatial dimensions, whereas we need more dimensions quantumly as we need to be protected from both X as well as Z errors. Of course, such a simple picture is appealing but may be ultimately misleading. There are at least three caveats, from a pure theoretical perspective.

First of all, we have a vision of active error correction for 2D quantum systems encoded in the surface code (or similar 2D topological quantum codes). This is the surface code architecture [12,20,13] in which one actively determines the presence and location of excitations. Ideally this architecture is implemented at the most physical level, that is, with a naturally suited dissipative mechanism which drives or keep the system in the code space without inducing logical errors. One could say that we get around the dimensional obstruction by active inclusion of the time-dimension and classical processing. This machinery of error correction will be challenging to implement but several qubits under construction, such as ion-trap and superconducting transmon qubits, are coming close the noise rate of 10^{-4} which would be required to start benefitting from this scheme.

Secondly, the situation in 3D concerning quantum self-correction, i.e. the presence of system-size dependent energy barriers for topologically-ordered many-body systems, is not clearcut. Results in [9] left open the question whether there would exist 3D lattice models where both logical operators were surface-like, even though this would seem hard to realize. On the other hand, from the picture of the toric code family, one can envision a certain no-go result, based on dualities. In D dimensions, if one logical operator, say $\overline{X}$, has $d \leq D$-dimensional support, then $\overline{Z}$ is only left with at most $D - d$-dimensional support. This duality was proved for 3D translationally-invariant stabilizer codes in [23], under the restriction that the number of qubits encoded in the code is independent of lattice size (and thus only dependent on topology). Again, this leaves the possibility that there are 3D codes in which the number of encoded qubits depends nontrivially on lattice size and whose logical operators divide the available 3D space more equally. How? As Haah and later Haah and Bravyi showed in a 3D model by having logical operators with *fractal* support. The Haah model has an energy barrier proportional to $\log L$ [7]. From numerical and analytical studies, Bravyi and Haah found that the storage time $\tau \sim L^{\frac{c}{T}}$ for a constant c, thus increasing with system size L as long as L is less than some critical size $L^* \sim e^{\frac{3}{T}}$ [6].

Last but not least, the spin models that we consider are gross oversimplifications, or toy models, of the physical reality of interacting fermions and bosons and details of these more realistic models can crucially matter. For example, we have seen a different minimal dimension for spontaneous magnetization for the ferromagnetic Heisenberg model, namely three dimensions, and the Ising model, namely two dimensions. This difference relates to the fact that in the Heisenberg model, one breaks a local continuous symmetry (the commutation of the Heisenberg Hamiltonian with $U^{\otimes n}$ for any unitary U) while in the Ising model one breaks a discrete symmetry (the commutation of the Ising Hamiltonian H with $X^{\otimes n}$) [3]. Another example is the dimensional dependence of superconductivity in which a non-zero value of the superconducting order parameter is only thermally stable in three dimensions. In two dimensions, a finite-temperature phase transition, a so-called Kosterlitz-Thouless transition, does still occur due to the attractive (logarithmically-scaling with distance) interaction between excitations (vortex anti-vortex pairs) [21], which counteracts the entropic contribution below the transition temperature.

Ultimately, the question of how to build a stable quantum memory will be decided in the lab, but I hope that our theoretical understanding can guide us in identifying approaches and physical systems which are likely to lead to succeed. I thank David DiVincenzo for interesting discussions clarifying some finer points of condensed matter physics.

References

1. Alicki, R., Fannes, M., Horodecki, M.: On thermalization in Kitaev's 2D model. Journal of Physics A Mathematical General 42(6), 065303 (2009)
2. Alicki, R., Horodecki, M., Horodecki, P., Horodecki, R.: On thermal stability of topological qubit in Kitaev's 4D model. Open Sys.Inf. Dyn. 17, 1 (2010)
3. Anderson, P.W.: Basic notions of condensed matter physics. Frontiers in Physics, vol. 55. Benjamin/Cummings, Menlo Park (1984)
4. Ashcroft, N.W., Mermin, N.D.: Solid State Physics. Saunders College, Philadelphia (1976)
5. Bacon, D.: Operator quantum error-correcting subsystems for self-correcting quantum memories. Physical Review A 73(1), 012340 (2006)
6. Bravyi, S., Haah, J.: Analytic and numerical demonstration of quantum self-correction in the 3D Cubic Code. ArXiv e-prints (2011), http://arxiv.org/abs/1112.3252
7. Bravyi, S., Haah, J.: Energy Landscape of 3D Spin Hamiltonians with Topological Order. Physical Review Letters 107(15), 150504 (2011)
8. Bravyi, S., Hastings, M.B., Michalakis, S.: Topological quantum order: Stability under local perturbations. Journal of Mathematical Physics 51(9), 093512 (2010)
9. Bravyi, S., Terhal, B.: A no-go theorem for a two-dimensional self-correcting quantum memory based on stabilizer codes. New Journal of Physics 11, 043029 (2009)
10. Castelnovo, C., Chamon, C.: Topological order in a three-dimensional toric code at finite temperature. Phys. Rev. B 78(15), 155120 (2008)
11. Levin, D.A., Peres, Y., Wilmer, E.L.: Markov Chains and Mixing Times. American Mathematical Society, Providence (2008)

---

[3] In a quantum memory model encoding one qubit, the symmetry is continuous but non-local, i.e. H commutes with any $\overline{U} = e^{i\theta \hat{n} \cdot \overline{S}}$ with $\overline{S} = (\overline{X}, \overline{Y}, \overline{Z})$ and the system is gapped unlike in models with local continuous symmetries.

12. Dennis, E., Kitaev, A., Landahl, A., Preskill, J.: Topological quantum memory. J. Math. Phys. 43, 4452–4505 (2002)
13. Fowler, A.G., Stephens, A.M., Groszkowski, P.: High-threshold universal quantum computation on the surface code. Physical Review A 80(5), 052312 (2009)
14. Kitaev, A.: Fault-tolerant quantum computation by anyons. Annals of Physics 303(1), 2–30 (2003), http://arxiv.org/abs/quant-ph/9707021
15. Kogut, J.B.: An introduction to lattice gauge theory and spin systems. Rev. Mod. Phys. 51(4), 659–713 (1979)
16. Likharev, K., Semenov, V.: RSFQ logic/memory family: a new josephson-junction technology for sub-terahertz-clock-frequency digital systems. IEEE Transactions on Applied Superconductivity 1(1), 3–28 (1991)
17. Mooij, J.E., Orlando, T.P., Levitov, L., Tian, L., van der Wal, C.H., Lloyd, S.: Josephson persistent-current qubit. Science 285(5430), 1036–1039 (1999), http://www.sciencemag.org/content/285/5430/1036.abstract
18. Nielsen, M.A., Chuang, I.L.: Quantum computation and quantum information. Cambridge University Press, Cambridge (2000)
19. Peierls, R.: On Ising's model of ferromagnetism. Mathematical Proceedings of the Cambridge Philosophical Society 32(03), 477–481 (1936)
20. Raussendorf, R., Harrington, J., Goyal, K.: Topological fault-tolerance in cluster state quantum computation. New J. Phys. 9, 199–219 (2007)
21. Tinkham, M.: Introduction to superconductivity. McGraw-Hill, New York (1975)
22. Wegner, F.: Duality in generalized Ising models and phase transitions without local order parameter. J. Math. Phys. 12, 2259–2272 (1971)
23. Yoshida, B.: Feasibility of self-correcting quantum memory and thermal stability of topological order. Annals of Physics 326, 2566–2633 (2011)

Computational Intelligence in Astronomy – A Win-Win Situation

Peter Tiňo[1] and Somak Raychaudhury[2]

[1] School of Computer Science,
[2] School of Physics and Astronomy
University of Birmingham, Birmingham B15 2TT, UK
{P.Tino@cs,somak@star.sr}.bham.ac.uk
http://www.birmingham.ac.uk

Abstract. Large archives of astronomical data (images, spectra and catalogues of derived parameters) are being assembled worldwide as part of the Virtual Observatory project. In order for such massive heterogeneous data collections to be of use to astronomers, development of Computational Intelligence techniques that would combine modern machine learning with deep domain knowledge is crucial. Both fields - Computer Science and Astronomy - can hugely benefit from such a research program. Astronomers can gain new insights into structures buried deeply in the data collections that would, without the help of Computational Intelligence, stay masked. On the other hand, computer scientists can get inspiration and motivation for development of new techniques driven by the specific characteristics of astronomical data and the need to include domain knowledge in a fundamental way. In this review we present three diverse examples of such successful symbiosis.

1 Introduction

The field of Computational Intelligence is not only concerned with the theoretical basis of intelligent data processing and machine learning, but it has also made substantial contributions to a wide variety of disciplines, with new subject areas emerging from these interactions (e.g. bioinformatics, computational finance), with their own dedicated journals, conferences etc. In the field of Astrophysics, some of the fundamental research problems involve the discovery of unusual sources or patterns in multivariate data, where dimensionality is high and, due to the heterogeneous ways of acquisition, significant portions of the data might be in the form of limits ("censored data") or missing altogether.

Large archives of astronomical data (images, spectra and catalogues of derived parameters) are being assembled worldwide as part of the Virtual Observatory (www.ivoa.net), to be made available to the wider community over the coming decade. This necessitates the development of fast automated techniques for feature extraction, classification and outlier detection for very large datasets. Computational Intelligence will enable the visualisation of the structure of high dimensional and structured data, as well as flexible extraction and study of relevant patterns and substructures. As with experimental data in other branches

A.-H. Dediu, C. Martín-Vide, and B. Truthe (Eds.): TPNC 2012, LNCS 7505, pp. 57–71, 2012.

of the physical sciences, the quantifiable systematic and random errors of measurement inherent in the data have to be taken into account in most problems [33].

One of the earliest areas of Astrophysics in which machine learning methods were used was in the morphological classification of galaxies, where the norm has been that of visual classification by experts, till the number of galaxies required to be classified for the purposes of the study of galaxy evolution exceeded 10^4. Artificial neural networks [19,1] or support vector machines [36] have been popular in studying the nature of galaxy evolution from photometric images. In recent years, with the availability of optical spectra of $> 10^6$ galaxies, the study of individual stellar populations within galaxies have been helped by incorporating independent component analysis and other data-driven techniques [21,22].

In this review, we give examples from three areas of astronomical problems where our computational intelligence research has provided unique solutions, which, informed by the knowledge of physics, have helped understand the underlying astrophysical phenomena.

2   Automated Calibration of Galaxy Disruption Simulations [38]

In the hierarchical growth of structure of the Universe, galaxies grow by merging. A giant galaxy, like the Milky Way, grows predominantly by minor mergers (i.e. involving smaller dwarf galaxies or satellites). When a satellite merges with a giant galaxy, it gets tidally disrupted in the process and eventually is completely assimilated in the giant galaxy [20]. Deep observations of the nearby Universe have revealed many examples of such tidal streams that resulting from tidal disruptions. Detailed studies of these tidal streams and debris can provide valuable insight into the detailed mechanism of galaxy formation and evolution.

Other than the satellite system of our own galaxy (Milky way), the most-studied system of streams involves the closest (spiral) galaxy M31, where structures such as shells and streams of stars have been discovered in abundance in its vicinity. These exciting discoveries have led astronomers to investigate the possibility that such structures are in fact remnants of disrupted smaller satellite galaxies [8]. Models involving dark matter and stars are use simulate the process of satellite galaxy disruption in the vicinity of a large galaxy [8]. There are models with a large number of particles, representing groups of stars. The simulation space is 6-dimensional ("phase space"), three describing the spatial position of each particle, the other three describing the velocity along the spatial coordinates. The particle evolution is governed by gravitational dynamics and hydrodynamics. To track the evolution process starting from a particular initial condition, the state of the simulation (values of all six phase space parameters) are recorded successive evolution stages. Hence, the disruption process is captured in a series of simulated datasets.

In these simulations, the observed low-dimensional structures evolve along with the satellite galaxy, differing slightly from pone simulation to another according to the different initial conditions. It makes that the low-dimensional structure in these simulated datasets looks very similar, but not identical. The observational astronomer, however, observed only one snapshot in time, i.e., the current state of the evolution. The ultimate goal of astronomers is to identify the most plausible set of initial conditions leading to the distribution of stars currently observed by the astronomers.

One possible way of learning the most plausible set of initial conditions is to identify the simulated stars having the most similar distribution to that of the currently observed stars. Obviously, it is impossible to compare the particles in simulation to the real observations on a point by point bases, but the observed *density* of stars can be compared with that of the simulated particles. In [38] we reported first results from an ongoing work concentrating on measuring the 'similarity' between the simulated datasets and the observation dataset through non-parametric probability density estimation.

The approach stands and falls on the quality of density models on the simulated data. Unfortunately, parametric density estimation cannot be used, as the disrupted satellites can produce complex low-dimensional manifolds along which the stars are organized (tidal streams, shells). Semi-parametric approaches such as Gaussian mixture modelling, fitted in the maximum likelihood framework via EM algorithm, are not capable of capturing such complex density structure because of the high sensitivity to initialization. Unless we provide good estimates of the positions and shapes of low dimensional structures floating in the cloud of high dimensional points, already before the mixture fitting, there is no hope of finding a satisfactory density estimate.

Non-parametric density estimation methods seem like a plausible approach - unfortunately they cannot be directly used since they typically put a local density kernel on each observation and the number of simulated particles makes such an approach computationally prohibitive. To reduce the computational cost, several algorithms have been devised to either reduce the sample size, or to reduce the amount of components (kernels) in the original complex Parzen Windows model. The latter approaches, introduced recently, have proved successful in several applications [11,40,39]. The idea is to simplify a complex model (Parzen Windows in density estimation) while minimizing the distance between the new model and the target function. However, this process usually has complexity of $\mathcal{O}(N^2)$ or larger, where N is the size of the dataset. Compared with considering fewer points in the estimation, optimizing the simplified density model by using all of the available observations could avoid sacrificing useful information, but it also loses the simplicity of the non-parametric density model. On the other hand, the limitation of Parzen Windows could also be noticed when the data points distribute along, or partially along, low dimensional structures [35]. In such cases, spherical smoothing kernels are not optimal.

In [38], we proposed a simple new algorithm to reduce the computational cost of PW, but also to keep the simplicity of the nonparametric model by avoiding complex model construction procedures. The main idea was to cover the entire data space by a set of hyper-balls of fixed (carefully chosen) radii. For each hyper-ball, the local density was captured by a full covariance Gaussian kernel. Our model is formed by a mixture of such locally fitted Gaussians with appropriately set mixing priors.

The densities fitted in the 6-dimensional simulation can be projected into the observation space (typically two spatial coordinates + the line of sight velocity) and the likelihood given the real observations calculated. We tested the approach on 22 simulation sets representing 22 stages of galaxy disruption in a single simulation run. Each set had 32, 768 data points (particles).

In the first set of experiments we used 10-fold cross-validation in each simulation data set to measure the quality of the estimated density models. The average log-likelihoods (ALL) on each individual set estimated by Parzen Window (PW), our approach - Fast PW (FPW) and Simplified Mixture Model (SMM) [40] are plotted in figure 1. We actually used two versions of FPW: (1) a simple 'hard' FPW (FPW-H) which estimated local means and covariances solely on the points within the covering hyperballs; (2) a 'soft' version (FPW-S) in which local means and covariances are estimated in a soft manner by positioning Gaussian weighting kernels in the hyperball centers. The hyper parameters were estimated through 10-fold cross validation within the training folds. The X-axes indicates the simulation set index (numbered from 0 to 21), the Y-axes shows the ALLs estimated by the models. Both FPW versions show a superior performance relative to both PW and SMM estimators.

In the second set of experiments, we investigated how reliably a stage in the galaxy disruption process can be detected, based on 'observations' not used in the model building process. We run a rolling window of size 3 over the series

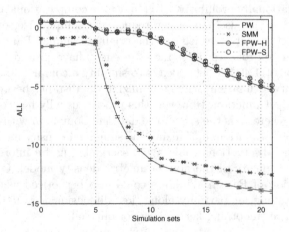

Fig. 1. Average log-likelihood on 22 simulation sets

of 22 simulation data sets, obtaining a set of 20 simulation set triplets (f, g, h), starting with simulation sets (f, g, h) at stages (0,1,2) and ending with the triplet (f, g, h) containing simulation set for stages (20,21,22). For each triplet of consecutive simulation sets (f, g, h), we estimated 3 models, one on 90% of data from f, one on 90% of data from g, and one on 90% of data from h. We also compared with Gaussian Mixture Model initialized randomly from the data (GMM) or initialized with K-means (GMM^k). To make experiments computationally feasible only 10% of the data was used to estimate the GMM models. All the models were then tested on the 10% hold-out set from g. In this way we could determine how well could the 'true' source density g be distinguished from the densities at the nearby stages f and h. This process was repeated 10 times.

We stress that the task is quite complicated as the densities corresponding to the nearby stages of galaxy disruption can be quite 'similar' and obtaining an accurate density model is essential for further investigations by the astronomers. As an illustration, we present in figure 2 two sets of 3-dimensional projections of the simulation data for the triplet $(f, g, h) = (20, 21, 22)$. The first projection is onto the spatial coordinates, the second is onto the leading 3 eigenvectors found by the Principal Component Analysis of the merged f, g and h sets.

All the models constructed on the set g have the highest hold-out ALL in each of the 20 triplets (f, g, h). However, the margin with which the set g was proclaimed the 'winner' was quite different across the models. The margins of the two FPW versions were almost the same and the variations in in the margins due to different experimental runs were negligible. The FPW methods outperformed the classical PW estimation and showed performance levels very similar to those of GMM, but with much less computational effort. The number of components in FPW-H and FPW-S varied from 150 to 850 and 700 to 4000, respectively. Note that the number of components in PW estimates was $\approx 30,000$.

3   Time Delay Estimation in Gravitationally Lensed Signals [4,5]

Time delay estimation between arrival times of two signals that originate from the same source but travel along different paths to the observer is a real-world problem in Astronomy. Signals to be analysed can represent repeated measurement, over many months or years, of the flux of radiation (optical light or radio waves) from a very distant quasar - a very bright source of light usually a few trillion light-years away. Some of these quasars appear as a set of multiple nearby images on the sky, due to the fact that the trajectory of light coming from the source gets bent as it passes a massive galaxy on the way (the "gravitational lens"). As a result, the observer receives the light from various directions, resulting in the detection of several images [16,32]. This phenomenon is called *gravitational lensing*. It is a natural consequence of a prediction of the General theory of Relativity, which postulates that massive objects distort space-time and thus cause the bending of trajectories of light rays passing near them.

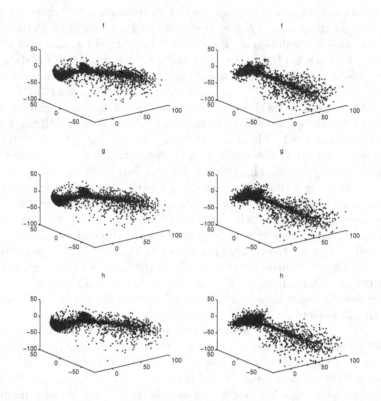

Fig. 2. 3-dimensional projections of the simulation data for the triplet $(f, g, h) = (20, 21, 22)$. The first projection (1st column) is onto the 3 spatial coordinates, the second (2nd column) is onto the leading 3 eigenvectors found by the Principal Component Analysis of the merged f, g and h sets.

Quasars are variable sources, and the same sequence of variations is detected at different times in the different images, according to the travel time along the various paths. Crucially, the time delay between the signals depends on the mass of the lens, and thus it is the most direct method to measure the distribution of matter in the Universe, which is often dark [31,16].

In this context, the underlying temporal pattern of emitted radiation fluxes from a quasar gets delayed, and the process of observation adds all kinds of noise. Moreover, like all astronomical time series measurements, they are also typically irregularly sampled with possibly large observational gaps (missing data) [24,29,23,15]. This is due to practical limitations of observation such as equipment availability, weather conditions, the brightness of the moon, among many other factors [7]. Currently, over a hundred systems of lensed quasars are currently known and about a dozen of these have been monitored for long periods. In some of these cases, the measurement of a time delay has been claimed.

In [5,4] we introduced a model based technique for estimating time delays in fluxes from gravitationally lensed objects (such as quasars). The main idea of the method was to impose an internal model on the quasar variability in time and then expect that the multiple images will follow that model, up to observational noise and time delays. We formulated the internal model of quasar variability in the framework of kernel regression (with free parameters determined from available data). Our approach was compared with currently popular methods of estimating time delays from real astronomical data: **(1)** *Dispersion spectra* method [26,27,25], and **(2)** the structure-function-based method (*PRH*, [30]). Two versions of Dispersion spectra were used; D_1^2 is free of parameters [26,27] and $D_{4,2}^2$ has a decorrelation length parameter δ involving only nearby points in the weighted correlation [27,25]. In the case of PRH method, we used the image A from the data to estimate the structure function [30].

For experimental (observational) data, we focused on Q0957+561, the first multiply-imaged quasar to be discovered [37]. This source, which has a pair of images (that we refer to as A and B), has been monitored for over twenty years (in both radio and optical range). In figure 3 we show an example of real optical data measured from Q0957+561. The optical fluxes observed from images A and B are given in the astronomical unit of magnitude (mag m), defined as $m = -2.5 \log_{10} f$, where f is the flux measured when observed through a green filter [18] (g-band). The measurement errors are shown as error bars. The source was monitored nightly, but many observations were missed due to cloudy weather and telescope scheduling. The big gap in Fig. 3 is an intentional gap in the nightly monitoring, since a delay of about 400 days, the pattern, was known 'a priori' – monitoring programs on this quasar started in 1979. Therefore, the peak in the light curve of image A, between 700 and 800 days, corresponds to the peak in that of image B between 1,100 and 1,200 days.

Despite numerous claims, a universally agreed value for the time delay in the Q0957+561 system has not emerged [18,5]. Indeed, a major problem with time delay estimation in astrophysics literature has been that these estimates are routinely produced for individual quasars, for which we have no idea what the 'true' time delay is (e.g. [30,28,3,7,13]). The uncertainty bounds in the reported estimates are mostly due to assumed noise model on the observations - the estimation has been repeated in a series of Monte Carlo experimental data generated from the measured flux values, under the noise model. However, for an unbiased comparison of alternative methods, before they are employed to the analysis of real data, they should be subjected to a large data collection in a controlled experimental setting where the time delay is externally imposed and known.

In [4] we generated a large number of flux times series resembling fluxes from real quasars. Three data generation mechanisms were considered:

- We simulated optical observations as in [24]. The data sets were irregularly sampled with three levels of noise and observational gaps of different size. 50 data set realisations per noise level were generated, yielding 38,505 data sets

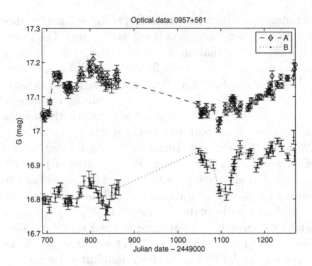

Fig. 3. Optical observations of the brightness of the doubly-imaged quasar Q0957+561, in the g-band, as a function of time (Top - Image A; Bottom - Image B). The time is measured in days (Julian days–2,449,000 days).

– Data streams were generated by Gaussian process, following [30], with a fixed covariance matrix given by a structure function according to [29]. The data was highly sampled with periodic gaps [7], simulating a monitoring campaign of eight months; yielding 61 samples per time series. We imposed seven 'true' delays and 100 realisations for each value of true delay [5].
– The data was generated from a Bayesian model [13], simulating three levels of noise with 225 data sets per level of noise (there were 3 levels of noise). The data were irregularly sampled with 100 observations per time series.

It is remarkable how the imposition of a unifying smooth internal model in our method stabilized the delay estimation. After tests for statistical significance, the machine learning based method employing kernel regression emerged as a clear overall winner in the large set of controlled experiments on synthetic data with known time delay. We stress that this method was able to sometimes outperform even methods that were used to generate the data sets themselves (Gaussian process or the Bayesian model of [13]).

In terms of real data from Q0957+561, the best (smallest estimated error) time delay quotes were 417±3 [18] and 419.5±0.8 [6]. Our results were consistent with these findings. However, we speculate that the estimate of 417±3 days constitutes an underestimate. For the quasar Q0957+561, the latest reports also give estimates around 420 days by using other data sets [24]. The delay estimates should be robust across the wavelength range since the gravitational lensing theory predicts that the time delay must be the same regardless of the wavelength of observation [31,16,32].

4 Clustering and Topographic Mapping of Light Curves from Eclipsing Binary Stars [9]

A binary is a gravitationally bound pair of stars that orbit a common centre of mass. Astronomical observations suggest that almost half of the stars are in binary systems [12]. Thus, the study of such systems is a crucial element for understanding a significant proportion of stars. Amongst other reasons, binary stars are important to astrophysics because they allow calculation of fundamental quantities such as masses and radii. The increasing number of binary star discoveries provides samples for testing theoretical models for stellar formation and evolution. Also, by measuring their fundamental parameters they can serve as distance indicators to galaxies. Moreover, the study of binaries has led to the discovery of extrasolar planets. A particular subclass of binary stars are eclipsing binary stars. The luminosity of such stars varies over time and forms a graph called light curve. Light curves are important because they provide information on the characteristics of stars and help in the identification of their type. It is therefore of great importance for the astronomers to have tools for automated analysis of large repositories of light curves from binary systems, e.g. tools for grouping and topographic mapping of such systems.

While clustering of a data set is mainly concerned with finding natural groups of data items e.g. according to some 'similarity' measure, topographic mapping is concerned with the construction of low-dimensional maps of the data where the distances on the map between data items reveal the structure of their relationships. Both approaches can provide valuable tools in initial mining complex data sets. The Self-Organizing map (SOM) [17] and its extensions are examples of tools for topographic map construction.

Several probabilistic analogues of SOM have been proposed, seeking to address some of the limitations of SOM[1] (e.g. [2]). One formulates a mixture of Gaussian densities constrained on a smooth image of a low-dimensional latent space. Each point in the latent space is mapped via a smooth non-linear mapping to its image in the high-dimensional data space. This image plays the role of the mean of a local spherical Gaussian noise model capturing data points in its vicinity. Due to the smoothness of the mapping, when latent points are mapped to the high-dimensional data space, they retain their local neighborhood structure. The model is trained by maximizing the model likelihood for the given data. Once the model has been trained, each data item is represented in the latent space by a point given as the mean position of latent points weighted by their posterior probabilities (responsibilities) given the data item.

Such approaches provide a framework that is readily extensible to structured data by adopting alternative formulations of noise models in the place of Gaussian densities. Such extensions have been proposed in [34] for the visualization of symbolic sequences and in [10] for the visualization of tree-structured data, where hidden Markov models and hidden Markov tree models play the role of local noise models respectively. In the same spirit, in [9] we formulated a

---

[1] E.g. the absence of a principled cost function.

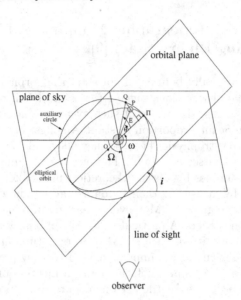

Fig. 4. Angles orientating the orbital plane with respect to the plane of sky, and angles associated with the orbits. Adapted from [14].

generative probabilistic model for clustering and topographic mapping of light curves from eclipsing binary stars. We adopted a specialized noise model based on the physical Kepler model that describes the generation of such light curves.

The core of the noise model is given by the basics of two-body gravitational dynamics, i.e. the Kepler model parametrized by the masses of the two stars (primary mass + mass ratio), the eccentricity of their relative orbit and other dynamical parameters, plus the geometry of viewing, i.e., the inclination of the orbit to the line of sight, as illustrated in figure 4. The overall model - a constrained and unconstrained mixture of such parametrized probabilistic models of fluxes from binary star models - can then be readily used for clustering and topographic mapping of binary systems, respectively. Since all the parameters are physically interpretable with universally known priors, the overall models were fitted in the MAP (maximum a-posteriori) framework.

The methodology was applied to a dataset of light curves from two resources:

(1) The *Catalog and Archive of Eclipsing Binaries* at http://ebola.eastern.edu/ which is a collection of light curves of the brightest eclipsing binary stars in the sky, compiled from the literature, based on several decades of photometric data;
(2) *All Sky Automated Survey* at http://archive.princeton.edu/~asas/. This is a survey of the brightest stars visible in the sky in the Southern hemisphere from a dedicated telescope in Chile.

Figure 5 presents clustering of the fluxes into 6 clusters. For each cluster, we show all lightcurves assigned to it. The clusters represent a natural grouping of binary systems into 4 groups according to their physical properties. The first three clusters group binaries with low eccentricity (symmetrical normalized fluxes). Cluster 2 represents binary systems with smaller primary and secondary stars and well-separated systems with large semi-major axis. On the other hand, cluster 3 groups binary systems with larger primary and secondary stars and systems with small separation between the primary and secondary stars. Cluster 1 represent binary systems in between the extremes characterized by clusters 2 and 3. Cluster 4 collects binaries of higher eccentricity. The binaries in cluster 4 have smaller primary and secondary stars and/or a large semi-major axis. Clusters 5 and 6 play the role of "garbage collectors" and collect binary systems that are either 'atypical' or represent low frequency binary star types in the data set that could not be naturally grouped together based on the given data.

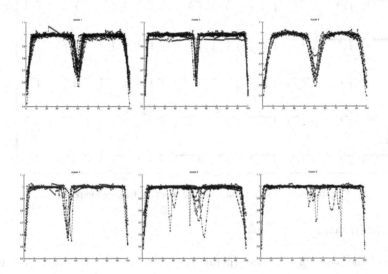

Fig. 5. Lightcurves belonging to each of the 6 clusters ordered from top left to bottom right

Visualization of the binary systems through their topographic mapping is shown in figure 6. The 2-dimensional manifold of binary star models (visualization space) is represented by the regular grid of fluxes generated at the corresponding positions on the visualization space. Superposed on this grid are some projections of the fluxes from real binary systems. A detailed discussion of this visualization is beyond the scope of this paper, we only mention that to the best of our knowledge, our methodology represents the first fully principled approach to physics based data driven automated clustering and topographic mapping of binary complexes.

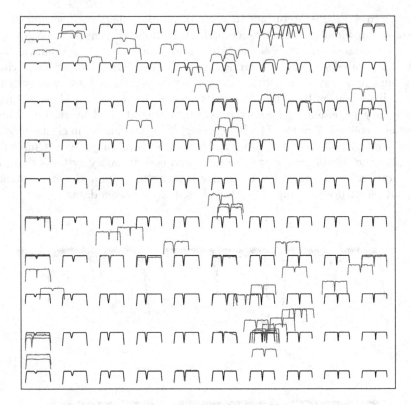

Fig. 6. Topographic mapping of a set of binary systems

5   Conclusions

In view of the assembly of large (petabytes) astronomical data archives, as in the Virtual Observatory, where observations across the electromagnetic spectrum (i.e. radio, infrared, optical, X-rays etc) of planets, stars and galaxies, the need has arisen for the application of computational intelligence to the automated analysis of these large multivariate datasets. These data will be in the form of images and spectra, and the combination of a large number of observations of the same parts of sky will give rise to measurements of variability in the form of multivariate time series, as well as various catalogues of derived parameters, whether directly derived from the observations or through detailed physical modelling of the observations.

Fast automated methods of classification, parameter extraction, characterisation and visualisation of multi-dimensional and multi-type datasets are necessary for advances in this field, and they have to be tailored to the particular problems with the help of the knowledge of the domain. One particular requirement of astrophysics is the handling of systematic and random errors introduced by the process of measurement as well as the inherent diversity of various systems. Learning algorithms are essential is characterising the inputs of experts, since many sub-fields still depend on visual characterisation of features in the observed morphology, spectra and time-series acquired in astronomical datasets. In this review, we have shown three diverse examples where such methods have been successful in understanding the physical problem, which in turn have helped in the development of new approaches in computational intelligence.

References

1. Banerji, M., Lahav, O., Lintott, C.J., Abdalla, F.B., Schawinski, K., Bamford, S.P., Andreescu, D., Murray, P., Raddick, M.J., Slosar, A., Szalay, A., Thomas, D., Vandenberg, J.: Galaxy Zoo: reproducing galaxy morphologies via machine learning. Monthly Notices of the Royal Astronomical Society 406, 342–353 (2010)
2. Bishop, C.M., Svensén, M., Williams, C.K.I.: GTM: The generative topographic mapping. Neural Computation 10(1), 215–234 (1998)
3. Burud, I., Magain, P., Sohy, S., Hjorth, J.: A novel approach for extracting time-delays from lightcurves of lensed quasar images. Astronomy and Astrophysics 380(2), 805–810 (2001)
4. Cuevas-Tello, J.C., Tiño, P., Raychaudhury, S., Yao, X., Harva, M.: Uncovering delayed patterns in noisy and irregularly sampled time series: An astronomy application. Pattern Recognition 43(3), 1165–1179 (2010)
5. Cuevas-Tello, J.C., Tiño, P., Raychaudhury, S.: How accurate are the time delay estimates in gravitational lensing? Astronomy and Astrophysics 454, 695–706 (2006)
6. Cuevas-Tello, J.C., Tiño, P., Raychaudhury, S.: A Kernel-Based Approach to Estimating Phase Shifts Between Irregularly Sampled Time Series: An Application to Gravitational Lenses. In: Fürnkranz, J., Scheffer, T., Spiliopoulou, M. (eds.) ECML 2006. LNCS (LNAI), vol. 4212, pp. 614–621. Springer, Heidelberg (2006)
7. Eigenbrod, A., Courbin, F., Vuissoz, C., Meylan, G., Saha, P., Dye, S.: COSMO-GRAIL: The COSmological MOnitoring of GRAvItational Lenses. I. How to sample the light curves of gravitationally lensed quasars to measure accurate time delays. Astronomy and Astrophysics 436, 25–35 (2005)
8. Fardal, M.A., Babul, A., Geehan, J.J., Guhathakurt, P.: Investigating the andromeda stream - ii. orbital fits and properties of the progenitor. Monthly Notices of the Royal Astronomical Society 366, 1012–1028 (2006)
9. Gianniotis, N., Tiño, P., Spreckley, S., Raychaudhury, S.: Topographic Mapping of Astronomical Light Curves via a Physically Inspired Probabilistic Model. In: Alippi, C., Polycarpou, M., Panayiotou, C., Ellinas, G. (eds.) ICANN 2009, Part I. LNCS, vol. 5768, pp. 567–576. Springer, Heidelberg (2009)
10. Gianniotis, N., Tiño, P.: Visualisation of tree-structured data through generative probabilistic modelling. In: Verleysen, M. (ed.) European Symposium on Artificial Neural Networks, pp. 97–102. D-Facto (2007)
11. Girolami, M., He, C.: Probability density estimation from optimally condensed data samples. IEEE Transactions on Pattern Analysis and Machine Intelligence 25, 1253–1264 (2003)
12. Guinan, E.F., Engle, S.G.: The brave new world of binary star studies. Astrophysics Space Science 304, 5–11 (2006)
13. Harva, M., Raychaudhury, S.: Bayesian estimation of time delays between unevenly sampled signals. In: IEEE International Workshop on Machine Learning for Signal Processing, pp. 111–116. IEEE (2006)

14. Hilditch, R.W.: An introduction to close binary stars. Cambridge University Press (2001)
15. Inada, N., Oguri, M., Becker, R.H., Shin, M.-S., Richards, G.T., Hennawi, J.F., White, R.L., Pindor, B., Strauss, M.A., Kochanek, C.S., Johnston, D.E., Gregg, M.D., Kayo, I., Eisenstein, D., Hall, P.B., Castander, F.J., Clocchiatti, A., Anderson, S.F., Schneider, D.P., York, D.G., Lupton, R., Chiu, K., Kawano, Y., Scranton, R., Frieman, J.A., Keeton, C.R., Morokuma, T., Rix, H.-W., Turner, E.L., Burles, S., Brunner, R.J., Sheldon, E.S., Bahcall, N.A., Masataka, F.: The Sloan Digital Sky Survey Quasar Lens Search. II. Statistical Lens Sample from the Third Data Release. Astronomical Journal 135, 496–511 (2008)
16. Kochanek, C., Schechter, P.: The Hubble constant from gravitational lens time delays. In: Freedman, W.L. (ed.) Measuring and Modeling the Universe, from the Carnegie Observatories Centennial Symposia, vol. 2, p. 117. Cambridge University Press (2004)
17. Kohonen, T.: The self-organizing map. Proceedings of the IEEE 78(9), 1464–1480 (1990)
18. Kundic, T., Turner, E.L., Colley, W.N., Gott-III, J.R., Rhoads, J.E., Wang, Y., Bergeron, L.E., Gloria, K.A., Long, D.C., Malhorta, S., Wambsganss, J.: A robust determination of the time delay in 0957+561A,B and a measurement of the global value of Hubble's constant. Astrophysical Journal 482(1), 75–82 (1997)
19. Lahav, O., Naim, A., Buta, R.J., Corwin, H.G., de Vaucouleurs, G., Dressler, A., Huchra, J.P., van den Bergh, S., Raychaudhury, S., Sodre Jr., L., Storrie-Lombardi, M.C.: Galaxies, Human Eyes, and Artificial Neural Networks. Science 267, 859–862 (1995)
20. McConnachie, A.W., Irwin, M.J., Ibata, R.A., Dubinski, J., Widrow, L.M., Martin, N.F., Côté, P., Dotter, A.L., Navarro, J.F., Ferguson, A.M.N., Puzia, T.H., Lewis, G.F., Babul, A., Barmby, P., Bienaymé, O., Chapman, S.C., Cockcroft, R., Collins, M.L.M., Fardal, M.A., Harris, W.E., Huxor, A., Mackey, A.D., Peñarrubia, J., Rich, R.M., Richer, H.B., Siebert, A., Tanvir, N., Valls-Gabaud, D., Venn, K.A.: The remnants of galaxy formation from a panoramic survey of the region around M31. Nature 461, 66–69 (2009)
21. Nolan, L.A., Harva, M.O., Kabán, A., Raychaudhury, S.: A data-driven Bayesian approach for finding young stellar populations in early-type galaxies from their ultraviolet-optical spectra. Monthly Notices of the Royal Astronomical Society 366, 321–338 (2006)
22. Nolan, L.A., Raychaudhury, S., Kabán, A.: Young stellar populations in early-type galaxies in the Sloan Digital Sky Survey. Monthly Notices of the Royal Astronomical Society 375, 381–387 (2007)
23. Oguri, M.: Gravitational Lens Time Delays: A Statistical Assessment of Lens Model Dependences and Implications for the Global Hubble Constant. Astrophysical Journal 660, 1–15 (2007)
24. Ovaldsen, J.E., Teuber, J., Schild, R.E., Stabell, R.: New aperture photometry of QSO 0957+561; application to time delay and microlensing. Astronomy and Astrophysics 402(3), 891–904 (2003)
25. Pelt, J., Hjorth, J., Refsdal, S., Schild, R., Stabell, R.: Estimation of multiple time delays in complex gravitational lens systems. Astronomy and Astrophysics 337(3), 681–684 (1998)
26. Pelt, J., Kayser, R., Refsdal, S., Schramm, T.: Time delay controversy on QSO 0957+561 not yet decided. Astronomy and Astrophysics 286(1), 775–785 (1994)
27. Pelt, J., Kayser, R., Refsdal, S., Schramm, T.: The light curve and the time delay of QSO 0957+561. Astronomy and Astrophysics 305(1), 97–106 (1996)

28. Pijpers, F.P.: The determination of time delays as an inverse problem - the case of the double quasar 0957+561. Monthly Notices of the Royal Astronomical Society 289(4), 933–944 (1997)
29. Pindor, B.: Discovering Gravitational Lenses through Measurements of Their Time Delays. Astrophysical Journal 626, 649–656 (2005)
30. Press, W.H., Rybicki, G.B., Hewitt, J.N.: The time delay of gravitational lens 0957+561, I. Methodology and analysis of optical photometric Data. Astrophysical Journal 385(1), 404–415 (1992)
31. Refsdal, S.: On the possibility of determining the distances and masses of stars from the gravitational lens effect. Monthly Notices of the Royal Astronomical Society 134, 315–319 (1966)
32. Saha, P.: Gravitational Lensing. In: Murdin, P. (ed.) Encyclopedia of Astronomy and Astrophysics. Nature Publishing, London (2001)
33. Sun, J., Kaban, A., Raychaudhury, S.: Robust Mixtures in the Presence of Measurement Errors. In: International Conference on Machine Learning, pp. 847–854 (June 2007)
34. Tiňo, P., Kaban, A., Sun, Y.: A generative probabilistic approach to visualizing sets of symbolic sequences. In: KDD 2004: Proceedings of the Tenth ACM SIGKDD International Conference on Knowledge Discovery and Data Mining, pp. 701–706. ACM Press (2004)
35. Vincent, P., Bengio, Y.: Manifold parzen windows. Advances in Neural Information Processing Systems 15, 825–832 (2003)
36. Wadadekar, Y.: Estimating Photometric Redshifts Using Support Vector Machines. Publications of the Astronomical Society of the Pacific 117, 79–85 (2005)
37. Walsh, D., Carswell, R.F., Weymann, R.J.: 0957 + 561 A, B - Twin quasistellar objects or gravitational lens. Nature 279, 381–384 (1979)
38. Wang, X., Tiňo, P., Fardal, M., Raychaudhury, S., Babul, A.: Fast Parzen Window Density Estimator. In: Proceedings of the International Joint Conference on Neural Networks - IJCNN 2009, Atlanta, Georgia, pp. 473–475. IEEE Computer Society (2009)
39. Chen, S., Hong, X., Harris, C.J.: A forward-constrained regression algorithm for sparse kernel density estimation. IEEE Transactions on Neural Networks 19, 193–198 (2008)
40. Zhang, K., Kwok, J.T.: Simplifying mixture models through function approximation. Advances in Neural Information Processing Systems 15, 825–832 (2006)

A Multi-objective Approach
to Solve the Location Areas Problem

Víctor Berrocal-Plaza, Miguel A. Vega-Rodríguez,
Juan M. Sánchez-Pérez, and Juan A. Gómez-Pulido

Dept. Technologies of Computers & Communications, University of Extremadura
Escuela Politécnica, Campus Universitario S/N, 10003, Cáceres, Spain
{vicberpla,mavega,sanperez,jangomez}@unex.es

Abstract. The Public Land Mobile Networks (PLMN) are designed to provide anywhere, any kind, and anytime services to either static or moving users, therefore mobile location management is a fundamental tool in these systems. One of the techniques used in mobile location management is the location areas strategy, which set out the problem as an optimization problem with two costs, location update and paging. In this paper we resort to a multi-objective evolutionary algorithm, Non-dominated Sorting Genetic Algorithm II (NSGA-II), for finding quasi-optimal solutions of this optimization problem. At present, there is not any previous work that addresses the problem in a multi-objective manner, so we compare our results with those obtained by mono-objective algorithms from other authors. Results show that, for this problem, better solutions are achieved when each objective is treated separately.

Keywords: Mobile Location Management, Multi-Objective Optimization, Non-Dominated Sorting Genetic Algorithm, Location Areas Problem.

1   Introduction

The terrestrial mobile communication systems, as Public Land Mobile Networks (PLMN), allow a high information exchange among mobile terminals with limited radioelectric resources, because of the systematic frequency reuse by applying the Cell Theory. With Cell Theory, the coverage area is divided into several smaller areas, known as cells, among which resources are distributed and reused. Therefore, due to user mobility, a management system that automatically controls the tracking and the location of all users takes on a fundamental role, especially in the last few years because of a vertiginous increase in the number of mobile users.

These cells are grouped into regions in a way that each region has all available spectrum while a cell has got associated a fraction of it. Therefore, cells from different regions that are separated a specified distance, the so-called co-channel or reuse distance, can use the same frequencies. Moreover, each cell has an associated Base Station (BS), the network entity through which the user receives or makes calls, and may be of different size depending on the area traffic density, high traffic densities requires small cells, and hence a high reuse level, while large cells are required with low traffic densities.

A.-H. Dediu, C. Martín-Vide, and B. Truthe (Eds.): TPNC 2012, LNCS 7505, pp. 72–83, 2012.

The location management problem consists in two parts: location update, when a mobile terminal notifies the network a change of cell, and location inquiry, performed by the network for locating the user when it has an incoming call [1]. Ideally, the network should know the cell associated with each user at anytime, but this implies a high signaling cost, so other strategies are used.

This paper focuses on solving one of the most common strategies of location management, the Location Areas (LA) scheme, which set out the problem as an optimization problem with two cost, location update and paging, associated with two minimization and conflicting objectives. For it, we resort to a multi-objective genetic algorithm that treats each objective separately known as Non-dominated Sorting Genetic Algorithm II (NSGA-II), since it is one of the most popular algorithms in the multi-objective evolutionary computation field.

Furthermore, we compare our results with those obtained by other authors, which applied mono-objective optimization techniques to solve the same test networks. There exist several works in which computationally efficient algorithms are applied to the mono-objective LA problem, e.g. Differential Evolution (DE) [2], Simulated Annealing (SA) [3-4], Genetic Algorithms (GAs) [5-6] or Hopfield Neural Network (HNN) [7].

The paper is organized as follows. Section 2 defines the LA scheme. An adaptation of NSGA-II to solve the LA problem is presented in Section 3. Section 4 shows our results and comparisons with those results obtained by other authors. Finally, the conclusions and future work are discussed in Section 5.

2   Location Areas Scheme

The Location Areas (LA) scheme is one of the most common strategies to solve the location management problem, it has been applied into mobile networks as Groupe Spéciale Mobile (GSM), which objective is to minimize the signaling traffic associated with the user location update and tracking.

In the LA strategy, cells are grouped into connected areas, see Fig. 1, such that the network only updates the user location when it enters in a new area, reducing the location update cost at the expense of complicating the location inquiry procedure, also known as paging cost, since a user must be searched in the whole area. Therefore, the LA management considered handles two costs, location update and paging costs, so it may be expressed as an optimization problem. It should be noted the existence of other location management costs not considered in this paper, as the database management costs associated with the user location update, the cost of communications among BSs, the handoff and call diverting costs, etc., because of location update and paging costs are sufficient to compare the different strategies.

In this work, location areas constituted only by one cell, namely single cell areas, are not allowed so they are merged with its smallest neighbor location area.

Let us define the following variables:

- $N_{i,j}$: number of users that move from cell i to cell j.
- $\rho_{i,j}$: binary variable that indicates whether the cell i and cell j belong to different areas, if it is equal to 1, or not, if it is equal to 0.

- NIC_i: number of incoming calls of the cell i.
- NA_k: number of cells belonging to area k.
- CA_k: vector that stores the cells associated with the area k.
- NCell: number of cells.
- NArea: number of areas.

From the above variables, the location update and paging costs can be defined as (1) and (2) respectively.

$$N_{LU} = \sum_{i=1}^{NCell} \sum_{j=1}^{NCell} \rho_{i,j} \times N_{i,j} \tag{1}$$

$$N_P = \sum_{k=1}^{NArea} \sum_{i \in CA_k} NIC_i \times NA_k \tag{2}$$

Then, the LA optimization problem consists in finding the best possible areas configuration that minimizes these costs. In previous works, both costs are combined into an only weighted cost, see (3), where β is a ratio constant defined to take into account that the location update cost may be higher than the paging cost and commonly is set to 10.

$$Cost_{tot} = \beta \times N_{LU} + N_P \tag{3}$$

However, in this paper we treat separately each cost by a multi-objective algorithm, which allows us to provide a wide range of possibilities to the network operator.

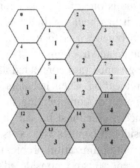

Fig. 1. Example of an LA configuration
Centre number: Area identifier. Upper left number: Cell identifier

3   Non-dominated Sorting Genetic Algorithm - II

When a multi-objective problem is solved by an only weighted objective function, a good knowledge of the problem is required because of the solutions obtained are very sensitive to the weight coefficients used. A multi-objective algorithm avoids this problem by treating independently each objective, leading to a set of equivalent solutions, known as non-dominated solutions, which are superior to the rest, see Fig. 2. A solution is defined equivalent to another when the former is better than the second in at least one goal and vice versa, whereas a solution is defined as dominated when exists a solution that achieves the same results in all goals and has at least a better result in one of the objectives. Also, the set of non-dominated solutions are grouped in the known as Pareto front.

In this paper we have implemented the Non-dominated Sorting Genetic Algorithm - II (NSGA-II) to solve the LA optimization problem. This algorithm has been proposed by K. Deb et al. in [8] as an improved version of the original NSGA defined by N. Srinivas and K. Deb in [9]. Basically NSGA-II is an elitist Genetic Algorithm (GA) with another selection operator based on the non-dominance (ND) described before and the crowding distance (CD), a parameter which favors the Pareto front spread and allows discrimination among equivalent solutions. Therefore, NSGA-II maintains the crossover and mutation operators of a generic GA.

Section 3.1 shows the individual representation and the individual initialization. Section 3.2 and Section 3.3 present a description of our crossover and mutation operators respectively. Section 3.4 exhibits the pseudo-code of the implemented NSGA-II.

Please note that when we refer to a random process, it is always associated with a uniform probability density function.

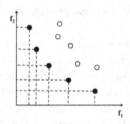

Fig. 2. Example of Pareto front where both objectives, f_1 and f_2, must be minimized
Black points: non-dominated solutions. White points: dominated solutions

3.1   Individual Representation and Initialization

In order to simplify the crossover and mutation operations, we use a simple individual representation which consists of a vector with a fixed length, equal to the network size in terms of number of cells [1], where every vector position is associated with a network cell and stores the location area assigned to it. Fig. 3 shows the individual representation of the LA configuration presented in Fig. 1.

For the initial population, each individual vector is filled with 0s and 1s generated according to a uniform probability distribution and then, this random pattern is used to determine the associated LA configuration. As we mentioned in Section 2, non-connected LA and single cell areas are not allowed so we have defined a repair operation to avoid them, see Fig.4.

3.2   Crossover Operation

The crossover operation considered here is similar to the crossover used in a generic elitist GA, see Fig. 5. First, an elitist selection of the parents involved in the crossover operation is performed, i.e. we randomly select four individuals grouped in pairs and then the best of each group is chosen. Subsequently, the crossover operation is applied according to the crossover probability, P_c, i.e. we generate a random value in the range [0, 1] and if it is less than or equal to P_c the crossover operation is performed, where the number and positions of breakpoints are randomly determined in the range [1, 4] and [0, NCell-1] respectively, otherwise the best parent is copied into the offspring population. The crossover operation provides two offspring; we select the best offspring by elitism. Finally, a repair operation is performed to remove non-connected LA and single cell areas.

It must be taken into account that, in the multi-objective field, a solution is better than another when the first dominates the second. If non-dominance is found, the best solution is the one with greater crowding distance.

3.3   Mutation Operation

Through an experimental study we determined that the crossover operator described before provides a high number of small LA, to compensate this effect we have defined two mutation operators that increase the LA size, gene mutation and merge LA mutation [1].

Gene mutation is similar to the mutation procedure used in traditional GAs but endowed with some intelligence. First, a boundary cell is randomly selected and then its gene value is set to the smallest neighbor location area, see Fig. 6. With this operator, new solutions are searched in a reduced region of the solution space.

On the other hand, merge LA mutation consists of merging the smallest location area with its smallest neighbor location area, see Fig. 7, allowing us to increase the search range with respect to gene mutation. The LA identifiers should be consecutive numbers, so the individual vector must be updated after this operation.

For notation, P_{GM} and P_{MLAM} are the probability of performing the gene and merge LA mutation procedures respectively.

Mutation operations have been implemented in a way that only one operation must be performed at a given time, i.e. we generate a random value in a range [0, 1], if it is in the range [0, P_{GM}] the gene mutation is performed, if it is in the range (P_{GM}, P_{GM}+ P_{MLAM}] the merge LA mutation is performed, otherwise no mutation operation is performed.

Cell ID	0	1	2	3	4	5	6	7	8	9	10	11	12	13	14	15
LA ID	1	1	2	2	1	1	2	2	3	3	2	4	3	3	3	4

Fig. 3. Example of individual representation

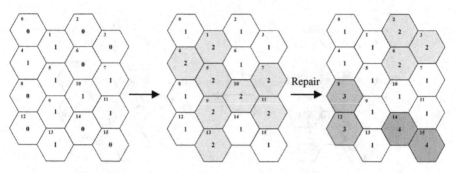

Fig. 4. Example of individual initialization with repair operation

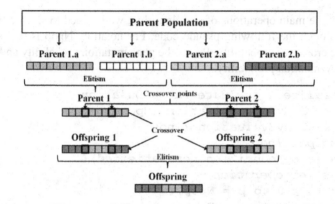

Fig. 5. Crossover operation scheme

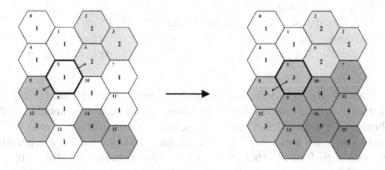

Fig. 6. Example of gene mutation

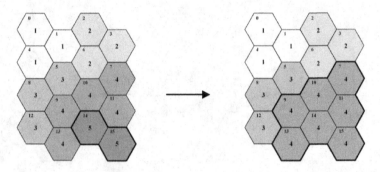

Fig. 7. Example of merge LA mutation

3.4   NSGA-II Pseudo-code

Once defined the main operations of our algorithm, we proceed to show a brief summary of it through the following pseudo-code. For notation, Npop is the population size, P_c is the crossover probability, P_{GM} is the gene mutation probability and P_{MLAM} is the merge LA mutation probability.

```
1:  %Initialize & evaluate the population
2:  Indv <- IndvInitialization (Npop);
3:  Indv <- IndvEvaluation (Indv);
4:  %Principal loop
5:  while (stop condition not satisfied){
6:  %Crossover operation
7:    for (p = 0 to p = Npop){
8:        Offspring(p) <- ElitistCrossover (Indv, P_c);
9:  %Mutation Operation
10:       Offspring(p) <- Mutation (Offspring(p),P_GM, P_MLAM);
11:   }
12: %Offspring Evaluation
13:   Offspring <- IndvEvaluation (Offspring);
14: %Combine, ND Sort and CD, and filter the population
15:   Indv <- SortPopulation (Indv, Offspring, Npop);
16: }
```

The above pseudo-code defines an iterative algorithm that runs until a stop condition is achieved. In our case, as well as the works with which we compare, the Maximum Number of Cycles (MNC) executed is selected as our stop condition.

In the first step, the initial population is generated and evaluated. Subsequently, the principal loop is performed, where the crossover and mutation operations are used to obtain the offspring. Then, the offspring is evaluated and finally, in order to keep constant the population size, the best Npop individuals are selected as the parent population of the next iteration.

4 Numerical Results

In this section we present our results obtained in different test networks and a comparison with results provided by other authors over the same instances. Although in this paper we have developed a multi-objective algorithm, comparisons with mono-objective algorithms, [1, 2, 4, 6, 7], have been performed since there are not other multi-objective algorithms applied to the LA management problem. Therefore metrics related to both research fields have been determined, as the best fitness value found (BF), calculated through (3) and used when we compare with mono-objective algorithms, and the hypervolume (HV) value, which is an indicator that measures the area covered by the Pareto front considered and we use it to determine the quality of our multi-objective algorithm.

The parametric study performed to configure our algorithm is discussed in Section 4.1. Section 4.2 presents a description of the used test networks. Section 4.3 shows our results and comparisons with those results obtained by other authors.

4.1 NSGA-II Parametric Study

As can be observed in Section 3, our NSGA-II has five setup parameters: population size (Npop), Maximum Number of Cycles (MNC), crossover probability (P_c), gene mutation probability (P_{GM}), and merge LA mutation probability (P_{MLAM}). To simplify the configuration task, we assume that $2xP_{GM} = 2xP_{MLAM} = P_M$, where P_M is the total mutation probability.

Npop and MNC are set as in [2], Npop = 250 and MNC = 5000, to perform suitable comparisons, so P_c and P_M are the only parameters involved in the parametric study, where the possible values are [1, 0.8, 0.6, 0.4, 0.2, 0].

This study is performed over the four test networks defined in Section 4.2, and for each parameter combination, 30 independent runs have been executed in order to obtain relevant statistical information associated with the best fitness found and with the hypervolume value.

Through the parametric study, $P_c = 0.8$ and $P_M = 0.4$, that is $P_{GM} = P_{MLAM} = 0.2$, have been selected as the best parameters configuration for all instances.

4.2 Problem Instances

In order to properly compare with other authors we have used the same instances, all of them provided by [1], where four test networks of different complexity are defined: LA25, a test network with 5x5 cells, LA35, a test network with 5x7 cells, LA49 a test network with 7x7 cells, and LA63, a test network with 7x9 cells. Each instance has a data set, see Table 1 as an example for the LA25 test network (the simplest one), where for each cell it provides the total updates that this cell may have (UpP), the number of incoming calls (NIC_i), and the number of users that moves from a neighbor cell to the considered cell ($N_{i,j}$). For more details, please, see [1].

Table 1. Data set for the LA25 test network

#Cell	UpP	NIC_i	$N_{i,i}$
0	129	50	(0:1,70) (1:5,46)
1	279	73	(0:0,76) (1:2,41) (2:5,31) (3:6,69) (4:7,55)
2	100	44	(0:1,29) (1:3,35) (2:7,22)
3	265	52	(0:2,31) (1:4,61) (2:7,63) (3:8,73) (4:9,27)
4	120	73	(0:3,63) (1:9,50)
5	202	52	(0:0,42) (1:1,29) (2:6,66) (3:10,59)
6	341	44	(0:1,77) (1:5,60) (2:7,32) (3:10,22) (4:11,63) (5:12,74)
7	284	34	(0:1,66) (1:2,19) (2:3,52) (3:6,38) (4:8,33) (5:12,65)
8	347	46	(0:3,70) (1:7,42) (2:9,60) (3:12,79) (4:13,61) (5:14,25)
9	199	52	(0:3,34) (1:4,44) (2:8,72) (3:14,45)
10	167	69	(0:5,51) (1:6,27) (2:11,29) (3:15,46)
11	327	41	(0:6,54) (1:10,37) (2:12,66) (3:15,26) (4:16,85) (5:17,47)
12	454	84	(0:6,83) (1:7,61) (2:8,71) (3:11,77) (4:13,51) (5:17,101)
13	336	55	(0:8,68) (1:12,65) (2:14,40) (3:17,44) (4:18,76) (5:19,29)
14	151	69	(0:8,20) (1:9,45) (2:13,33) (3:19,34)
15	158	52	(0:10,39) (1:11,32) (2:16,29) (3:20,42)
16	365	92	(0:11,83) (1:15,42) (2:17,83) (3:20,47) (4:21,61) (5:22,43)
17	401	56	(0:11,37) (1:12,96) (2:13,49) (3:16,79) (4:18,76) (5:22,49)
18	364	80	(0:13,98) (1:17,71) (2:19,25) (3:22,46) (4:23,59) (5:24,53)
19	135	51	(0:13,34) (1:14,30) (2:18,21) (3:24,36)
20	124	63	(0:15,34) (1:16,60) (2:21,24)
21	150	82	(0:16,61) (1:20,25) (2:22,57)
22	253	59	(0:16,41) (1:17,46) (2:18,34) (3:21,50) (4:23,68)
23	159	52	(0:18,71) (1:22,49) (2:24,33)
24	138	59	(0:18,72) (1:19,40) (2:23,20)

4.3   Results

Table 2 shows our comparisons with several mono-objective algorithms developed by other authors, as S. M. Almeida-Luz et al. [2], who implemented the DE algorithm, and J. Taheri and A. Zomaya [1, 4, 6, 7], who developed respectively genetic algorithms, simulated annealing, genetic algorithm-neural network combination and Hopfield neural network approaches, all of them applied to the same instances. Furthermore, Fig. 8 displays a graphical representation of the solutions associated with the BF values obtained by our algorithm. Table 2 reveals that our NSGA-II achieves similar results to the considered mono-objective algorithms in all test networks except in the most complex one, LA63, where we obtain significantly better results.

Table 3 shows statistical data of the hypervolume (HV), mean and standard deviation (σ), for 30 independent runs by experiment. As discussed before, HV comparison is not performed since there are no other multi-objective algorithms applied to the LA management problem. Moreover, Fig. 9 displays a graphical representation of the Pareto front associated with the nearest HV to the HV_{mean} for each test network. Also, each reference point used to calculate the HV is displayed in Fig. 9. These reference points are associated with the maximum value of both costs, N_{LU} (1) and N_P (2), and have been determined through the extreme LA configurations, i.e. all cells belong to an only location area ($N_{LU} = 0$, $N_{P,max}$), also known as never-update strategy, and single cell areas ($N_{LU, max}$, $N_P = 0$), also known as always-update strategy.

Fig. 9 reveals that increasing the LA size, i.e. solutions with high N_P value, decreases the number of possible combinations, resulting in less dense Pareto regions.

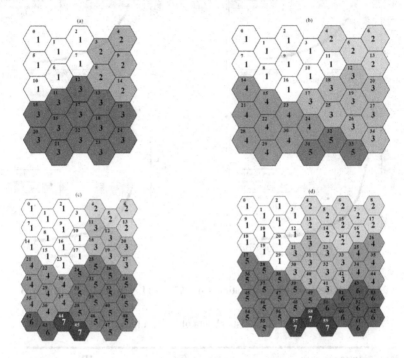

Fig. 8. Best LA configuration: (a) LA25, (b) LA35, (c) LA49, (d) LA63

Table 2. Comparisons with other algorithms. Best Fitness (BF) found (3)

Instance	Algorithm							
	NSGA-II	DE[2]	GA[1]	HNN[7]	SA[4]	GA-HNN1[6]	GA-HNN2[6]	GA-HNN3[6]
LA25	26990	26990	28299	27249	26990	26990	26990	26990
LA35	39832	39859	40085	39832	42750	40117	39832	39832
LA49	60849	61037	61938	63516	60694	62916	62253	60696
LA63	89085	89973	90318	92493	90506	92659	91916	91819

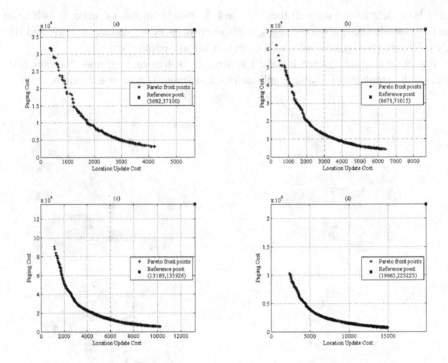

Fig. 9. Pareto front representation: (a) LA25, (b) LA35, (c) LA49, (d) LA63

Table 3. Statistical data of hypervolume (HV)

Instance	$HV_{mean}(\%)$	HV_σ
LA25	0.7207 (72.07%)	0.00009
LA35	0.7731 (77.31%)	0.00946
LA49	0.7916 (79.16%)	0.01299
LA63	0.7914 (79.14%)	0.01863

5   Conclusion and Future Work

In this paper, we have implemented a multi-objective genetic algorithm (NSGA-II) to solve the Location Areas management problem with the objective of minimizing two of the involved cost, location update and paging costs. In order to check the quality of our algorithm we have compared it with several mono-objective algorithms, since there are no other multi-objective approaches proposed in the literature, over four test networks of different complexity.

In contrast to mono-objective optimization techniques, a multi-objective approach provides a set of non-dominated solutions among which the network operator can select the one that not only minimizes costs but also best fits the network real state in every moment, since the location management system must coexist and share resources with other control and management systems. Furthermore, results show that our solutions equal or outperform the solutions obtained by other authors.

As a future work, we propose to solve more complex instances and other location management schemes, as reporting cells scheme, with our algorithm. Also, it would be interesting to implement other multi-objective algorithms and compare their results with those provided by NSGA-II.

Acknowledgement. The work of Víctor Berrocal-Plaza has been developed under Grant FPU-AP2010-5841 from the Spanish Government. The authors would like to thank the Gobierno de Extremadura (Spain) for the GR10025 grant provided to the research group TIC015.

References

1. Taheri, J., Zomaya, A.: A genetic algorithm for finding optimal location area configurations for mobility management. In: Proceedings of the IEEE Conference on Local Computer Networks 30th Anniversary, pp. 568–577. IEEE Computer Society, Washington (2005)
2. Almeida-Luz, S.M., Vega-Rodríguez, M.A., Gómez-Pulido, J.A., Sánchez-Pérez, J.M.: Differential evolution for solving the mobile location management. Applied Soft Computing 11(1), 410–427 (2011)
3. Demestichas, P., Georgantas, N., Tzifa, E., Demesticha, V., Striki, M., Kilanioti, M., Theologou, M.: Computationally efficient algorithms for location area planning in future cellular systems. Computer Communications 23(13), 1263–1280 (2000)
4. Taheri, J., Zomaya, A.: A Simulated Annealing approach for mobile location management. In: Proceedings of the 19th IEEE International Parallel and Distributed Processing Symposium, pp. 194–201. IEEE Computer Society, Washington (2005)
5. Gondim, P.: Genetic algorithms and the location area partitioning problem in cellular networks. In: Proceedings of IEEE 46th Vehicular Technology Conference, 'Mobile Technology for the Human Race', vol. 3, pp. 1835–1838 (1996)
6. Taheri, J., Zomaya, A.: A combined genetic-neural algorithm for mobility management. Journal of Mathematical Modeling and Algorithms 6(3), 481–507 (2007)
7. Taheri, J., Zomaya, A.: The use of a Hopfield neural network in solving the mobility management problem. In: Proceedings of The IEEE/ACS International Conference on Pervasive Services, pp. 141–150. IEEE Computer Society, Washington (2004)
8. Deb, K., Agrawal, S., Pratap, A., Meyarivan, T.: A fast and elitist multiobjective genetic algorithm: NSGA-II. IEEE Transactions on Evolutionary Computation 6(2), 182–197 (2002)
9. Srinivas, N., Deb, K.: Multiobjective optimization using nondominated sorting in genetic algorithms. Evolutionary Computation 2(3), 221–248 (1994)

Nature-Inspired Algorithms Applied to an Efficient and Self-adaptive Resources Selection Model for Grid Applications

María Botón-Fernández[1], Francisco Prieto Castrillo[1],
and Miguel A. Vega-Rodríguez[2]

[1] Ceta-Ciemat, Department of Science and Technology
Trujillo, Spain
{maria.boton,francisco.prieto}@ciemat.es
http://www.ceta-ciemat.es

[2] University of Extremadura, Dept. Technologies of Computers and Communications
Cáceres, Spain
mavega@unex.es
http://arco.unex.es

Abstract. Grid computing infrastructures are systems composed by an heterogeneous and geographically distributed resource set. Despite the advantages of such paradigm, several challenges related to grid resources selection and resources availability still demand active research.

The aim of this article is to provide an efficient and self-adaptive resources selection strategy for grid applications deployment. This resources adaptation capability is provided by applying nature-inspired algorithms during the selection process. Specifically, both the preferential attachment technique from Complex Network field and a cellular automata model are used.

Finally, the results obtained during tests in a real grid show that the proposed model achieves an effective use of grid resources, resulting in a reduction of application execution time and in an increased rate of successfully finished tasks. In conclusion, the model improves the infrastructure throughput for grid applications.

Keywords: Self-adaptivity, nature-inspired computing, grid computing, complex network, resources selection.

1 Introduction

Grid computing environments [1][2] are distributed systems composed by many heterogeneous and geographically dispersed resources cooperating to perform very large tasks. Basically, these environments bring up a new approach for solving massive computational problems using a large amount of resources organized by the so-called Virtual Organizations (*VO*). In this regard, grid computing allows to process data-intensive applications from various scientific fields such as physics, biology, chemistry, etc. A paradigmatic example of massive scientific

A.-H. Dediu, C. Martín-Vide, and B. Truthe (Eds.): TPNC 2012, LNCS 7505, pp. 84–96, 2012.

application carried out by using this computing solution is the Large Hadron Collider (*LHC*) experiment set. However, the dynamic nature of these infrastructures along with the heterogeneous and changing characteristics of grid resources lead to non-trivial task scheduling limitations. In fact, this is a challenging topic which is being thoroughly investigated by the grid community due to the fact that the performance, efficiency and availability of grid resources vary over time, resulting in a worse applications performance. An extensively used alternative to solve this issue is to provide a self-adaptive capability to applications, so that, they can deal with the constantly changing environment.

In relation to this, the research developed in [3] presents an adaptive grid execution by defining a new Globus based framework which manages jobs in a more efficiently way. In [4] the investigation is focussed on both monitoring and discovering processes using the Autonomic Computing paradigm. A new Grid Information Service (*GIS*) is also proposed. The study in [5] provides a software system design that dynamically fits to the application parallelism. This way, the system handles the environmental changes. Two planning policies are described: one is focussed on tasks suspension/cancellation and the other manages the tasks migration process. Other works investigate the adaptation ability of grid applications. In [6], a resources selection approach is exposed. The main idea is that the information related to resources communication and processing times are collected with certain periodicity during application execution. Based on this information, the resource set is adjusted by adding or deleting nodes. The goal is to solve bottleneck and resources overload improving the infrastructure performance. A similar study is presented in [7], where an approach for an autonomous management of grid applications is described. This method uses the infrastructure internal state and the knowledge from external sensors to select the resource set. The concept of *living* simulation (which implies application migrations at runtime from a computer to another) using the referred information is also introduced. Finally, a survey of adaptive systems able to handle the grid environment changing conditions by taking autonomous decisions can be found in [8].

The different studies mentioned above have a common purpose: to improve the infrastructure performance. As stated, this improvement is accomplished by using scheduling techniques, avoiding bottleneck fails, reducing resources workload, etc. However, the present contribution proposes an Efficient Resources Selection (*ERS*) model based on improving the infrastructure throughput enhancing grid applications with a self-adaptive capability. Furthermore, the model is designed from the user point of view which implies that it does not have control on the internal grid components. This is an important difference with respect to the works discussed above: the model simply chooses resources based on several efficiency metrics but it does not change neither the characteristics nor the behaviour of grid elements.

The paper is structured as follows. In Section 2 a description of the *ERS* model with further information about the implemented versions is addressed. In every version a nature-inspired algorithm is applied. Then, the experiments and resulting data from the model evaluation are discussed in Section 3. The different model versions are compared with the usual resources selection in grid. Finally, Section 4 concludes this paper.

2 The Self-adaptive and Efficient Resources Selection Model

As stated, the present approach has been designed to select a suitable resource set for a given application in an efficient way. The *ERS* design is guided by nature-inspired algorithms and it is composed by biological evolution mechanisms such as *mutation, recombination* and *selection.* Afterwards, certain basic concepts related to grid infrastructure are described. They are useful for a better understanding of the model.

2.1 Grid Infrastructure Concepts

Grid infrastructures are heterogeneous distributed systems emerging from the aggregation of both computational and storage resources belonging to several centres, each of them with a different geographical location. A particular centre provides resources that can be assigned to different projects, which implies that these resources are used by different grid infrastructures. For that reason, grid resources are managed by Virtual Organizations. A *VO* refers to a dynamic set of institutions associated with a particular project.

The grid architecture is divided into 4 main layers: the **network layer** is considered the lowest one and connects the grid resources. Above this layer lies the **resources layer** containing the computational elements, storage systems, digital data catalogues, etc (Table 1 summarizes the basic elements). The middle layer known as **middleware** provides the tools that allow the different grid elements to act as a whole. Finally, on the top is the **application layer**, in which scientific applications, frameworks and development tools are placed. Users interact with this layer.

2.2 Background and Assumptions

The *ERS* model is based on the mapping between two spaces; on the one hand, a task space **J** composes by n independent and parallel tasks of the corresponding application. On the other hand, a resource space **R** composed by m heterogeneous elements belonging to the grid infrastructure. In particular, the resources handle by the model are those called Computing Element (*CE*) (Table 1). The space **J** is partitioned into several equally sized subsets denoted as *"processing units"* or $\mathbf{P}_\alpha$. For each P_α a subset $\mathbf{RP}_\alpha \subset R$ is chosen by the model in an efficient way. Besides, the resources-tasks matching is a *one-to-many* relationship.

Now, the different steps performed by the model are described (Figure 1). Once the application environment is prepared (which means to discover infrastructure resources, to divide the space J and to select the first P_α), a RP_α is

Table 1. Basic grid elements

Acronym	Element	Function
UI	User Interface	The access point to grid infrastructure for users.
CE	Computing Element	The scheduler that manages the jobs queue within a resources centre.
WN	Worker Node	Element in which tasks are executed. They are managed by CEs within a resources centre.
SE	Storage Element	Element with storage capacity.
RB	Resource Broker	Metascheduler which deals with computing load balancing and manages the infrastructure storage.
BDII	Berkeley DB Information Index	The global information system that maintains resources status and information.
LFC	LHC File Catalog	Distributed file catalog which handles an unique global name space in the grid.

randomly selected for the initial P_α because at this step no resources efficiency metrics are available. In fact, these metrics are calculated during the application execution. Next, the corresponding P_α is launched into execution. At this point, it should be noted that every RP_α has associated a *lifetime lt*. This value is the maximum execution time available to complete the corresponding P_α. When this *lifetime* ends or the P_α tasks are finished, the efficiency metrics for the corresponding resources are updated. From now on, these metrics are used to select the successive RP_α sets. Finally, these processes of selection, launching, monitoring and updating are repeated until all the P_α are executed. This loop (*selection-execution-monitoring-classification*), in which resources efficiency metrics are updated leading to new and more efficient RP_α, provides the self-adaptive capability to grid applications. At the end, all the information gathered during the application execution is registered in output files.

In order to obtain the fitness value of a particular CE **i**, it is computed the resource *processing time* $\mathbf{T_i}$, as shown in (1), where $\mathbf{NT_i}$ is the set of assigned tasks, $\mathbf{Tcomm_i}$ is the communication time between the CE_i and other grid services and $\mathbf{Tcomp_{j,i}}$ is the processing time of a task **j** in the CE_i.

$$T_i = Tcomm_i + \sum_{j \in NT_i} Tcomp_{j,i} . \tag{1}$$

Now, the increment of the *processing time* $\mathbf{\Delta T_i}$ (2) for CE_i, which depends on maximum and minimum time values from the corresponding RP_α, is defined as:

$$\Delta T_i = (T_{max} - T_i)/(T_{max} - T_{min}) . \tag{2}$$

The fitness $\mathbf{F_i}$ is then calculated by using ΔT_i along with other three parameters as it can be observed in (3). On the one hand, ϵ_i is the percentage of successfully completed tasks of CE_i. On the other hand, two *relevance parameters* a and b are introduced. They are specified by users and indicate the relative weight of ϵ_i and

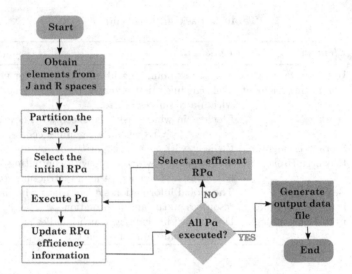

Fig. 1. The execution flow diagram for the *ERS* model describing the main actions and routines. It can be observed the loop enhancing self-adaptivity to the infrastructure changes while there are tasks to be performed.

ΔT_i. Thus, users can decide the highest priority condition in their experiments.

$$F_i = (a \cdot \epsilon_i + b\Delta T_i)/(a + b) \ . \tag{3}$$

Finally, applying these metrics the *ERS* model is able to discard those resources that perform inappropriately (either by overloading, availability or other situations), providing a self-adaptive capability to grid applications. Hence, the model acts as a sublayer within the application layer guiding applications execution in grid environments.

2.3   Applying a Cellular Automata Technique on the ERS Model

A cellular Automata (*CA*) is a mathematical model for a dynamical system which evolves in discrete steps. It is suitable for modelling natural systems which can be described as a massive collection of simple objects that interact locally with each other. The theory of cellular automata was initiated by John Von Neumann in his seminal work *Theory of Self-Reproducing Automata* [9]. However, although John Von Neumann established the basic formalism for *CAs*, they were introduced in 1951 by Stanislaw Ulam [10] and in the 60s by Konrad Zuse [11]. Later, in 1970, the British mathematician John Conway proposed his famous *game of life* [12], considered one of the best cellular automata examples. The design of the rules for the *ERS* model is based on this idea. In this work, we represent the grid infrastructure behaviour as a cellular automata, specifically as a cellular automata network [13] [14]. This way, the grid of cells that composes our *CA* consists of a finite resource set (i.e., each cell of the *CA* corresponds to a grid resource). Furthermore, it has been determined that two resources which are physical neighbours in the grid infrastructure will be neighbours in the *CA*. Grid resources are grouped into a given number of subnetworks, so that, an evaluation of a reasonable amount of resources is realized at every execution cycle. Then, considering the resources belonging to the National Grid Initiative [15], our resulting *CA* network is composed by 8 subnetworks (Figure 2). As it can be observed, every subnetwork includes at least three resources belonging to sites arranged by geographical proximity.

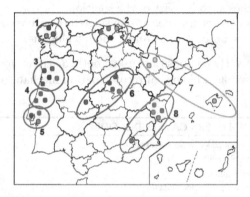

Fig. 2. Illustration showing the different subnetworks that compose the cellular automata network in the *ERS-CA* version

The *CA* rules (Figure 3) for this particular version (denoted as *ERS-CA - Efficient Resources Selection based on Cellular Automata*) are described in the following paragraphs. As it is known, in every *CA* the cells may or may not change their state at every iteration, depending on *CA* rules an their neighbours. The possible values this state can take depend on the problem to be solved. In *ERS-CA* the cells have three feasible states: *inactive, alive or dead.* We consider that a cell is inactive when its corresponding *CE* is not operating; an alive cell is a selected *CE* for a particular RP_α and, finally, a cell is dead if it is not efficient enough for be part of a RP_α. Next, the transition rules applied in every subnetwork at each time step are specified:

– Every inactive resource is a dead cell.
– Every live cell with overload (a condition/state determined by the *ERS model*) dies - the model considers that the corresponding *CE* is overloaded.
– Only the two resources holding the minimal load will survive.
– Cells with all their neighbours dead survives.

According to the *ERS-CA* behaviour, when the first RP_α (the one chosen in an uniformly random way) finishes its execution, the model evaluates the workload of all resources. This criterion is then used in the subnetworks rules mentioned above. Next, the fitness values of the resources belonging to the RP_α are updated using the mathematical formulation exposed in section 2.2. After that, an efficient resources selection is performed as follows:

1. A **candidate set** is composed by using the surviving cells from the 8 subnetworks. In a given subnetwork only two cells must survive: the resources holding the smallest load.
2. From this candidate set two rules are applied to obtain the next RP_α:
   - **Selective pressure:** the most efficient 50% of the resources promotes to the next RP_α, which is an evolutionary mechanism of selection.
   - **Scout resource:** as long as there are unused resources one of them is randomly chosen to be part of the solution.
3. Finally, the **selected resources** are considered the **alive cells**. The resources-tasks allocation is based on the *round robin* technique.

In this regard, the RP_α composition using both *Selective pressure* and *Scout resource* is considered as a biological recombination mechanism.

ALGORITHM 1:   ERS-CA PSEUDOCODE

Input: application tasks, infrastructure resources
Output: set of solutions

1. Prepare environment;
2. while there are processing units **do**
      2.1 Execute and monitor the processing unit P_α ;
      2.2 Update resources efficiency metrics;
      2.3 Efficient selection of RP_α using CA;
         2.3.1 Evaluate the resources workload;
         2.3.2 **Survivors:** the two resources less loaded promote in every subnetwork ;
         2.3.3 **Selective pressure:** only the most efficient resources from the surviving set will be part of the solution;
         2.3.4 **Scout:** an unsued resource will be chosen randomly to be part of the solution;
      3. End while

Fig. 3. The main rules for governing the *ERS-CA* version. These steps determine the *CA* network behaviour within our model.

2.4   The ERS Model Using the Preferential Attachment Algorithm

As mentioned before, the algorithm used in the selection process for the *ERS-PA* (*Efficient Resources Selection based on Preferential Attachment*) [16] is inspired on the Preferential Attachment (*PA*) technique [17], which has been extensively used in *Complex Networks* for understanding the evolution and structure of networks. The main idea of this mechanism is that network nodes with a higher degree acquire new nodes with more probability than those with a lower degree. The following assumptions are considered for representing the grid infrastructure as a Complex Network:

- The *CEs* are considered as nodes of a complex network.
- Thus, a resources network is built during application execution by selecting resources from the R space. The RP_α set built at every execution cycle is a subset of this network.
- Furthermore, nodes belonging to a particular RP_α are interconnected composing a complete graph in the resources network. RP_α resources may be new elements to be tested or classified as efficient resources (due to *PA* behaviour). This way, every RP_α emerges from a sort of recombination procedure.
- Network edges represent the constraint "*executing tasks from the same P_α*" or "*resources belong from the same RP_α*".

Moreover, to determine if a resource is efficient it should be considered not only the rate of successfully completed tasks ϵ_i and the increment of *processing time* ΔT_i but also the degree value k_i; so that, in this case we merged the degree and the fitness (3) for obtaining the resource efficiency $\mathbf{E_i}$ as shown in (4).

$$E_i(k, F) = (k_i \cdot F_i)/k_{max} \ . \tag{4}$$

where $\mathbf{k_{max}}$ is the maximum degree value for a specific RP_α. Thus, the link probability is determined by the resources efficiency because the best elements should be selected.

Related to *ERS-PA* scheme (Figure 4), as well as in *ERS-CA*, first the application environment is prepared and the initial P_α is launched into execution. Once the RP_α is monitored the resources efficiency is computed. A global maximum value of efficiency $\mathbf{E_{max}}$ is fixed and used in the selection process. Then, an efficiency value $\mathbf{E_r}$ within the range $(0, E_{max})$ is chosen from a uniform probability distribution. Next, a resource $\subset R$ is randomly selected and if its efficiency value $\mathbf{E_n}$ is greater or equal than E_r, it will be part of the new RP_α (this step is considered as a biological selection). Therefore, by using this strategy the *most popular* nodes are selected generating hubs in the resulting Complex Network.

Finally, it should be mentioned that this new version of the *PA* in which additional node features are superposed to the link probability, is known as Heterogeneous Preferential Attachment (*HPA*) [18].

3 Experiments and Results

During the evaluation phase an effort to ensure that the *ERS* model guides grid applications (specifically parametric sweep applications) along its execution is done, selecting resources (*CE*) efficiently. Furthermore, the following two objectives: *execution time reduction* and *increase of the number of successfully completed tasks* are expected to be verified. These assumptions emerged at the definition stage; it is assumed a reduction in execution time due to overloaded and failed *CE* are neglected (best performing resources are selected). On that basis, the complete tasks rate would increase.

ALGORITHM 2: ERS-PA PSEUDOCODE

Input: application tasks, infrastructure resources

Output: set of solutions

1. Prepare environment;

2. while there are processing units do

    2.1 Execute and monitor the processing unit P_α ;

    2.2 Update resources efficiency metrics;

    2.3 Efficient selection of RP_α using PA;

        2.3.1 Obtain the maximum efficiency value labelled as E_{max};

        2.3.2 Within the range $(0, E_{max})$ an efficiency value E_r is chosen;

        2.3.3 A resource is randomly selected and its efficiency E_n is compared with E_r ;

        2.3.4 If $E_n \geq E_r$ then the resource is added to the solution;

        otherwise is neglected;

3. End while

Fig. 4. The implemented algorithmic of the *ERS-PA* version where the main actions are summarized

The model has been tested in a real grid infrastructure with a relatively large number of *CEs*. This experimental testbed is the grid infrastructure of the National Grid Initiative (*NGI*) of Spain [15]. The Spanish *NGI* aims to coordinate and to promote the development of scientific activity through the collaborative use of geographically distributed resources. It contains a significant amount of Virtual Organizations, the majority of them created for specific research projects or topics (three of them with a generic nature). From the range of available *VO* in the project, we selected the one belonging to the IBERGRID project (*iber.vo.ibergrid.eu*) [19].

The testing application used in this evaluating phase is based on the Runge-Kutta method [20], a well-known procedure for solving systems of ordinary differential equations numerically. In particular, the version applied is the fourth-order implicit approximation, which provides very good results despite its simplicity. It must be highlighted that we focus on analysing the model behaviour within the defined scenarios. That means, the executable application plays the role of a testing element and no further considerations about the scientific production are considered. Finally, to corroborate that the model achieves an efficient selection the *ERS-PA* and *ERS-CA* implementations are compared with the traditional resources selection (*TRS*) in grid. In *TRS* the criteria for selecting *CEs* are mainly based on resources availability, resources closeness and tasks requirements (specified by users).

3.1   Scenario 1: Model Iterations Effect

In this first scenario the aim is to monitor the influence of the model iterations over the application execution. Namely, the minimum iterations number to achieve a greater time reduction compared to the *TRS* approach is determined. Five tests have been defined, every of them with a size of 200 tasks for space **J**. In each test, the model iterations number is varied (5, 10, 15, 20, 40) and, consequently, the size of the $\mathbf{P}_\alpha$ changes (40, 20, 13, 10, 5). The values of the parameters **a** and **b** (3) have been set to 60% and 40% respectively. It should be mentioned that in both scenarios each graphical point is the average value obtained from 10 repetitions of every experiment.

From the obtained results (Figure 5), it is clear that both model versions improve the execution time compared to the *TRS* version. Both *ERS-CA* and *ERS-PA* execution times include not only the application execution time but also the communication time between the model and the application as well as the time used by the model for monitoring and classifying the grid resources. It must also be highlighted that not only a reduction in execution time is achieved but also an improvement in the number of successfully completed tasks (as intended). In the case of the *TRS* this rate is around 73% while *ERS-PA* and *ERS-CA* reach 92.7% and 87.2% respectively.

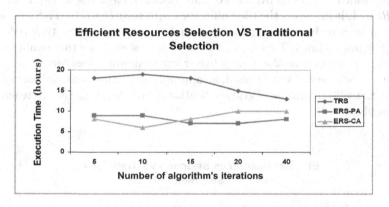

Fig. 5. Graph showing the obtained results within scenario 1. The two efficient versions improve the *TRS* approach.

Next, we analyse the behaviour of both developed model versions. On one hand, the *ERS-PA* version presents a fairly constant behaviour with the exception of the point of 15 iterations, in which it achieves its minimum value. From this iteration value the algorithm stagnates in the time reduction with respect to the *TRS*. Due to its overall behaviour it can be interpreted that from certain point the *ERS-PA* does not learn any more. On the other hand, the *ERS-CA* attains its minimum values in early tests (with 5 and 10 iterations). This is due to the rules of survival and selective pressure, which ensure that for every $\mathbf{P}_\alpha$ a certain number of resources is evaluated. Moreover, considering that the tasks allocation follows the *round robin* technique, we find that the larger the number of tasks in $\mathbf{P}_\alpha$, the more resources will be loaded, causing new elements get involved more quickly. Hence, the most efficient resources are found faster in early tests.

3.2   Scenario 2: Effect of Task Space Size

The objective for this scenario is to gauge the effect of **J** space size within the application performance. Both the size of the processing units P_α and the J space size are key parameters to determine the minimum application length (in term of tasks quantity) to obtain optimal results. The size of $\mathbf{P}_\alpha$ has been set to 10 tasks (common value for all tests) while the task space **J** is ranged through 6 different tests (50, 100, 200, 300, 400, 500). It is assumed that the larger **J** size, the greater difference in execution time (between *ERS* and *TRS*) is achieved. This is due to the fact that the model is executed a greater number of times (there is a larger learning phase within the model).

Figure 6 plots the results obtained in hours for the three selection strategies under comparison. It is noticed that J sizes larger than 200 tasks involve execution times of the order of days. Concerning to execution times obtained for both *ERS* versions, a significant time reduction compared to the *TRS* version is appreciated. In the first tests *ERS-PA* and *ERS-CA* acquire similar results. However, a stagnation is noticed in *ERS-PA* from the size of 300 tasks because of its fast learning, which implies an overload of hubs (most efficient resources). Related to the *ERS-CA*, it improves the time difference with respect to the *TRS* solution in a continuous way. In general terms, this version achieves a better time reduction for higher productions. That is, as the task space size grows the number of the model iterations increases, so that, a better knowledge of infrastructure resources efficiency is achieved. As mentioned, an appropriate resources specialization, considering the self-adaptation of grid applications as needed, is the key to reach such good results.

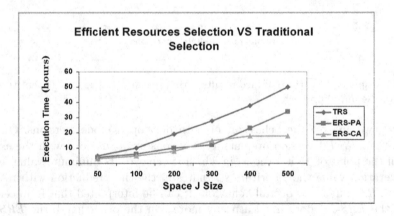

Fig. 6. Obtained results for the second scenario showing that the two efficient proposed versions achieve a better performance

Finally, from the two implemented scenarios it can be concluded that the model makes an efficient use of grid resources, resulting in applications able to handle the changing environmental characteristics. Moreover, an execution time reduction is achieved improving the number of successfully completed tasks.

4   Conclusions

The present study is focused on the resources selection problem providing a self-adaptive capability to grid applications. To accomplish this intelligent strategy the fitness and efficiency of every resource are continuously monitored. The fitness of a resource is determined by both its successfully completed tasks rate and its processing time. The efficient and self-adaptive resources selection in grid environments is a feasible solution ensuring applications to adapt to environmental changes, therefore, improving the infrastructure throughput. This can be deduced from the obtained results during the testing of the proposed model. The two developed versions (*ERS-PA* and *ERS-CA*) are compared with the traditional resources selection technique, characteristic of grid infrastructures. Significant improvements have been achieved using our model.

Future work will involve studying the implementation of other algorithms and to improve the functionalities of the different modules included in the *ERS* model. Additionally, other grid deployments or new grid services will be considered.

Acknowledgment. María Botón-Fernández is supported by the PhD research grant of the Spanish Ministry of Economy and Competitiveness at the Research Centre for Energy, Environment and Technology (CIEMAT). The authors would also like to acknowledge the support of the European Funds for Regional Development.

References

1. Foster, I.: What is the Grid? A three Point Checklist. GRIDtoday 1(6), 22–25 (2002)
2. Foster, I.: The Anatomy of the Grid: Enabling Scalable Virtual Organizations. In: Sakellariou, R., Keane, J.A., Gurd, J.R., Freeman, L. (eds.) Euro-Par 2001. LNCS, vol. 2150, pp. 1–4. Springer, Heidelberg (2001)
3. Huedo, E., Montero, R.S., Llorente, I.M.: A Framework for Adaptive Execution in Grids. Software: Practice & Experience 34(7), 631–651 (2004)
4. Keung, H.N.L.C., Dyson, J.R.D., Jarvis, S.A., Nudd, G.R.: Self-Adaptive and Self-Optimising Resource Monitoring for Dynamic Grid Environments. In: DEXA 2004 Proceedings of the Database and Expert Systems Applications, 15th International Workshop, pp. 689–693. IEEE Computer Society, Zaragoza (2004)
5. Vadhiyar, S.S., Dongarra, J.J.: Self Adaptivity in Grid Computing. Concurrency and Computation: Practice & Experience 17(2-4), 235–257 (2005)
6. Wrzesinska, G., Maassen, J., Bal, H.E.: Self-adaptive Applications on the Grid. In: 12th ACM SIGPLAN Symposium on Principles and Practice of Parallel Programming, San Jose, California, USA, pp. 121–129 (2007)
7. Groen, D., Harfst, S., Zwart, S.P.: On the Origin of Grid Species: The Living Application. In: Allen, G., Nabrzyski, J., Seidel, E., van Albada, G.D., Dongarra, J., Sloot, P.M.A. (eds.) ICCS 2009, Part I. LNCS, vol. 5544, pp. 205–212. Springer, Heidelberg (2009)

8. Batista, D.M., Da Fonseca, L.S.: A Survey of Self-adaptive Grids. IEEE Communications Magazine 48(7), 94–100 (2010)
9. Neuman, J.V.: The Theory of Self-Reproducing Automata. In: Burks, A.W. (ed.). University of Illinois Press, Champaign (1966)
10. Beyer, W.A., Sellers, P.H., Waterman, M.S.: Stanislaw M. Ulams Contributions to Theoretical Theory. Letters in Mathematical Physics 10, 231–242 (1985)
11. Zuse, K.: Rechnender Raum. Elektronische Datenverarbeitung 8, 336–344 (1967); MIT Technical Translation (1970)
12. Gardner, M.: Mathematical Games: the Fantastic Combinations of John Conway's New Solitaire Game "Life". Scientific American 223(4), 120–123 (1970)
13. Yang, X.S., Yang, Y.Z.L.: Cellular Automata Networks. In: Adamatzky, A., Bull, L., De Lacy Costello, B., Stepney, S., Teuscher, C. (eds.) Proceedings of Unconventional Computing, pp. 280–302. Luniver Press, UWE and EPSRC (2007)
14. Tomassini, M.: Generalized Automata Networks. In: El Yacoubi, S., Chopard, B., Bandini, S. (eds.) ACRI 2006. LNCS, vol. 4173, pp. 14–28. Springer, Heidelberg (2006)
15. National Grid Initiative of Spain, http://www.es-ngi.es
16. Botón-Fernández, M., Castrillo, F.P., Vega-Rodríguez, M.A.: Self-Adaptive Deployment of Parametric Sweep Applications through a Complex Networks Perspective. In: Murgante, B., Gervasi, O., Iglesias, A., Taniar, D., Apduhan, B.O. (eds.) ICCSA 2011, Part II. LNCS, vol. 6783, pp. 475–489. Springer, Heidelberg (2011)
17. Barabási, A.-L., Réka, A.: Emergence of Scaling in Random Networks. Science 286(5439), 509–512 (1999)
18. Santiago, A., Benito, R.M.: An Extended Formalism for Preferential Attachment in Heterogeneous Complex Networks. Europhysics Letters 82(5) (2008)
19. The Iberian Grid Infrastructure Initiative, http://www.ibergrid.eu/
20. Press, W.H., Flannery, B.P., Teukolsky, S.A., Vetterling, W.T.: Numerical Recipies in C. Press Syndicate of the University of Cambridge, New York (1992)

Attacks on Fixed Apparatus Quantum Key Distribution Schemes

Michel Boyer[1], Ran Gelles[2,*], and Tal Mor[3]

[1] Département IRO, Université de Montréal (Québec), Canada
Michel.Boyer@umontreal.ca
[2] Computer Science Department, University of California, Los Angeles, USA
gelles@cs.ucla.edu
[3] Computer Science Department, Technion, Haifa, Israel
talmo@cs.technion.ac.il

Abstract. We consider quantum key distribution implementations in which the receiver's apparatus is fixed and does not depend on a choice of basis at each qubit transmission. We show that, although theoretical quantum key distribution (QKD) is proven secure, such implementations are totally insecure against a strong eavesdropper that has a one-time (single) access to the receiver's equipment. The attack we present here, the "fixed-apparatus attack" causes a potential risk to the usefulness of several recent QKD implementations.

Keywords: Quantum Key Distribution, Security, Implementation loopholes, Quantum Cryptography.

1 Introduction: A Fixed-Apparatus Attack

Quantum key distribution (QKD) is probably the best known application of quantum cryptography, for it has already given rise to commercial implementations for securing communications. In prepare and measure QKD protocols a sender, conventionally named Alice, prepares non orthogonal quantum states to be measured by the receiver, conventionally named Bob. The security of the transmission is in principle guaranteed by the fact that an eavesdropper cannot spy the state being sent without inducing errors and be detected. Such protocols comprise the BB84 protocol [3], the B92 protocol [2], a six-state protocol [7], etc.

Given a mathematical description of the BB84 protocol, its security can indeed be proven rigorously. Its physical implementations may nevertheless be insecure; for instance if states are encoded as photon pulses, critical security problems emerge from pulses containing two photons [6], or from the possibility of an eavesdropper to shift pulses in time [20].

---

* Part of this work done while at Technion, Israel.

A.-H. Dediu, C. Martín-Vide, and B. Truthe (Eds.): TPNC 2012, LNCS 7505, pp. 97–107, 2012.
© Springer-Verlag Berlin Heidelberg 2012

Assuming ideal devices are used, it is generally taken for granted that if sources whose states are all ideal qubits in $\mathcal{H}_2$ could be guaranteed, so would be the security of BB84 implementations. We show this is not the case, the problem now is lying on the receiver's side. More generally, let $\mathcal{H}_A$ be the Hilbert space corresponding to those states $|\varphi\rangle$ Alice sends to Bob according to their protocol. The eavesdropper (Eve) may send Bob states in a Hilbert space larger than $\mathcal{H}_A$ and by doing so, alter the assumed behavior of Bob's device [11]. This problem is inherent when using photons, since even if Alice sends an ideal qubit, each pulse can potentially contain more than a single photon and be shifted in time, and her (ideal) space $\mathcal{H}_2$ is merely a subspace of a larger Hilbert space exploitable by Eve.

Protocols (in particular BB84) require Bob to make random choices. In BB84 the choice made by Bob is performing the measurement in one of two measurement bases, the computation basis or the Hadamard basis. This can also be described as randomly choosing a unitary transformation (either the identity transformation or the Hadamard transformation) followed by a measurement which is always done in the computation basis. That random choice is Bob's input to the protocol. In most automated QKD implementations, a random number generator or a pseudo random number generator is used by Bob for generating his random input. However, to guarantee a faster bit-rate in some implementations, those random choices were made by the QKD equipment itself, rather than be given by Bob as an input. Indeed, apparata for which there is no input from Bob have been proposed and implemented in the literature [29,8,16,15,25,19,1,27,23,24,18]. Such an apparatus, with no input from Bob, is what we call a "fixed apparatus"; it simply gives outputs.

A simple behavior of Bob's fixed-apparatus procedure can be described as follows: when Alice sends some state $|\varphi\rangle \in \mathcal{H}_A$, Bob adds an ancillary state $|0\rangle_{anc} \in \mathcal{H}_{anc}$ and performs a measurement, in the computation basis, of $\mathcal{U}|\varphi\rangle_A|0\rangle_{anc}$, where $\mathcal{H}_B = \mathcal{H}_A \otimes \mathcal{H}_{anc}$ and $\mathcal{U} : \mathcal{H}_B \to \mathcal{H}_B$ is a unitary. If Eve has a secret access to $\mathcal{H}_{anc}$ then nothing prevents her from generating a state in $\mathcal{H}_B$ instead of sending a state in $\mathcal{H}_A$, and Bob may be unable to notice or prevent it, due to the fact his apparatus is fixed (Theorem 1).

In a more realistic case which is particularly relevant when the quantum carriers are photons, as mentioned above, the space $\mathcal{H}_A$ spanned by Alice states is a subspace of a larger space $\mathcal{H}'_A$, which also contains basis states corresponding to a vacuum pulse (0 photons) or pulses with two or more photons.[1] Here, when Alice sends some state $|\varphi\rangle \in \mathcal{H}_A$, Bob actually processes $|\varphi'\rangle = \mathcal{I}_A|\varphi\rangle \in \mathcal{H}'_A$, where $\mathcal{I}_A : \mathcal{H}_A \to \mathcal{H}'_A$ is the inclusion. The process then continues as before: an ancilla $|0\rangle_{anc} \in \mathcal{H}_{anc}$ is attached to the input, which gives the state $|\varphi'\rangle|0\rangle_{anc}$ in the joint space $\mathcal{H}_B = \mathcal{H}'_A \otimes \mathcal{H}_{anc}$; a unitary transform $\mathcal{U} : \mathcal{H}_B \to \mathcal{H}_B$ is then applied on $|\varphi'\rangle|0\rangle_{anc}$ and finally a measurement in the standard basis of $\mathcal{H}_B$ is performed.

---

[1] The space $\mathcal{H}'_A$ is equivalent to the Fock space of the specific photonic mode. See for instance the full version of [11].

If Eve knows about $\mathcal{H}'_A$ and can access $\mathcal{H}_{anc}$ then nothing prevents her from generating a state in $\mathcal{H}_B$ instead of sending a state in $\mathcal{H}_A$, and Bob may be unable to notice or prevent it. This leads to our attack, which is a special and very interesting case of a "reversed-sapce attack" [11]:

Theorem 1 (informal). *If Bob's setting is "fixed" and Eve has access to $\mathcal{H}_{anc}$ in addition to $\mathcal{H}'_A$, then Eve can get full information about Bob's measured outcomes without changing their statistics.*

Each state $|r\rangle$ measured by Bob (where $|r\rangle \in \mathcal{H}_B$) can be "reversed in time" to yield a specific state in $\mathcal{H}'_A \otimes \mathcal{H}_{anc}$ that, if generated by Eve and given to Bob as input, results in Bob measuring exactly the state $|r\rangle$. Hence, once Eve controls $\mathcal{H}_{anc}$ and $\mathcal{H}'_A$, she has full control on Bob's measured states. Note that Eve only sends information into Bob's lab but is not getting information out of it, thus it is a special type of a Trojan Pony attack [13,17].

We can further generalize the attack: in fact there is no reason to require that $\mathcal{H}_B$ is composed of two subsystems, namely $\mathcal{H}'_A \otimes \mathcal{H}_{anc}$, or make any assumption on the structure of $\mathcal{H}_B$; all that we need is that $\mathcal{H}_B$ is some space "containing" $\mathcal{H}_A$.

Definition 2. *A map $\mathcal{I} : \mathcal{H}_A \to \mathcal{H}_B$ is called* unitary embedding *or* isometry *if $\mathcal{I}$ preserves inner products; equivalently, if $\mathcal{I}^\dagger \mathcal{I} = I_{\mathcal{H}_A}$, where $I_{\mathcal{H}_A}$ is the identity operator on $\mathcal{H}_A$.*

If $\mathcal{I}$ is a unitary embedding, the subspace $\mathcal{I}(\mathcal{H}_A)$ of $\mathcal{H}_B$ is isomorphic to $\mathcal{H}_A$ by $\mathcal{I}$. Notice that the map $\mathcal{I} : \mathcal{H}_A \to \mathcal{H}_B$ defined by $\mathcal{I}|\varphi\rangle = \mathcal{I}_A|\varphi\rangle|0\rangle_{anc}$ is always a unitary embedding. In addition there is no need to perform a complete measurement of $\mathcal{U}\mathcal{I}|\varphi\rangle \in \mathcal{H}_B$ in the standard basis. Instead, any projective measurement defined by a family $(P_m)_{m \in M}$ of orthogonal projectors (i.e. such that $P_m P_{m'} = \delta_{mm'} P_m$ and $\sum_{m \in M} P_m = I_{\mathcal{H}_B}$), can be used.

Theorem 3 (fixed-apparatus attack). *Let $\mathcal{H}_A$ be Alice's space, let $\mathcal{H}_B$ be Bob's full working space, with $(P_m)_{m \in M}$ an associated fixed projective measurement, and $\mathcal{U} : \mathcal{H}_B \to \mathcal{H}_B$ a unitary. When Alice sends $|\varphi\rangle \in \mathcal{H}_A$, Bob inputs $\mathcal{I}|\varphi\rangle$ to his device where $\mathcal{I} : \mathcal{H}_A \to \mathcal{H}_B$ is a unitary embedding; the device applies $\mathcal{U}$ on it and then measures. If for all $m \in M$, Eve can produce a state $|\psi_m\rangle$ such that $P_m|\psi_m\rangle = |\psi_m\rangle$ and make it so that Bob's input is $\mathcal{U}^\dagger|\psi_m\rangle$, then Eve can get full information of Bob's measured outcomes without changing their statistics.*

Proof. Eve simply captures the incoming state $|\varphi\rangle$ and applies the same measurement as Bob on $\mathcal{U}\mathcal{I}|\varphi\rangle$, getting some output $m \in M$. She then sends Bob $\mathcal{U}^\dagger|\psi_m\rangle$. Bob applies $\mathcal{U}$ on it, gets $|\psi_m\rangle$ which necessarily gives him output m. Indeed for any $m' \neq m$, $P_{m'}|\psi_m\rangle = P_{m'}P_m|\psi_m\rangle = 0$ since P_m and $P_{m'}$ are orthogonal, hence measurement m' has probability 0; the only possible measurement for Bob is m.   □

Theorem 3 applies to many QKD experiments in which a fixed-apparatus is used by Bob, such as [8,16,15,25,19,1,27,23,24,18]. We stress that we don't claim the above implementations to be insecure. Rather, we point out weak-points of such realizations.

In order to clarify the suggested attack and its implications, let us focus on BB84 protocols in which Alice sends Bob photons in one of two bases, while Bob measures an incoming qubit with a fixed apparatus independently of its basis. We note that in many such apparata [29,8,16,15,25,19,1,27,23,24,18], Bob's ancillary input is of a certain type, namely, it is a vacuous pulse that contains no photons (i.e., a vacuum ancilla). Commonly, such a vacuum pulse is "added" each time the data-path goes through a beamsplitter in which one of the inputs is blocked.[2] This specific type of ancillary input makes our attack highly relevant since all Eve has to do in order to obtain full control over $\mathcal{H}_B$ is to drill a small hole in Bob's device, right where the other input of the beamsplitter is located. If Eve is some technician or service person that has a one time access to Bob's lab, the device may be compromised.

As a different justification for the feasibility of the suggested attack, consider a situation where Alice and Bob purchase their devices from Eve, who in turn wires the other input of the beamsplitter to the channel, such that pulses that arrive at specific timings will go through the other input.[3] Alice and Bob may be blind to such an attack even if they proactively test the behavior of their devices: unless they know the specific timings, the device will behave exactly as expected and they will not find out Eve's hack.

2   Applications: QKD Implementations with Fixed Apparatus

In this section we recall several common QKD implementations in which the apparatus is fixed. These realizations are susceptible to the fixed-apparatus attack (Theorem 3).

2.1   Polarization-Based BB84

Polarization-based QKD is realized by many experiments (e.g. [21,22,28,12] and references therein), many of which [8,16,15,25,19,1] suffer from the above weakness. Specifically, recall the implementation of the 'standard' polarized-based BB84 [3], based on polarization beamsplitters (PBS). Each qubit sent by Alice either has a horizontal/vertical polarization (the z basis), or a diagonal polarization, i.e., $\pm 45°$ (the x basis). Bob's apparatus (as outlined in Fig. 1) is composed of two PBSs: one separates horizontal polarization from a vertical one and the other separates $+45°$ from $-45°$ (say, via a polarization rotator that rotates the

---

[2] The beamsplitter's output is the interference of both its inputs, thus a blocked input means a vacuum pulse.

[3] Of course, if Eve *builds* the device she has a lot of power and can perform much stronger attacks.

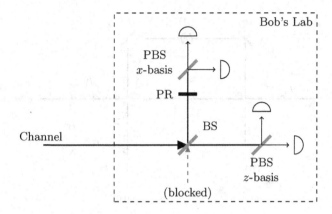

Fig. 1. A simple fixed detection apparatus that splits the channel into two basis-dependent detection arrays [8,16,15,25,19,1], one for the vertical/horizontal (z) basis, and one for the diagonal (x) basis. PBS = polarization beam splitter, PR=polarization rotator.

photon's polarization by $45°$). Both PBSs are connected to the channel via a (standard) beamsplitter, with one blocked arm [8,16,15,25,19,1].

In order to have full control on Bob's space $\mathcal{H}_B$, all Eve has to do is to access the other arm of the beamsplitter (the arm that is supposed to be blocked). By generating a superposition of pulses in *both* input arms Eve can "choose" whether the photon is transmitted to the z-basis detectors or reflected to the x-basis detectors.

Eve can cause any detector to click. To see that, consider a single photon originated at some specific detector. If we 'reverse' the direction the photon travels (i.e., assume it goes from the detector and to the channel), it is easy to see that the photon ends as superposition of pulses in both the beamsplitter inputs. Due to the symmetry in time of quantum mechanics, in the real (un-reversed) setting, if Eve creates exactly that superposition the photon will end up at the desired detector.

The above attack can be generalizes to any QKD setting in which a beamsplitter is used to connect the channel into two (or more) different basis-dependent measurement apparatus.

2.2   Interferometric BB84

Another interesting example for a fixed-apparatus setting which suffers from the fixed-apparatus attack is *interferometric QKD*, realized via an interferometer (Fig. 2). The most common interferometric realization is for BB84 with x and y bases [26] (see also [14,12,10,9]), in which Bob changes the phase φ of the phase-shifter according to the basis he wishes to measure (see [11] for a detailed description of this setting).

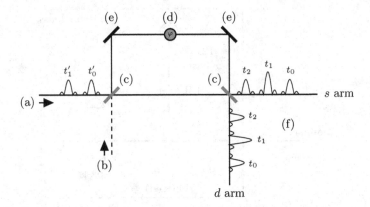

Fig. 2. A Mach-Zender interferometer. (a) An input qubit. The time-difference between the two incoming modes is identical to the difference between the two arms; (b) a vacuum state entering the second (blocked) arm; (c) beamsplitters; (d) phase shifter P_φ; (e) mirrors; (f) six output modes.

However, motivated by the need to increase the key rate and other reasons[4], *fixed* implementations of BB84 with x and z bases were suggested and implemented as well [12,27,23,24,18]. At each transmission, Alice sends a single photon in a superposition of two time-modes $|t'_0\rangle \equiv |0\rangle$ and $|t'_1\rangle \equiv |1\rangle$. Bob fixes φ to the x-basis and performs a complete measurement of the space. Later Alice reveals the basis she used. When the x basis is used Bob ignores clicks at time t_0 and t_2 as those measurements are inconclusive. Similarly, when the z basis is used, Bob ignores clicks at t_1.

Now that the apparatus is fixed, the implementation suffers from our attack (Theorem 3). As in the case of polarization-based BB84, one of the interferometer's input arms is assumed to be blocked, and if this is not the case then the scheme is totally insecure.[5] In a way similar to above, each one of the states Bob may detect can be 'reversed in time' into a superposition of four modes at the interferometer inputs. Eve that controls the other (blocked) input of the interferometer can generate such a superposition and force a detection of a specific state. See Appendix A for full details.

---

[4] Measuring the z basis might be required, for instance, in order to implement the 6-state QKD protocol [7], in which Alice sends a qubit using the x, y and z bases at random; or in order to perform "QKD with classical Bob" [4,5,30] in which one party is restricted to use only the (classical) z-basis, and either performs measurements in that basis or returns the qubits (unchanged) to the other party.

[5] We note that such a scheme might not be secure even when the second input arm is blocked [11].

Appendix

A   Interferometric BB84 with z-Basis and x-Basis

A.1   The Setting

Consider a BB84 implementation which uses two time-separated modes (Fig. 3). For every transmission, the first mode arrives to Bob's lab at time t'_0, and the second mode at $t'_1 = t'_0 + \Delta T$. We denote these pulses as $|s'_0\rangle$ and $|s'_1\rangle$ respectively. It is also assumed that after some fixed time T, the pulse $|s'_0\rangle$ produces pulse $|s_0\rangle$ if it goes straight (s) through the two beam splitters. It is also assumed that the upper detour causes a delay equal to ΔT. Finally, it is known that every reflection on a beam splitter (BS) produces a phase factor equal to i. For instance, if $|s'_0\rangle$ goes through the first BS and then is reflected by the second BS, it ends in state $i|d_0\rangle$; it can also be reflected by the first BS (phase factor i), be delayed ΔT by the upper detour, go throughout the second BS (phase factor 1) and then end in state $i|d_1\rangle$. Note that an additional phase of i is added each time the photon is reflected from a mirror. To compensate for these extra phases we add a (fixed) phase-shift of π and neglect the effect of the mirrors hereinafter.

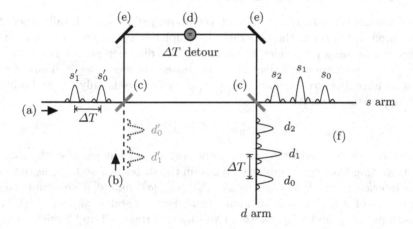

Fig. 3. A Mach-Zender interferometer. (a) An input qubit. The time-difference between the two incoming modes is identical to the difference between the two arms; (b) a vacuum state entering the second (blocked) arm; (c) beamsplitters; (d) ΔT time detour plus a phase shift (to compensate phase shift done by mirrors); (e) mirrors; (f) six output modes.

Taking the four possible paths, and taking into account the delay and the beamsplitter's phase factors, gives the following resulting states

$$
\begin{aligned}
|s'_0\rangle &\mapsto (|s_0\rangle_B - |s_1\rangle_B & + i|d_0\rangle_B + i|d_1\rangle_B &)/2 \\
|s'_1\rangle &\mapsto (& |s_1\rangle_B - |s_2\rangle_B & + i|d_1\rangle_B + i|d_2\rangle_B)/2.
\end{aligned}
\tag{1}
$$

Alice and Bob use the x and z bases encoded as follows:

$$|0_z\rangle_A \equiv |s_0'\rangle \qquad\qquad |0_x\rangle_A \equiv (|s_0'\rangle + |s_1'\rangle)/\sqrt{2}$$
$$|1_z\rangle_A \equiv |s_1'\rangle \qquad\qquad |1_x\rangle_A \equiv (|s_0'\rangle - |s_1'\rangle)/\sqrt{2}.$$

The output of the interferometer on inputs $|0\rangle_x$ and $|1\rangle_x$ is the following linear combinations of the right-hand side of (1):

$$
\begin{aligned}
|0_x\rangle_A &\mapsto (|s_0\rangle_B \qquad\qquad - |s_2\rangle_B + i|d_0\rangle_B + 2i|d_1\rangle_B + i|d_2\rangle_B)/\sqrt{8} \\
|1_x\rangle_A &\mapsto (|s_0\rangle_B - 2\,|s_1\rangle_B + |s_2\rangle_B + i|d_0\rangle_B \qquad\qquad - i|d_2\rangle_B)/\sqrt{8}
\end{aligned}
\tag{2}
$$

If Bob measures those outputs in the $|s_0\rangle$, $|s_1\rangle$, $|s_2\rangle$, $|d_0\rangle$, $|d_1\rangle$ and $|d_2\rangle$ basis, i.e. simply looks at his detectors at times t_0, t_1 and t_2, then

1. if Alice used the z basis, measurements $|s_0\rangle$ and $|d_0\rangle$ imply she sent $|0_z\rangle$.
2. if Alice used the z basis, measurements $|s_2\rangle$ and $|d_2\rangle$ imply she sent $|1_z\rangle$.
3. if Alice used the x basis, measurement $|d_1\rangle$ implies she sent $|0_x\rangle$.
4. if Alice used the x basis, measurement $|s_1\rangle$ implies she sent $|1_x\rangle$.
5. otherwise, the measurement is inconclusive.

A.2   A Fixed Apparatus Attack

If Eve controls the arm at the (b) end, the above realization is totally insecure. If that input is left open, the apparatus is completely symmetric; however, since a reflection causes a phase factor of i, the reverse direction gives a factor of $-i$. Taking the detour back also decreases time instead of increasing it. Thus, if Eve wants to force Bob to measure, say, $|s_1\rangle$, then she needs only set as input of Bob's apparatus the state

$$(|s_1'\rangle - |s_0'\rangle - i|d_1'\rangle - i|d_0'\rangle)/2.$$

That state can be calculated in the same way as (1) but going backwards in Fig. 3, starting from $|s_1\rangle$. Similarly, to obtain the states $|s_2\rangle$ and $|d_2\rangle$ as outputs of the interferometer, Eve needs to use $|s_2'\rangle$, $|s_1'\rangle$, $|d_2'\rangle$ and $|d_1'\rangle$, i.e. input pulses with delays of 2 and 1 in both input arms; For the states $|s_0\rangle$ and $|d_0\rangle$, Eve needs to use $|s_{-1}'\rangle$ and $|d_{-1}'\rangle$ as well. Eve's need of times -1 and 2 might pose a problem if Bob uses a shutter to allow only pulses at times 0 and 1 (since Alice only uses these times).

Let us complete the details and show a concrete attack on the fixed setting above, using Theorem 3. The space $\mathcal{H}_A$ is taken to be the span of $|s_0\rangle$, $|s_1\rangle$; all the states Alice intends to send are in $\mathcal{H}_A$. The unitary $\mathcal{U} : \mathcal{H}_B \to \mathcal{H}_B$ should describe the effect of Bob's device on pulses; $\mathcal{U}$ must be defined on all states in $\mathcal{H}_B$, return a state in $\mathcal{H}_B$, and be onto, else the theorem does not apply. One can rewrite Equation (1) for an arbitrary time t as follows:

$$
\begin{aligned}
\mathcal{U}|s_t\rangle &= (\,|s_t\rangle - |s_{t+1}\rangle + i|d_t\rangle + i|d_{t+1}\rangle)/2 \\
\mathcal{U}|d_t\rangle &= (i|s_t\rangle + i|s_{t+1}\rangle - |d_t\rangle + |d_{t+1}\rangle)/2
\end{aligned}
\tag{3}
$$

The reverse transformation $\mathcal{U}^\dagger$, giving the inputs that Eve needs to fix to get the proper output of the interferometer are given by

$$\mathcal{U}^\dagger|s_t\rangle = (\quad|s_t\rangle - |s_{t-1}\rangle - i|d_t\rangle - i|d_{t-1}\rangle)/2$$
$$\mathcal{U}^\dagger|d_t\rangle = (-i|s_t\rangle - i|s_{t-1}\rangle - |d_t\rangle + |d_{t-1}\rangle)/2 \tag{4}$$

where the formulas are written so that the input and the output be in the same space; if those formulas are to be defined for $t = 0, 1$, then they eventually need to be defined for all times t, positive and negative. Equations (3) and (4) define a unitary map $\mathcal{U} : \mathcal{H}_B \to \mathcal{H}_B$ if $\mathcal{H}_B$ is taken to have basis all states $|s_t\rangle$ and $|d_t\rangle$ for all $t \in \mathbb{Z}$. That is our choice for $\mathcal{H}_B$. The embedding $\mathcal{I} : \mathcal{H}_A \to \mathcal{H}_B$ is the straightforward inclusion, and Bob's measurement with outputs $M = \{z0, z1, x0, x1, \emptyset\}$ is defined by $(P_m)_{m \in M}$ where

$$P_{z0} = |s_0\rangle\langle s_0| + |d_0\rangle\langle d_0|, \qquad P_{z1} = |s_2\rangle\langle s_2| + |d_2\rangle\langle d_2|,$$
$$P_{x0} = |d_1\rangle\langle d_1|, \qquad P_{x1} = |s_1\rangle\langle s_1|,$$

$$P_\emptyset = \sum_{t \notin \{0,1,2\}} [|s_t\rangle\langle s_t| + |d_t\rangle\langle d_t|].$$

The operators P_m are clearly orthogonal projectors and they sum to $I_{\mathcal{H}_B}$, the identity of $\mathcal{H}_B$. Since states such as $|s_{-1}\rangle$ and $|d_{-1}\rangle$ must be in $\mathcal{H}_B$, the measurement needs to specify some output on them, which here is denoted $\emptyset$ for "nothing". Eve however never gets output $m = \emptyset$ on any state sent by Alice, and neither should Bob.

The conditions of Theorem 3 are now all satisfied and thus, if Eve can fix the input of both arms of Bob's measuring device at times of her choice, she gets full information. To do so, she measures the qubit sent by Alice as Bob would do, getting some output m, chooses $|\psi_m\rangle$ such that $P_m|\psi_m\rangle = |\psi_m\rangle$ and sends $\mathcal{U}^\dagger|\psi_m\rangle$ to Bob. Here are valid choices:

m	$\|\psi_m\rangle$	$\mathcal{U}^\dagger\|\psi_m\rangle$
$z0$	$[\|d_0\rangle - i\|s_0\rangle]/\sqrt{2}$	$[-i\|s_0\rangle - \|d_0\rangle]/\sqrt{2}$
$z1$	$[\|d_2\rangle + i\|s_2\rangle]/\sqrt{2}$	$[-i\|s_1\rangle + \|d_1\rangle]/\sqrt{2}$
$x0$	$\|d_1\rangle$	$[-i\|s_1\rangle - i\|s_0\rangle - \|d_1\rangle + \|d_0\rangle]/2$
$x1$	$\|s_1\rangle$	$[\quad\|s_1\rangle - \|s_0\rangle - i\|d_1\rangle - i\|d_0\rangle]/2$

The states $|\psi_{z0}\rangle$ and $|\psi_{z1}\rangle$ were chosen so that the states $\mathcal{U}^\dagger|\psi_m\rangle$ Eve sends Bob be all in the span of $|s_0\rangle$, $|s_1\rangle$, $|d_0\rangle$ and $|d_1\rangle$, i.e. within times 0 and 1. Hence, Eve's attack works even if Bob uses a shutter to forbid other time slots and simply forgets to block the (b) arm. The states $|\psi_m\rangle$ Bob will measure also guarantee the right statistics if Bob made a full measurement in the standard basis: on measuring state $|\psi_{z0}\rangle$, Bob would get randomly $|d_0\rangle$ or $|s_0\rangle$, as expected;

on measuring $|\psi_{z1}\rangle$, he would get randomly $|s_2\rangle$ or $|d_2\rangle$, as expected. Using Theorem 3 and an incomplete measurement, we thus eventually produced an attack that works even if Bob uses a shutter and makes a complete measurement in the standard basis.

References

1. Alléaume, R., Treussart, F., Messin, G., Dumeige, Y., Roch, J.F., Beveratos, A., Brouri-Tualle, R., Poizat, J.P., Grangier, P.: Experimental open-air quantum key distribution with a single-photon source. New Journal of Physics 6(1), 92 (2004)
2. Bennett, C.H.: Quantum cryptography using any two nonorthogonal states. Physical Review Letters 68(21), 3121–3124 (1992)
3. Bennett, C.H., Brassard, G.: Quantum Cryptography: Public key distribution and coin tossing. In: Proceedings of IEEE International Conference on Computers, Systems and Signal Processing, pp. 175–179 (December 1984)
4. Boyer, M., Kenigsberg, D., Mor, T.: Quantum Key Distribution with Classical Bob. Physical Review Letters 99(14), 140501 (2007)
5. Boyer, M., Gelles, R., Kenigsberg, D., Mor, T.: Semiquantum key distribution. Phys. Rev. A 79(3), 032341 (2009)
6. Brassard, G., Lütkenhaus, N., Mor, T., Sanders, B.C.: Limitations on practical quantum cryptography. Physical Review Letters 85(6), 1330–1333 (2000)
7. Bruß, D.: Optimal Eavesdropping in Quantum Cryptography with Six States. Physical Review Letters 81, 3018–3021 (1998)
8. Buttler, W.T., Hughes, R.J., Kwiat, P.G., Lamoreaux, S.K., Luther, G.G., Morgan, G.L., Nordholt, J.E., Peterson, C.G., Simmons, C.M.: Practical free-space quantum key distribution over 1 km. Phys. Rev. Lett. 81, 3283–3286 (1998)
9. Dusek, M., Lütkenhaus, N., Hendrych, M.: Chapter 5 quantum cryptography. In: Wolf, E. (ed.) Progress in Optics, vol. 49, pp. 381–454. Elsevier (2006)
10. Elliott, C., Pearson, D., Troxel, G.: Quantum cryptography in practice. In: SIG-COMM 2003: Proceedings of the 2003 Conference on Applications, Technologies, Architectures, and Protocols for Computer Communications, pp. 227–238. ACM Press, New York (2003)
11. Gelles, R., Mor, T.: On the security of interferometric quantum key distribution. In: Dediu, A.-H., Martín-Vide, C., Truthe, B. (eds.): TPNC 2012. LNCS, vol. 7505, pp. 133–146. Springer, Heidelberg (2012)
12. Gisin, N., Ribordy, G., Tittel, W., Zbinden, H.: Quantum cryptography. Reviews of Modern Physics 74(1), 145–195 (2002)
13. Gottesman, D., Lo, H.K., Lütkenhaus, N., Preskill, J.: Security of quantum key distribution with imperfect devices. Quantum Information and Computation 5, 325–360 (2004), arXiv:quant-ph/0212066
14. Hughes, R.J., Morgan, G.L., Peterson, C.G.: Quantum key distribution over a 48 km optical fibre network. Journal of Modern Optics 47(2-3), 533–547 (2000)
15. Hughes, R.J., Nordholt, J.E., Derkacs, D., Peterson, C.G.: Practical free-space quantum key distribution over 10 km in daylight and at night. New Journal of Physics 4(1), 43 (2002)
16. Hughes, R., Nordholt, J., Morgan, G., Peterson, C.: Free space quantum key distribution in daylight. Summaries of Papers Presented at the Quantum Electronics and Laser Science Conference, QELS 2002. Technical Digest, p. 266 (2002)

17. Hwang, W.Y., Lim, I.T., Park, J.W.: No-clicking event in quantum key distribution. ArXiv:quant-ph/0412206 (2004)
18. Jaeger, G., Sergienko, A.: Entangled states in quantum key distribution. In: AIP Conference Proceedings, vol. 810(1), pp. 161–167 (2006)
19. Kurtsiefer, C., Zarda, P., Halder, M., Weinfurter, H., Gorman, P.M., Tapster, P.R., Rarity, J.G.: Quantum cryptography: A step towards global key distribution. Nature 419 (2002)
20. Makarov, V., Hjelme, D.R.: Faked states attack on quantum cryptosystems. Journal of Modern Optics 52, 691–705 (2005)
21. Muller, A., Breguet, J., Gisin, N.: Experimental demonstration of quantum cryptography using polarized photons in optical fibre over more than 1 km. EPL (Europhysics Letters) 23(6), 383 (1993)
22. Muller, A., Zbinden, H., Gisin, N.: Quantum cryptography over 23 km in installed under-lake telecom fibre. EPL (Europhysics Letters) 33(5), 335 (1996)
23. Nambu, Y., Hatanaka, T., Nakamura, K.: Planar lightwave circuits for quantum cryptographic systems. ArXiv:quant-ph/0307074 (2003)
24. Nambu, Y., Hatanaka, T., Nakamura, K.: Bb84 quantum key distribution system based on silica-based planar lightwave circuits. Japanese Journal of Applied Physics 43(8B), L1109–L1110 (2004)
25. Rarity, J., Tapster, P., Gorman, P., Knight, P.: Ground to satellite secure key exchange using quantum cryptography. New Journal of Physics 4, 82 (2002)
26. Townsend, P.D.: Secure key distribution system based on quantum cryptography. Electronics Letters 30, 809–811 (1994)
27. Walton, Z.D., Abouraddy, A.F., Sergienko, A.V., Saleh, B.E.A., Teich, M.C.: Decoherence-free subspaces in quantum key distribution. Phys. Rev. Lett. 91(8), 087901 (2003)
28. Zbinden, H.: Experimental quantum cryptography. In: Lo, H., Spiller, T., Popescu, S. (eds.) Introduction to Quantum Computation and Information, pp. 120–142. World Scientific (1998)
29. Zbinden, H., Bechmann-Pasquinucci, H., Gisin, N., Ribordy, G.: Quantum cryptography. Applied Physics B: Lasers and Optics 67, 743–748 (1998)
30. Zou, X., Qiu, D., Li, L., Wu, L., Li, L.: Semiquantum-key distribution using less than four quantum states. Phys. Rev. A 79(5), 052312 (2009)

Cellular Automaton Based Motion Planning Algorithms for Mobile Sensor Networks

Salimur Choudhury, Kai Salomaa, and Selim G. Akl

Queen's University, Kingston, ON, Canada
{salimur,ksalomaa,akl}@cs.queensu.ca

Abstract. We develop a set of probabilistic and deterministic cellular automaton based algorithms for an optimization problem of mobile wireless sensor networks (MWSN). We consider a scenario where the sensors are initially randomly distributed and the mobile sensors need to disperse autonomously to both maximize coverage of the network and to maintain connectivity. We perform extensive simulations of both deterministic and randomized variants of the algorithm and argue that randomized algorithms have better overall performance. Cellular automaton algorithms rely only on local information about the network and, hence, they can be used in practice for MWSN problems. On the other hand, locality of the algorithm implies that maintaining connectivity becomes a non-trivial problem.

Keywords: Cellular Automata, Wireless Sensor Networks, Coverage, Connectivity.

1 Introduction

Mobile wireless sensor networks (MWSN) have a wide range of applications [6,8] and there has been much research on this topic. One of the important optimization problems in a MWSN is to maximize its coverage. A typical MWSN consists of a number of tiny mobile nodes that have quite different characteristics from the nodes of a traditional computer network. The attributes (for example, energy, transmission range, memory, processing power, etc.) of these nodes are very limited. Mobile wireless sensor networks can be used in smart transport systems, security of our daily life, environmental monitoring, etc. [9].

Typically, a sensor is deployed in a network to cover some region of the network. The coverage of a network is defined as the area that is covered by its sensors. In different applications of MWSN, it is not possible to deploy the sensors deterministically so that they can maximize the coverage. More commonly, they are deployed randomly and the sensors are required to disperse autonomously using algorithms to maximize the coverage of the network [8]. The major concern of this dispersion is the preservation of the network's connectivity. Once the sensors try to move by themselves, they can break the connectivity. The latter is an important aspect of the network as it is used to route the data among the nodes. We call this problem *the Mobile Dispersion Problem*. Most of the solutions that

A.-H. Dediu, C. Martín-Vide, and B. Truthe (Eds.): TPNC 2012, LNCS 7505, pp. 108–120, 2012.

have been proposed for this problem are either global or distributed algorithms that are also, arguably, highly complex [7,10,5,12,3,13].

A cellular automaton model provides more realistic algorithms than the non-local algorithms because sensors have only local information about the network. Cellular automata (CA) constitute a natural model for MWSN algorithms where the sensors need to make decisions based on information from a local neighbourhood. In this paper, we always use a CA model with a Moore neighbourhood [4]. Also, an advantage of CA based algorithms is that they allow extensive simulations to be performed.

As far as we know, the first CA based algorithms to maximize the coverage of MWSN appeared in [11], and [1] continued this work. In the set-up of [11,1] the connectivity of the network is not a major concern. A different CA based algorithm for connectivity preserving deployment of mobile sensors was developed in [2]. A limitation of the experimental set-up of [2] is that there the sensors are initially deployed as a "regular" $n \times n$ square formation. Here we study systematically more realistic random initial deployments of sensors and for the realistic initial deployments it is not equally easy to obtain an optimal solution. We need to add features to the algorithm that try to prevent the creation of "holes" in the network and also, in this context, it turns out to be useful to consider randomized variants of the algorithm. The problems caused by holes will be discussed in section 3.

2   CA Algorithms for the Mobile Dispersion Problem

We use 2-dimensional cellular automata to model MWSN. The sensors move on a 2-dimensional square grid and one square (or cell) can contain more than one sensor. In one time step, a sensor can move one square in any direction (also diagonally). The sensors have communication radius R_c and sensing radius R_s. The sensing radius refers to the monitoring function of the network and a sensor is said to cover the cells within its sensing radius. On the other hand, the sensors can communicate with other sensors that are within their communication radius. The network is connected if any two sensors can be connected by a path of sensors $s_1, \ldots, s_k$ where s_{i+1} is within the communication radius of s_i, $i = 1, \ldots, k - 1$. The coverage of the network is the area covered by the largest connected component of the network.

When $R_s \geq \frac{1}{2}R_c$, the sensor deployments that maximize coverage are, essentially, long chains which can be considered "bad" for most applications. For this reason, instead of connectivity, our algorithm tries to maximize strongly connected coverage as defined in section 3. In this section, we give a high-level description of our algorithm that disperses sensors from an initial configuration while trying to maintain the connectivity. In particular, for simplicity, below we talk about the movement of an individual sensor. However, in the general case, one cell may contain more than one sensor and the state of the cell needs to remember the information for each sensor it contains. We consider a scenario where $R_c > R_s$.

The algorithm determines the movement direction of a sensor s based on the weighted number of neighbours of s in the positive and in the negative x-direction (respectively, y-direction). The weights assigned to neighbours in case of $R_c = 3$ are as follows: The weights for neighbours at distance 1, 2, 3 are 4, 2, 1 respectively. In case of $R_c = 2$, the weights for neighbours at distance 1, 2 are 2, 1 respectively.

In an ideal case, one sensor can have neighbours at distance 3 away in case of $R_c = 3$ and $R_s = 1$ to maximize the coverage while maintaining connectivity. For this reason we assign the weights to be inversely proportional to the distance.

The state representing an individual sensor is a pair $(x, y), x, y \in \{-1, 0, 1\}$. The state remembers the last move of the sensor. For example, a pair $(0, 1)$ means that in the last time step the sensor did not move in the x-direction and moved upwards along the y-direction. The next movement step of a sensor s is determined by the weighted neighbourhood of s and the previous movement direction of s that is stored in the pair of integers representing s. When a cell has more than one sensor, each represented by a pair (x, y), $x, y \in \{-1, 0, 1\}$, the algorithm computes the potential movement direction for each of these sensors. (The movement direction depends on (x, y) and, thus, may be different for different sensors in the same cell.)

2.1   Local Rules Defining the Movement of Sensors

The algorithm uses a parameter (a multiplier), $M \geq 2$, that is used to encourage the sensor to keep moving in the direction of its previous movement step. We define the movement rule as follows.

Suppose a sensor s is represented by pair (s_x, s_y). Suppose that w_1 is the sum of weights of neighbours of s in the negative x-direction (to the left of s). Suppose that w_2 is the sum of basic weights of neighbours of s in the positive x-direction (to the right of s). The potential movement of s in the x-direction depends on the value of s_x, i.e. by remembering the last move, the sensor tries to keep moving in the same direction, unless there is a really good reason to change direction. So the movement of a sensor along the x-direction depends on its neighbours in the positive and negative x-direction and the current value of s_x. If we use a multiplier M, then the decision of movement in the x-direction is determined by a value x-move(s) defined as

- if $s_x = 0$, x-move(s) $= w_2 - w_1$
- if $s_x = -1$, x-move(s) $= (M * w_2) - w_1$
- if $s_x = 1$, x-move(s) $= w_2 - (M * w_1)$

Now, if x-move(s)$= 0$ then the sensor does not move in the x-direction. If x-move(s)≥ 1 and x-move(s)≤ -1 then the sensor moves in the negative and positive direction, respectively. Movement in the y-direction is determined analogously.

If we do not have multipliers, that is, if we set $M = 1$, the movement rules defined by the weighted neighbourhood of a sensor can lead to infinite cycles. This is illustrated by the following example.

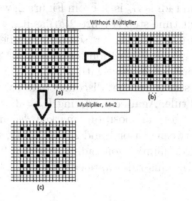

Fig. 1. An example of a cycle and the usefulness of multiplication factor

We consider a network with communication radius 3 and the initial configuration consists of sensors in a 6×6 square. After some t time steps the configuration is depicted in Figure 1(a) (the cell marked as black contains a sensor) and in the next time step the configuration is as in Figure 1(b). Note that in 1(a) we have a situation that is discussed later in Figure 5 and the connectivity of the network is broken in Figure 1(b). Hence the network applies the move back rules (discussed later), and the resulting configuration is the same as Figure 1(a), which means that the network has entered into an infinite cycle. For this reason the algorithm introduces a multiplier $M \geq 2$ that encourages a sensor to keep moving in its previous direction. The sensor (*i.e.*, the state of the cell containing this sensor) remembers the previous movement direction, and weights of neighbours in the opposite direction are multiplied with M. Going back to the example depicted in Figure 1, the computation step from configuration 1(a) using a multiplier, $M = 2$ yields a configuration as in 1(c).

2.2   Rules for Blocking Movement

We introduce rules that attempt to prevent the network from losing connectivity. Below we consider a movement step in the positive x-direction. The same rules apply to the three other directions. If a sensor s does not see any neighbours within distance $R_c - 1$ in the negative x-direction, a movement step in the positive x-direction is blocked.

Consider a cell with m sensors s_1, s_2, ..., s_m. Each sensor determines independently whether it should move or not. If all the sensors move in the positive x-direction then sensor s_1 checks within distance $R_c - 1$ in the negative x-direction for the connectivity, and if there is no sensor within distance $R_c - 1$ then only sensor s_1 will not move in the positive x-direction. In case all sensor in the cell try to move in one of the other three directions, a similar control step is done in the opposite direction.

Additionally, if we have a situation as described in Figure 2, the movement of s in the positive x-direction is blocked. In Figure 2, we consider a situation where the communication radius R_c is 3. From Figure 2, we can see that sensor 3 does not move in the next time step (Figure 2(b)) as it does not satisfy the rules of the algorithm in Figure 2(a). However, sensor 2 satisfies the rules and moves in the positive x and negative y-directions (Figure 2(b)) which makes sensor 3 disconnected as it was only connected with sensor 2. As a result, without any movement of its own, a sensor can get disconnected. To solve this problem, we introduce one additional rule. Again considering $R_c = 3$, when we have the same configuration in Figure 3 and all positions marked "e" in the figure (common communication range between sensor 1 and 2) are empty, sensor 1 is not allowed to move away from the communication radius of sensor 2 (independently of its weighted neighbourhood). This rules applies symmetrically to 3 other orientations.

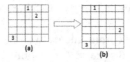

(a)   (b)

Fig. 2. Example: Connectivity breaks

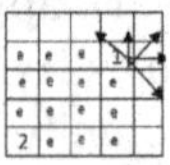

Fig. 3. Example: Additional Blocking Rule

In case of multiple sensors in a cell, if we have a situation that sensors $s_1, ..., s_m$ in a cell C_1 see a neighbour diagonally to the south west at distance R_c in cell C_2 and all the cells of the square with corners C_1 and C_2 are empty, then the algorithm prevents sensor s_1 from moving in the positive x-direction (or the positive y-direction). Other sensors in cell C_1 follow the movement rule. This situation, with $R_c = 3$, is illustrated in Figure 4. Here the cells marked as "e" are empty.

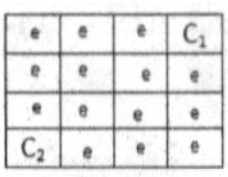

Fig. 4. A situation where sensor s_1 in C_1 cannot move in the positive x (or y) direction

Fig. 5. Neighbours break connectivity for $R_c = 3$

Note that here it is quite possible that there are other sensors to the north west of C_1 and the original rule for preserving connectivity does not apply. The same rule is used for movement in the other three directions.

2.3 Move-Back Rules

The above blocking conditions still do not guarantee the preservation of connectivity because the sensors that are within distance $R_c - 1$ of each other can move in the opposite directions as in Figure 5. For this reason we introduce the following *quadrant move back* rules. At any given time period t, before moving in the positive x-direction, a sensor s remembers whether or not it has a neighbour in two different quadrants (marked as circles Q_1 and Q_2 in Figure 6) in the negative x-direction. In the next time period $t + 1$, if the sensor finds that there is no sensor in one of these quadrants but there was at least one sensor in the same quadrant at period t, then the sensor moves back in the negative x-direction. The same rule applies to the three other directions.

Fig. 6. Quadrant move back rule

If we are concerned only about the loss of connectivity, the move back rule can be simplified by remembering only whether or not there were neighbours in the direction opposite to the current movement, that is, in the case of Figure 6, quadrants Q_1 and Q_2 can be combined together. We call this simplified rule the 180°-*move back rule*. The purpose of the quadrant-rules is to prevent the creation of holes in the network. Large holes increase the hop-distance between individual sensors and, thus, worsen the strong connectivity of the network (defined in the next section).

If we have a cell with m sensors and x-move(s_i) = 1 for all $i = 1 \ldots k$, where $k \leq m$, then in the case of the 180°-move back rule, only sensor s_1 checks cells for a distance R_c in the negative direction, and if it finds that there is no sensor in the negative direction then it moves back in the negative direction. All other sensors move according to the other rules. On the other hand, in the case of

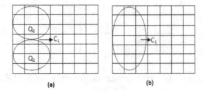

Fig. 7. Move back rules for a cell with multiple sensors. (a) Quadrant move back, (b) 180°-move back

quadrant move back, before moving to a new direction each sensor remembers whether there is any sensor in the quadrants of the opposite direction.

At any period t, s_1 checks the quadrants of the opposite direction, and if it finds that there is no sensor in one of the quadrants at that time period but there was at least one in that quadrant at time $t-1$, then only sensor s_1 moves back in the negative x-direction. Other sensors continue with other rules. These rules are applied similarly in the other three directions.

For example, in Figure 7, a cell C_1 contains multiple sensors and all came from the west then, in the case of the 180°-move back rule, sensor s_1 (one of the sensors in C_1) checks cells at a distance R_c in the west, and in the case of the quadrant move back rule, it checks Q_1 and Q_2 quadrants in the west.

In a deterministic version of the algorithm, one sensor checks the rules at each time period to decide whether it should move from the current location or not. We also consider the probabilistic versions of the algorithms where at each time period, each sensor verifies the rules with some probability. While the probabilistic version takes more time than the deterministic one to reach a final position, we find that it gives a better result, and the probability of being in a cycle is much smaller than in the deterministic case. In the case of 1000 sensors, typically, a deterministic algorithm takes 2000 time steps on average, while a probabilistic algorithm with 0.2 probability takes around 7500 time steps on average. Different parameters considered in the experiments with the probabilistic algorithms are discussed in more details in the next section.

3   Experimental Results of Mobile Dispersion Algorithms

We study the sensor dispersal problem experimentally for cases where (R_c, R_s) is $(3, 2)$, $(3, 1)$ or $(2, 1)$. The general idea is that the sensors are initially deployed in a dense and random "clump", and the local algorithm should disperse the sensors to maximize coverage while, at the same time, maintaining connectivity of the network. In this section, we give an overview of the results for the different algorithms and explain the reasoning behind adding various features in the algorithms. It is easy to see that when $R_s \geq \frac{1}{2} R_c$, the sensor deployments that maximize total coverage of the network consist of long chains of sensors that would not be useful in practice because, for example, they become easily disconnected. For this reason we measure the performance of the algorithms in terms of strongly connected coverage.

The *strongly connected coverage* of a network (aSCC) is defined as the ratio between the average coverage of the network and the average hop distance of the network. The average coverage of a network (aCOV) is the ratio between the total coverage of the network, and the number of sensors of the network and the average hop distance of a network (aHD) consisting of n sensors is

$$\frac{\sum_{r_1 \neq r_2} \mathrm{hd}(r_1, r_2)}{n(n-1)}.$$

where the hop distance, between r_1 and r_2, $\mathrm{hd}(r_1, r_2)$, is the length of the shortest path of sensors connecting r_1 and r_2.

We compare the results of the algorithms with a benchmark configuration where n sensors are placed in a square formation and the distance between adjacent sensors is R_c, or a "close to square" formation when n is not a perfect square. Note that, except in the case, $R_c = 3$, $R_s = 1$, the square formation does not provide optimal total coverage, because the area sensed by two adjacent sensors overlaps when the sensors are within the communication radius of each other. However, the square formation gives reasonably good strongly connected coverage with respect to the strongly connected coverage measure.

The average results for the deterministic algorithm with the 180°-move back rule were not very impressive and due to this we consider other variants of the algorithm below. A possible reason why the results for the deterministic algorithm with the 180°-move back rule are not very good is that the multiplication factors cause the sensors to expand aggressively and this often results in holes in the network. One of the holes is illustrated in Figure 8 (by a curve). Figure 8 is one of the final configurations for 20 sensors using a multiplier, $M = 3$, which gives the best aSCC among all the multipliers we considered for this configuration. The existence of holes unnecessarily increases the hop distance between sensors in different parts of the network and, thus, reduces strong connectivity. In Figure 8 the hop distance between the sensors at the two end points of the curve is 8. For the deterministic algorithm with the 180°-move back rule we get the best strongly connected coverage with multiplier $M = 3$.

Recall that the multipliers were needed to prevent cycles in the algorithm. As an alternative way to avoid the cycles, we use a probabilistic algorithm where at a given time step, each sensor checks movement rules with some probability p (that is, a given sensor s with probability p follows the rules of the algorithm to determine whether or not s should move). Another modification that tries to prevent the creation of holes is the quadrant rules. As we expect better results from the quadrant move back rules in terms of average hop distance, we apply this variant of the algorithm on 20 different random initial configurations. We find that this does not give competitive results in deterministic cases because some cycles occur in the solutions quite early. While we do not get competitive results for the deterministic quadrant move back version of the algorithm, we get better results for the probabilistic quadrant move back version compared to the other variants of the algorithm including the probabilistic 180°-move back rule.

Fig. 8. Example of a big hole

The probabilistic variant of the algorithm and the quadrant rules were introduced to reduce holes in the final configuration and, thus, to improve strong coverage. A typical final configuration is illustrated in Figure 9. The configuration of Figure 9(a) has smaller holes than the configuration produced by the 180°-move back rule in the Figure 9(b). The reason why even the quadrant algorithm cannot completely prevent the creation of holes is illustrated by Figure 10. In this example, sensor 2 satisfies the rules and moves north west in the next time period. Sensor 7 loses its neighbours in that quadrant in the next time period as sensor 2 will not move back, since it will still find sensor 4 as a neighbour in the opposite quadrant.

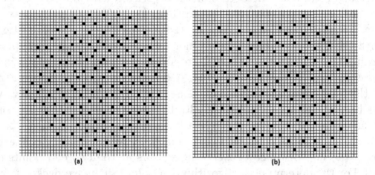

Fig. 9. Comparison of the final Configurations: (a) Probabilistic quadrant move back, (b)180°-move back rule

We used various numbers of sensors in our experiments. For each case we considered 20 different initial configurations for a given probability value p, and we took the average of these 20 experiments. We found that the probabilistic quadrant move back algorithm gives us better results for $p = 0.2$ compared to all other variants of the algorithms.

Figure 11 shows the average coverage of a network for several numbers of sensors for two probabilistic algorithms with $R_c = 3$ and $R_s = 2$. In the case of multipliers algorithms, we can get an early cycle in the simulations. For this reason we do not include them in Figure 11. We find that in terms of average coverage the probabilistic 180°-move back rule gives us better results but in terms of strongly connected coverage, quadrant move back performs better because of

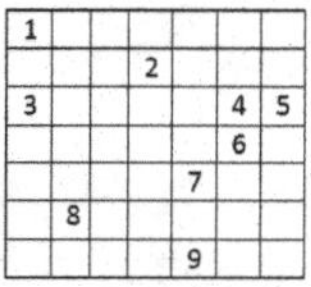

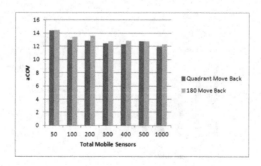

Fig. 10. Example of a hole in quadrant move back

the lower average hop distance of a network (Figure 12). Note that to show the comparison we consider the best result from both algorithms ($p = 0.2$). We show the strongly connected coverage of a network for both probabilistic algorithms with (R_c, R_s) pairs $(2, 1)$ and $(3, 1)$ in Figures 13 and 14.

In fact, both versions of our probabilistic algorithm give on average slightly better strongly connected connectivity than the square benchmark configuration for the $(3, 2)$ and $(2, 1)$ pairs. Figure 15 illustrates final configurations with 1000 sensors, where the result is, roughly, 4% better than in the benchmark configuration. The explanation is that when the ratio R_c/R_s becomes smaller, the increase in hop-distance caused by holes in the network is more than compensated for by less overlap between the sensing radii of adjacent sensors. With a larger sensing radius, the algorithm should try to disperse the sensors more aggressively. Finally, we compare the best results of the probabilistic algorithm (quadrant move back rule with $p = 0.2$) with the benchmark square configuration in Figure 16. The Y axis represents the ratio (raSCC) of the average strongly connected connectivity for the results produced by the algorithm and for the benchmark square configurations, respectively. Note than in the case of both $(3, 2)$ and $(2, 1)$, the strongly connected coverage of the network produced by the probabilistic algorithm is better than for the benchmark square configuration because, in this case, though aHD (average hop distance) is better in the benchmark, the latter gives less average coverage than the probabilistic algorithm.

Fig. 11. Comparison of aCOV among two probabilistic algorithms for various numbers of mobile sensors with $R_c = 3$ and $R_s = 2$

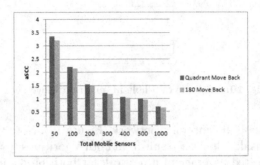

Fig. 12. Comparison of aSCC among two probabilistic algorithms for various numbers of mobile sensors with $R_c = 3$ and $R_s = 2$

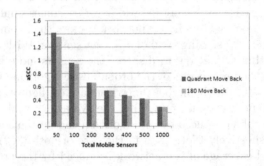

Fig. 13. Comparison of aSCC for various numbers of mobile sensors with $R_c = 2$ and $R_s = 1$

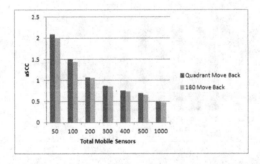

Fig. 14. Comparison of aSCC for various numbers of mobile sensors with $R_c = 3$ and $R_s = 1$

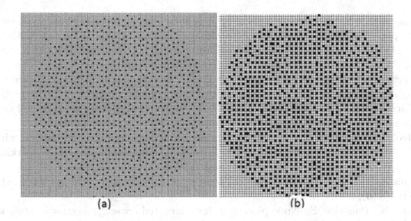

Fig. 15. Example: Final configurations with 1000 sensors for a) (3,2) and b) (2,1)

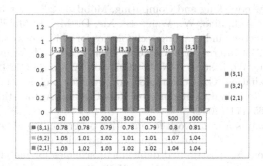

	50	100	200	300	400	500	1000
■ (3,1)	0.78	0.78	0.79	0.78	0.79	0.8	0.81
▦ (3,2)	1.05	1.01	1.02	1.01	1.01	1.07	1.04
■ (2,1)	1.03	1.02	1.03	1.02	1.02	1.04	1.04

Fig. 16. raSCC for Probabilistic with Quadrant Move Back algorithm for different (R_c, R_s) pairs

4 Conclusion

We proposed cellular automaton based algorithms for the mobile dispersion problem. Our experiments showed that the probabilistic variants give better results in terms of the strongly connected coverage metric. In future work, we plan to consider the synchronous gathering problem, where after dispersing in a network, all the sensors try to gather in a location where they can communicate with each other directly.

References

1. Choudhury, S., Akl, S., Salomaa, K.: Energy efficient cellular automaton based algorithms for mobile wireless sensor networks. In: 2012 IEEE Wireless Communications and Networking Conference (WCNC 2012), Paris, France, April 1-4, pp. 2341–2346 (2012)

2. Choudhury, S., Salomaa, K., Akl, S.: A cellular automaton model for connectivity preserving deployment of mobile wireless sensors. In: 2nd IEEE International Workshop on Smart Communication Protocols and Algorithms (ICC 2012 WS - SCPA), Ottawa, Canada, June 10-15, pp. 6643–6647 (2012)
3. Cortes, J., Martinez, S., Karatas, T., Bullo, F.: Coverage control for mobile sensing networks. IEEE Transactions on Robotics and Automation 20(2), 243–255 (2004)
4. Garzon, M.: Models of massive parallelism, Analysis of cellular automata and neural networks. Texts in Theoretical Computer Science. Springer (1995)
5. Heo, N., Varshney, P.: A distributed self spreading algorithm for mobile wireless sensor networks. In: 2003 IEEE Wireless Communications and Networking, WCNC 2003, vol. 3, pp. 1597–1602 (March 2003)
6. Huang, G.: Casting the wireless sensor net. Technology Reviw-Manchester NH 106(6), 50–57 (2003)
7. Kar, K., Banerjee, S.: Node placement for connected coverage in sensor networks. In: Proceedings of WiOpt, vol. 3 (2003)
8. Liu, B., Brass, P., Dousse, O., Nain, P., Towsley, D.: Mobility improves coverage of sensor networks. In: Proceedings of the 6th ACM International Symposium on Mobile ad Hoc Networking and Computing, MobiHoc 2005, pp. 300–308 (2005)
9. Munir, S.A., Ren, B., Jiao, W., Wang, B., Xie, D., Ma, J.: Mobile wireless sensor network: Architecture and enabling technologies for ubiquitous computing. In: Proceedings of the 21st International Conference on Advanced Information Networking and Applications Workshops, AINAW 2007, vol. 02, pp. 113–120 (2007)
10. Poduri, S., Sukhatme, G.: Constrained coverage for mobile sensor networks. In: 2004 IEEE International Conference on Robotics and Automation, April 26-May 1, vol. 1, pp. 165–171 (2004)
11. Torbey, S.: Towards a framework for intuitive programming of cellular automata. M.Sc thesis, School of Computing, Queen's University (2007)
12. Wang, Y., Tseng, Y.: Distributed deployment schemes for mobile wireless sensor networks to ensure multilevel coverage. IEEE Transactions on Parallel and Distributed Systems 19(9), 1280–1294 (2008)
13. Wiedermann, J., Petrů, L.: On the universal computing power of amorphous computing systems. Theory of Computing Systems 45, 995–1010 (2009)

An Easy Automata Based Algorithm
for Testing Coding Properties
of Infinite Sets of (DNA) Words[*]

Michelangelo Cianciulli, Rocco Zaccagnino, and Rosalba Zizza

Dipartimento di Informatica
Università di Salerno, via Ponte Don Melillo
84084 Fisciano (SA), Italy
{zaccagnino,zizza}@dia.unisa.it

Abstract. Recently a new interest towards the design of efficient algorithms for testing whether a language X is a code, has arisen from (wet) DNA Computing. Indeed, in this context, the final computation is a concatenation of DNA strands (words) that must satisfy some restrictions (DNA properties) to prevent them from interacting in undesirable ways. Efficient algorithms (and implementations) have been designed when X is a finite set. In this paper we provide an algorithm (and a Java implementation) for testing whether an infinite but regular set of words is a code that avoids some unwanted cross hybridizations. The algorithm runs in $O(n^2)$, where n is the sum of the numbers of states and transitions in a finite state automaton recognizing X.

Keywords: DNA codeword design problem, DNA Computing, Codes, Finite State Automata.

1 Introduction

Variable-length codes were investigated in depth for the first time by Schützenberger (1955), by linking the theory of codes with classical noncommutative algebra. Informally, a code is a set of words X such that any message composed from its elements is uniquely decipherable (UD) and so guarantees a secure and economic transmission. Sardinas and Patterson [13] characterized codes through a decidable property for a regular set. When X is a finite set, efficient algorithms have been designed for testing UD property, by using different approaches (see [2]). Others are known in the regular case [1,2,10].

Recently a new interest with respect to the design and implementation of efficient algorithms for testing the UD property has arisen from (wet) DNA Computing [12]. Briefly, every DNA molecule can be viewed as an oriented

[*] Partially supported by the FARB Project *"Automi e Linguaggi Formali: aspetti emergenti e fondazionali"* (University of Salerno, 2009-2011), and by the FARB Project *"Aspetti emergenti e fondazionali nella teoria degli automi e dei linguaggi formali"* (University of Salerno, 2010-2012).

A.-H. Dediu, C. Martín-Vide, and B. Truthe (Eds.): TPNC 2012, LNCS 7505, pp. 121–132, 2012.

single-stranded sequence of nucleotides, i.e., a word over the finite alphabet $\Sigma = \{A, C, G, T\}$. The simple property of Watson-Crick complementary (C and T are respectively complementary to G and A), which allows the precise matching between two oppositely-oriented complementary strands, can be used to assemble DNA strands (hybridation). One aspect of DNA Computing is the possibility of using DNA for solving some "complicated" computational problems (like showed by Adleman in his seminal paper - Science, 1994). The input data for DNA computing must be encoded into the form of single or double DNA strands. Due to the importance of this step for the success of computations much attention has been devoted to define suitable sets of codewords. The first property that a set of words should respect, in order to be used for coding the problem, is the UD property: otherwise, starting from the final computation, which is a concatenation of DNA strands, we are not able to uniquely recover how the solution of the problem is built. In addition, as complementary parts of single strands can bind together forming a double stranded DNA sequence, we have to impose some restrictions (in the sequel, DNA properties) on these sets of codewords languages to prevent them from interacting in undesirable ways. As an example, *hairpins* occur when a factor of a long single stranded DNA molecule is complementary to another factor of the same length; or a single strand which is the complement of a factor of another single strand. In both situations these hybridations are unwanted. Furthermore, molecular processes are not error-free: two DNA sequences which are not perfectly Watson-Crick complementary may hybridize, producing false positives or negatives. Different approaches have been used to investigate "good" DNA encodings. This problem has been faced from a formal language point of view firstly in [7,8], by defining a list of properties of words and languages, which if fulfilled by a given set of DNA strands, can guarantee the robustness during computation: among them, θ-compliance and θ-freedom, where θ is a morphism or antimorphism on the alphabet (e.g., the Watson-Crick complementary rule). These properties avoid two intermolecular hybridations for which the Watson-Crick complement of a word v in X cannot be a factor of another word of X (resp. the concatenation of two words of X). It is already known that the problem of deciding whether a regular language X is θ-compliant or θ-free is decidable and can be solved in quadratic time with respect to the size of a finite state automaton recognizing X [7].

In the literature, all known algorithms (and implementations) testing these properties have been designed when X is a finite language [9,11]. In our opinion, in order to encode larger and larger instances of NP-complete problems through a (big) set of different words satisfying DNA properties, it could be more useful to test DNA properties of an infinite set of DNA words with the same structural description, provided by a regular expression. This is our motivation. However, the UD property cannot be efficiently tested for a regular set, if X is given by an ambiguous automaton (otherwise efficient techniques are known [2]). Here, we use the algorithm of [10] for testing UD property, that presents many advantages w.r.t. others (see Section 3 for details). We use McCloskey's tecnique also for testing the two DNA properties in [9] for the code words. The time complexity of our algorithm is $O(n^2)$, where n is the size of the finite state automaton recognizing X. Following the approach of CODEGEN [9], we also provide a Java implementation which takes care of space requirements for implementing automata. Our software implements automata by using primitive data types and no external library.

The paper is organized as follows. In Section 2 we gathered basics on words, automata and codes. Section 3 presents the problem of testing UD property and the algorithm of [10] is described in Section 4. DNA properties are defined in Section 5 and Section 6 shows how we can test them on a regular set. Conclusions give a glance at the implementation of the algorithm and work in progress. For the reader's convenience, the project can be downloaded at http://www.dia.unisa.it/professori/zizza/TPNC2012.

2   Basics on Languages, Codes and Automata

We denote by Σ^* the free monoid over a finite alphabet Σ and we set $\Sigma^+ = \Sigma^* \setminus \lambda$, where λ is the empty word. For a word $w \in \Sigma^*$ and $a \in \Sigma$, $|w|$ is the length of w and $|w|_a$ is the number of occurrences of a in w. Furthermore, for a finite subset X of Σ^*, $|X|$ is the cardinality of X.

We suppose the reader familiar with classical definitions on automata [6]. Here we fix only some notations. An NFA (*non-deterministic finite state automaton*) is a 5-tuple $\mathcal{A} = (\Sigma, Q, \delta, q_0, F)$, where Σ is a finite alphabet, Q is a finite set of states, $q_0 \in Q$ is the initial state, $F \subseteq Q$ is the set of final (or accepting) states, $\delta : Q \times (\Sigma \cup \lambda) \to 2^Q$ is the transition function. In the sequel, we will abuse the notation by not distinguishing between an NFA and its transition graph, i.e., the graph with node set Q and edge set composed by (p, a, s) for each transition from p to s labeled a. Thus, the *size* of $\mathcal{A}$ is the sum of the numbers of states and transitions in $\mathcal{A}$. (The number of symbols in $\mathcal{A}$'s alphabet is taken to be a constant.) If we classically extend the domain of δ to $Q \times \Sigma^*$ we get the function δ^*. $\mathcal{A}$ is deterministic (DFA) if for each state q there is at most one transition labeled by a letter. The language recognized by $\mathcal{A}$ is denoted by $L(\mathcal{A})$.

Definition 1. *[2] A code $X \subseteq \Sigma^*$ is a set of words such that any word in Σ^* has at most one factorization as a product of elements in X, i.e., for all $c_1, \ldots, c_h, c_1', \ldots, c_k' \in X$ we have*

$$c_1 \cdots c_h = c_1' \cdots c_k' \Rightarrow h = k, \quad and \quad \forall i \in \{1, \ldots, h\} \quad c_i = c_i'.$$

Classically, $X = \{a, ab, ba\}$ is not a code, since, for example, the word aba cannot be written uniquely as product of words in X. On the contrary, for any $p \geq 1$, the sets Σ^p of all words of length p are codes, named uniform codes. Also sets X such that no word in X is a prefix (resp. suffix) of another word in X, i.e., prefix (resp. suffix) sets, are codes, as well as biprefix sets (i.e., no word in X is a prefix or a suffix of another word in X). Finally, if X is a code, then $\lambda \notin X$ and each non-empty subset of X is a code.

3   The Problem

When X is a regular set, i.e., it is recognized by a finite state automaton, it is decidable whether X is a code or not [2]. The problem of testing whether a regular set is a code is a special case of a well-known problem in automata theory, namely testing whether a given rational expression is unambiguous. Standard decision procedures are known but, as noted in [2], the exact time complexity is unknown and so they cannot be used for our aim.

One approach uses the unambiguous automaton and it is presented in [1,2]. A finite state automaton $\mathcal{A}$ is an *unambiguous* automaton if for each pair (p, q) of states, there is no word which is the label of two different paths from p to q. The main idea of using automata to decide whether a language is a code is to replace the computation on words by a computation on paths labelled by words. Thus, the uniqueness of factorizations for a code corresponds to the uniqueness of paths in the unambiguous automaton. The real Achilles' heel of this algorithm is clear: if X is specified by means of an ambiguous finite state automaton $\mathcal{A}$, it cannot be directly applied. In order to make $\mathcal{A}$ unambiguous, in the worst case, it is not possible to avoid the exponential explosion of the number of the states. To our knowledge, no other technique is known to transform an ambiguous automaton into an unambiguous automaton which is different from the well-known procedure that determinizes the ambiguous automaton (see Question 1 in [3]). Indeed, by definition, each DFA is trivially an unambiguous automaton (see again [3] for details). A possible solution for this problem is presented in [2] and uses the *flower automaton* of X, an "universal" automaton constructed starting from X. Unfortunately, the flower automaton of a language has many states, and it can be also infinite. In particular, the flower automaton of an infinite code is infinite. To overcome these difficulties, Head and Weber proposed an efficient algorithm that involves the construction of nondeterministic finite transducer associated with X [5]. The complexity of the algorithm is $O(n^2)$, where n is the size of the input NFA.

We implement a technique, based on finite state automata only, which can be applied to regular (even infinite) languages. McCloskey's algorithm is suitable for our scope, as shown in the next sections.

4   UD and Restricted Automata

The algorithm given in [10] takes as input a finite state automaton $\mathcal{A}$ recognizing X and decides whether X is a code. Let n be the size of $\mathcal{A}$. A λ-transition is an edge of $\mathcal{A}$ labeled by λ.

Definition 2. *[10] A finite state automaton $\mathcal{A}$ is in restricted form if it has only one accepting state and there are no λ-transitions into that state and no transition of any kind out of that state.*

We often say that $\mathcal{A}$ is a *restricted automaton* if $\mathcal{A}$ is in restricted form. An example from [10] is reported in Figure 1. Observe that any X recognized by a restricted finite state automaton is λ-free.

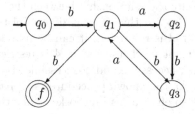

Fig. 1. An unambiguos NFA recognizing $b(aba + ba)^*b$

Following the procedure from [4] for the construction given in [10], we show how to transform an NFA in its restricted form. Let $\mathcal{A} = (\Sigma, Q', \delta', q'_0, F')$ be an NFA. We define $\mathcal{A}_\mathcal{R} = (\Sigma, Q, \delta, q_0, F)$ to be the NFA such that $Q = Q' \cup \{f\}$, $f \notin Q'$, $q_0 = q'_0$, $F = \{f\}$ and $\delta : Q \times (\Sigma \cup \{\lambda\}) \to 2^Q$, defined as follows.

   (a) For each $q' \in Q'$, for each $a \in \Sigma \cup \lambda$ such that $q \in \delta'(q', a)$, then $q \in \delta(q', a)$. Loosely speaking, all transitions in $\mathcal{A}$ are transitions in $\mathcal{A}_\mathcal{R}$.

   (b) For each $q' \in Q'$, for each $a \in \Sigma$ such that $q \in \delta'(q', a)$ and $q \in F'$, then $f \in \delta(q', a)$. Loosely speaking, each non λ-transition that in $\mathcal{A}$ reaches a final state (so a state in F'), is transformed into a transition that reaches f in $\mathcal{A}_\mathcal{R}$.

   (c) Finally, let $S \subseteq Q'$ such that for each $q' \in S$, we have $\delta'^*(q', \lambda) \cap F' \neq \emptyset$. Let $q'' \in Q'$ such that $\delta'(q'', a) \cap S \neq \emptyset$, $a \in \Sigma$. Thus $f \in \delta(q'', a)$. This step allows us to eliminate the λ-paths in $\mathcal{A}$ which end in a final state, making the path to end in f.

By using suitable Depth-First-Search visits, it is clear that this procedure can be done in $O(n)$ time [10]. As classically done for the flower automaton [2], a variant of the direct product of $\mathcal{A}$ can be used for detecting suitable paths in order to decide the UD property [10]. For a better typesetting, from now on, $[p, q]$ denotes the pair of states (p, q).

Definition 3. *[10] Let* $\mathcal{A} = (\Sigma, Q, \delta, q_0, \{f\})$ *be in restricted form. We define* $\langle \mathcal{A} \times \mathcal{A} \rangle = (Q \times Q, \Sigma, \delta', [q_0, q_0], [f, f])$, *where, for each* $p, q \in Q$, $a \in \Sigma$,

$$\delta'([p, q], a) = \delta(p, a) \times \delta(q, a),$$
$$\delta'([p, q], \lambda) = ((\delta(p, \lambda) \cup \{p\}) \times (\delta(q, \lambda) \cup \{q\})) - \{[p, q]\}$$

That is, there is a walk in $\langle \mathcal{A} \times \mathcal{A} \rangle$ from $[p, q]$ to $[r, s]$ labeled x if and only if $\mathcal{A}$ has walks from p to r and from q to s, both of which are labeled x.

   Finally, let us consider $\langle \mathcal{A} \times \mathcal{A} \rangle$. Insert, for each $s \neq f$, an edge (λ-transition) from each of $[s, f]$ and $[f, s]$ to $[q_0, s]$. (Refer to a state $[s, f]$ or $[f, s]$, where $s \neq f$, as a *semi-final state*). Let us consider $\langle \mathcal{A} \times \mathcal{A} \rangle$. It follows from $\mathcal{A}$ being in restricted form that any transition out of a semi-final state must be a λ-transition to another semi-final state. The directed graph obtained as above is denoted by $\hat{\mathcal{A}}$ and named here the *square automaton* of $\mathcal{A}$. It is easy to check that it can be constructed in $O(n^2)$ time.

Remark 4. It is natural to investigate the relationship between the determinism and the restricted form. It is easy to see that if $\mathcal{A}$ is deterministic, it is still possible that $\mathcal{A}$ is not restricted. If $\mathcal{A}$ is restricted, it can be non-deterministic (see Fig.1). However, it is not difficult to check that if $\mathcal{A}$ is restricted and deterministic, the trim part of $\hat{\mathcal{A}}$, i.e., accessible and coaccessible states, which is restricted, has the same size of $\mathcal{A}$. So, the known procedure as [2] based on (star and) unambiguous automata is as so efficient as McCloskey's algorithm.

Theorem 5. *[10] Let $\mathcal{A}$ be in restricted form. Then $L(\mathcal{A})$ is a code if and only if there are no walks in $\hat{\mathcal{A}}$ from $[q_0, q_0]$ to $[f, f]$ that pass through at least one semi-final state.*

McCloskey's algorithm runs as follows. Let $\mathcal{A}$ be a finite state automaton recognizing X. **(1)** Check whether $\lambda \in L(\mathcal{A})$. If it is so, X is not a code (by definition). This step can be implemented by using a Depth-First-Search (DFS) visit on (the graph underlying) $\mathcal{A}$, by considering only the paths labelled by λ. **(2)** Check whether $\mathcal{A}$ is in restricted form (this can be trivially done by using Definition 2). If it is not so, construct the restricted automaton $\mathcal{A}_{\mathcal{R}}$ equivalent to $\mathcal{A}$. **(3)** Construct the product automaton $\hat{\mathcal{A}}$ of $\mathcal{A}_{\mathcal{R}}$. **(4)** Find a path in $\hat{\mathcal{A}}$ from the initial state to the (unique) final state, which passes through a *semi-final state*, i.e., a state $[p, q]$ in $\hat{\mathcal{A}}$ with $p \neq q$ and $p = f$ or $q = f$, f being the final state of $\mathcal{A}_{\mathcal{R}}$. If such a path exists, X is not a code; otherwise, X is a code. Also this step can be implemented by using DFS visits.

Steps 1-2 can be performed in time linear in the size of $\mathcal{A}$, whereas Steps 3-4 in time linear in the size of $\hat{\mathcal{A}}$, i.e., in $O(n^2)$ time [10].

5   DNA Code Words

In the following, we suppose X to be a regular set and we denote by $\theta \colon \Sigma \to \Sigma$ an *involution* on Σ, i.e., satisfying $\theta(\theta(x)) = x$ for all $x \in \Sigma$. Two natural extensions on Σ^* can be considered. If for each $x, y \in \Sigma^*$, $\theta(xy) = \theta(x)\theta(y)$, θ is a *morphism*. If $\theta(xy) = \theta(y)\theta(x)$, then θ is an *antimorphism*. We consider only two basic properties, called DNA properties.

Definition 6. *[7,9] Let Σ be an alphabet, X a code on Σ. Let θ be a morphism or antimorphism on Σ. The code X is θ-compliant if $\Sigma^+ \theta(X)\Sigma^* \cap X = \emptyset$ and $\Sigma^* \theta(X)\Sigma^+ \cap X = \emptyset$.*

Loosely speaking, the involution of a word in X is not a proper factor of an element of X.

Definition 7. *[7,9] Let Σ be an alphabet, X a code on Σ. Let θ be a morphism or antimorphism on Σ. The code X is θ-free if $\Sigma^+ \theta(X)\Sigma^* \cap X^2 = \emptyset$ and $\Sigma^* \theta(X)\Sigma^+ \cap X^2 = \emptyset$.*

Loosely speaking, the involution of a word in X is not a factor of the concatenation of two elements of X. Clearly, if the factor appears inside one of the two words, then X is also not θ-compliant, either.

As in [9], we will work only on the *strictly forms* of the DNA properties above. Precisely, if Σ^+ is replaced by Σ^* in the above definitions, then X is said to be strictly θ-*compliant* and strictly θ-*free*, respectively. Additional considerations are to be done for non strictly forms, and are work in progress.

In the Examples 8-10 below, we use the Watson-Crick complementary relation as involution.

Example 8. [7] Let us consider the code $X = \{ACCAA, ACCGT\}$. It is easy to check that the DNA properties are both satisfied.

Example 9. Let us consider the code $X = \{TT, AGA\}$. It is easy to check that the θ-*compliance* property is satisfied. On the contrary, the word TT allows us to detect the failure of the θ-*freedom* property, since $\theta(TT) = AA$ and $AG\mathbf{AA}GA \in X^2$.

Example 10. Let $X = \{GA, CTG\}$. Thus we have $\theta(X) = \{CT, GAC\}$ and $X^2 = \{GAGA, CTGCTG, GACTG, CTGGA\}$. The factor CT, involution of GA, makes X not θ-*compliant* (and so not θ-*free*). However, X is θ-*compliant* in the non-strictly form, since CT is a prefix in X. As another example, $GAC = \theta(CTG)$ and $\mathbf{GAC}TG = GA \cdot CTG \in X^2$, thus X is not θ-*free*.

Example 11. Let us consider again the restricted automaton of Fig. 1 recognizing the code $X = b(aba + ba)^*b$ and $\theta(X) = a(bab + ab)^*a$, where we fix the natural involution $\theta(a) = b, \theta(b) = a$. We have that X is not θ-*compliant*, since $bb\mathbf{aaba}b \in X$ and $aaba = \theta(bbab)$, with $bbab \in X$. In addition, X is not θ-*free*, since $bab\mathbf{ababb}babab = bababab \cdot babab \in X^2$ and $ababbaba = \theta(babaabab)$, with $babaabab \in X$.

Some closure properties are studied for these DNA properties [7] and it is already known that are decidable for regular languages [7]. Precisely, the time complexity of the decision procedure is quadratic in the size of the finite state automaton recognizing X. Now, recall that in this context, X must also satisfy the UD property. Thus, we can ask for efficient algorithms for testing DNA properties of regular codes. Known algorithms, such as the one in [11], works only for finite sets of words (and test the DNA properties by using a technique which is different from the one used for the UD). On the contrary, here we apply to restricted automata a technique which is similar to the one used for CODEGEN and applied to flower automata [9]. In this way, the algorithm tests both UD and DNA properties by using the same structures and still remains within the same time complexity.

6   Testing Properties of an Infinite Set of (DNA) Words

Let us introduce two automata that we use for testing the DNA properties.

Definition 12. *[9] Let $\mathcal{A} = (\Sigma, Q, \delta, q_0, F)$ be an NFA recognizing $X \subseteq \Sigma^*$ and let θ be a morphism or antimorphism on Σ. The Theta automaton $\mathcal{A}_\theta(X)$ of X is an NFA automaton $(\Sigma, Q, \delta', q_0, F)$ such that $p \in \delta(q, a)$ if and only if $p \in \delta'(q, \theta(a))$.*

It is clear that the Theta automaton $\mathcal{A}_\theta(X)$ recognizes $\theta(X)$ and it can be naturally constructed starting from $\mathcal{A}$ by replacing each letter a with $\theta(a)$. Obviously, if $\mathcal{A}$ is in restricted form, also $\mathcal{A}_\theta(X)$ is in restricted form. Let us consider a variant of Definition 3, where instead of considering only $\mathcal{A}$, we define the same operation between $\mathcal{A}_\theta(X)$ and $\mathcal{A}$. In this way we can constuct $\langle \mathcal{A}_\theta(X) \times \mathcal{A} \rangle$.

Definition 13. *Let $X \subseteq \Sigma^*$ be a regular language recognized by $\mathcal{A}$ in restricted form. Let $\mathcal{A}_\theta(X)$ be the Theta automaton of X naturally constructed starting from $\mathcal{A}$. The involution square automaton of X is the automaton $P_\theta(X)$ where the following edges are added to $\langle \mathcal{A}_\theta(X) \times \mathcal{A} \rangle$. For each $q \neq f$, insert a λ-transition from each of $[q, f]$ to $[q, q_0]$.*

These λ-transitions allow us to simulate the concatenation of two paths which are "successfull" w.r.t. $\mathcal{A}$. As in the case of the square automaton $\hat{\mathcal{A}}$, it follows that in the involution square automaton of $\mathcal{A}$, any transition out of a semi-final state must be a λ-transition to another semi-final state. In addition these out-transitions are only of the form given in Definition 13.

Similarly to CODEGEN, we can check the DNA properties in this context as follows.

a) *θ-compliance.*

In the involution square automaton $P_\theta(X)$, we look for paths from a state $[q_0, p]$ to a state $[f, q]$, $p, q \in Q$, which never pass through states of the form $[k, f]$, and so $[k, q_0]$, with $k \neq q_0$. In the sequel such paths will be named θ-*compliant*-paths.

Such a path is labeled by a word w accepted by the Theta automaton $\mathcal{A}_\theta(X)$ (so $\theta(w) = w' \in X$ is accepted by $\mathcal{A}$, being θ an involution). Moreover, there exist a word $z = xwy \in X$ and so X is not θ-*compliant.*

b) *θ-freedom.*

In the involution square automaton $P_\theta(X)$, we look for paths from a state $[q_0, p]$ to a state $[f, q]$, $p, q \in Q$, which passes at most once through a state of the form $[k, f]$, and so $[k, q_0]$, with $k \neq q_0$. In the sequel such paths will be named θ-*free*-paths.

Such a path is labeled by a word w accepted by the Theta automaton $\mathcal{A}_\theta(X)$ (so $\theta(w) = w' \in X$ is accepted by $\mathcal{A}$, being θ an involution). Moreover, there are two words $x, y \in X$, such that w is a factor of $xy \in X^2$ (the path from p to f is labeled by w_1 and it is a suffix of some $x \in X$, while the path from q_0 to q is labeled by w_2 and it is a prefix of some $y \in X$). So X is not θ-*free.* Obviously, if no state of the form $[k, f]$, with $k \neq q_0$, is found in such paths, we have θ-*compliant*-paths.

Theorem 14. *Let X be a code on Σ and let $\mathcal{A} = (\Sigma, Q, \delta, q_0, F)$ be in restricted form such that $X = L(\mathcal{A})$. The language X is θ-compliant if and only if in the involution square automaton $P_\theta(X)$ there exists no θ-compliant-path, i.e., no path π that starts from a state $[q_0, p]$, ends in $[f, q]$, $p, q \in Q$ which never pass through states of the form $[k, f]$, with $k \neq q_0$.*

The language X is θ-free if and only if there exists no θ-free-path, i.e., no path π that starts from a state $[q_0, p]$, ends in $[f, q]$, $p, q \in Q$ and passes at most once through a state of the form $[k, f]$, with $k \neq q_0$.

(Sketch of the) Proof. Observations in items a) and b) above allow us to conclude that if $P_\theta(X)$ contains a θ-*compliant*-path (resp. θ-*free*-path), then X cannot be θ-*compliant* (resp. θ-*free*).

Let us now prove that if such a θ-*compliant*-path does not exist, we can conclude that X is θ-*compliant*. By contradiction, let us suppose that X is not θ-*compliant*. By definition, there exist $z \in X$ and $w' \in X$, such that $z = xwy$ and $\theta(w') = w$. In other words, there is a successfull path in the Theta automaton $\mathcal{A}_\theta(X)$ labeled by $\theta(w') = w$, i.e., $q_0 \stackrel{w}{\twoheadrightarrow} f$. Moreover, there is a successfull path in $\mathcal{A}$ labeled by $z = xwy$, i.e., $q_0 \stackrel{xwy}{\twoheadrightarrow} f = q_0 \stackrel{x}{\twoheadrightarrow} p \stackrel{w}{\twoheadrightarrow} q \stackrel{y}{\twoheadrightarrow} f$. Observe that both $\mathcal{A}$ and $\mathcal{A}_\theta(X)$ are in restricted form, i.e., f in not an intermediate state in these paths. Let us now consider the involution square automaton $P_\theta(X)$. By construction, a transition from $[q_0, p]$ to $[f, q]$ labeled by w exists. We can easily check that a state of the form $[k, f]$ cannot belong to this path, otherwise the path in $\mathcal{A}$ from p to q labeled by w should pass through the state f. Thus we have found a θ-*compliant*-path in the involution square automaton, a contradiction.

The case of θ-*freedom* works similarly, by taking care of the λ-transitions from each of $[q, f]$ to $[q, q_0]$ in the involution square automaton of X (see Definition 13). Indeed, let us suppose that X is not θ-*free*. By definition, there exist $x, y \in X$ and $w' \in X$, such that $xy = x'w_1w_2y' \in X^2$, with $x = x'w_1$, $y = w_2y'$, and $\theta(w') = w_1w_2$. Thus, $\theta(w') = w_1w_2$ is the label of a (successfull) path in the Theta automaton $\mathcal{A}_\theta(X)$. The λ-transitions in the involution square automaton $P_\theta(X)$, added to $\langle \mathcal{A}_\theta(X) \times \mathcal{A} \rangle$, allow us to paste the path labeled by w_1 (that ends in f in $\mathcal{A}$) with the path labeled by w_2 (that starts in q_0 in $\mathcal{A}$). Thus we find a θ-*free*-path in the involution square automaton, a contradiction. $\qquad \square$

Example 15. (Example 8 continued). Let us consider the restricted finite state automaton recognizing $X = \{ACCAA, ACCGT\}$, constructed by considering the path $q_0 \stackrel{A}{\rightarrow} q_1 \stackrel{C}{\rightarrow} q_2 \stackrel{C}{\rightarrow} q_3$, and then $q_3 \stackrel{A}{\rightarrow} q_4 \stackrel{A}{\rightarrow} f$ and $q_3 \stackrel{G}{\rightarrow} q_5 \stackrel{T}{\rightarrow} f$. If we consider the Theta automaton of X and the involution square automaton of X, we can easily check that $[q_0, q_5]$ is the unique non isolated state of the form $[q_0, p]$. The unique path starting from $[q_0, q_5]$ is $[q_0, q_5] \rightarrow [q_1, f] \rightarrow [q_1, q_0]$ labeled by $T\lambda$. Thus both conditions a) and b) are satisfied (no path is found), and so X is θ-*free* (and θ-*compliant*).

Example 16. (Example 9 continued) Figure 2 contains the automata for applying Theorem 14 to the language $X = \{TT, AGA\}$. We can easily check that, in the involution square automaton of X, there exists the θ-*free*-path $[q_0, q_3] \rightarrow [q_1, f] \rightarrow [q_1, q_0] \rightarrow [f, q_2]$ labeled by $A\lambda A$, since it passes through a state of the form $[k, f]$, $k \neq q_0$. (This is exactly the factor AA detected in the Example 9.) So X is not θ-*free*. No θ-*compliant*-path is found, and so X is θ-*compliant*.

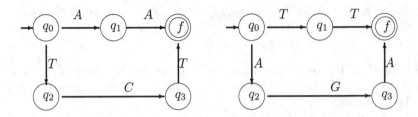

Fig. 2. (left) The Theta automaton $\mathcal{A}_\theta(X)$ constructed from the reduced automaton recognizing $X = \{TT, AGA\}$ (on the right)

Example 17. (Example 10 continued) Figure 3 contains the automata for applying Theorem 14 to $X = \{GA, CTG\}$. We can easily check that, in the involution square automaton of X, there exists the θ-*compliant*-path $[q_0, q_0] \rightarrow [q_1, q_2] \rightarrow [f, q_3]$ labeled by CT, since it does not pass through a state of the form $[k, f]$, $k \neq q_0$. (This is exactly the factor CT detected in the Example 10.) So X is not θ-*compliant*. Clearly, this path is also a θ-*free*-path, and so it allows to say that X is also not θ-*free*. However, also the path $[q_0, q_0] \rightarrow [q_2, q_1] \rightarrow [q_3, f] \rightarrow [q_3, q_0] \rightarrow [f, q_2]$ (labeled $GA\lambda C$) is a θ-*free*-path.

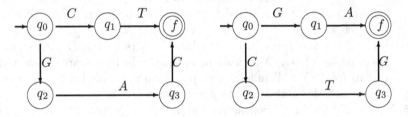

Fig. 3. (left) The Theta automaton $\mathcal{A}_\theta(X)$ constructed from the reduced automaton recognizing $X = \{GA, CTG\}$ (on the right)

Example 18. (Example 11 continued) We already know that the code $X = \{b(aba + ba)^*b\}$ is not θ-*compliant*. Let us consider the construction of the involution square automaton of X, starting from the restricted automaton of Figure 1. We can check that the path $[q_0, q_3] \rightarrow [q_1, q_1] \rightarrow [q_3, q_2] \rightarrow [q_1, q_3] \rightarrow [f, q_1]$ labeled by $aaba$ is a θ-*compliant*-path.

In addition, we already know that X is not θ-*free*. We can check that the path $[q_0, q_3] \rightarrow [q_1, q_1] \rightarrow [q_2, q_3] \rightarrow [q_3, q_1] \rightarrow [q_1, f] \rightarrow [q_1, q_0] \rightarrow [q_2, q_1] \rightarrow [q_1, q_3] \rightarrow [f, q_1]$ labeled by $abab\lambda baba$ is a θ-*free*-path.

7   Conclusion

In this paper we have faced the problem of detecting some undesiderable bonds between DNA molecules which are used in the design of good DNA encodings.

We have proposed a technique for testing an infinite (regular) set of words instead of a (large amount of) finite words. For the UD property, we have used McCloskey's algorithm, and for the DNA properties we have adapted the technique of CODEGEN in this new context.

The software has been implemented using Java as programming language (JDK 1.7, JFlap library for the graphical interface and IDE Eclipse). The object oriented aspect of such language is often an advantage in the choice of the architecture and the composition of the classes. Nevertheless, there are many aspects for which such choice should be handled with care. The natural choice of implementing automata as graphs represented by adjacency lists (and so by using for example java.util.AdjacencyListGraph) has been considered (firstly in [4] only for the UD property), but discarded here for another representation that represents a good compromise between run-time and memory usage.

The pitfall of the algorithm is the construction of the (involution) square automaton, due to the cardinality of the set $Q \times Q$. Briefly, we describe $\mathcal{A}$ by building three parallel arrays V_1, V_2, L as follows: for each edge (q_i, a, q_j), insert q_i into V_1, insert q_j into V_2, insert a into L (precisely, we insert the integer index of these states). This means that for each index i, $(V_1[i], L[i], V_2[i])$ is an edge of $\mathcal{A}$. This simple representation has many advantages in the construction of the square automaton. In fact, given the states $q_0, q_1, \ldots, q_{|Q|-1}$ of $\mathcal{A}$, we obtain the new states $q'_0, q'_1, \ldots, q'_{(|Q|-1) \times (|Q|-1)}$ of the (involution) square automaton, as follows. By using the representation based on the three arrays, given q_i, q_j two states of $\mathcal{A}$, we can calculate immediately the index k of corresponding state $q'_k = [q_i, q_j]$ into the (involution) square automaton as follows: $k = (i \times |Q|) + j$.

Our Java implementation takes care of the memory space requirement, by involving primitive data types. Future investigations regard both theory and implementations, e.g., a more space efficient implementation and the possibility of testing other properties with this technique.

Acknowledgements. We wish to thank the anonymous referees whose comments helped us in improving the readability of our paper. The third author wish also to thank an anonimous referee of [4] for encouraging a more depth implementation of McCloskey's algorithm and to continue the investigation into how the various algorithms for the coding property compare to one another, in practice, in terms of their running times (and space usage).

References

1. Béal, M.P., Perrin, D.: Codes, unambiguous automata and sofic systems. Theor. Comput. Sci. 356(1-2), 6–13 (2006)
2. Berstel, J., Perrin, D., Reutenauer, C.: Codes and Automata, Encyclopedia od Mathematics and its Applications, vol. 129. Cambridge University Press (2009)
3. Colcombet, T.: Forms of determinism for automata. In: STACS 2012. pp. 1–23 (2012) (invited talk)
4. D'Auria, L., Zizza, R.: A note on the McCloskey's algorithm for deciding whether a regular language is a code. In: ICTCS 2010, Camerino, Italy (2010)

5. Head, T., Weber, A.: Deciding code related properties by means of finite transducers. In: Capocelli, R., De Santis, A., Vaccaro, U. (eds.) Sequences II, pp. 260–272. Springer (1993)

6. Hopcroft, J.E., Motwani, R., Ullman, J.D.: Introduction to Automata Theory, Languages, and Computation. Addison-Wesley, Reading (2001)

7. Hussini, S., Kari, L., Konstantinidis, S.: Coding properties of DNA languages. Theor. Comput. Sci. 290(3), 1557–1579 (2003)

8. Jonoska, N., Mahalingam, K.: Languages of DNA Based Code Words. In: Chen, J., Reif, J.H. (eds.) DNA 9. LNCS, vol. 2943, pp. 61–73. Springer, Heidelberg (2004)

9. Kephart, D.E., LeFevre, J.: CODEGEN: The generation and testing of DNA code words. In: IEEE Congress on Evolutionary Computation (2004)

10. McCloskey, R.: An $O(n^2)$ time algorithm for deciding whether a regular language is a code. Journal of Computing and Information 2(10), 79–89 (1996), updated version downloaded http://www.cs.uofs.edu/ mccloske/publications/ code_alg_header_mar2011.pdf

11. Oprocha, P.: Fast solutions for DNA code words test. Schedae Informaticae 15 (2006)

12. Păun, G., Rozenberg, G., Salomaa, A.: DNA Computing, new computing paradigms. Springer (1996)

13. Sardinas, A.A., Patterson, G.W.: A necessary and sufficient condition for the unique decomposition of coded messages. IRE Convention Record (Pt. 8), 104–108 (1953)

On the Security of Interferometric Quantum Key Distribution

Ran Gelles[1],[*] and Tal Mor[2]

[1] Computer Science Department, University of California, Los Angeles, USA
gelles@cs.ucla.edu
[2] Computer Science Department, Technion, Haifa, Israel
talmo@cs.technion.ac.il

Abstract. Photonic quantum key distribution (QKD) is commonly implemented using interferometers, devices that inherently cause the addition of vacuum ancillas, thus enlarging the quantum space in use. This enlargement sometimes exposes the implemented protocol to new kinds of attacks that have not yet been analyzed.

We consider several QKD implementations that use interferometers, and analyze the enlargement of the quantum space caused by the interferometers. While we show that some interferometric implementations are robust (against simple attacks), our main finding is that several other implementations used in QKD experiments *are totally insecure*.

This result is somewhat surprising since although we assume ideal devices and an underlying protocol which is proven secure (e.g., the Bennett-Brassard QKD), the realization is insecure. Our novel attack demonstrates the risks of using practical realizations without performing an extensive security analysis of the specific setup in use.

Keywords: Quantum Key Distribution, Security, Implementation loopholes, Quantum Cryptography.

1 Introduction

Quantum Key Distribution (QKD) is a cryptographic protocol for expanding a pre-shared secret between two users (Alice and Bob) by transferring quantum systems. Once an adversary (Eve) tries to acquire information about a transferred quantum system, she inevitably disturbs it in a way that can be detected by the legitimate users, and causes the abortion of the protocol. This principle is known as "Information Vs. Disturbance" [18,17,12,6].

The first and most popular QKD protocol is the BB84 protocol [5], in which Alice sends qubits to Bob using two conjugate bases. In the real world, qubits are implemented via various methods. A very common QKD implementation is the *phase-encoded, time-multiplexed* scheme: a pulse that contains a single photon is sent in a superposition of two possible times, so that the encoded bit is the phase difference between these superpositions. This was initially suggested by

---

[*] Part of this work done while at Technion, Israel.

A.-H. Dediu, C. Martín-Vide, and B. Truthe (Eds.): TPNC 2012, LNCS 7505, pp. 133–146, 2012.
© Springer-Verlag Berlin Heidelberg 2012

Bennett [4] and implemented by Townsend and others [44,23,21]. In order to produce and measure such superpositioned pulses, it is common to use an *interferometer* (see Section 5.1). In addition to the basic (phase-encoded, time-multiplexed) setup, interferometers are also used in more complex QKD setups. For instance, they are used in *Differential Phase Shift QKD (DPS-QKD)* [25,42,43], which generalizes the time-multiplexing scheme by encoding each bit as a phase shift of three superpositioned pulses (instead of two). Another variant which uses interferometer is the *Plug & Play* protocol used in many experiments [33,41] and commercial products, in which the signal is generated by Bob, sent over to Alice who modulates its phase, then sent back to be measured by Bob.

In this paper we analyze interferometric based QKD schemes. Mainly, we discuss different ways to implement the BB84 protocol. We also discuss implementations of more general schemes, such as the six-state QKD protocol. Once a protocol is implemented via photons and interferometers, the implementation differs from the ideal protocol (that uses abstract qubits) since the "ideal world" two-dimensional qubit space is replaced with a "real world" larger quantum space. This is due to two reasons: first, interferometers inherently introduce a higher-dimension space; and second, having pulses with zero photons, or more than one photon, implies a higher dimension as well. Here we focus on the first space enlargement.

This deviation from the theoretical protocol requires us to revisit the security analysis. Eve possibly controls the large space, rather than the ideal qubit space, and can perform a much stronger attack. In this paper we design a novel type of attack, the *reversed-space attack*, based on considering this large space. we demonstrate a reversed-space attack on several BB84 implementations used in recent experiments [8,34,35,37] proving them to be insecure.

This work joins a line of research that examines the security of QKD implementations. Although BB84 has been proven secure against the most powerful attacks [40,31,39,3,6], these proofs do not apply to realistic variants, and specific attacks that exploit limitations of specific implementations were presented (e.g., [13]). Several security analyses have been published for special cases [27,45]: e.g., a specific protocol variant (DPS-QKD, Plug&Play, etc.), or a specific eavesdropping method. In addition, recent analyses have considered the security of protocols realized using imperfect equipment, such as faulty sources and detectors [32,22,24]. Finally, a recent work [30] analyzes the security of BB84 with arbitrary individual imperfections. That work also considers attacks that allow Eve to control additional degrees of freedom in the detector (i.e., an "enlarged space").

2   Preliminaries and Model

The BB84 Protocol. We mainly focus on implementations of the BB84 protocol [5]. In BB84 Alice uses two conjugate bases (say, z and x) to encode each of her bits as one of the states $|0_z\rangle$, $|1_z\rangle$, $|0_x\rangle = \frac{1}{\sqrt{2}}(|0_z\rangle + |1_z\rangle)$, or $|1_x\rangle = \frac{1}{\sqrt{2}}(|0_z\rangle - |1_z\rangle)$. Let H^A be the quantum space Alice holds (here Alice is ideal, therefore $H^A = H_2$). The qubits reach Bob's lab where he measures them, each in a separately and randomly chosen basis (x or z). After all the qubits have been received by Bob, Alice announces the bases she used over an authenticated public channel. Qubits that have been measured by Bob in a wrong basis are discarded. Next, the parties estimate the error rate by revealing part of the bits and abort the scheme if the error rate exceeds some predetermined threshold. Finally, Alice and Bob generate a final key out of the shared bitstring by performing (classical) error correction and privacy amplification.

Note that in the theoretical (ideal) protocol, Alice and Bob use the same two-dimensional space H_2. However, in a non-ideal world, the spaces H^A and H^B, held by Alice and Bob respectively, might be larger. An important demonstration of such a case is given in [13], where a realistic photonic source is analyzed, such that the cases of zero photons and two photons are added, and as a result $\dim H^A = 6$. Surprisingly, when interferometers are used, even in the case where $\dim H^A = 2$ and all the devices are ideal, Bob measures six orthogonal states that are correlated to the pulse sent by Alice. If Bob actually measures these 6 states, his measured-space becomes much larger than H_2, specifically, $\dim H^B = 6$.

Robustness. The criterion of *robustness* is often used when analyzing the security of QKD protocols. We follow the robustness definition of [9] to analyze interferometric QKD implementations.

Definition 1. *A protocol is said to be* **completely robust** *if nonzero information acquired by Eve implies nonzero probability that the legitimate participants find errors on the bits tested by the protocol. A protocol is said to be* **completely nonrobust** *if Eve can acquire the entire information transmitted in the protocol (namely, the entire information string), without inducing any errors on the bits tested by the protocol.*

Model and Assumptions. The focus of this paper is QKD implementations based on single *photons* as the quantum carriers. In order to describe a qubit using a single photon, one needs to define two orthogonal states. These orthogonal states (called *modes*) are commonly either an intrinsic property (e.g. the polarization of the photon, $|\updownarrow\rangle$ and $|\leftrightarrow\rangle$), or a spatial separation (e.g., $|t_0\rangle$ and $|t_1\rangle$ for different times t_0, t_1). A very convenient way to describe photonic qubits is the *Fock Space* notations, however in this paper we limit the analysis to the case of a single photon and use the standard qubit notations. We refer the reader to the full version of this paper [19] for more details regarding Fock notations.

For simplicity, we assume throughout the paper that Alice's operations are ideal, namely she always succeeds in generating a qubit in the exact desired state. Under this assumption, it is easier to see the novelty and importance of the attack that we suggest and analyze here.

We restrict the adversary to sending only pulses with a single photon, namely, a *single-photon-limited Eve*. Nevertheless, the adversary is capable of receiving, holding and manipulating quantum systems of higher dimensions. Moreover, all our robustness proofs are against individual-particle attacks.

Finally, we discuss the way losses are treated and differentiated from errors, since it can sometimes influence the robustness (and security) analysis. Security proofs (e.g., [40,31,6]) determine the maximal error rate (attributed to Eve's attack) that keeps Eve's knowledge negligible. If Bob considers each loss as a random bit obtained from Alice, he adds an error with probability half, and increases the error-rate. In reality, the loss-rate is too high (commonly, 90% or even 99%) for considering each loss as half-an-error, since the resulting error-rate will exceed the allowed threshold, and the protocol will always abort. Allowing losses without defining a loss-rate threshold might allow Eve to perform useful attacks that result in losses yet no errors, and thus cannot be detected [13,28]. In such cases, one might be able to define a loss-rate threshold such that for a high loss-rate the protocol is completely nonrobust, while for a low loss-rate the protocol is partly robust, and might yield a secure final key.

3   Attacks in an Enlarged Space

We now extend the standard security analysis to the case where Alice is ideal and Bob measures a larger space (for instance, Bob uses interferometer for his measurements). As a first step we define the set of Eve's attacks on that large space that cannot be identified by the legitimate users, that is, attacks that cause no errors. Later we consider the maximal amount of information Eve may obtain by performing such an attack.

3.1   Formulating Eve's Attack

Assume that Alice is ideal, and denote the basis states of her system by $|i\rangle_A$ with $i \in \{0, 1\}$. Eve adds an ancilla in the state $|0\rangle_{\tilde{E}}$ and performs her attack on the joint system $A\tilde{E}$. Eve continues her attack by sending the subsystem A to Bob.

However, Eve can use an enlarged system (e.g. by adding photons or modes). Eve may want to send states beyond the qubit of Alice if those states influence Bob's measurement. A more general attack can be described as

$$|0\rangle_{\tilde{E}} |i\rangle_A \xrightarrow{\mathcal{U}_E} \sum_k \epsilon_{i,k} |E_{i,k}\rangle_E |k\rangle_P, \tag{1}$$

where the subsystem P (rather than A) is sent over to Bob, and $|k\rangle_P$ are basis states of the system P. Obviously, $P = A$ is merely a special case, while in the more general case Eve might send Bob a system with different dimensions than A. The subsystem E, which remains in Eve's hands to be measured afterwards, can therefore differ from the subsystem $\tilde{E}$ she initially had. Moreover, both can be of any dimension as long as the dimension of the entire system does not change, $H^{\tilde{E}} \otimes H^A = H^E \otimes H^P$. Let a general qubit sent by Alice be $|\psi\rangle_A = \sum_i \alpha_i |i\rangle$ with $\sum_i |\alpha_i|^2 = 1$, then due to linearity, the attack on that qubit is

$$\mathcal{U}_E \left(\sum_i \alpha_i |0\rangle_{\tilde{E}} |i\rangle_A \right) = \sum_{i,k} \alpha_i \epsilon_{i,k} |E_{i,k}\rangle_E |k\rangle_P. \tag{2}$$

3.2   Formulating Bob's Measurement

We model Bob's measurement as *(i)* adding the ancilla[1] $|0\rangle_{B'}$; *(ii)* performing a unitary transformation $\mathcal{U}_B$ on $|\psi\rangle_A|0\rangle_{B'}$; and then *(iii)* measuring the joint system in the computation basis. Note that $\mathcal{U}_B$ changes according to the specific basis used by Bob. For the case of BB84, where Bob uses a separate setup for the x and the z basis, we get

$$|i\rangle_A|0\rangle_{B'} \xrightarrow{\;\mathcal{U}_{B_z}\;} \sum_j \beta_{i,j}^z |j\rangle_{AB'} \quad ; \quad |i\rangle_A|0\rangle_{B'} \xrightarrow{\;\mathcal{U}_{B_x}\;} \sum_j \beta_{i,j}^x |j\rangle_{AB'}\,. \qquad (3)$$

The β's are determined by the specific setup used by Bob, and the states $|j\rangle_{AB'}$ are Bob's basis states in the computation basis of $H^A \otimes H^{B'}$.

As an illustrative example, assume that Bob adds no ancilla and his detectors are set to the z-basis. Therefore, for measuring the z basis Bob performs no transformation (i.e. $\mathcal{U}_{B_z} = I$, the identity matrix), while for measuring the x-basis he must perform the Hadamard transformation $\mathcal{U}_{B_x} = \mathcal{H} \triangleq \frac{1}{\sqrt{2}}\left(\begin{smallmatrix} 1 & 1 \\ 1 & -1 \end{smallmatrix}\right)$, so that $|0_x\rangle \xrightarrow{\;\mathcal{U}_{B_x}\;} |0_z\rangle$ and $|1_x\rangle \xrightarrow{\;\mathcal{U}_{B_x}\;} |1_z\rangle$. Since Bob adds no ancilla, $H^{AB'} = H^A$. Using the notations of Equation (3), we get $\mathcal{U}_{B_z}|0\rangle_A = |0\rangle_{AB'}$ thus $\beta_{0,0}^z = 1$ and $\beta_{0,1}^z = 0$; $\mathcal{U}_{B_z}|1\rangle_A = |1\rangle_{AB'}$ thus $\beta_{1,1}^z = 1$ and $\beta_{1,0}^z = 0$. We can write β as a matrix $\beta = (\beta_{i,j})_{i,j=0..1}$ which gives $\beta_{i,j}^z = I$, and similarly $\beta_{i,j}^x = \mathcal{H}$.

It should be noted that Bob's transformation $\mathcal{U}_B$ is actually defined on Bob's ancilla and the space entering his lab, H^P (rather than H^A). Eve has no incentive to send Bob states that can *never* affect his measurement and we can assume Eve sends exactly H^P to Bob (any other system that cannot affect Bob is sent back to Eve and considered as part of her ancilla H^E). In this case, Bob performs a measurement of $B = PB'$, rather than of AB'.

While a fully powerful Eve knows the protocol space of Alice and Bob, and their equipment limitations, Alice and Bob themselves might not be aware of the fact that the system A is replaced by the enlarged system P. The above formulas (3) immediately generalize to this case, simply by replacing the subscript A by P. The general final state $|\Psi_{EB}\rangle$ (held by Bob and Eve), can be written as

$$|\Psi_{EB}\rangle = (I_E \otimes \mathcal{U}_B) \sum_{i,k} \alpha_i \epsilon_{i,k} |E_{i,k}\rangle_E |k\rangle_P |0\rangle_{B'} = \sum_{i,k,j} \alpha_i \epsilon_{i,k} \beta_{k,j} |E_{i,k}\rangle_E |j\rangle_B. \qquad (4)$$

There is a great deal of importance regarding the way Bob interprets his measurement outcomes. The states $|j\rangle_B$ can be classified into sets according to Bob's interpretation: some of these states indicate "Alice has sent the bit 0", others indicate "Alice has sent the bit 1". Let us denote these two sets by J_0 and J_1, respectively. An error occurs when Alice sends a bit b, while Bob measures a state in J_{1-b}. Generally, for a specific transmission, we define by J_{error} the set of all states that imply an error, so in the above example $J_{\text{error}} = J_{1-b}$.

---

[1] Without loss of generality, we assume that Bob uses the same ancilla $|0\rangle_{B'}$ for all of his setups. This can always be justified, e.g., by using a sufficiently large ancilla, such that the different setups potentially use different subsystems of that ancilla.

3.3   Attacks that Cause No Error

When considering real implementations, there may be some outcomes that are not interpreted as valid outcomes:

1. losses: failed transmissions that are not considered to be errors because they naturally occur even when no eavesdropper interferes (e.g. a vacuum state). These outcomes are included in the set J_{loss}.
2. invalid-erroneous outcomes J_{invalid}: outcomes that can never occur if the quantum system sent by Alice reaches Bob intact, e.g., when Alice sends a single photon pulse but Bob's detectors click twice. It is Bob's choice of interpretation that determines whether a specific outcome is to be considered as a loss or as an invalid result. Generally speaking, when an invalid outcome increases the error rate, it is in J_{invalid}, and otherwise it is in J_{loss}.

In order to analyze the robustness of QKD protocols, we consider attacks that cause no errors or invalid outcomes at Bob's end. Formally, for any $|j'\rangle$ in J_{error} or J_{invalid}, we require the overlap $\langle j'|\Psi_{BE}\rangle$ to be zero. Using Equation (4) we see that Eve's attack causes no errors if and only if $\langle j'|\sum_{i,k,j}\alpha_i\epsilon_{i,k}\beta_{k,j}|E_{i,k}\rangle_E|j\rangle_B = 0$, for any $j' \in J_{\text{error}} \cup J_{\text{invalid}}$.

Corollary 2. *For a given QKD implementation, Eve's attack $\mathcal{U}_E$ causes no errors if and only if for every state $|\psi\rangle_A = \sum_i \alpha_i|i\rangle_A$ sent by Alice,*

$$\sum_{i,k}\alpha_i\epsilon_{i,k}\beta_{k,j}|E_{i,k}\rangle_E = 0, \tag{5}$$

for any $j \in J_{\text{error}} \cup J_{\text{invalid}}$ (corresponding to the specific state $|\psi\rangle_A$).

Given a specific QKD implementation, the (expected) error rate is exclusively determined by the attack $\mathcal{U}_E$ performed by Eve.

Definition 3. *Let $\mathbf{U}_{\text{zero}}$ be the set of attacks on a given protocol, that cause no errors (in all the possible setups of the protocol).*

A scheme is robust if $\mathbf{U}_{\text{zero}}$ only consists of attacks that give Eve no information about the key. For BB84 with bases z and x, $\mathbf{U}_{\text{zero}}$ is determined by the intersection of the zero-error attacks for z-basis and x-basis.

4   The Power of Reversed-Space Attacks

One can apply the reversed transformation $(\mathcal{U}_B)^{-1} = \mathcal{U}_B^\dagger$ on each possible $|j\rangle_B$, in order to identify the space that influences Bob's outcome. We call an attack, designed according to this observation, a *reversed-space attack*. The term "reversed" here is borrowed from the "time reversal symmetry" of quantum theory. The symmetry of quantum mechanics to the exchange of the prepared (preselected) state and the measured (postselected) state was suggested by [1,2] (and was already used in quantum cryptography as well, see the time-reversed EPR scheme [7]).

To clarify this point, we note that in the above attack Eve sends Bob a quantum system with space H^P (instead of H^A), which is exactly the space given by the reverse method (i.e., the space obtained by considering $(\mathcal{U}_B)^{-1}$, and tracing out the ancilla $H^{B'}$). As said, Eve has no incentive in sending systems of higher-dimension, since those will be ignored by Bob. This simplifies any security analysis, since there is no use in analyzing spaces with dimension larger than the dimension of the reversed-space.

In the following sections we describe various BB84 implementations that use interferometers, and analyze their robustness via the reverse-space method, against an adversary limited to sending pulses with at most one photon.

5   Analysis of Phase-Encoded Interferometric BB84

In this section we analyze several different implementation variants such as phase-encoded time-multiplexed [44] and time-bin encoded schemes. As a preparatory step we show that the tools developed above are useful to show the robustness of some of these implementation (it should be noted that their robustness also follows from previous works [30]). More interestingly, we use the same techniques to devise a successful "reversed-space attack" on a specific BB84 implementation that uses interferometers [46,34,35,26,37], proving its insecurity.

5.1   Interferometric Implementation of the xy-BB84 Scheme

Consider a BB84 implementation which uses two time-separated modes (pulses). For every transmission, the first mode arrives to Bob's lab at time t'_0, and the second mode at $t'_1 = t'_0 + \Delta T$. We denote these pulses as $|t'_0\rangle$ and $|t'_1\rangle$ respectively. The users use the x and y bases, so that an ideal Alice sends one of the following four states,

$$|0_x\rangle_A \equiv (|t'_0\rangle + |t'_1\rangle)/\sqrt{2} \qquad\qquad |0_y\rangle_A \equiv (|t'_0\rangle + i|t'_1\rangle)/\sqrt{2}$$
$$|1_x\rangle_A \equiv (|t'_0\rangle - |t'_1\rangle)/\sqrt{2} \qquad\qquad |1_y\rangle_A \equiv (|t'_0\rangle - i|t'_1\rangle)/\sqrt{2}.$$

Bob measures the qubit using a Mach-Zender interferometer, which consists of two beam splitters (BS) with one short path, one long path, and a controlled phase shifter P_ϕ, that is placed at the long arm of the interferometer. (See the full version of this paper [19] for a detailed description of interferometers, and analysis of their operation on single-photon modes). The length difference between the two arms is determined by ΔT: when the first pulse travels through the long arm, and the second through the short arm, they arrive together at the output. Due to that exact timing of the pulses, each incoming qubit is transformed into a superposition of 6 possible modes (Figure 1): 3 time modes (t_0, t_1, t_2) at the straight (s) output arm of the interferometer, and 3 modes at the down (d) output arm.

For the sake of simplicity we denote these modes as $s_0, s_1, s_2, d_0, d_1, d_2$, and since we only consider pulses with zero or one photons, we can use the states,

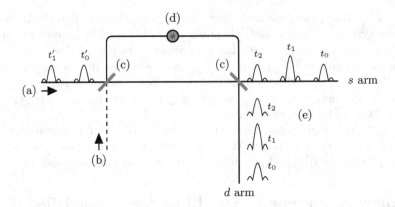

Fig. 1. A Mach-Zender interferometer. (a) An input qubit. The time-difference between the two incoming modes is identical to the difference between the two arms; (b) a vacuum state entering the second (blocked) arm; (c) beam-splitters; (d) phase shifter P_ϕ; (e) six output modes.

$|s_0\rangle, |d_0\rangle$, etc., along with the vacuum state $|V\rangle$ (a pulse that contains no photons in any of the modes).

The intereferometer's operation (see [19]) is defined by $|V\rangle \mapsto |V\rangle_B$ and

$$|t_0'\rangle \mapsto (|s_0\rangle_B - e^{i\phi}|s_1\rangle_B + i|d_0\rangle_B + ie^{i\phi}|d_1\rangle_B)/2$$
$$|t_1'\rangle \mapsto (|s_1\rangle_B - e^{i\phi}|s_2\rangle_B + i|d_1\rangle_B + ie^{i\phi}|d_2\rangle_B)/2. \tag{6}$$

Bob sets the phase ϕ according to the basis he wishes to measure: $\phi = 0$ for the x-basis and $\phi = \pi/2$ for the y-basis. When Alice's and Bob's bases match, the input qubit evolves in the interferometer as

$$
\begin{aligned}
|0_x\rangle_A &\xrightarrow{\phi=0} (|s_0\rangle_B &&- |s_2\rangle_B + i|d_0\rangle_B + 2i|d_1\rangle_B + i|d_2\rangle_B)/\sqrt{8} \\
|1_x\rangle_A &\xrightarrow{\phi=0} (|s_0\rangle_B - 2|s_1\rangle_B + |s_2\rangle_B + i|d_0\rangle_B &&- i|d_2\rangle_B)/\sqrt{8} \\
|0_y\rangle_A &\xrightarrow{\phi=\pi/2} (|s_0\rangle_B &&+ |s_2\rangle_B + i|d_0\rangle_B - 2|d_1\rangle_B - i|d_2\rangle_B)/\sqrt{8} \\
|1_y\rangle_A &\xrightarrow{\phi=\pi/2} (|s_0\rangle_B - 2i|s_1\rangle_B - |s_2\rangle_B + i|d_0\rangle_B &&+ i|d_2\rangle_B)/\sqrt{8}
\end{aligned}
\tag{7}
$$

Bob opens his detectors at time t_1 at both the arms. A click at the "down" direction (i.e., measuring the state $|d_1\rangle$) means the bit-value 0, while a click at the "straight" direction ($|s_1\rangle$) means 1. The other modes are commonly considered as a loss (namely, they are not measured) since they do not reveal the value of the original qubit. The above implementation is commonly used for QKD experiments, and products [20,16,15]. We denote this implementation by xy-BB84.

Since measuring the other modes ($|s_0\rangle$, etc.) does not reveal the bit Alice has sent, measuring these modes can only help Bob in noticing some eavesdropping attacks. On the other hand, considering these modes complicates the security analysis since Eve might send superpositions of the time-modes $t_2' = t_1' + \Delta T$, and $t_{-1}' = t_0' - \Delta T$, which will not result in $|V\rangle$.

We show the above xy-BB84 implementation is completely robust against a single-photon limited Eve.

Theorem 4. *Assuming a single-photon-limited adversary, the xy-BB84 scheme is completely robust*

The proof is done via the tools constructed in Section 3, that is, by considering all possible *reversed-space attacks* on the scheme. Specifically we define the set $\mathbf{U}_{\text{zero}}$ of attacks that induce no errors, according to Definition 3, and show that all the attacks in $\mathbf{U}_{\text{zero}}$ leak no information to Eve.

Since we limit the parties to single-photon pulses, we only need to consider the sub-space that contains the vacuum state and the single-photon states, i.e., the states $|V\rangle$, $|s_0\rangle$, $|s_1\rangle$, $|s_2\rangle$, $|d_0\rangle$, $|d_1\rangle$ and $|d_2\rangle$ defined above. The analysis must consider the states (sent by Alice or Eve) that, after the interferometer, have a non-zero overlap with the modes measured by Bob. This idea is what differentiates our analysis from previous methods of analyzing (theoretical) protocols.

A detailed proof of Theorem 4 appears in the full version of this paper [19].

5.2 "Native" Implementation for x and z Bases

Let us now extend the analysis to implementations that use the z-basis. This might be required, for instance, in order to implement the 6-state QKD protocol [14], in which Alice sends qubits using the x, y and z bases at random; or in order to perform "QKD with classical Bob" [9,10,48] in which one party is restricted to use only the (classical) z-basis, and either performs measurements in that basis or returns the qubits (unchanged) to the other party.

We now describe a possible setup for measuring the z-basis, e.g. the states $|0_z\rangle = |t'_0\rangle$ and $|1_z\rangle = |t'_1\rangle$. The implementation is rather straightforward—Bob measures the pulses after the appropriate delay, so that the measurement of $|0_z\rangle$ ($|1_z\rangle$) is done by opening a detector at time t_0 (t_1); see Figure 2.

The respective transformation $\mathcal{U}_{B_z}$ is

$$|0_z\rangle \xrightarrow{\mathcal{U}_{B_z}} |d_1\rangle \quad ; \quad |1_z\rangle \xrightarrow{\mathcal{U}_{B_z}} |s_1\rangle, \tag{8}$$

where the other modes are not measured by Bob, and are not relevant for this scheme. We use the mode $|d_1\rangle$ instead of the more intuitive $|s_0\rangle$ in order to be consistent with the modes representing the bit values 0 and 1 when the x (or y) setup is used[2].

We denote the BB84 protocol that uses x and z bases by alternating the setups (adding and removing beam-splitters as needed), as native-xz-BB84. In the same manner, a six-state protocol implemented by alternating the above setups (e.g., [38]) is denoted as native-six-state scheme.

---

[2] This can be justified by placing and removing a mirror, such that the pulse entering the lab at time t'_1 is reflected to the d arm.

It is rather straightforward to extend the robustness proof of the xy-BB84 scheme to the above native-xz-BB84 setting, which also implies the robustness of the native-six-state scheme. In the full version [19] we show the following.

Theorem 5. *Assuming a single-photon-limited adversary, the* native-six-state *scheme is completely robust.*

5.3   "Unified" Implementation for the xz-Bases

The native implementation suffers from one main caveat: the need of a mechanical operation after each qubit-transmission, as the basis must be chosen at random. Such an operation might take a lot of time and substantially decrease the maximal bit-rate allowed in the protocol. Other implementations do not involve mechanical operation but use a beam-splitter to split the channel such that each output reaches a different setup (see for instance [38,36,47]). These kinds of implementations suffer from high loss-rate and low bit-rate.

Let us describe a BB84 protocol that uses the z and x bases, in which Bob's interferometric setup is fixed and independent of the basis used [20,46,34,35,26]. The idea is to use the setup $\mathcal{U}_{B_x}$ for measuring both bases in the following manner. In order to perform a measurement in the x basis, Bob opens his two detectors at time-bin t_1, so that he measures the states $|s_1\rangle$ and $|d_1\rangle$. In addition, for measuring the z basis, Bob measures $|s_0\rangle, |d_0\rangle$ which implies the bit-value '0' and $|s_2\rangle, |d_2\rangle$ that implies '1', (see Equations (6) and (7)). We denote this scheme as unified-xz-BB84.

Bob measures different time-bins than t_1, namely times t_0 and t_2. In contrast to previous schemes, here the input modes t'_{-1} and t'_2 might have a non-zero overlap with the modes measured by Bob. The reversed-space attack implies that time modes -1 to 2 may affect Bob, and other time modes will always yield a loss. Hence, a state sent by Eve needs only be a superposition of modes t'_{-1} to t'_2.

5.4   (Non-)Robustness of xz-BB84-Unified Scheme for a Single-Photon-Limited Eve

Theorem 6. *The unified-xz-BB84 scheme is completely nonrobust*

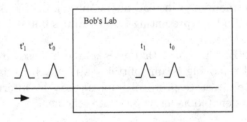

Fig. 2. Bob's laboratory setup for the z basis

Proof. For the non-robustness proof, it suffices to restrict Eve (as well as any natural noise) to single photon pulses.

We use Corollary 2 to define attacks that cause no errors at all. For this specific implementation, $\mathbf{U}_{\text{zero}}$ consists of the attacks that satisfy Equation (5) in four cases, matching the four BB84 states sent by Alice. Bob's setup (i.e. the constants $\beta_{k,j}$) is basis-independent and can be written using Equation (6) in a matrix form as[3]

$$\beta_{\substack{k=\{t'_{-1},t'_0,t'_1,t'_2\},\\ j=\{s_0,s_1,s_2,d_0,d_1,d_2\}}} = \frac{1}{2}\begin{pmatrix} -1 & 0 & 0 & i & 0 & 0 \\ 1 & -1 & 0 & i & i & 0 \\ 0 & 1 & -1 & 0 & i & i \\ 0 & 0 & 1 & 0 & 0 & i \end{pmatrix}.$$

We describe the measurement Bob performs, for the x basis, as $J_0 = \{|d_1\rangle\}$; $J_1 = \{|s_1\rangle\}$; $J_{\text{loss}} = I - J_0 - J_1$; and $J_{\text{invalid}} = \emptyset$, where I represents the computation basis of H^B, and the minus stands for set difference. Furthermore, when Bob measures the z basis, he interprets his outcome according to $J_0 = \{|d_0\rangle, |s_0\rangle\}$, $J_1 = \{|d_2\rangle, |s_2\rangle\}$, $J_{\text{invalid}} = \emptyset$ (due to the single-photon assumption), and $J_{\text{loss}} = I - J_0 - J_1$.

Consider the case where Alice sends $|0_x\rangle$, namely, $\alpha_0 = \alpha_1 = \frac{1}{\sqrt{2}}$. An error occurs if Bob measures $J_{\text{error}} = \{|s_1\rangle\}$, and by Equation (5), the attack causes no error if

$$-\frac{1}{2\sqrt{2}}(\epsilon_{t'_0,t'_0}|E_{t'_0,t'_0}\rangle_E + \epsilon_{t'_1,t'_0}|E_{t'_1,t'_0}\rangle_E) + \frac{1}{2\sqrt{2}}(\epsilon_{t'_0,t'_1}|E_{t'_0,t'_1}\rangle_E + \epsilon_{t'_1,t'_1}|E_{t'_1,t'_1}\rangle_E) = 0.$$

Similarly, when Alice sends $|1_x\rangle$, $J_{\text{error}} = \{|d_1\rangle\}$, and we require

$$\frac{i}{2\sqrt{2}}(\epsilon_{t'_0,t'_0}|E_{t'_0,t'_0}\rangle_E - \epsilon_{t'_1,t'_0}|E_{t'_1,t'_0}\rangle_E) + \frac{i}{2\sqrt{2}}(\epsilon_{t'_0,t'_1}|E_{t'_0,t'_1}\rangle_E - \epsilon_{t'_1,t'_1}|E_{t'_1,t'_1}\rangle_E) = 0.$$

As for the z-basis, following Corollary 2, an attack $\mathcal{U}_E$ causes no errors if

$$i\epsilon_{t'_0,t'_1}|E_{t'_0,t'_1}\rangle + i\epsilon_{t'_0,t'_2}|E_{t'_0,t'_2}\rangle = 0 \quad \text{and} \quad -\epsilon_{t'_0,t'_1}|E_{t'_0,t'_1}\rangle + \epsilon_{t'_0,t'_2}|E_{t'_0,t'_2}\rangle = 0, \quad (9)$$

corresponding to the case where Alice sends $|0_z\rangle$, i.e. $\alpha_0 = 1$, $\alpha_1 = 0$, and $J_{\text{error}} = \{|d_2\rangle, |s_2\rangle\}$, as well as

$$\begin{aligned} i\epsilon_{t'_1,t'_{-1}}|E_{t'_1,t'_{-1}}\rangle + i\epsilon_{t'_1,t'_0}|E_{t'_1,t'_0}\rangle = 0 \quad \text{and} \\ -\epsilon_{t'_1,t'_{-1}}|E_{t'_1,t'_{-1}}\rangle + \epsilon_{t'_1,t'_0}|E_{t'_1,t'_0}\rangle = 0, \end{aligned} \quad (10)$$

corresponding to the case where Alice sends $|1_z\rangle$, i.e. $\alpha_0 = 0$, $\alpha_1 = 1$, and $J_{\text{error}} = \{|d_0\rangle, |s_0\rangle\}$. This leads to the constraints $\epsilon_{t'_0,t'_1} = \epsilon_{t'_0,t'_2} = 0$ and $\epsilon_{t'_1,t'_{-1}} = \epsilon_{t'_1,t'_0} = 0$. Attacks that satisfy all the above requirements are of the form

$$|0\rangle_{\bar{E}}|0_z\rangle_A \xrightarrow{\mathcal{U}_E} p|\phi\rangle_E|t'_0\rangle_P + p_1|\phi_1\rangle|t'_{-1}\rangle_P + p_2|\psi_0\rangle_E|V\rangle_P$$
$$|0\rangle_E|1_z\rangle_A \xrightarrow{\mathcal{U}_E} p|\phi\rangle_E|t'_1\rangle_P + p_3|\phi_2\rangle|t'_2\rangle_P + p_4|\psi_1\rangle_E|V\rangle_P \quad (11)$$

---

[3] We omit the vacuum state, since in any possible setup, $|V\rangle \to |V\rangle$; also, $\mathcal{U}_B$ is defined for any time mode $t \in \mathbb{Z}$, yet any time $t \notin \{-1, 0, 1, 2\}$ is always measured as a loss and can be omitted by the analysis.

with $|p|^2 + |p_1|^2 + |p_2|^2 = |p|^2 + |p_3|^2 + |p_4|^2 = 1$. It is now easy to devise an attack and show that the protocol is completely non-robust. For instance, let

$$|0\rangle_{\tilde{E}}|0_z\rangle_A \xrightarrow{U_E} |E_1\rangle_E|t'_{-1}\rangle_P \qquad\qquad |0\rangle_{\tilde{E}}|1_z\rangle_A \xrightarrow{U_E} |E_2\rangle_E|t'_2\rangle_P \qquad (12)$$

with orthogonal $|E_1\rangle$, $|E_2\rangle$. This attack never causes an error, yet it increases the loss rate—Bob always gets a loss when using the x basis. This means that only bits encoded using the z basis are used for transferring information, and Eve can copy the information. It follows that the unified-xz-BB84 is *completely nonrobust* according to Definition 1. $\qquad\qquad\qquad\qquad\qquad\qquad\qquad\qquad\qquad$ □

This specific attack is somewhat related to the "fake state" attack [28,29], and can be avoided if Bob adds a shutter to block the channel at times other than 0 and 1. This might however result in decreasing the key rate according to the shutter speed. Additionally, adding a shutter modifies the protocol and could expose it to weaknesses not analyzed here. Other reversed-space attacks might exist even when Bob uses a shutter, e.g., if Eve has (one-time) access to the blocked arm of the interferometer [11].

As mentioned above all qubits sent by Eve are in the z-basis (i.e., the loss-rate Bob sees for the x-basis is 1). We can compose an attack that doesn't have such a property (for instance, by letting $p > 0$), in which Eve does not force a loss in the x-basis, yet she does not learn the information for that basis.

Finally, note that the above attack also applies to the unified six-state QKD scheme (see [37], for instance), making such realizations totally insecure. Going beyond the schemes presented here is left for future research.

Acknowledgment. The authors thank Michel Boyer for many useful suggestions. We also thank Akshay Wadia, Alan Roytman and Niek Bouman for miscellaneous comments.

References

1. Aharonov, Y., Bergmann, P.G., Lebowitz, J.L.: Time symmetry in the quantum process of measurement. Phys. Rev. 134(6B), B1410–B1416 (1964)
2. Aharonov, Y., Vaidman, L.: Properties of a quantum system during the time interval between two measurements. Physical Review A 41(1), 11–20 (1990)
3. Ben-Or, M., Horodecki, M., Leung, D.W., Mayers, D., Oppenheim, J.: The Universal Composable Security of Quantum Key Distribution. In: Kilian, J. (ed.) TCC 2005. LNCS, vol. 3378, pp. 386–406. Springer, Heidelberg (2005)
4. Bennett, C.H.: Quantum cryptography using any two nonorthogonal states. Physical Review Letters 68(21), 3121–3124 (1992)
5. Bennett, C.H., Brassard, G.: Quantum Cryptography: Public key distribution and coin tossing. In: Proceedings of IEEE International Conference on Computers, Systems and Signal Processing, pp. 175–179 (December 1984)
6. Biham, E., Boyer, M., Boykin, P.O., Mor, T., Roychowdhury, V.P.: A proof of the security of quantum key distribution. J. Cryptology 19(4), 381–439 (2006)

7. Biham, E., Huttner, B., Mor, T.: Quantum cryptographic network based on quantum memories. Physical Review A 54(4), 2651–2658 (1996)
8. Bonfrate, G., Harlow, M., Ford, C., Maxwell, G., Townsend, P.: Asymmetric machzehnder germano-silicate channel waveguide interferometers for quantum cryptography systems. Electronics Letters 37(13), 846–847 (2001)
9. Boyer, M., Kenigsberg, D., Mor, T.: Quantum Key Distribution with Classical Bob. Physical Review Letters 99(14), 140501 (2007)
10. Boyer, M., Gelles, R., Kenigsberg, D., Mor, T.: Semiquantum key distribution. Physical Review A 79(3), 032341 (2009)
11. Boyer, M., Gelles, R., Mor, T.: Attacks on Fixed Apparatus Quantum Key Distribution Schemes. In: Dediu, A.-H., Martín-Vide, C., Truthe, B. (eds.): TPNC 2012. LNCS, 7505, pp. 97–107. Springer, Heidelberg (2012)
12. Boykin, P.O., Roychowdhury, V.P.: Information vs. disturbance in dimension d. Quantum Info. Comput. 5(4), 396–412 (2005)
13. Brassard, G., Lütkenhaus, N., Mor, T., Sanders, B.C.: Limitations on practical quantum cryptography. Physical Review Letters 85(6), 1330–1333 (2000)
14. Bruß, D.: Optimal Eavesdropping in Quantum Cryptography with Six States. Physical Review Letters 81, 3018–3021 (1998)
15. Dusek, M., Lütkenhaus, N., Hendrych, M.: Chapter 5 quantum cryptography. In: Wolf, E. (ed.) Progress in Optics, vol. 49, pp. 381–454. Elsevier (2006)
16. Elliott, C., Pearson, D., Troxel, G.: Quantum cryptography in practice. In: SIGCOMM 2003, pp. 227–238 (2003)
17. Fuchs, C.A., Gisin, N., Griffiths, R.B., Niu, C.S., Peres, A.: Optimal eavesdropping in quantum cryptography. i. information bound and optimal strategy. Physical Review A 56(2), 1163–1172 (1997)
18. Fuchs, C.A., Peres, A.: Quantum-state disturbance versus information gain: Uncertainty relations for quantum information. Physical Review A 53(4), 2038–2045 (1996)
19. Gelles, R., Mor, T.: On the security of interferometric quantum key distribution (2011), (full version) arXiv:1110.6573
20. Gisin, N., Ribordy, G., Tittel, W., Zbinden, H.: Quantum cryptography. Reviews of Modern Physics 74(1), 145–195 (2002)
21. Gobby, C., Yuan, Z.L., Shields, A.J.: Quantum key distribution over 122 km of standard telecom fiber. Applied Physics Letters 84(19), 3762–3764 (2004)
22. Gottesman, D., Lo, H.-K., Lütkenhaus, N., Preskill, J.: Security of quantum key distribution with imperfect devices. Quantum Information and Computation 5, 325–360 (2004)
23. Hughes, R.J., Luther, G.G., Morgan, G.L., Simmons, C.: Quantum cryptography over 14km of installed optical fiber. In: Rochester Conference on Coherence and Quantum Optics, pp. 7–10 (June 1995)
24. Inamori, H., Lütkenhaus, N., Mayers, D.: Unconditional security of practical quantum key distribution. European Physical Journal D 41, 599–627 (2007)
25. Inoue, K., Waks, E., Yamamoto, Y.: Differential phase shift quantum key distribution. Physical Review Letters 89(3), 037902 (2002)
26. Jaeger, G., Sergienko, A.: Entangled states in quantum key distribution. In: AIP Conference Proceedings, vol. 810(1), pp. 161–167 (2006)
27. Lütkenhaus, N.: Security against individual attacks for realistic quantum key distribution. Physical Review A 61(5), 052304 (2000)
28. Makarov, V., Hjelme, D.R.: Faked states attack on quantum cryptosystems. Journal of Modern Optics 52, 691–705 (2005)

29. Makarov, V., Anisimov, A., Skaar, J.: Effects of detector efficiency mismatch on security of quantum cryptosystems. Physical Review A 74, 022313 (2006)

30. Marøy, Ø., Lydersen, L., Skaar, J.: Security of quantum key distribution with arbitrary individual imperfections. Physical Review A 82, 032337 (2010)

31. Mayers, D.: Unconditional security in quantum cryptography. J. ACM 48(3), 351–406 (2001)

32. Mayers, D., Yao, A.: Quantum cryptography with imperfect apparatus. In: FOCS 1998, p. 503 (1998)

33. Muller, A., Herzog, T., Huttner, B., Tittel, W., Zbinden, H., Gisin, N.: "Plug and play" systems for quantum cryptography. Applied Physics Letters 70(7), 793–795 (1997)

34. Nambu, Y., Hatanaka, T., Nakamura, K.: Planar lightwave circuits for quantum cryptographic systems. Arxiv:quant-ph/0307074 (2003)

35. Nambu, Y., Hatanaka, T., Nakamura, K.: BB84 quantum key distribution system based on silica-based planar lightwave circuits. Japanese Journal of Applied Physics 43(8B), L1109–L1110 (2004)

36. Nambu, Y., Yoshino, K., Tomita, A.: Quantum encoder and decoder for practical quantum key distribution using a planar lightwave circuit. Journal of Modern Optics 55(12), 1953–1970 (2008)

37. Nazarathy, M., Tselniker, I., Regev, Y., Orenstein, M., Katz, M.: Integrated-optical realizations of quantum key distribution over maximally unbiased bases. IEEE Journal of Selected Topics in Quantum Electronics 12(4), 897–913 (2006)

38. Nazarathy, M.: Quantum key distribution over a fiber-optic channel by means of pulse position modulation. Opt. Lett. 30(12), 1533–1535 (2005)

39. Renner, R.: Security of Quantum Key Distribution. Ph.D. thesis, Swiss Federal Institute of Technology, Zurich (2005)

40. Shor, P.W., Preskill, J.: Simple proof of security of the BB84 quantum key distribution protocol. Physical Review Letters 85(2), 441–444 (2000)

41. Stucki, D., Gisin, N., Guinnard, O., Ribordy, G., Zbinden, H.: Quantum key distribution over 67 km with a plug&play system. New Journal of Physics 4, 41 (2002)

42. Takesue, H., Diamanti, E., Honjo, T., Langrock, C., Fejer, M.M., Inoue, K., Yamamoto, Y.: Differential phase shift quantum key distribution experiment over 105km fibre. New Journal of Physics 7, 232 (2005)

43. Takesue, H., Honjo, T., Kamada, H.: Differential phase shift quantum key distribution using 1.3-μm up-conversion detectors. Japanese Journal of Applied Physics 45, 5757 (2006)

44. Townsend, P.D.: Secure key distribution system based on quantum cryptography. Electronics Letters 30, 809–811 (1994)

45. Waks, E., Takesue, H., Yamamoto, Y.: Security of differential-phase-shift quantum key distribution against individual attacks. Physical Review A (Atomic, Molecular, and Optical Physics) 73(1), 012344 (2006)

46. Walton, Z.D., Abouraddy, A.F., Sergienko, A.V., Saleh, B.E.A., Teich, M.C.: Decoherence-free subspaces in quantum key distribution. Physical Review Letters 91(8), 087901 (2003)

47. Yoshino, K., Fujiwara, M., Tanaka, A., Takahashi, S., Nambu, Y., Tomita, A., Miki, S., Yamashita, T., Wang, Z., Sasaki, M., Tajima, A.: High-speed wavelength-division multiplexing quantum key distribution system. Opt. Lett. 37(2), 223–225 (2012)

48. Zou, X., Qiu, D., Li, L., Wu, L., Li, L.: Semiquantum-key distribution using less than four quantum states. Physical Review A 79(5), 052312 (2009)

Generating DNA Code Words
Using Forbidding and Enforcing Systems

Daniela Genova[1] and Kalpana Mahalingam[2]

[1] Department of Mathematics and Statistics
University of North Florida
Jacksonville, FL 32224, USA
d.genova@unf.edu
[2] Department of Mathematics
Indian Institute of Technology
Chennai, TN 600036, India
kmahalingam@iitm.ac.in

Abstract. Research in DNA computing was initiated by Leonard Adleman in 1994 when he solved an instance of an NP-complete problem solely by molecules. DNA code words arose in the attempt to avoid unwanted hybridizations of DNA strands for DNA based computations. Given a set of constraints, generating a large set of DNA strands that satisfy the constraints is an important problem in DNA computing. On the other hand, motivated by the non-determinism of molecular reactions, A. Ehrenfeucht and G. Rozenberg introduced forbidding and enforcing systems (fe-systems) as a model of computation that defines classes of languages based on two sets of constraints. We attempt to establish a connection between these two areas of research in natural computing by characterizing a variety of DNA codes that avoid certain types of cross hybridizations by fe-systems. We show that one fe-system can generate the entire class of DNA codes of a certain property, for example θ-k-codes, and confirm some properties of DNA codes through fe-systems. We generalize by fe-systems some known methods of generating good DNA code words which have been tested experimentally.

Keywords: fe-systems, fe-families, Biomolecular computing, Watson-Crick involution, Hybridization, DNA codes.

1 Introduction

In 1994, Adleman [1] solved an instance of an NP-problem by encoding information into DNA strands and using these strands to perform the computation by themselves. Since then, research on DNA computing has had a tremendous growth. Problems are solved by encoding information on DNA strands. One of the challenges is choosing the right set of strands for computational purposes, as the strands may bind to each other in undesirable ways due to Watson-Crick complementarity. This type of hybridization can occur during a polymerase chain reaction, a self-assembly step, or in the extraction process. Several authors have

A.-H. Dediu, C. Martín-Vide, and B. Truthe (Eds.): TPNC 2012, LNCS 7505, pp. 147–160, 2012.

addressed this issue and proposed various solutions [3,6,17,18]. Generating a large set of DNA code words is a difficult problem. Recently, in [8], a large set of DNA code words was designed using DNA metric spaces and it was shown that such a problem is NP-complete.

In [13], Kari et al. introduced a theoretical approach to the problem of designing code words. Following this approach, a DNA code that avoids all kinds of unwanted partial bindings was introduced in [14] and was called a θ-k-code (see Figure 1). Note that for any word w over the alphabet $\Delta = \{A, C, G, T\}$ and for an antimorphic involution θ such that $\theta(A) = T$, $\theta(C) = G$ and vice versa, $\theta(w)$ denotes the Watson-Crick complement of the strand w.

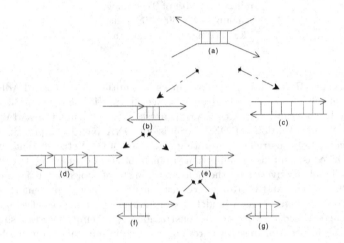

Fig. 1. Various cross hybridizations of molecules avoided by: (a): θ-k-code - one molecule contains a subword of length k and the other its complement. For a suitable k, a θ-k-code also avoids cross bindings of type avoided by (b): θ-comma-free, (c): θ-strict, (d): θ-intercode, (e): θ-infix, (f): θ-prefix, (g): θ-suffix code.

Motivated by the non-determinism in molecular reactions, A. Ehrenfeucht and G. Rozenberg introduced forbidding-enforcing systems, fe-systems, in [4,5] as a model of computation that defines classes of languages. This model uses a forbidding set to exclude combinations of subwords from the subwords of each language in the family and uses an enforcing set to require certain words to be in the language, provided some pre-specified sets of words are already contained in the language. One fe-system consisting of a forbidding set and an enforcing set defines a class of languages, fe-family. These classes were shown in [11] to be completely different than Chomsky's classes. On the other hand, fe-systems were shown to be suitable for defining the solutions to combinatorial problems and for modeling DNA molecules and splicing with an enzyme [5,9,12]. Fe-systems models in membrane computing were introduced in [2] and [7] proposed modeling self-assembly of graphs by fe-systems.

The purpose of this paper is to show that the theory of forbidding and enforcing systems is very suitable for generating DNA codes and to initiate research at the interplay of both areas. We use the fe-systems defined in [4,5] to characterize the types of DNA codes presented in [13,14,16]. We show that one can generate the entire family of DNA codes that avoid certain unwanted cross-hybridizations by a single fe-system, as opposed to classical language theory where one grammar (automaton) generates (accepts) only one language (DNA code). In the process, we also confirm some properties of DNA codes, deriving them through fe-systems. The definitions are recalled in Section 2 and various DNA codes characterizations are presented in Section 3. In Section 4, as an illustration, we present fe-systems that characterize DNA code words generated using methods proposed in [14]. These code words were experimentally tested in [14] and were shown to have no visible cross-hybridizations.

2   Basic Concepts and Definitions

An alphabet is denoted by Σ, the length of a word w over Σ by $|w|$ and the empty word by λ. The free monoid Σ^* contains all words over Σ and the free semigroup $\Sigma^+ = \Sigma^* \setminus \{\lambda\}$. For $k \geq 1$, $\Sigma^k = \{w \in \Sigma^* \mid |w| = k\}$ and $\Sigma^{\leq k} = \{w \in \Sigma^* \mid |w| \leq k\}$. The set of all languages over Σ is $\mathcal{P}(\Sigma^*)$. For $w \in \Sigma^*$, the set of subwords of w is $\mathrm{Sub}\,(w)$ and $\mathrm{Sub}\,_k(w) = \mathrm{Sub}\,(w) \cap \Sigma^k$. Extended to languages, $\mathrm{Sub}\,(L)$ denotes all subwords of the language L.

2.1   DNA Involution Codes

We follow the definitions from [13,14,16,15]. An involution $\theta : \Sigma \to \Sigma$ of a set Σ is a mapping such that θ^2 equals the identity mapping, i.e. $\theta(\theta(x)) = x$, for all $x \in \Sigma$. For words $u, v \in \Sigma^*$ and morphic θ we have that $\theta(uv) = \theta(u)\theta(v)$ and for an antimorphic θ, $\theta(uv) = \theta(v)\theta(u)$.

Definition 1. Given an alphabet Σ, let $\theta : \Sigma^* \to \Sigma^*$ be a morphic or an antimorphic involution and $X \subseteq \Sigma^+$. Then the set (language) X is called a:

1. θ-*subword-k-m-code* for some positive integers k and m if for all $u \in \Sigma^k$ we have $\Sigma^* u \Sigma^i \theta(u) \Sigma^* \cap X = \emptyset$ for all $1 \leq i \leq m$.
2. θ-*subword-k-code* for some positive integer k if for all $u \in \Sigma^k$ we have $\Sigma^* u \Sigma^i \theta(u) \Sigma^* \cap X = \emptyset$ for all $i \geq 1$.
3. θ-*strict-code* if $X \cap \theta(X) = \emptyset$.
4. θ-*prefix-code* if $X \cap \theta(X)\Sigma^+ = \emptyset$.
5. θ-*suffix-code* if $X \cap \Sigma^+\theta(X) = \emptyset$.
6. θ-*bifix-code* if X is both a θ-prefix-code and a θ-suffix-code.
7. θ-*intercode of index m* for some integer $m \geq 1$ if $X^{m+1} \cap \Sigma^+\theta(X^m)\Sigma^+ = \emptyset$.
8. θ-*infix-code* if $\Sigma^*\theta(X)\Sigma^+ \cap X = \emptyset$ and $\Sigma^+\theta(X)\Sigma^* \cap X = \emptyset$.
9. θ-*comma-free-code* if $X^2 \cap \Sigma^+\theta(X)\Sigma^+ = \emptyset$.
10. θ-*k-code* for some integer $k > 0$ if $\mathrm{Sub}_k(X) \cap \mathrm{Sub}_k(\theta(X)) = \emptyset$.

A set $X \subseteq \Sigma^+$ is said to be a θ-*strict-P-code* if X is both a θ-P-code and a θ-strict-code, where $P \in \{$prefix, suffix, infix, bifix, comma-free, intercode, k-(code)$\}$.

Example 2. Let $X = \{aa, baa\}$ be a language over the alphabet $\Sigma = \{a, b\}$ and θ be a morphic involution on Σ with $\theta(a) = b$ and $\theta(b) = a$. Then $\theta(X) = \{bb, abb\}$. Note that X is a θ-infix-code since none of the subwords of X are in $\theta(X)$ and X is a θ-comma-free-code since $X^2 = \{a^4, a^2ba^2, ba^4, ba^2ba^2\}$ and none of the words in $\theta(X)$ appears as a subword of any word in X^2. Also, note that $\mathrm{Sub}_3(X) \cap \mathrm{Sub}_3(\theta(X)) = \emptyset$. Hence, X is a θ-3-code. The word $baa = ba\theta(b)$ and hence X is not a θ-subword-1-code but there is no word of the type $uxv\theta(x)w$ in X with $u, w \in \Sigma^*$, $v \in \Sigma^+$ and $|x| = 2$. Thus, X is a θ-subword-2-code.

2.2   Forbidding-Enforcing Systems

Similar to grammars and automata, forbidding-enforcing systems can be used as a language defining tool. Unlike grammars and automata, they define languages based on the principle that "everything that is not forbidden is allowed" as opposed to "everything that is not allowed is forbidden". In this paper, we use the model of fe-systems introduced in [4,5] where one fe-system defines a family of languages. The relevant definitions are recalled below.

Definition 3. A *forbidding set* is a family of finite nonempty subsets of Σ^+ for some alphabet Σ; each element of a forbidding set is called a *forbidder*.

Given a forbidding set $\mathcal{F}$ and a language K: (i) for $F \in \mathcal{F}$, we say that K *is consistent with the forbidder* F, written $K \, con \, F$, if and only if $F \not\subseteq \mathrm{Sub}(K)$ and (ii) we say that K *is consistent with the forbidding set* $\mathcal{F}$, denoted $K \, con \, \mathcal{F}$, if and only if $K \, con \, F$ for each $F \in \mathcal{F}$.

The family of languages consistent with the forbidding set $\mathcal{F}$ is denoted by $\mathcal{L}(\mathcal{F})$, i.e. $\mathcal{L}(\mathcal{F}) = \{K \mid K \, con \, \mathcal{F}\}$. The class (family) of languages $\mathcal{L}(\mathcal{F})$ is an *f-family* and is said to be *defined by* $\mathcal{F}$.

If a language $L \notin \mathcal{L}(\mathcal{F})$ then L *is not consistent with* $\mathcal{F}$, denoted $L \, ncon \, \mathcal{F}$.

Note that if $K \, con \, \mathcal{F}$, every subset of K is also consistent with $\mathcal{F}$ [5]. Also, $\mathcal{F} = \emptyset$ if and only if $\mathcal{L}(\mathcal{F}) = \mathcal{P}(\Sigma^*)$.

Example 4. Let $\Sigma = \{a, b\}$. For the forbidding set $\mathcal{F} = \{\{ab, ba\}, \{aa, bb\}\}$ from [5], the languages in $\mathcal{L}(\mathcal{F})$ are precisely the subsets of the languages $K_1 = a^*b \cup a^*$, $K_2 = ba^* \cup a^*$, $K_3 = b^*a \cup b^*$, and $K_4 = ab^* \cup b^*$.

Definition 5. An *enforcing set* is a family of ordered pairs (X, Y) such that for some alphabet Σ all $X, Y \subseteq \Sigma^+$, X, Y are finite, and each $Y \neq \emptyset$; each element of an enforcing set is called an *enforcer*.

Given an enforcing set $\mathcal{E}$ over Σ and a language K: (i) for $(X, Y) \in \mathcal{E}$ we say that a language K *satisfies the enforcer* (X, Y), written $K \, sat \, (X, Y)$, if and only if $X \subseteq K$ implies $Y \cap K \neq \emptyset$ and (ii) we say that K *satisfies the enforcing set* $\mathcal{E}$, written $K \, sat \, \mathcal{E}$, if and only if $K \, sat \, (X, Y)$ for each $(X, Y) \in \mathcal{E}$.

The class (family) of all languages that satisfy the enforcing set $\mathcal{E}$ is denoted by $\mathcal{L}(\mathcal{E})$, i.e. $\mathcal{L}(\mathcal{E}) = \{K \mid K \ sat \ \mathcal{E}\}$. The class of languages $\mathcal{L}(\mathcal{E})$ is an *e-family* and is said to be *defined by* $\mathcal{E}$.

If a language $L \notin \mathcal{L}(\mathcal{E})$, then L *does not satisfy* $\mathcal{E}$, denoted by $L \ nsat \ \mathcal{E}$.

For enforcers $(\emptyset, Y)$, $K \cap Y \neq \emptyset$ for all $K \in \mathcal{L}(\mathcal{E})$. Assume that all $(X, Y) \in \mathcal{E}$ are non-trivial, i.e. $X \cap Y = \emptyset$. Thus, $\mathcal{L}(\mathcal{E}) = \mathcal{P}(\Sigma^*)$ if and only if $\mathcal{E} = \emptyset$.

Example 6. Let $\Sigma = \{a, b\}$ and $\mathcal{E} = \{(\emptyset, \{b\}), (\{b\}, \{b^2\}), \ldots, (\{b^n\}, \{b^{n+1}\}), \ldots\}$. Then, $\mathcal{E}$ "enforces" b^* in every language in $\mathcal{L}(\mathcal{E})$, i.e. $\mathcal{L}(\mathcal{E}) = \{K \mid b^* \subseteq K\}$.

Definition 7. A *forbidding-enforcing system* (fe-system) over an alphabet Σ is a construct $(\mathcal{F}, \mathcal{E})$, where $\mathcal{F}$ is a forbidding set and $\mathcal{E}$ is an enforcing set over Σ. The class of languages $\mathcal{L}(\mathcal{F}, \mathcal{E})$, the *fe-family*, defined by this fe-system consists of all languages that are consistent with $\mathcal{F}$ and satisfy $\mathcal{E}$, i.e $\mathcal{L}(\mathcal{F}, \mathcal{E}) = \mathcal{L}(\mathcal{F}) \cap \mathcal{L}(\mathcal{E})$.

Example 8. For $\Sigma = \{a, b\}$, $\mathcal{F}$, K_3, and K_4 from Example 4 and $\mathcal{E}$ from Example 6, we have that $\mathcal{L}(\mathcal{F}, \mathcal{E}) = \{K \mid K \subseteq K_3, K_4 \text{ and } b^* \subseteq K\}$.

Observe that $\mathcal{L}(\emptyset, \mathcal{E}) = \mathcal{L}(\mathcal{E})$ for all $\mathcal{E}$ and $\mathcal{L}(\mathcal{F}, \emptyset) = \mathcal{L}(\mathcal{F})$ for all $\mathcal{F}$. In this respect, every f-family and every e-family can be regarded as an fe-family.

3 Characterizing Involution Codes with fe-Systems

One benefit of studying DNA codes with fe-systems is that one fe-system can define an entire class of DNA codes $\mathcal{L}(\mathcal{F}, \mathcal{E})$ as opposed to just one DNA code X that has been the norm in constructing/studying DNA code words using classical formal language theory.

3.1 Characterizations by f-Families

We begin with a finite forbidding set that defines the entire class of θ-subword-k-m-codes, i.e. for given positive integers k and m one can construct a forbidding set $\mathcal{F}$ such that any language L in the f-family $\mathcal{L}(\mathcal{F})$ is a θ-subword-k-m-code and any θ-subword-k-m-code is in the f-family $\mathcal{L}(\mathcal{F})$.

For the rest of this paper, assume that the alphabet Σ is given and θ is a morphic or an antimorphic involution on Σ extended to Σ^*, unless stated otherwise. Also, to ease notation, by $L \in \mathcal{L}(\mathcal{F})$ (resp. $L \in \mathcal{L}(\mathcal{E})$, $L \in \mathcal{L}(\mathcal{F}, \mathcal{E})$) we mean those L for which $\lambda \notin L$ and $L \neq \emptyset$.

Proposition 9. *Let $k, m \geq 1$ be integers. For every $u \in \Sigma^k$ construct $\mathcal{F}_u = \{\{uw\theta(u)\} \mid w \in (\Sigma^{\leq m} \setminus \{\lambda\})\}$ and let $\mathcal{F} = \cup_{u \in \Sigma^k} \mathcal{F}_u$. Then L is a θ-subword-k-m-code if and only if $L \in \mathcal{L}(\mathcal{F})$.*

Proof. Note that L is a θ-subword-k-m-code if and only if $\Sigma^* u \Sigma^i \theta(u) \Sigma^* \cap L = \emptyset$ for all $1 \leq i \leq m$, which holds if and only if no word in L has a subword of the kind $uw\theta(u)$, where $u \in \Sigma^k$ and $w \in (\Sigma^{\leq m} \setminus \{\lambda\})$, i.e. if and only if $L \ con \ F$ for every $F \in \mathcal{F}$, i.e. if and only if $L \in \mathcal{L}(\mathcal{F})$. $\square$

The next result presents a way to construct a forbidding set that defines the entire class of θ-subword-k-codes.

Proposition 10. *Let $k \geq 1$ be an integer. For every $u \in \Sigma^k$ construct $\mathcal{F}_u = \{\{uw\theta(u)\} \mid w \in \Sigma^+\}$ and let $\mathcal{F} = \cup_{u \in \Sigma^k}\mathcal{F}_u$. Then L is a θ-subword-k-code if and only if $L \in \mathcal{L}(\mathcal{F})$.*

Proof. Observe that L is a θ-subword-k-code if and only if $\Sigma^* u \Sigma^i \theta(u) \Sigma^* \cap L = \emptyset$ for all $u \in \Sigma^k$ and for all $i \geq 1$, which holds if and only if no word in L has a subword of the kind $uw\theta(u)$, where $u \in \Sigma^k$ and $w \in \Sigma^+$, i.e. if and only if L con F for every forbidder $F \in \mathcal{F}$, i.e. if and only if $L \in \mathcal{L}(\mathcal{F})$.   □

Proposition 10 uses an infinite forbidding set. The next result uses a finite forbidding set, but provides only a sufficient condition for θ-subword-k-codes.

Proposition 11. *Let $k \geq 1$ be an integer. Consider $\mathcal{F} = \{\{u, \theta(u)\} \mid u \in \Sigma^k\}$. Then for every $L \in \mathcal{L}(\mathcal{F})$, L is a θ-subword-k-code.*

Proof. Assume that $L \in \mathcal{L}(\mathcal{F})$. Then, $\{u, \theta(u)\} \not\subseteq \text{Sub}(L)$ for every $u \in \Sigma^k$. Hence, for every $x \in L$ and for every $u \in \Sigma^k$, x cannot contain both u and $\theta(u)$ as subwords. Thus, $\Sigma^* u \Sigma^i \theta(u) \Sigma^* \cap L = \emptyset$ for all $u \in \Sigma^k$ and for all $i \geq 1$, i.e. L is a θ-subword-k-code.   □

Note that the converse of the above proposition does not necessarily hold, since a θ-subword-k-code X may have a word x with a subword $u_1u_2v_2$ such that $u = u_1u_2$ and $\theta(u) = v_1v_2$ with $u_2 = v_1$ for some $u \in \Sigma^k$, i.e. u and $\theta(u)$ overlap in x. Such X will not be consistent with the forbidding set $\mathcal{F}$ from Proposition 11 as illustrated in the next example.

Example 12. Consider $\Sigma = \{a, b\}$ and a morphic θ with $\theta(a) = b$ and $\theta(b) = a$. Note that the set $X = \{aa, aba\}$ is a θ-subword-2-code by Definition 1. Construct the forbidding set $\mathcal{F}$ from Proposition 11 for $k = 2$, namely $\mathcal{F} = \{\{aa, bb\}, \{ab, ba\}\}$. Notice that the second forbidder $\{ab, ba\} \subseteq \text{Sub}(X)$ since both ab and ba are in the subwords of aba. Hence, $X \notin \mathcal{L}(\mathcal{F})$.

Since the forbidding set of Example 4 is the same as $\mathcal{F}$ in Example 12, we note that every nonempty subset of K_i for $i = 1, \ldots, 4$ from Example 4, not containing λ, is a θ-subword-2-code for the morphic θ from Example 12, but $\mathcal{L}(\mathcal{F})$ does not contain all of the θ-subword-2-codes for this θ.

In the remainder of this section, the forbidding sets constructed from a given X are finite when X is a finite code.

Proposition 13. *Let $X \subset \Sigma^+$ be given and let $\mathcal{F} = \{\{u\} \mid u \in \theta(X)\}$. Then X is a θ-strict-infix-code if and only if $X \in \mathcal{L}(\mathcal{F})$.*

Proof. Consider $\mathcal{F} = \{\{u\} \mid u \in \theta(X)\}$. Note that X is a θ-strict-infix-code if and only if $\Sigma^* \theta(X) \Sigma^* \cap X = \emptyset$, which holds if and only if $\theta(X) \cap \text{Sub}(X) = \emptyset$, if and only if $F \not\subseteq \text{Sub}(X)$ for every $F \in \mathcal{F}$ if and only if $X \in \mathcal{L}(\mathcal{F})$.   □

The next characterization follows directly from the definitions in Section 2.

Proposition 14. *Let $X \subset \Sigma^+$ be given and let $\mathcal{F}_u = \{\{ua\} \mid a \in \Sigma\} \cup \{\{au\} \mid a \in \Sigma\}$ and let $\mathcal{F} = \cup_{u \in \theta(X)} \mathcal{F}_u$. Then X is a θ-infix-code if and only if $X \in \mathcal{L}(\mathcal{F})$.*

Proof. Consider $\mathcal{F}$ as defined in the proposition. Assume X is a θ-infix-code. Then, $\Sigma^*\theta(X)\Sigma^+ \cap X = \emptyset$ and $\Sigma^+\theta(X)\Sigma^* \cap X = \emptyset$. This implies that u is not a proper prefix and not a proper suffix of a word in X and $u \notin (\mathrm{Sub}\,(X) \setminus X)$ for every $u \in \theta(X)$, i.e. for every $u \in \theta(X)$, $u \notin \mathrm{Sub}\,(X)$ unless $u = x$ for some $x \in X$. Hence, $X \, con \, F$ for every $F \in \mathcal{F}$. Therefore, $X \in \mathcal{L}(\mathcal{F})$. Conversely, assume $X \in \mathcal{L}(\mathcal{F})$. Then, for every $u \in \theta(X)$ it holds that $u \notin \mathrm{Sub}\,(X)$ unless $u = x$ for some $x \in X$. Therefore, X is a θ-infix-code. $\qquad\square$

Proposition 15. *Let $X \subset \Sigma^+$ be given, $m \geq 1$ be an integer and $\mathcal{F} = \{\{u\} \mid u \in \theta(X^m)\}$. Then X is a θ-strict-intercode of index m if and only if $X^{m+1} \in \mathcal{L}(\mathcal{F})$.*

Proof. Let $\mathcal{F} = \{\{u\} \mid u \in \theta(X^m)\}$. Note that X is a θ-strict-intercode of index m if and only if $\Sigma^*\theta(X^m)\Sigma^* \cap X^{m+1} = \emptyset$, which holds if and only if $\theta(X^m) \cap \mathrm{Sub}\,(X^{m+1}) = \emptyset$, i.e. if and only if $X^{m+1} \, con \, F$ for every $F \in \mathcal{F}$. $\qquad\square$

Similarly, one can define a θ-intercode by a forbidding set.

Proposition 16. *Let $X \subset \Sigma^+$ be given, $m \geq 1$ be an integer and for every $u \in \theta(X^m)$ let $\mathcal{F}_u = \{\{aub\} \mid a, b \in \Sigma\}$ and let $\mathcal{F} = \cup_{u \in \theta(X^m)} \mathcal{F}_u$. Then X is a θ-intercode of index m if and only if $X^{m+1} \in \mathcal{L}(\mathcal{F})$.*

Proof. Consider $\mathcal{F}$ as defined in the proposition. Assume X is a θ-intercode of index m. Then, $\Sigma^+\theta(X^m)\Sigma^+ \cap X^{m+1} = \emptyset$. This implies that $aub \notin \mathrm{Sub}\,(X^{m+1})$ for every $a, b \in \Sigma$, where a and b are not necessarily distinct, and every $u \in \theta(X^m)$. Hence, $X^{m+1} \, con \, F$ for every $F \in \mathcal{F}$. Therefore, $X^{m+1} \in \mathcal{L}(\mathcal{F})$. Conversely, assume $X^{m+1} \in \mathcal{L}(\mathcal{F})$. Then, for every $u \in \theta(X^m)$ and every $a, b \in \Sigma$ it holds that $aub \notin \mathrm{Sub}\,(X^{m+1})$. Therefore, $\Sigma^+\theta(X^m)\Sigma^+ \cap X^{m+1} = \emptyset$. Hence, X is a θ-intercode. $\qquad\square$

Remark 17. Note that a θ-strict-intercode of index 1 is a θ-strict-comma-free-code and a θ-intercode of index 1 is a θ-comma-free-code.

The corollaries below follow from Propositions 15 and 16 and the above remark.

Corollary 18. *Let $X \subset \Sigma^+$ be given and let $\mathcal{F} = \{\{u\} \mid u \in \theta(X)\}$. Then X is a θ-strict-comma-free-code if and only if $X^2 \in \mathcal{L}(\mathcal{F})$.*

Corollary 19. *Let $X \subset \Sigma^+$ be given and for every $u \in \theta(X)$ construct $\mathcal{F}_u = \{\{aub\} \mid a, b \in \Sigma\}$ and let $\mathcal{F} = \cup_{u \in \theta(X)} \mathcal{F}_u$. Then X is a θ-comma-free-code if and only if $X^2 \in \mathcal{L}(\mathcal{F})$.*

We present some θ-k-codes characterizations next. Note that the forbidding set in the following proposition is finite, even if X is infinite.

Proposition 20. *Let $X \subset \Sigma^+$ and $k \geq 1$ be given and let $\mathcal{F} = \{\{u\} \mid u \in \mathrm{Sub}_k \theta(X)\}$. Then X is a θ-k-code if and only if $X \in \mathcal{L}(\mathcal{F})$.*

Proof. By definition, X is a θ-k-code if and only if $\mathrm{Sub}_k(X) \cap \mathrm{Sub}_k(\theta(X)) = \emptyset$, which holds if and only if $u \notin \mathrm{Sub}(X)$ for every $u \in \mathrm{Sub}_k\theta(X)$, i.e. if and only if $F \not\subseteq \mathrm{Sub}(X)$ for every $F \in \mathcal{F}$ if and only if $X \in \mathcal{L}(\mathcal{F})$. $\qquad\square$

Observe that if X is a θ-m-code for some fixed $m \geq 1$, then X is a θ-k-code for any $k \geq m$. This fact is confirmed by the forbidding-enforcing theory, since if one constructs $\mathcal{F}_k = \{\{u\} \mid u \in \mathrm{Sub}_k\theta(X)\}$ and lets $\mathcal{F} = \cup_{k \geq m}\mathcal{F}_k$, the resulting forbidding set will not be subword incomparable and according to [4], it will be equivalent to the forbidding set from Proposition 20 for $k = m$.

While Proposition 20 is a direct "restatement" of the definition for θ-k-codes in terms of fe-systems, the following proposition presents a sufficient condition for θ-k-codes that can be used for generating θ-k-codes with specific additional restrictions on the subwords. It provides a forbidding set, which for a given k defines a family of θ-k-codes.

Proposition 21. *Given a finite alphabet Σ and a fixed $k \geq 1$ let $\Sigma^k = P \cup Q \cup R$ such that $\theta(P) = Q$ and $\theta(x) = x$ for all $x \in R$ and P, Q, and R are pairwise disjoint. Let $H = Q \cup R$ and let $\mathcal{F} = \{\{u\} \mid u \in H\}$. Then, for all $L \in \mathcal{L}(\mathcal{F})$, L is a θ-k-code.*

Proof. Assume $L \in \mathcal{L}(\mathcal{F})$. Suppose there exists $v \in \mathrm{Sub}_k(\theta(L))$ such that $v \in \mathrm{Sub}(L)$. Then, $v \notin H$, since $\{u\} \not\subseteq \mathrm{Sub}(L)$ for every $u \in H$. Hence, $v \in P$. Therefore, $\theta(v) \in Q$. Since $v \in \mathrm{Sub}_k(\theta(L))$, there exists $y \in L$ such that $v \in \mathrm{Sub}(\theta(y))$. Thus, there exists $x \in \mathrm{Sub}(y)$ such that $v = \theta(x)$. Then, $\theta(v) = \theta(\theta(x)) = x$. Since $\theta(v) \in Q$, it follows that $\{x\} \in \mathcal{F}$ and $x \notin \mathrm{Sub}(L)$, which contradicts our supposition that $v \in \mathrm{Sub}(\theta(L))$ and hence $\theta(v) \in \mathrm{Sub}(L)$. Thus, L is a θ-k-code. $\qquad\square$

We conclude this subsection with a necessary and sufficient condition for θ-k-codes. Observe that the forbidding set in the next proposition is finite.

Proposition 22. *Let $k \geq 1$ be an integer. Consider $\mathcal{F} = \{\{u, \theta(u)\} \mid u \in \Sigma^k\}$. Then, L is a θ-k-code if and only if $L \in \mathcal{L}(\mathcal{F})$.*

Proof. Let L be a θ-k-code and take an arbitrary forbidder $F \in \mathcal{F}$. Then $F = \{u, \theta(u)\}$ for some $u \in \Sigma^k$. Suppose $\{u, \theta(u)\} \subseteq \mathrm{Sub}(L)$. Then $u \in \mathrm{Sub}(L)$ implies $\theta(u) \in \mathrm{Sub}(\theta(L))$. Hence, $\theta(u) \in \mathrm{Sub}_k(L) \cap \mathrm{Sub}_k(\theta(L))$, which contradicts the assumption that L is a θ-k-code. Therefore, $\{u, \theta(u)\} \not\subseteq \mathrm{Sub}(L)$ and $L \in \mathcal{L}(\mathcal{F})$. Conversely, assume L is not a θ-k-code. This implies that there exists $u \in \mathrm{Sub}_k(L) \cap \mathrm{Sub}_k(\theta(L))$. Since $u \in \mathrm{Sub}_k(\theta(L))$, there exists $v \in \mathrm{Sub}_k(L)$ such that $u = \theta(v)$. Then $\theta(u) = \theta(\theta(v)) = v \in \mathrm{Sub}_k(L)$, implying $\{u, \theta(u)\} \subseteq \mathrm{Sub}(L)$. Hence, $L \notin \mathcal{L}(\mathcal{F})$. $\qquad\square$

Example 23. Let $\Sigma = \{a, b\}$, $k = 2$, and θ be a morphic involution that maps $a \to b$ and $b \to a$. Then $\mathcal{F}$ is precisely the forbidding set from Example 4 (and from Example 12) and the θ-2-codes are precisely the subsets of the languages K_i for $i = 1, \ldots, 4$. If θ is antimorphic, $\mathcal{F} = \{\{aa, bb\}, \{ab\}, \{ba\}\}$ and every θ-2-code is either a subset of a^* or a subset of b^*. For $k = 3$ and morphic θ

with $a \to b$ and $b \to a$, $\mathcal{F} = \{\{aaa, bbb\}, \{aab, bba\}, \{aba, bab\}, \{baa, abb\}\}$ and for antimorphic θ we have $\mathcal{F} = \{\{aaa, bbb\}, \{aab, abb\}, \{aba, bab\}, \{baa, bba\}\}$. Observe that the latter $\mathcal{L}(\mathcal{F})$ contains X from Example 30.

Notice that Propositions 22 and 11 confirm the fact that every θ-k-code is a θ-subword-k-code through fe-systems.

3.2 Characterizations by e-Families

While the previous subsection showed that fe-systems with empty enforcing sets are capable of characterizing DNA codes, this subsection focuses on DNA code characterizations obtained by enforcing sets only. Recall that one can view enforcing sets as fe-systems with empty forbidding sets. We begin with a characterization of θ-strict-codes.

Proposition 24. *Let $X \subseteq \Sigma^+$ and let $z \in \Sigma^+$ such that $z \notin X$. For each $w \in X$ construct $\mathcal{E}_w = \{(\{w, u\}, \{z\}) \mid u \in \theta(X)\}$ and let $\mathcal{E} = \cup_{w \in X} \mathcal{E}_w$. Then, X is a θ-strict-code if and only if $X \in \mathcal{L}(\mathcal{E})$.*

Proof. Assume that X is a θ-strict-code. Then, $X \cap \theta(X) = \emptyset$ implies that $\{w, u\} \not\subseteq X$ for every enforcer $(\{w, u\}, \{z\}) \in \mathcal{E}$, since $u \notin X$ for all $u \in \theta(X)$. Thus, X satisfies every enforcer in $\mathcal{E}$ trivially. Therefore, $X \in \mathcal{L}(\mathcal{E})$. Conversely, assume that X is not a θ-strict-code. This implies that $X \cap \theta(X) \neq \emptyset$. Hence, there exists $y \in X \cap \theta(X)$. Thus, there exists an enforcer $(\{y\}, \{z\}) \in \mathcal{E}$ with $y \in X$ and $z \notin X$. It follows that $X \, nsat \, (\{y\}, \{z\})$. Hence, $X \notin \mathcal{L}(\mathcal{E})$. □

Proposition 25. *Let $X \subseteq \Sigma^+$ and let $z \in \Sigma^+$ such that $z \notin X$. For each $w \in X$ construct $\mathcal{E}'_w = \{(\{w, ut\}, \{z\}) \mid u \in \theta(X), t \in \Sigma^+\}$ and $\mathcal{E}''_w = \{(\{w, su\}, \{z\}) \mid u \in \theta(X), s \in \Sigma^+\}$. Let $\mathcal{E}' = \cup_{w \in X} \mathcal{E}'_w$, $\mathcal{E}'' = \cup_{w \in X} \mathcal{E}''_w$, and let $\mathcal{E} = \mathcal{E}' \cup \mathcal{E}''$. Then, the following statements hold.*

1. *X is a θ-prefix-code if and only if $X \in \mathcal{L}(\mathcal{E}')$.*
2. *X is a θ-suffix-code if and only if $X \in \mathcal{L}(\mathcal{E}'')$.*
3. *X is a θ-bifix-code if and only if $X \in \mathcal{L}(\mathcal{E})$.*

Proof. 1. Assume that X is a θ-prefix-code. Then, $X \cap \theta(X)\Sigma^+ = \emptyset$ implies that $\{w, ut\} \not\subseteq X$ for every enforcer $(\{w, u\}, \{z\}) \in \mathcal{E}'$, since $ut \notin X$ for all $u \in \theta(X)$ and all $t \in \Sigma^+$. Thus, X satisfies every enforcer in $\mathcal{E}'$ trivially. Therefore, $X \in \mathcal{L}(\mathcal{E}')$. Conversely, assume that X is not a θ-prefix-code. This implies that $X \cap \theta(X)\Sigma^+ \neq \emptyset$. Hence, there exists $y \in X \cap \theta(X)\Sigma^+$. Thus, there exists an enforcer $(\{y\}, \{z\}) \in \mathcal{E}'$ with $y \in X$ and $z \notin X$. It follows that $X \, nsat \, (\{y\}, \{z\})$. Hence, $X \notin \mathcal{L}(\mathcal{E}')$.
2. Similar to 1.
3. Follows from 1. and 2. above and the property for enforcing sets $\mathcal{L}(\mathcal{E}' \cup \mathcal{E}'') = \mathcal{L}(\mathcal{E}') \cap (\mathcal{E}'')$. □

The following result can be proved in a similar way.

Proposition 26. *Let $X \subseteq \Sigma^+$ and let $z \in \Sigma^+$ such that $z \notin X$. For each $w \in X$ construct $\mathcal{E}'_w = \{(\{w, ut\}, \{z\}) \mid u \in \theta(X), t \in \Sigma^+\}$, $\mathcal{E}''_w = \{(\{w, su\}, \{z\}) \mid u \in \theta(X), s \in \Sigma^+\}$, and $\mathcal{E}'''_w = \{(\{w, puq\}, \{z\}) \mid u \in \theta(X), p, q \in \Sigma^+\}$. Let $\mathcal{E}' = \cup_{w \in X} \mathcal{E}'_w$, $\mathcal{E}'' = \cup_{w \in X} \mathcal{E}''_w$, $\mathcal{E}''' = \cup_{w \in X} \mathcal{E}'''_w$ and let $\tilde{\mathcal{E}} = \mathcal{E}' \cup \mathcal{E}'' \cup \mathcal{E}'''$. Then, X is a θ-infix-code if and only if $X \in \mathcal{L}(\tilde{\mathcal{E}})$.*

Since, $\mathcal{E} \subseteq \tilde{\mathcal{E}}$ for $\mathcal{E}$ and $\tilde{\mathcal{E}}$ from Propositions 25 and 26 respectively, and since $\mathcal{E} \subseteq \tilde{\mathcal{E}}$ implies $\mathcal{L}(\tilde{\mathcal{E}}) \subseteq \mathcal{L}(\mathcal{E})$, the forbidding-enforcing theory confirms the known fact that every θ-infix-code is a θ-bifix-code.

Similarly, we obtain the following characterization.

Proposition 27. *Let $X \subseteq \Sigma^+$ and let $m \geq 1$ be an integer. Let $z \in \Sigma^+$ such that $z \notin X^{m+1}$. For each $w \in X^{m+1}$ construct $\mathcal{E}_w = \{(\{w, sut\}, \{z\}) \mid u \in \theta(X^m), s, t \in \Sigma^+\}$ and let $\mathcal{E} = \cup_{w \in X^{m+1}} \mathcal{E}_w$, Then, X is a θ-intercode of index m if and only if $X^{m+1} \in \mathcal{L}(\mathcal{E})$.*

The following corollary is a consequence of Proposition 27 and Remark 17.

Corollary 28. *Let $X \subseteq \Sigma^+$ and $z \in \Sigma^+$ such that $z \notin X^2$. For each $w \in X^2$ construct $\mathcal{E}_w = \{(\{w, sut\}, \{z\}) \mid u \in \theta(X), s, t \in \Sigma^+\}$ and let $\mathcal{E} = \cup_{w \in X^2} \mathcal{E}_w$. Then, X is a θ-comma-free-code if and only if $X^2 \in \mathcal{L}(\mathcal{E})$.*

In the previous subsection, some ways to present θ-k-codes as f-families were proposed. We conclude this section with characterizing θ-k-codes by enforcing sets only and present an example. Note that the enforcing set in the next proposition is finite, even if X is infinite.

Proposition 29. *Let $X \subseteq \Sigma^+$ and $k > 0$ be an integer. Let $z \in \Sigma^+$ such that $z \notin \mathrm{Sub}_k(X)$. For each $w \in \mathrm{Sub}_k(X)$ construct $\mathcal{E}_w = \{(\{w, u\}, \{z\}) \mid u \in \mathrm{Sub}_k(\theta(X))\}$ and let $\mathcal{E} = \cup_{w \in \mathrm{Sub}_k(X)} \mathcal{E}_w$. Then, X is a θ-k-code if and only if $\mathrm{Sub}_k(X) \in \mathcal{L}(\mathcal{E})$.*

Proof. Assume X is a θ-k-code. Then, $\mathrm{Sub}_k(X) \cap \mathrm{Sub}_k(\theta(X)) = \emptyset$ implies that for every $u \in \mathrm{Sub}_k(\theta(X))$, $u \notin \mathrm{Sub}_k(X)$. Hence, for every enforcer $\{w, u\} \in \mathcal{E}$ we have that $\{w, u\} \not\subseteq \mathrm{Sub}_k(X)$ and thus $\mathrm{Sub}_k(X)$ satisfies every enforcer trivially. Therefore, $\mathrm{Sub}_k(X) \in \mathcal{L}(\mathcal{E})$. Conversely, assume that X is not a θ-k-code. Then, there exists $y \in \mathrm{Sub}_k(X) \cap \mathrm{Sub}_k(\theta(X))$, which implies that there exists an enforcer $(\{y\}, \{z\}) \in \mathcal{E}$ with $\{y\} \subseteq \mathrm{Sub}_k(X)$ and $z \notin \mathrm{Sub}_k(X)$. Since $\mathrm{Sub}_k(X)$ does not satisfy $(\{y\}, \{z\})$, we have that $\mathrm{Sub}_k(X) \notin \mathcal{L}(\mathcal{E})$. $\square$

Example 30. Consider $X = \{aab, baab\}$ over the alphabet $\Sigma = \{a, b\}$ and let θ be an antimorphic involution that maps $a \to b$ and $b \to a$. Then $\theta(X) = \{abb, abba\}$ and it is clear that $\mathrm{Sub}_3(X) \cap \mathrm{Sub}_3(\theta(X)) = \emptyset$. Hence, X is a θ-3-code by Definition 1. Since $\mathrm{Sub}_3(X) = \{aab, baa\}$, we construct $\mathcal{E}_{aab} = \{(\{aab, abb\}, \{z\}), (\{aab, bba\}, \{z\})\}$ and $\mathcal{E}_{baa} = \{(\{baa, abb\}, \{z\}), (\{baa, bba\}, \{z\})\}$ where $z \notin \mathrm{Sub}_3(X)$. One can verify that for $\mathcal{E} = \mathcal{E}_{aab} \cup \mathcal{E}_{baa}$, $\mathrm{Sub}_3(X) \in \mathcal{L}(\mathcal{E})$.

4 Generating Good Codes by fe-Systems

In the previous section, we characterized some DNA codes through forbidding sets only and/or through enforcing sets only. In this section, we show how an fe-system with a nonempty forbidding set and a nonempty enforcing set can generate θ-k-codes. In contrast to the very special kind of enforcers used in the previous section, where the strictly enforced word z was chosen not to belong to the given set, we use a more general type of enforcers to emphasize the computational, rather than definitional capabilities of fe-systems.

In [14], the authors introduced some methods to generate DNA code words X such that X^+ has the same property. These theoretically generated codes were also tested experimentally in [14] and were shown to have no visible cross-hybridizations. In this section, we construct fe-systems that generalize the methods in [14]. As an illustration, the sets of DNA code words X, X^+ generated in Proposition 4.9 in [14] are in the fe-family. Similar fe-systems constructions can be given for various other methods described in [14].

Proposition 31. *Let Σ be an alphabet and θ a morphic or an antimorphic involution such that $\theta(a) \neq a$ for each symbol $a \in \Sigma$. Let $b, c \in \Sigma$ such that $\theta(b) = c$. Consider the forbidding set $\mathcal{F} = \{\{c\}\} \cup \{\{u\} \mid u \in (\Sigma \setminus \{b, c\})^k\}$. Then $L \in \mathcal{L}(\mathcal{F})$ implies L is a θ-k code.*

Proof. Assume L is not a θ-k-code. Then there exists $u \in \Sigma^k$ such that $u \in \mathrm{Sub}_k(L) \cap \mathrm{Sub}_k(\theta(L))$. If u contains the symbol c, then $L \, ncon \, \mathcal{F}$, so we may assume that $u \in (\Sigma \setminus \{c\})^k$. Since $u \in \mathrm{Sub}(\theta(L))$ there exists $v \in \mathrm{Sub}(L)$ such that $u = \theta(v)$. This implies that $\theta(u) = \theta(\theta(v)) = v \in \mathrm{Sub}(L)$. So, both u and $\theta(u)$ are in the subwords of L. If u contains the symbol b, then $\theta(u)$ contains c, which implies that $L \, ncon \, \mathcal{F}$. Otherwise, $u \in (\Sigma \setminus \{b, c\})^k$ and thus $\{u\} \in \mathcal{F}$, which also implies $L \, ncon \, \mathcal{F}$. In all cases, $L \notin \mathcal{L}(\mathcal{F})$. □

Note that the above condition is sufficient for θ-k-codes but not necessary, i.e. there exist θ-k-codes that are not in $\mathcal{L}(\mathcal{F})$, as shown in the next example.

Example 32. Let b, c, Σ and θ be as in Proposition 31. Let $Y = (\Sigma \setminus \{b, c\})^k$ and let $Y = P \cup Q \cup R$ where for all $x \in R$, $\theta(x) = x$, and for all $x \in P$, $\theta(x) \in Q$ and vice versa with P, Q, and R pairwise disjoint. Then for $Z = P \cup \{c^+\}$, $Z \notin \mathcal{L}(\mathcal{F})$ since both $c, u \in \mathrm{Sub}(Z)$ for $u \in P \subseteq (\Sigma \setminus \{b, c\}^k)$. However, one can verify that Z is indeed a θ-k-code.

Given $\Delta = \{A, C, T, G\}$, let θ be a morphic or an antimorphic involution. In particular, θ can be the Watson-Crick complementarity such that $\theta(A) = T$, $\theta(T) = A$, $\theta(C) = G$, and $\theta(G) = C$, where θ is antimorphic. We obtain the following consequence of Proposition 31.

Corollary 33. *Let the forbidding set $\mathcal{F} = \{\{G\}\} \cup \{\{u\} \mid u \in (\Delta \setminus \{G, C\})^k\}$ be given. Then $L \in \mathcal{L}(\mathcal{F})$ implies L is a θ-k code.*

Corollary 33 generalizes the experiment performed in [14] in that the forbidder $\{G\}$ models the fact that only three types of nucleotides were used in the sequence design and the rest of the forbidders ensure that every k consecutive nucleotides contain a C. It imposes less restrictions on the set of strands compared to the stricter requirements proposed in Proposition 4.9 in [14]. Note that X, X^+ from Proposition 4.9 in [14] are in the above $\mathcal{L}(\mathcal{F})$, but there is $L \in \mathcal{L}(\mathcal{F})$, such that $L^+ \notin \mathcal{L}(\mathcal{F})$. Hence, the following stronger condition.

Proposition 34. *Let Σ be an alphabet and θ a morphic or an antimorphic involution such that $\theta(a) \neq a$ for each symbol $a \in \Sigma$. Let $b, c \in \Sigma$ such that $\theta(b) = c$ and $k \geq 2$. Consider the forbidding set $\mathcal{F} = \{\{c\}\} \cup \{\{u\} \mid u \in (\Sigma \setminus \{b, c\})^k\}$ and the enforcing set $\mathcal{E} = (\emptyset, \{ub \mid u \in (\Sigma \setminus \{c\})^{k-1}\}) \cup \{(\{u, v\}, \{uv\}) \mid u, v \in \Sigma^*\}$. If $L \in \mathcal{L}(\mathcal{F}, \mathcal{E})$ then L is a θ-k-code. Furthermore, if $L \in \mathcal{L}(\mathcal{F}, \mathcal{E})$ then $L = L^+$.*

Proof. If L is not a θ-k-code, then by Proposition 31, $L \notin \mathcal{L}(\mathcal{F})$ and hence $L \notin \mathcal{L}(\mathcal{F}, \mathcal{E})$. Assume that $L \in \mathcal{L}(\mathcal{F}, \mathcal{E})$. Then L sat $\mathcal{E}$ and hence if any two words u and v are in L, their concatenation uv is also in L, which is the definition of L^+. Consequently, $L = L^+$. $\qquad\qquad\square$

Corollary 35. *Let the alphabet be Δ, $\mathcal{F} = \{\{G\}\} \cup \{\{u\} \mid u \in \{A, T\}^k\}$, and $\mathcal{E} = (\emptyset, \{uC \mid u \in \{A, T, C\}^{k-1}\}) \cup \{(\{u, v\}, \{uv\}) \mid u, v \in \Delta^*\}$. Then, $L \in \mathcal{L}(\mathcal{F}, \mathcal{E})$ implies that L is a θ-k-code. Furthermore, if $L \in \mathcal{L}(\mathcal{F}, \mathcal{E})$ then $L = L^+$.*

Fe-systems can be used as a definitional tool or viewed as a one-step computation, but they can also be used as a computational tool which models the evolution of a molecular system. The Γ-tree presented in [5] is based on the idea that one can start with smaller sets of strands and "build" larger sets by applying enforcers in such a way that the resulting sets comply with the forbidden conditions.

In [14], 10 θ-5-codes of length 20 were selected from X (Prop. 4.9) and were tested experimentally. It was shown that no duplexes were detected when all 10 θ-5-codes were annealed and also no cross-hybridizations were observed.

Corollary 35 generalizes this experiment and can be used for a Γ-tree computation as follows. Fix an integer $k \geq 1$. Let $S = Y$, where $(\emptyset, Y)$ is the first enforcer of $\mathcal{E}$. Input S. Observe that S con $\mathcal{F}$. Apply all applicable enforcers from $\mathcal{E}$ (denote them by $\mathcal{E}_1$), i.e. the enforcers of the kind (X, Y) with $X \subseteq S$. Observe that S sat $(\emptyset, S)$. The rest of the applicable enforcers ensure that any two strands from S can now anneal. The resulting set of strands S_1 contains all the strands from S and from S^2 and $S_1 \in \mathcal{L}(\mathcal{F}, \mathcal{E}_1)$. In the next step, apply all applicable enforcers to S_1 (denote them by $\mathcal{E}_2$). Apply these enforcers in one step again, i.e. allow all possible annealing of strands from S and S^2 to occur. The resulting set S_2 contains all the strands from S, S^2, S^3, and S^4, i.e. $S_2 = S \cup S^2 \cup S^3 \cup S^4$ and $S_2 \in \mathcal{L}(\mathcal{F}, \mathcal{E}_2)$. The process can be applied as many steps as desired, e.g. until sequences of a desired length have been generated. After the ith step, the resulting set S_i is in the fe-family $\mathcal{L}(\mathcal{F}, \mathcal{E}_i)$ and S_i is a θ-k-code. The process can terminate at any step n by discarding all enforcers that are not applicable up to step n to obtain an enforcing set $\mathcal{E}_n$. We observe that $S_n \in \mathcal{L}(\mathcal{F}, \mathcal{E}_n)$, S_n is a θ-k-code and the fe-system $(\mathcal{F}, \mathcal{E}_n)$ is finite for any $n \geq 1$.

Note that in the experiment performed in [14] the input S consisted of 10 θ-5-codes of length 20. The above algorithm can be modified by replacing the first enforcer by $(\emptyset, S)$ and continuing until a desired set of strands has been generated, i.e. a predetermined length of strands has been reached.

5   Concluding Remarks

Since forbidding-enforcing systems impose restrictions on the subwords and words of a language, they can be used to model the restrictions imposed by unwanted hybridizations and thus, provide a natural framework to study DNA codes. This paper investigated ways to generate DNA codes using fe-systems that define classes of languages (classes of DNA codes). We showed that one fe-system can define an entire class of codes, for example θ-k-codes for a given k, as opposed to just one language (code) generated by a grammar or accepted by an automaton. We see this work as the beginning of research connecting the two areas. Using fe-systems, we confirmed some known properties of DNA codes, which shows a potential for discovering new properties of these codes through fe-systems. DNA codes can also be studied through other variants of fe-systems, such as the single-language fe-system model as defined in [9]. Using the connection between a family of languages defined by a forbidding set as in [5] and a set of words defined by the same forbidding set as described in [9,10] and the results in this paper, one can generate all words (strands) complying with a certain type of codes, any subset of which will be a desired code. Computation using fe-systems was described through evolving along the Γ-tree introduced in [5]. Defining Γ-tree computations that generate specific DNA codes can have applications in laboratory experiments.

On the other hand, applying fe-systems to DNA codes may enrich the theory of forbidding and enforcing by suggesting new directions in investigating proposed fe-systems, as well as, a need for defining and studying new fe-system models. Different variants of fe-systems defining languages, words, or graphs were shown to be capable of defining solutions to NP-complete problems [5,9,12]. Since laboratory experiments in DNA computing can be modeled by languages and graphs, including DNA codes in the set of structures defined by fe-systems adds to the development of the theory of fe-systems as a natural framework to study molecular computation.

Acknowledgement. The authors thank Nataša Jonoska for numerous discussions and helpful suggestions to link our results with experimental work. This work has been partially supported by a UNF Faculty Development Scholarship Grant for Daniela Genova.

References

1. Adleman, L.: Molecular computation of solutions to combinatorial problems. Science 266, 1021–1024 (1994)
2. Cavaliere, M., Jonoska, N.: Forbidding and enforcing in membrane computing. Natural Computing 2, 215–228 (2003)

3. Deaton, R., Murphy, R., Rose, J., Garzon, M., Franceschetti, D., Stevens Jr., S.: A DNA based implementation of an evolutionary search for good encodings for DNA computation. In: Proc. IEEE Conference on Evolutionary Computation ICEC 1997, pp. 267–271. Institute of Electrical and Electronics Engineers (1997)
4. Ehrenfeucht, A., Hoogeboom, H.J., Rozenberg, G., van Vugt, N.: Forbidding and enforcing. In: DNA Based Computers V, vol. 54, pp. 195–206. AMS DIMACS, Providence (2000)
5. Ehrenfeucht, A., Rozenberg, G.: Forbidding-enforcing systems. Theoretical Computer Science 292, 611–638 (2003)
6. Faulhammer, D., Cukras, A.R., Lipton, R.J., Landweber, L.F.: Molecular computation: RNA solutions to chess problems. Proceedings of the National Academy of Sciences, USA 97(4), 1385–1389 (2000)
7. Franco, G., Jonoska, N.: Forbidding and enforcing conditions in DNA self-assembly of graphs. In: Nanotechnology: Science and Computation. Natural Computing Series Part I, pp. 105–118 (2006)
8. Garzon, M.: On codeword design in metric spaces. Natural Computing 8(3), 571–588 (2009)
9. Genova, D.: Defining Languages by Forbidding-Enforcing Systems. In: Löwe, B., Normann, D., Soskov, I., Soskova, A. (eds.) CiE 2011. LNCS, vol. 6735, pp. 92–101. Springer, Heidelberg (2011)
10. Genova, D.: Forbidding Sets and Normal Forms for Language Forbidding-Enforcing Systems. In: Dediu, A.-H., Martín-Vide, C. (eds.) LATA 2012. LNCS, vol. 7183, pp. 289–300. Springer, Heidelberg (2012)
11. Genova, D., Jonoska, N.: Topological properties of forbidding-enforcing systems. Journal of Automata, Languages and Combinatorics 11(4), 375–397 (2006)
12. Genova, D., Jonoska, N.: Forbidding and enforcing on graphs. Theoretical Computer Science 429, 108–117 (2012)
13. Hussini, S., Kari, L., Konstantinidis, S.: Coding properties of DNA languages. Theoretical Computer Science 290, 1557–1579 (2003)
14. Jonoska, N., Mahalingam, K., Chen, J.: Involution codes: with application to DNA coded languages. Natural Computing 4, 141–162 (2005)
15. Kari, L., Konstantinidis, S., Losseva, E., Wozniak, G.: Sticky-free and overhang-free DNA languages. Acta Informatica 40, 119–157 (2003)
16. Kari, L., Mahalingam, K.: DNA Codes and Their Properties. In: Mao, C., Yokomori, T. (eds.) DNA12. LNCS, vol. 4287, pp. 127–142. Springer, Heidelberg (2006)
17. Liu, Q., Wang, L., Frutos, A.G., Condon, A., Corn, R.M., Smith, L.M.: DNA computing on surfaces. Nature 403, 175–179 (2000)
18. Marathe, A., Condon, A.E., Corn, R.M.: On combinatorial word design. Preliminary Preproceedings of the 5th International Meeting on DNA Based Computers, Boston, pp. 75–88 (1999)

Wolbachia Infection Improves Genetic Algorithms as Optimization Procedure

Mauricio Guevara-Souza and Edgar E. Vallejo

Tecnológico de Monterrey, Campus Estado de México
Computer Science Department
Atizapan de Zaragoza, Edo. de Mexico, 52926, México
{A00456476,vallejo}@itesm.mx

Abstract. This paper shows how the addition of *Wolbachia* infection can improve evolutionary function optimization by preventing the system from sticking at local optima. Firstly a variant of genetic algorithms that allows the introduction of *Wolbachia* is described. Then an application of this system to the optimization of a collection of mutimodal functions is described. Finally, we show how the introduction of *Wolbachia* infection improves the procedure in terms of both fitness and the number of generations required to obtain the solutions.

Keywords: *Wolbachia*, function optimization, genetic algorithms.

1 Introduction

We are engaged in a research program that aims at constructing computational models that are useful for understanding the population dynamics of disease vectors and its application to the control of vector borne diseases such as malaria and dengue.

One promising strategy for disease control is the introduction of transgenic vectors that are refractory to the disease into wild populations so as to achieve the replacement of the disease carrying populations [9].

An alternative promising avenue is the introduction of mosquitoes infected with the *Wolbachia* bacteria into wild populations for dengue disease control [8] [10]. The endosymbiont bacteria *Wolbachia* contributes to the establishment of the immune populations using a variety of reproduction and fitness altering mechanisms [3].

Over the last few years we have developed and tested computer simulation models for a variety of gene drive mechanisms such as transposable elements and the maternal effect dominant embryonic arrest (MEDEA) so as to predict the effectiveness of a population replacement strategy for disease control [7] [6].

We believe that these mechanism hold much promise for improving the performance of evolutionary algorithms at solving complex optimization problems. Based on observations and inspirations drawn from nature and our own previous experiments, we predict that the incorporation of a simulated *Wolbachia* infection can contribute to improve the performance of evolutionary algorithms by preventing the procedure from sticking at local optima.

A.-H. Dediu, C. Martín-Vide, and B. Truthe (Eds.): TPNC 2012, LNCS 7505, pp. 161–173, 2012.
© Springer-Verlag Berlin Heidelberg 2012

In this paper we present a series of experiments on the optimization of non-linear multi-modal function optimization using the proposed model. The results are then compared with those produced by a simple genetic algorithm. The experiments presented here demonstrate that *Wolbachia* infection is capable of improving both the solutions and the number of generations of evolutionary algorithms.

2   Related Work

2.1   Wolbachia

Wolbachia pipientis is a widespread bacteria that infects more than half of all insect species [3]. This bacteria can spread rapidly into uninfected host population by inducing cytoplasmic incompatibility [5] [12]. This mechanism causes the progeny of *Wolbachia*-uninfected females to die when they are mated with infected males whereas infected females are not affected in this manner, as shown in Figure 1.

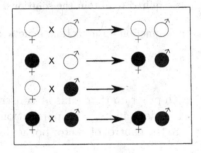

Fig. 1. Cytoplasmic incompatibility in *Wolbachia*. Filled figures represent infected individuals.

Moreover, it has been shown that *Wolbachia* provides the host with the advantage of reducing the ability of viruses to infect the hosts and thus contribute to overcoming a loss of fitness. These mechanisms results in the rapid invasion of the host population.

2.2   Mating Restrictions in Genetic Algorithms

There is a variety of mating restrictions mechanisms proposed in the literature for maintaining the variability in the populations of evolutionary algorithms [11][1]. The experiments presented here are focused on the simulation of the *Wolbachia* infection and its effects on the performance of genetic algorithms. To our knowledge, no empirical research on this topic has been reported in the literature of evolutionary algorithms.

3   Methods

The proposed computer model is a variation of the canonical genetic algorithm. We simulated the Wolbachia mechanism during reproduction to help the genetic algorithm to surpass local minima and achieve better solutions in less generations. In addition, a couple of features are incorporated to the individuals of the population to make them more alike to living beings.We also propose a novel population structure that mimics in a more realistic way the manner in which an animal population is distributed in their environment.

3.1   Representation of Individuals

The most important part of the individuals is its chromosome. We represented the chromosome of each individual as an array of floating point numbers of the same length as the dimensions of the function we wanted to minimize. Each floating point number in the chromosome were forced to be within a desired range and all the genetic operators used were carefully designed to preserve this requirement. This is because the space of solution is theoretically infinite so we wanted to establish some boundaries to make the problem more tractable.

Another important feature of the individuals is its gender. Since we want to emulate a natural population as close as possible, we decided to include this important distinction between individuals.

We also kept track of the position of each individual in the population with a couple of variables. Location is important in the reproduction stage and population structure.

For the *Wolbachia* process simulation we used a boolean flag to register if the individual was infected or not.

Finally, the fitness of the individual is calculated evaluating the function we wanted to minimize with the numbers stored in its chromosome.

3.2   Population Structure

To structure the population we used a two dimensional symmetric grid(Figure 2). The position of each individual on the grid is important because for reproduction we restricted the possible mates to a neighborhood. It is important to denote that in every generation, the distribution of males and females in the population changed randomly, but we preserve an even distribution of females and males of approximately 50% each.

We used this population structure to get a little closer to how the reproduction is done in real populations where the geographic location is important. The best adapted individuals of a population tend to get together and the less favored ones are relegated to remote locations in the population.

3.3   *Wolbachia* Infection

The *Wolbachia* infected individuals are introduced in the population periodically after a given number of generations. We estimated the number of generations by

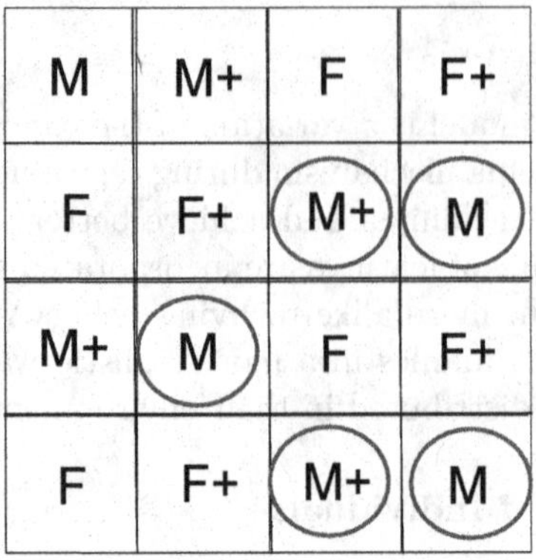

Fig. 2. Distribution of males and females in the population. Red circles indicate the possible mates of the female in the center of the neighborhood. Individuals with the plus sign are infected with *Wolbachia* bacteria.

running the algorithm without *Wolbachia* infection and observing in which generation the algorithm got stuck in a local minimum. When is time to introduce the infection, we selected a percentage of the best individuals in the population, infected them and let them reproduce. After the reproduction is done, we disinfect the entire population so no individual with *Wolbachia* is left. This is done to prevent the over spreading of those individuals as this would propitiate the loss of genetic diversity in the population.

3.4   Genetic Operators

Selection. A tournament selection [11] is used for reproduction in the experiments reported here but we used two main restrictions. The first one was the gender. The first parent we selected was always a female. Since we have a population with males and females, only males could be selected as the other parent. The second restriction is the neighborhood. Once the female is selected, the males that participated in the tournament were those located in the range of the neighborhood. This implies a limitation of the reproduction mates favoring the exploration over the exploitation to avoid rushing into a local minima in the earliest generations.

Crossover. Before performing the crossover, we checked over the *Wolbachia* infection status of the parents. As described above, if the female is not infected with *Wolbachia* and the male is, the cytoplasmic incompatibility would kill all the offspring so the crossover would not be necessary. If the offspring is feasible, we used a single point crossover operation. After the crossover is done, the *Wolbachia* infection of the offspring is updated according to the parent's status. It is important to highlight that the crossover is done with 100% of probability unlike the classical genetic algorithm that generally is $\sim$ 60%–75%. This is because in nature, the offspring always carry genetic material from both parents and we wanted to simulate reproduction as close as possible to the real thing.

Mutation. Uniform mutation [11] was implemented in our experiments. Given that our chromosome is not binary but contains floating point numbers, the mutation was a little different. For every number in the chromosome we generated a random number and if it was above a threshold the number was mutated. To perform the mutation we generated another random number between the ranges of the function, then we added or subtracted that number to the one in the chromosome depending on the result of a bit flip. If the mutated number fell out of the ranges of the function, the number was changed to the closest valid number within the range.

4   Experiments and Results

In this paper we tested our algorithm with four distinct complex functions: Rastrigin, Rosenbrock, Schwefel and Shifted Elliptic [4] [13]. We chose these functions because they are some of the most used for testing the performance of the optimization algorithms. For the first three functions, we made experiments with two different population sizes. For the last function we made experiments with only one population size. Several parameter variations were tested but for space limitations we are only reporting the experiments that yielded the best results.

4.1   Optimization of the Rastrigin Function

The Rastrigin function is a non-convex, non-linear and multimodal function with several local minima. Its global minima is 0 and is found when all the parameters of the function are 0(Figure 3). It is considered a hard function to minimize due to its large search space and the number of local minima. The equation for this function is defined as follows:

$$An + \sum_{i=1}^{n}[x_i^2 - A\cos(2\pi x_i)]$$

The goal of this experiment was to test our algorithm against a simple genetic algorithm to observe which one obtained better results in similar conditions using a Rastrigin function of 100 dimensions. We used two population sizes, 400 and 2,500 individuals respectively. In the case of the algorithm with *Wolbachia* infection, the population were distributed in a grid of 20 x 20 and 50 x 50. The chromosome of the individuals had a length of 100. We used a 1% probability of mutation, 100% probability of crossover and a tournament size of 100 in all cases. A 1% of infection rate for the *Wolbachia* algorithm was used. The A value that appears in the Rastrigin equation was 7. The neighborhoods used in our algorithm was of 10 for the 20x20 population grid and a neighborhood of 20 was used in the 50x50 population grid. In both algorithms, the values in the chromosome were between -5.12 and 5.12. The maximum offspring in our algorithm were determined by the female's fitness with a minimum of 0 and a maximum of 2 offspring per generation. The *Wolbachia* infection was introduced every 10,000 generation in the population of 400 individuals and every 1,000 generations in the population of 2,500 individuals. We let both algorithms ran for 50,000 generations.

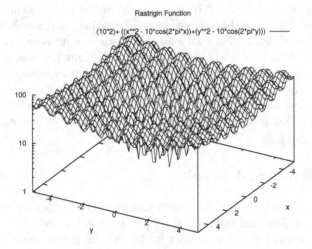

Fig. 3. Rastrigin function

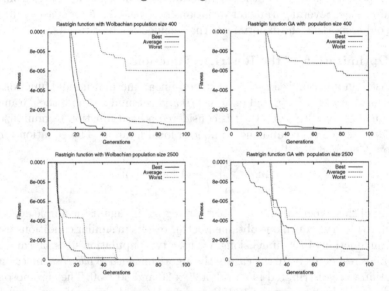

Fig. 4. Results of the Rastrigin function optimization. Every step in the x axis represents 500 generations, 30 independent runs were made. The best series is the average of the best 5 runs, similarly the worst series is the average of the 5 worst runs. The average series was calculated as the average of the 30 runs.

As can be seen in the figure 4, the *Wolbachia* algorithm is very superior in fitness. In the case of the 400 population size, both algorithms reached the optimal minimum but our algorithm reached it in less than half of the generations compared with the simple genetic algorithm. With a population of 2,500 individuals, the gap between the two algorithms is even bigger. Our algorithm reached the optimum in approximately a third of the generations required by the simple genetic algorithm.

4.2   Optimization of the Rosenbrock Function

The Rosenbrock function is a non-convex, non-linear and unimodal function (Figure 5). It is also known as the banana function. This function is considered to be very difficult to minimize because of its narrow ridge. The tip of the ridge is very sharp and is surrounded by a parabola. The global optimum is inside a flat valley that is easy to find, but reaching the global optimum is hard. The global optimum of this function is 0 and is located when all the parameters of the function are 1. The Rosenbrock function definition is as follows:

$$\sum_{i=1}^{n-1}[100(x_{i+1} - x_i^2)^2 + (1 - x_i)^2]$$

The goal of this experiment was also to test our algorithm against a simple genetic algorithm using the Rosenbrock function as benchmark. The parameters of this experiment are identical to the previous experiment with the only difference of values in the chromosome that are in the range of -2.48 and 2.48. The results of these experiments can be seen in Figure 6.

In this experiment none of the algorithms could reach the global minimum in any of the scenarios. Again, our algorithm is superior in fitness and number of generations. With a population of 400 individuals both algorithms got stuck in a local minima in approximately the same number of generations, but our algorithm reached a

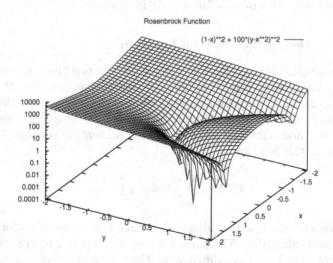

Fig. 5. Rosenbrock function

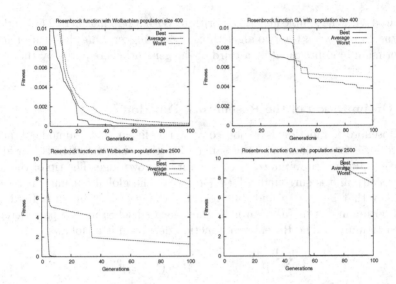

Fig. 6. Results of the Rosenbrock function optimization. Every step in the x axis represents 500 generations, 30 independent runs were made. The best series is the average of the best 5 runs, similarly the worst series is the average of the 5 worst runs. The average series was calculated as the average of the 30 runs.

local minima much closer to the global minima than the simple genetic algorithm. In the scenario of a population of 2,500 individuals, our algorithm not only reached a better local minima than the simple genetic algorithm, but it reached that local minima 6 times faster. An interesting result in this experiment was that the *Wolbachia* algorithm with a population of 400 individuals yielded better results that the same algorithm with a population of 2,500 individuals.

4.3   Optimization of the Schwefel Function

The Schwefel function is not as hard to optimize as the two functions mentioned above. It is considered a deceptive function due to the fact that the global minimum is geometrically distant from the center of the function and the second best minimum is very far from the optimal(Figure 7). The global minimum of this function is 0 and is reached when all the parameters are equal to 490.9687. The definition of this function is:

$$418.9829n + \sum_{i=1}^{n}(x_i \sin(\sqrt{||x_i||}))$$

As the two experiments described above, we wanted to test our algorithm against a classical genetic algorithm. The parameters of this experiment are equal than the experiment above with two differences. The length of the chromosome this time is 3, and the values that the genes in the chromosome can take are between -500 and 500.

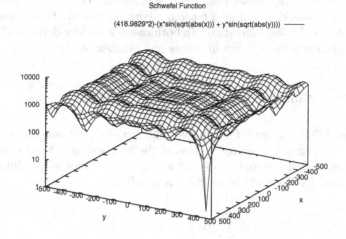

Fig. 7. Schwefel function

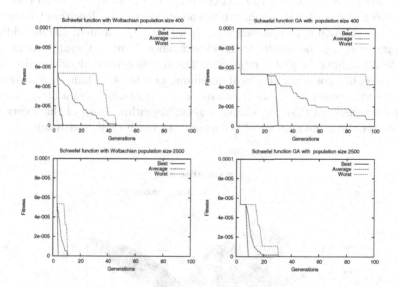

Fig. 8. Results of the Schwefel function optimization. Every step in the x axis represents 500 generations, 30 independent runs were made. The best series is the average of the best 5 runs, similarly the worst series is the average of the 5 worst runs. The average series was calculated as the average of the 30 runs.

As can be seen in figure 8, both of the algorithms reached the global minimum relatively fast. This is because this function is not as hard as the others but once again our algorithm was much faster. In the first scenario, the *Wolbachia* algorithm was four times faster than the simple genetic algorithm. In the second scenario the gap was closed quite a bit, our algorithm was two times faster when the population had 2,500 individuals. In both cases, it is clear that our algorithm produced better results in terms of fitness and number of generations.

4.4 Optimization of the Shifted Elliptic Function

The Shifted Elliptic function is a separable, scalable and unimodal function (Figure 9). Since it is the shifted version of the function, it is harder to find de global minimum that is 0 and it is found when all the values in the chromosome are 0 [13]. The definition of the function is as follows:

$$\sum_{i=1}^{n}(10^6)^{(i-1/n-1)}x_i^2$$

The parameters of this experiment are the same as the other experiments, the length of the chromosome is 100 and the range of the values of the chromosome are between -100 and 100. Again, we use a simple genetic algorithm to compete against our algorithm. In this case we only used a population of 400 individuals.

Figure 10 shows the results of the experiments. None of the algorithms were capable of reaching the global minimum. The simple genetic algorithm decreases much faster, but got stuck at a local minimum. On the other hand, our algorithm decreases at a slower rate until it got stuck in a local minimum a little closer to the global minimum than the simple genetic algorithm. Both of the algorithms took almost the same number of generations to reach their best result.

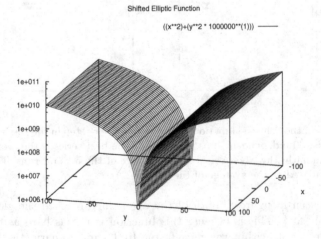

Fig. 9. Shifted Elliptic function

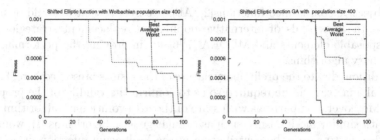

Fig. 10. Results of the Shifted Elliptic functionl function optimization. Every step in the x axis represents 500 generations, 18 independent runs were made. The best series is the average of the best 3 runs, similarly the worst series is the average of the 3 worst runs. The average series was calculated as the average of the 18 runs.

Table 1. Summary of results. Due to the power of representation of the computer used for the simulations, when we report a value of 0, this value is at least less than 1x10-9 but not necessarily 0.

Summary of results			
Function	**Population Size**	**Generations**	**Best Fitness**
Schwefel W	400	3,000	0
	2,500	3,000	0
Schwefel GA	400	12,500	0
	2,500	5,000	0
Rastrigin W	400	12,500	0
	2,500	5,500	0
Rastrigin GA	400	26,000	0
	2,500	15,500	0
Rosenbrock W	400	48,500	.00000143
	2,500	49,500	.0000535
Rosenbrock GA	400	45,000	.00186358
	2,500	49,500	.000216
Elliptic W	400	49,000	.000000757
Elliptic GA	400	49,000	.000024246

5 Discussion

This paper shows how the addition of *Wolbachia* infection can improve evolutionary function optimization by preventing the system from sticking at local optima. We tested the proposed model experimentally using a collection of benchmarking functions [4]. The proposed *Wolbachia* mechanisms have proven to contribute to the improvement of both the fitness and number of generations of genetic algorithms. In effect, the proposed model is capable of both providing better values of the optimization problems and to reaching the global optima faster than the simple genetic algorithm.

An immediate extension of this work would be to test the proposed model when confronting more complex optimization problems such as those posed by multi-objective constrained functions[2]. Also, we believe that it would be useful to assess the potentials of alternative population replacement strategies such as transposable elements and MEDEA [7][6] for improving the performance of evolutionary algorithms.

In addition, due to the preliminary nature of the results presented here, formal statistical analyses will be required so as to confirm the validity of the proposed model. Moreover, comparisons with state of the art evolutionary algorithms and those with similar mechanisms, such as cellular genetic algorithms [1], would be required so as to assess the contribution of the Wolbachia infection mechanism generally.

All in all, we believe that the population replacement strategies that have proven to be effective for controlling vector borne diseases hold the promise of improving the performance of evolutionary algorithms at solving optimization problems.

Acknowledgements. The authors would like to thank Charles E. Taylor for their invaluable contribution to this paper.

References

1. Alba, E., Dorronsoro, B.: Cellular Genetic Algorithms. Springer, Heidelberg (2008)
2. Coello, C.A., Lamont, G.B., Veldhuizen, D.V.: Evolutionary Algorithms for Solving Multi-Objective Problems. Springer, Heidelberg (2007)
3. Crain, P.R., Mains, J.W., Suh, E., et al.: Wolbachia infections that reduce immature insect survival: Predicted impacts on population replacement. BMC Evolutionary Biology 11, 290 (2011)
4. Digalakis, J.G., Margaritis, K.G.: An experimental study of benchmarking functions for genetic algorithms. In: IEEE International Conference on Systems, Man and Cybernetics, pp. 3810–3815. IEEE Press, New York (2000)
5. Dobson, S.L., Fox, W.C., Jiggins, F.M.: The effect of wolbachia-induced cytoplasmic incompatibility on host population size in natural and manipulated systems. Proc. Biol. Sci. 269(1490), 437–445 (2002)
6. Guevara, M., Vallejo, E.E.: Computer simulation on the maternal effect dominant embryonic arrest (medea) for disease vector population replacement. In: 11th Annual Conference on Genetic and Evolutionary Computation, GECCO 2009, pp. 1787–1788. ACM Press, New York (2009)
7. Guevara, M., Vallejo, E.E.: A computer simulation model of gene replacement in vector populations. In: 8th IEEE International Conference on BioInformatics and BioEngineering, BIBE 2008, pp. 1–6. IEEE Press, New York (2008)
8. Hoffman, A.A., Montgomery, B.L., Popovici, J., et al.: Successful establishment of wolbachia in aedes populations to suppress dengue transmission. Nature 476, 454–459 (2011)
9. Marshall, J.M., Taylor, C.E.: Malaria control with transgenic mosquitoes. PLoS Medicine 6, 164–168 (2009)

10. McMeniman, C.J., Lane, R.V., Cass, B.N., et al.: Stable introduction of a life-shortening wolbachia infection into the mosquito aedes aegypti. Science 323, 141–144 (2009)
11. Mitchell, M.: An Introduction to Genetic Algorithms. The MIT Press, Cambridge (1996)
12. Presgraves, D.C.: A genetic test of the mechanism of wolbachia-induced cytoplasmic incompatibility in drosophila. Genetics 154, 771–776 (2000)
13. Tang, K., Li, X., Suganthan, P.N., et al.: Benchmark functions for the cec 2010 special session and competition on large scale global optimization. Technical report. Nature Inspired Computation and Applications Laboratory, USTC, China (2009)

Neural Networks Solving Free Final Time Optimal Control Problem

Tibor Kmet and Maria Kmetova

Constantine the Philosopher University, Tr. A. Hlinku 1, 949 74 Nitra, Slovakia
{tkmet,mkmetova}@ukf.sk

Abstract. A neural network based optimal control synthesis is presented for solving free final time optimal control problems with control and state constraints. The optimal control problem is transcribed into nonlinear programming problem which is implemented with adaptive critic neural network. The proposed simulation methods is illustrated by the optimal control problem of photosynthetic production. Results show that adaptive critic based systematic approach holds promise for obtaining the free final time optimal control with control and state constraints.

Keywords: feed forward neural network, free final time optimal control problem, state and control constraints, numerical examples, photosynthetic production.

1 Introduction

Optimal control of nonlinear systems is one of the most active subjects in control theory. There is rarely an analytical solutions although several numerical computation approaches have been proposed (for example, see [7], [13]). The most of the literature dealing with numerical methods for the solution of general optimal control problems focuses on algorithms for solving discretized problems. The basic idea of these methods is to apply nonlinear programming techniques to the resulting finite dimensional optimization problem [2]. When *Euler* integration methods are used, the recursive structure of the resulting discrete time dynamic can be exploited in computing first-order necessary condition.

In the recent years the neural networks are used for obtaining numerical solutions to optimal control problem [11], [12]. For the neural network presented, a feed forward network with one hidden layer, a steepest descent error backpropagation rule, a hyperbolic tangent sigmoid transfer function and a linear transfer function were used.

The paper presented extends adaptive critic neural network architecture proposed by [12] to the optimal control problems with control and state constraints. The organization of the paper is as follows. In Section 2 optimal control problems with control and state constraints are being introduced. We summarize necessary optimality conditions and give a short overview on basic result including iterative numerical methods and discussed discretization methods for given optimal control problem and a form of resulting *nonlinear programming problems*.

A.-H. Dediu, C. Martín-Vide, and B. Truthe (Eds.): TPNC 2012, LNCS 7505, pp. 174–186, 2012.

Section 3 presented a short description of *adaptive critic neural network synthesis* for optimal problem with state and control constraints. Section 4 consists of mechanistic model of phytoplankton photosynthesis. We apply the methods to the model presented to compare short-term and long-term strategy of photosynthetic production with fixed and free final time, respectively. Conclusions are being presented in Section 5.

2   Optimal Control Problem

We consider nonlinear control problem subject to control and state constraints. Let $x(t) \in R^n$ denote the state of a system and $u(t) \in R^m$ the control in a given time interval $[t_0, t_f]$.

Optimal control problem is to minimize

$$F(x, u) = g(x(t_f)) + \int_{t_0}^{t_f} f_0(x(t), u(t))dt \qquad (1)$$

subject to

$$\dot{x}(t) = f(x(t), u(t)),$$
$$x(t_0) = x_0,$$
$$\psi(x(t_f)) = 0,$$
$$c(x(t), u(t)) \leq 0, \quad t \in [t_0, t_f].$$

The functions $g : R^n \to R$, $f_0 : R^{n+m} \to R$, $f : R^{n+m} \to R^n$, $c : R^{n+m} \to R^q$ and $\psi : R^{n+m} \to R^r$, $0 \leq r \leq n$ are assumed to be sufficiently smooth on appropriate open sets. The theory of necessary conditions for optimal control problem of form (1) is well developed (cf. [7], [14],).

We introduce an additional state variable

$$x_0(t) = \int_0^t f_0(x(s), u(s))ds$$

defined by the

$$\dot{x}_0(t) = f_0(x(t), u(t)), \quad x_0(0) = 0.$$

Then the *augmented Hamiltonian function* for problem (1) is

$$H(x, \lambda, \mu, u) = \sum_{j=0}^{n} \lambda_j f_j(x, u)$$

$$+ \sum_{j=0}^{q} \mu_j c_j(x, u),$$

where $\lambda \in R^{n+1}$ is the adjoint variable and $\mu \in R^q$ is a multiplier associated to the inequality constraints. Let $(\hat{x}, \hat{u})$ be an optimal solution for (1) then the necessary condition for (1) (cf. [7], [14]) implies that there exist a piecewise continuous and piecewise continuously differentiable *adjoint function* $\lambda : [t_0, t_f] \to R^{n+1}$, a piecewise continuous *multiplier function* $\mu : [t_0, t_f] \to R^q$, $\mu(t) \geq 0$ and a multiplier $\sigma \in R^r$ satisfying

$$\dot{\lambda}_j(t) = -\frac{\partial H}{\partial x_j}(\hat{x}(t), \lambda(t), \mu(t), \hat{u}(t))$$

$$\lambda_j(t_f) = g_{x_j}(\hat{x}(t_f)) + \sigma \psi_{x_j}(\hat{x}(t_f))$$

$$j = 0, \ldots, n$$

$$\dot{\lambda}_0(t) = 0$$

$$0 = \frac{\partial H}{\partial u}(\hat{x}(t), \lambda(t), \mu(t), \hat{u}(t)).$$

For free final time t_f, an additional condition need to be satisfied:

$$H(t_f) = (\sum_{j=0}^{n} \lambda_j f_j(x, u) + \sum_{j=0}^{q} \mu_j c_j(x, u))|_{t_f} = 0$$

Furthermore, the complementary conditions hold a.e. in $t \in [t_0, t_f]$ $\mu \geq 0$, $c(x, u) \leq 0$ *and* $\mu c(x, u) = 0$. Herein, the subscript x or u denotes the partial derivative with respect to x or u.

2.1   Discretization of Optimal Control Problem

Direct optimization methods for solving the optimal control problem are based on a suitable discretization of (1), see [1], [2]. Choose a natural number N and let $t_i \in [t_0, t_f]$, $i = 0, \ldots, N$, be a equidistant mesh point with $t_i = t_0 + ih, i = 1, \ldots, N$, where $h = \frac{t_f - t_0}{N}$. Let the vectors $x^i \in R^{n+1}$, $u^i \in R^m, i = 1, \ldots, N$, be approximation of state variable and control variable $x(t_i)$, $u(t_i)$, respectively at the mesh point. *Euler's* approximation applied to the differential equations yields

$$x^{i+1} = x^i + hf(x^i, u^i), \ i = 0, \ldots, N - 1.$$

Choosing the optimal variable
$z := (x^0, x^1, \ldots, x^{N-1}, u^0, \ldots, u^{N-1},) \in R^{N_s}$, $N_s = (n+1+m)N$, the optimal control problem is replaced by the following discretized control problem in the form of nonlinear programming problem with inequality constraints:

$$Minimize \ J(z) = G(x^N),$$

where

$$G(x^N) = g((x_1, \ldots, x_n)^N) + x_0^N,$$

subject to

$$-x^{i+1} + x^i + hf(x^i, u^i) = 0, \tag{2}$$
$$x^0 = x(t_0)$$
$$\psi(x^N)) = 0,$$
$$c(x^i, u^i) \le 0,$$
$$i = 0, \dots, N-1.$$

A free final time t_f can be handled as an additional optimization variable in z. In a discrete-time formulation we want to find an admissible control which minimize object function (2). Let us introduce the *Lagrangian function* for the nonlinear optimization problem (2):

$$L(z, \lambda, \sigma, \mu, h) = \sum_{i=0}^{N-1} \lambda^{i+1}(-x^{i+1} + x^i + hf(x^i, u^i)) +$$

$$G(x^N) + \sum_{i=0}^{N-1} \mu^i c(x^i, u^i) + \sigma\psi(x^N) \tag{3}$$

and define $H(i)$ and Φ as follows:

$$H(i) = \lambda^{i+1}(x^i + hf(x^i, u^i)) + \mu^i c(x^i, u^i),$$
$$\Phi(x^N) = G(x^N) + \sigma\psi(x^N). \tag{4}$$

The first order optimality conditions of Karush-Kuhn-Tucker [13] for the problem (2) are:

$$0 = L_{x^i}(s, \lambda, \mu, h) = \lambda^{i+1} + h\lambda^{i+1}f_{x^i}(x^i, u^i) -$$
$$\lambda^i + \mu^i c_{x^i}(x^i, u^i), \tag{5}$$
$$i = 0, \dots, N-1,$$
$$0 = L_{x^N}(s, \lambda, \mu, h) = G_{x^N}(x^N) + \tag{6}$$
$$\sigma\psi_{x_N}(x_N) - \lambda^N,$$
$$0 = L_{u^i}(s, \lambda, \mu, h) = h\lambda^{i+1}f_{u^i}(x^i, u^i)$$
$$+ \mu^i c_{u^i}(x^i, u^i), \tag{7}$$
$$i = 0, \dots, N-1.$$
$$0 = L_h(z, \lambda, \nu, \mu, h) = \Phi_h + \sum_{i=0}^{N-1} H_h(i). \tag{8}$$

Eq. $(5-8)$ represents the discrete version of necessary condition   for optimal control problem (1).

3   Adaptive Critic Neural Network for Optimal Control Problem with Control and State Constraints and Free Final Time

It is well known that a neural network can be used to approximate smooth time-invariant functions and uniformly time-varying function [6]. Neurons are grouped into distinct layers and interconnected according to a given architecture Fig. (1). Each connection between two neurons has a weight coefficient attached to it. The standard network structure for an approximation function is the multiple-layer perceptron (or feed forward network). The feed forward network often has one or more hidden layers of sigmoid neurons followed by an output layer of linear neurons.

Fig. (1) shows a feed forward neural network with n_i inputs nodes one layer of n_{hl} hidden units and n_o output units. Let $in = [in_1, \ldots, in_{n_i}]$ and $out = [out_1, \ldots, out_{n_o}]$ be the input and output vectors of the network, respectively. Let $V = [v_1, \ldots, v_{n_{hl}}]$ be the matrix of synaptic weights between the input nodes and the hidden units, where $v_j = [v_{j0}, v_{j1} \ldots, v_{jn_i}]$, v_{j0} is the bias of the jth hidden unit, and v_{ji} is the weight that connects the ith input node to the jth hidden unit.

Let also $W = [w_1, \ldots, w_{n_o}]$ be the matrix of synaptic weights between the hidden and output units, where $w_k = [w_{k0}, w_{k1} \ldots, w_{kn_o}]$, w_{k0} is the bias of the kth output unit, and w_{kj} is the weight that connects the jth hidden units to the kth output unit.

The response of the jth hidden unit is given by

$$hl_j = tanh(\sum_{i=0}^{n_i} v_{ji} in_k),$$

where $tanh(.)$ is the activation function for the hidden units. The response of the kth output unit is given by

$$out_k = \sum_{j=0}^{n_{hl}} w_{kj} hl_j.$$

Multiple layers of neurons with nonlinear transfer functions allow the network to learn nonlinear and linear relationships between input and output vectors. The number of neurons in the input and output layers is given, respectively, by the number of input and output variables in the process under investigation.

The multi-layered feed forward network shown in Fig. (1) is training using the steepest descent error backpropagation rule. Basically, it is a gradient descent, parallel distributed optimization technique to minimize the error between the network and the target output [15].

To solve equations (6-7) we are concerned the following nonlinear projection equation (for detail description see [18]):

$$\alpha F(P_X(u)) + u - P_X(u) = 0, \tag{9}$$

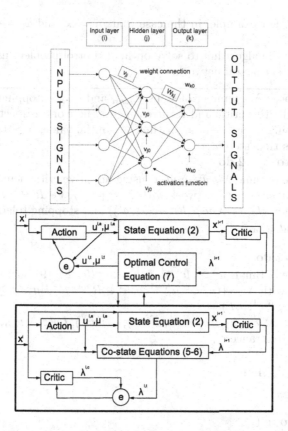

Fig. 1. Feed forward neural network topology with one hidden layer, v_{js}, w_{kj} are values of connection weights, v_{j0}, w_{k0} are values of bias. Architecture of adaptive critic feed forward network synthesis, x^i-input signal to the action and critic network, $u^{i,t}, \mu^{i,t}$ and $\lambda^{i,t}$ output signal from action and critic network, respectively.

where $\alpha > 0$ is a constant $F : R^l \to R^l$, $X = \{u \in R^l \mid d_i \le u_i \le h_i\}$ and $P_X : R^l \to X$ is a projection operator defined by $P_X(u) = (P_X(u_1), \ldots, P_X(u_l))$

$$P_X(u_i) = \begin{cases} d_i & : \quad u_i < d_i \\ u_i & : \quad d_i \le u_i \le h_i \\ h_i & : \quad u_i > h_i \end{cases}$$

which can be solved by the following dynamic model

$$\dot{u}(t) = -\beta(\alpha F(P_X(u)) + u - P_X(u)). \tag{10}$$

Note that d_i and h_i are lower and upper limits of u_i for $i = 1, \ldots, l$. A system described by (10) can be realized by a recurrent neural network with a single-layer structure. A asymptotic and exponencial stability of the present neural network in (10) are proven by [18]. Equilibrium points of (10) coincide with solutions of (9). For example, in the case that $h_i = \infty$ and $d_i = -\infty$, $X = R^l$ and $P_X(u) = u$.

We can state the algorithm to solve optimal control problem using adaptive critic and recurrent neural network.

---

input: Choose N - number of steps, ϵ_{acnn} and ϵ_{rnn} - stopping tolerance for adaptive critic and recurrent neural network, respectively, ϵ_h - stopping tolerance of algorithm, x^0 -initial value, $\alpha > 0$ and $\beta > 0$, Guess time step h.

*for $i \leftarrow 0$ to $N - 2$ do

   Compute optimal $\hat{\lambda}^i$, $\hat{u}^i$, and $\hat{\mu}^i$ using adaptive critic neural network and recurrent neural network with $X = \{(u^i, \mu^i) \in R^{m+q} | \mu^i \geq 0\}$, $F(u^i, \mu^i) = (L_{u^i}(z, \lambda, \nu, \mu, h), -c(x^i, u^i))$ and stopping tolerance ϵ_{acnn} and ϵ_{rnn}.

end

for $i = N - 1$ do

   Compute optimal $\hat{u}^{N-1}, \hat{\mu}^{N-1}, \hat{\nu}, \hat{h}$ using (5 - 8), (9) recurrent neural network with $X = \{(u^{N-1}, \mu^{N-1}, \nu, h) \in R^{m+q+r+1} | \mu^{N-1} \geq 0, h \geq 0\}$, $F(u^{N-1}, \mu^{N-1}, \nu, h) =$ $(L_{u^{N-1}}(z, \lambda, \nu, \mu, h), -c(x^{N-1}, u^{N-1}), -\psi(x^N), L_h(z, \lambda, \nu, \mu, h))$ and stopping tolerance ϵ_{rnn}.

end

if $|h - \hat{h}| < \epsilon_h$ then

   | end;

else

   | $h = \hat{h}$ Go to (*);

end

Algorithm 1: Algorithm to solve optimal control problem

In the Pontryagin's maximum principle for deriving an optimal control law, the interdependence of the state, costate and control dynamics is made clear. Indeed, the optimal control $\hat{u}$ and multiplier $\hat{\mu}$ is given by Eq. (7), while the costate Eqs. (5-6) evolves backward in time and depends on the state and control. The *adaptive critic neural network* is based on this relationship. It consists of two network at each node: an *action* network the inputs of which are the current states and outputs are the corresponding control $\hat{u}$ and multiplier $\hat{\mu}$, and the *critic* network for which the current states are inputs and current costates are outputs for normalizing the inputs and targets (zero mean and standard deviations). For detail explanation see [15].

From free final condition $(\psi(x) \equiv 0)$ and from Eqs. (5-6) we obtain that $\lambda_0^i = -1$, *for* $i = N, \ldots, 0$ *and* $\lambda_j^N = 0$, *for* $j = 1, \ldots, n$. We use this observation before proceeding to the actual training of the *adaptive critic neural network*.

Further discussion and detail explanation of this adaptive critic methods can be found in [8], [9], [11], [12].

4   A Mechanistic Model of Phytoplankton Photosynthesis

Mathematical models of photosynthesis in bioreactors are important for both basic science and the bioprocess industry [5]. There is a class of models based on the concept of the 'photosynthetic factories' developed by Eilers and Peeters [3]. The dynamic behaviour of the model has also been discussed in [4], [10], [16], [17]. Assuming that phytoplankton regulates its photosynthetic production rate with a certain strategy which maximize production, two such possible strategies is examined, i.e. instantaneous and the integral maximal production.

4.1   Description of the Model

Basic for the following consideration is the mechanistic model of phytoplankton photosynthesis. It is based on unit processes concerning the cellular reaction centres called $photo-synthetic\ factories-PSF$. It is known from algal physiology [3] that three states of a PSF are possible: x_i - resting, x_2 - activated and x_3 - inhibited. Transitions between states depend both on light intensity and time. The probabilities of the PSF being in the state x_1, x_2 or x_3, are given as p_1, p_2 and p_3, respectively. Transitions between states can be expressed as follows:

$$\dot{p}_1 = -\alpha I p_1 + \gamma p_2 + \delta p_3 \tag{11}$$
$$\dot{p}_2 = \alpha I p_1 - (\beta I + \gamma) p_2$$
$$\dot{p}_3 = \beta I p_2 - \delta p_3.$$

The parameters α, β, γ and δ occurring in this model are positive constants and I is a light intensity.

Let $p(t, p^0)$ be a solution of (11) with the initial condition $p(0, p^0) = p^0$, where $p_1^0 + p_2^0 + p_3^0 = 1$. Note that solutions of the system (11) exist for all $t \geq 0$. By adding up the right-hand side of (11) we get

$$\dot{p}_1 + \dot{p}_2 + \dot{p}_3 = 0,$$

i.e. $\sum p_i(t, p^0) = 1$ for all $t \geq 0$. Of course these equations are considered in $S = \{p \in R_+^3 : p_1 + p_2 + p_3 = 1\}$. The simplex S is positively invariant. System (11) for all $I \geq 0$ has a unique positive equilibrium $\bar{p}(I)$ with entries

$$\bar{p}_1(I) = \frac{\beta \delta I + \gamma \delta}{F} \tag{12}$$
$$\bar{p}_2(I) = \frac{\alpha \delta I}{F}$$
$$\bar{p}_3(I) = \frac{\alpha \beta I^2}{F},$$

where $F = \alpha \beta I^2 + (\alpha + \beta)\delta I + \gamma \delta$. The equilibrium $\bar{p}(I)$ is globally asymptotically stable on S, that means for fixed light intensity I all solutions with initial condition $p(0) \in S$ converge to $\bar{p}(I)$. For proof see [10].

4.2 Optimization of Photosynthetic Production

Let us assume that phytoplankton regulates its photosynthetic production rate (FP) with a certain strategy which maximizes production. The rate of the photosynthetic production FP is proportional to the number of transitions from x_2 to x_1. Let us investigate the optimal values of light intensity $I(t)$, for which the photosynthetic production $FP = \gamma p_2(t)$ is maximal under constraints $I \in [I_{min}, I_{max}]$.

We will examine two strategies:

1. instantaneous maximal photosynthetic production with respect to I, (local optimality), i.e., $\dot{p}_2 = f_2(p, I, t) \to max$ for all t, under the constraints $I \in [I_{min}, I_{max}]$.

2. integral maximal biomass (global optimality), i.e.

$$J(I) = \int_0^{t_f} \gamma p_2(t) \, dt,$$

under the constraints $I \in [I_{min}, I_{max}]$.

4.3 Local Optimality

In the case of strategy 1, we maximize the following function

$$J(I(t)) = I(t)\alpha p_1(t) - I(t)\beta p_2(t).$$

under the constraints $I \in [I_{min}, I_{max}]$. For $p(t) = \bar{p}(I)$ we examine the following function

$$FP(I) = \frac{\alpha \delta I \gamma}{\delta \gamma + (\beta \delta + \alpha \delta)I + \alpha \beta I^2}.$$

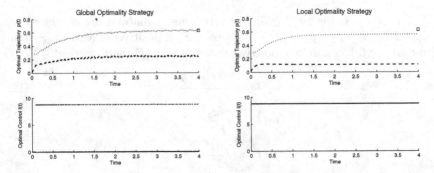

Fig. 2. Adaptive critic neural network simulation of optimal control I^* and $\hat{I}(t)$ for global and local strategies, respectively with fixed final time, dotted line $p_1^*(t)$, $\hat{p}_1(t)$, dashed line $p_2^*(t)$, $\hat{p}_2(t)$

By straightforward calculation we get that the optimal light intensity is given by:

$$I^* = \sqrt{\left(\tfrac{\gamma\delta}{\alpha\beta}\right)}.$$

4.4   Global Optimality

In case of strategy 2, we have the following optimal control problem: to find a function $\hat{I}(t)$, for which the goal function

$$J(I) = \int_0^{t_f} \gamma p_2(t)\, dt$$

attains its maximum, where t_f is fixed. We introduce an additional state variable

$$p_0(t) = \int_0^t \gamma p_2(s)ds \tag{13}$$

defined by the

$$\dot{p}_0(t) = \gamma p_2(t),\ \ p_0(0) = 0.$$

We are led to the following optimal control problems: Maximize

$$p_0(t_f) \tag{14}$$

under the   constraints

$$c_1(p, I) = I_{min} - I \leq 0$$
$$c_2(p, I) = I - I_{max} \leq 0.$$

Discretization of Eqs. (11 - 14) using Eqs. (5- 7) and state equation (2) leads to

$$Minimize\ \ -p_0^N$$

subject to

$$p^{i+1} = p^i + hf(p^i, I^i)$$
$$i = 0, \ldots, N - 1,$$
$$\lambda^i = \lambda^{i+1} + h\lambda^{i+1} f_{p^i}(p^i, I^i)$$
$$+ \mu^i c_{p^i}(p^i, I^i),$$
$$i = N - 1, \ldots, 0,$$
$$\lambda_0^i = -1,\ i = 0, \ldots, N - 1$$
$$\lambda^N = (-1, 0, 0, 0, 0, 0, 0),$$
$$0 = h\lambda^{i+1} f_{I^i}(p^i, I^i)$$
$$+ \mu^i c_{I^i}(p^i, I^i),$$

where the vector function

$$F(p, I) = (-\gamma p_2, f_1(p, I), \ldots, f_3(p, I))$$

is given by Eq. (13) and by right-hand side of Eq. (11). In the adaptive critic

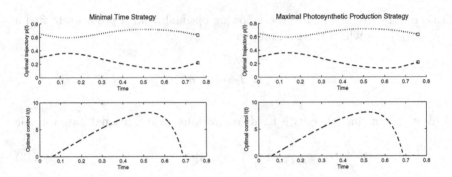

Fig. 3. Adaptive critic neural network simulation of optimal control $\hat{I}(t)$ for maximal photosynthetic production and minimal time, respectively to a point $\bar{p}(I^*)$ with initial condition $x(0) = (0.3, 0.65, 0.05)$ dotted line $\hat{p}_1(t)$, dashed line $\hat{p}_2(t)$

synthesis, the critic and action network were selected such that they consist of three and two subnetworks, respectively, each having 3-18-1 structure (i.e. three neurons in the input layer, eighteen neurons in the hidden layer and one neuron in the output layer). The results of numerical solutions (Fig. 2) have shown that the optimal strategies $\tilde{I}(t)$ and $\hat{I}(t)$ based on short or long-term perspective, respectively, have different time trajectory and for long-term strategy optimal trajectory $\hat{p}_2(t)$ converges to $\bar{p}_2(I^*)$. Therefore let us consider the following free final time optimal control problems

$$J(t_f, I) = \int_0^{t_f} \gamma p_2(t)\, dt$$

and

$$J(t_f, I) = \int_0^{t_f} dt,$$

with final condition $\psi(p(t_f)) = 0$, where $\psi(p) = (p_1 - \bar{p}_1(I^*), p_2 - \bar{p}_2(I^*))$. Results of adaptive-critic simulations are shown in Fig. 3. The results of numerical calculations have shown that the proposed *adaptive critic neural network* is able to meet the convergence tolerance values that we choose, which led to satisfactory simulation results. Simulations, using MATLAB show that proposed neural network is able to solve nonlinear free final time optimal control problem with state and control constraints.

5   Conclusion

A single network adaptive critic approach is presented for optimal control synthesis with control and state constraints. We have formulated, analysed and solved an optimal control problem related to optimal photosynthetic production. Using MATLAB, a simple simulation model based on adaptive critic neural network was constructed. Numerical simulations have shown that adaptive critic neural network is able to solve nonlinear optimal control problem with control and state constraints and free final time.

Acknowledgment. The author is grateful to the referee for his valuable suggestions. The paper was worked out as a part of the solution of the scientific project number KEGA 004UJS-4/2011.

References

1. Bryson Jr., A.E.: Dynamic Optimization. Addison-Wesley Longman Inc., New York (1999)
2. Buskens, C., Maurer, H.: Sqp-methods for solving optimal control problems with control and state constraints: adjoint variable, sensitivity analysis and real-time control. Jour. Comp. Appl. Math. 120, 85–108 (2000)
3. Eilers, P.H.C., Peeters, J.C.H.: A model for relationship between light intensity and the rate of photosynthesis in phytoplankton. Ecol. Modelling 42, 199–215 (1988)
4. Eilers, P.H.C., Peeters, J.C.H.: Dynamic behaviour of a model for photosynthesis and photoinhibition. Ecol. Modelling 69, 113–133 (1993)
5. Garcia-Camacho, F., Sanchez-Miron, A., Molina-Grima, E., Camacho-Rubio, F., Merchuck, J.C.: A mechanistic model of photosynthesis in microalgal including photoacclimation dynamics. Jour. Theor. Biol. 304, 1–15 (2012)
6. Hornik, M., Stichcombe, M., White, H.: Multilayer feed forward networks are universal approximators. Neural Networks 3, 256–366 (1989)
7. Kirk, D.E.: Optimal Control Theory: An Introduction. Dover Publications, Inc., Mineola (1989)
8. Kmet, T.: Neural network simulation of nitrogen transformation cycle. In: Otamendi, J., Bargiela, A., Montes, J.L., Pedrera, L. (eds.) ECMS 2009 - European Conference on Modelling and Simulation, pp. 352–358. ECMS, Madrid (2009)
9. Kmet, T.: Neural network simulation of optimal control problem with control and state constraints. In: Homelka, T., Duch, W., Girolami, M., Kaski, S. (eds.) ICANN 2011. LNCS, vol. 6791, pp. 261–268. Springer, Heidelberg (2011)
10. Kmet, T., Straskraba, M., Mauersberger, P.: A mechanistic model of the adaptation of phytoplankton photosynthesis. Bull. Math. Biol. 55, 259–275 (1993)
11. Padhi, R., Balakrishnan, S.N.: A single network adaptive critic (snac) architecture for optimal control synthesis for a class of nonlinear systems. Neural Networks 19, 1648–1660 (2006)
12. Padhi, R., Unnikrishnan, N., Wang, X., Balakrishnan, S.N.: Adaptive-critic based optimal control synthesis for distributed parameter systems. Automatica 37, 1223–1234 (2001)
13. Polak, E.: Optimization Algorithms and Consistent Approximation. Springer, Berlin (1997)

14. Pontryagin, L.S., Boltyanskii, V.G., Gamkrelidze, R.V., Mischenko, E.F.: The Mathematical Theory of Optimal Process. Nauka, Moscow (1983) (in Russian)

15. Rumelhart, D.F., Hinton, G.E., Wiliams, R.J.: Learning internal representation by error propagation. In: Rumelhart, D.E., McClelland, D.E., Group, P.R. (eds.) Parallel Distributed Processing. Foundation, vol. 1, pp. 318–362. Cambridge University Press, Cambridge (1987)

16. Papáček, Š., Čelikovský, S., Rehák, B., Štys, D.: Experimental design for parameter estimation of two time-scale model of photosynthesis and photoinhibition in microalgae. Math. Comp. Sim. 80, 1302–1309 (2010)

17. Wu, X., Merchuk, J.C.: A model integrating fluid dynamics in photosynthesis and photoinhibition. Chem. Ing. Scien. 56, 3527–3538 (2001)

18. Xia, Y., Feng, G.: A new neural network for solving nonlinear projection equations. Neural Network 20, 577–589 (2007)

Comparing Different Operators and Models to Improve a Multiobjective Artificial Bee Colony Algorithm for Inferring Phylogenies

Sergio Santander-Jiménez, Miguel A. Vega-Rodríguez,
Juan A. Gómez-Pulido, and Juan M. Sánchez-Pérez

University of Extremadura
Department of Technologies of Computers and Communications
ARCO Research Group, Escuela Politécnica
Campus Universitario s/n, 10003. Cáceres, Spain
{sesaji,mavega,jangomez,sanperez}@unex.es

Abstract. Maximum parsimony and maximum likelihood approaches to phylogenetic reconstruction were proposed with the aim of describing the evolutionary history of species by using different optimality principles. These discrepant points of view can lead to situations where discordant topologies are inferred from a same dataset. In recent years, research efforts in Phylogenetics try to apply multiobjective optimization techniques to generate phylogenetic topologies which suppose a consensus among different criteria. In order to generate high quality topologies, it is necessary to perform an exhaustive study about topological search strategies as well as to decide the most fitting molecular evolutionary model in agreement with statistical measurements. In this paper we report a study on different operators and models to improve a Multiobjective Artificial Bee Colony algorithm for inferring phylogenies according to the parsimony and likelihood criteria. Experimental results have been evaluated using the hypervolume metrics and compared with other multiobjective proposals and state-of-the-art phylogenetic software.

Keywords: Phylogenetic inference, swarm intelligence, multiobjective optimization, artificial bee colony.

1 Introduction

Many scientists agree that phylogenetic inference is one of the most important research topics in Bioinformatics, and the centrepiece of research in many areas of biology. The main goal of phylogenetic procedures is the description of ancestral relationships among related organisms [1]. These techniques take as input sequences of molecular characteristics (known as sites) from several species and generate as output a mathematical structure which defines relationships among them by defining hypothetical ancestors over the course of evolutionary history: the *phylogenetic tree*. Phylogenetics can contribute significantly useful knowledge in a variety of fields, such as evolutionary biology, molecular evolution, paleontology, ecology, and physiology.

A.-H. Dediu, C. Martín-Vide, and B. Truthe (Eds.): TPNC 2012, LNCS 7505, pp. 187–200, 2012.
© Springer-Verlag Berlin Heidelberg 2012

In recent decades, researchers in Phylogenetics have proposed the definition of optimality criteria methods to carry out topological searches with the aim of generating the most accurate trees in accordance with some principles, such as parsimony and likelihood [2]. Searching for the best phylogenetic trees according to optimality criteria is considered as an NP-hard problem, so exhaustive approaches cannot be applied on large datasets. The first evolutionary approaches proposed to overcome this issue were reported by Matsuda in 1995 [3] and Lewis [4] in 1998. Several studies suggested different mutation operators as well as new crossover strategies to carry out topological searches and escape from local optima [5]. For example, Cotta and Moscato analyzed the use of several operators for crossover and mutation applied to distance-based methods [6]. In addition to this, maximum likelihood analyses rely on mathematical models to approximate the evolutionary process that gave rise to the input data. Selecting the most accurate model depends on a number of features and must be done according to statistical metrics [7].

A major drawback that arises when applying these approaches to phylogenetic reconstruction is the occurrence of possible incongruences among the inferred phylogenetic topologies for a same dataset. We can find in literature different sources of incoherence when tackling the phylogenetic inference problem, such as the choice of the optimality criterion and conflicting taxon sampling [8]. Multi-objective optimization techniques [9] were proposed to address these issues. The first multiobjective algorithm applied to Phylogenetics was reported by Poladian and Jermiin in 2006 [10]. One year later, Coelho et al. published a multiobjective immune-inspired algorithm under the minimal evolution and mean-squared error criteria [11]. Finally, Cancino and Delbem reported high-quality phylogenetic results using PhyloMOEA, a multiobjective genetic algorithm for maximum parsimony and maximum likelihood reconstruction [12].

In this work we report a study of several techniques for topological search and evolutionary models to improve a multiobjective approach to phylogenetic inference based on the Artificial Bee Colony (ABC) algorithm [13]. Our main purpose is the selection of the most accurate strategies for inferring phylogenetic trees by the maximum parsimony and maximum likelihood criteria. These principles represent two of the most widely-used criteria for phylogenetic reconstruction. Meanwhile parsimony seeks to find the simplest explanation to the evolution of species, maximum likelihood techniques try to reconstruct the most likely evolutionary history of the organisms. Biologists often analyze their data sets and publish phylogenies using a variety of single-criterion software [14] due to the fact that these different approaches can lead to discordant explanations to the observed data. Multiobjective optimization represents a way to address this issue, as the reconstruction of phylogenetic trees considering, simultaneously, the parsimony and likelihood principles can help to overcome the limitations [15] that each criterion presents separately when analyzing real data sets.

The ABC algorithm was chosen because of the promising results it has achieved in a variety of problems, including multiobjective phylogenetic inference [16]. Unlike that previous study, we discuss in this paper the impact on the performance achieved by the algorithm when using different neighbourhood-based strategies for exploring the tree search space and several evolutionary models, running experiments on four nucleotide data sets. Results will be assessed using the hypervolume metrics and applying several statistical tests to select the most fitting model to the input data.

This paper is organized in the following way. The next section details the basis of optimality criteria approaches and proposals to address the search for optimal phylogenetic trees. In Section 3 we summarize the characteristics of the Multiobjective Artificial Bee Colony (MOABC) algorithm, and explain the way we use different strategies to explore the tree search space. Experimental results, discussion and comparisons with other authors can be found in Section 4. Finally, Section 5 provides some conclusions and future work.

2 Inferring Phylogenies

Optimality criteria methods for phylogenetic reconstruction were proposed with the aim of inferring optimal phylogenetic trees according to a specific criterion, an objective function which will be used to guide the inference process. Heuristics defined to guide the search in the space of possible topologies are usually the main core of these methods. When researchers deal with large data sets of species, heuristic-based methods are used to address the inference process, as exhaustive methods cannot be applied for this purpose due to two key factors [17]:

1. By increasing the number of species in the dataset, the tree search space grows exponentially. If we consider a collection of n species to be processed, the number of possible topologies is given by $(2n - 5)!/(n - 3)!2^{n-3}$ [10].
2. By increasing the number of sites in molecular sequences, the assessment of phylogenetic trees will require more processing times and memory consumption. If the inference process is carried out in agreement with complex criteria which use a huge number of parameters and mathematical models, the method will be computationally expensive.

Computational complexity and possible incongruences are the two main issues that can be addressed by using multiobjective metaheuristics applied to the phylogenetic inference problem. Now, we will introduce the basis of the optimality criteria for phylogenetic reconstruction which are the scope of this study: maximum parsimony and maximum likelihood.

2.1 Maximum Parsimony Criterion

Inspired by the Occam's razor principle, maximum parsimony approaches look for those phylogenetic trees that minimize the amount of molecular changes needed to explain the observed data [17]. Given a phylogenetic tree τ, inferred from a set of n nucleotide sequences characterized by N aligned sites, we can formulate the parsimony score for τ as follows [12]:

$$P(\tau) = \sum_{i=1}^{N} \sum_{(a,b) \in B(\tau)} C(a_i, b_i) \qquad (1)$$

where (a, b) is a branch in set B which represents an evolutionary relationship between the nodes a and b, a_i and b_i the state of the ith site for a and b, and $C(a_i, b_i)$ the cost of evolving from the state a_i to b_i. A tree which *minimizes* the parsimony value would represent a simpler evolutionary hypothesis than the proposed by other topologies with higher scores, so we will prefer those trees with low parsimony values. To compute the parsimony for a phylogenetic topology we can use the Fitch's algorithm [2].

In order to explore the search space for most parsimonious phylogenetic trees, several topological operators have been proposed in literature [1]:

- *Approaches based on local moves.* These techniques allow to quickly generate new neighbour topologies, so they usually do not imply an intensive search of the tree space. For this reason, these operators involve small changes in the tree topology to generate new phylogenetic trees. One of the most widely-used local operators is the Nearest Neighbour Interchange (NNI), which takes an internal branch of the tree and executes a swap between the nodes in the subtrees situated at the sides of the chosen branch.
- *Approaches based on global moves.* These proposals aim to avoid phylogenetic algorithms to be trapped on local optima, allowing intensive processing of the tree search space. The classical representative of these operators is the Subtree Pruning and Regrafting (SPR) proposal. SPR consists of removing a subtree from the original topology and regraft it in all possible places. Then, each tree is evaluated according to the chosen optimality criterion.

Recent studies have introduced new methodologies to maximize the percentage of the search space processed while reducing processing times. One of the most modern techniques is the Parametric Progressive Tree Neighbourhood (PPN) proposed by Goëffon et al. [18]. These authors define PPN as the set of possible SPR moves such that the distance between the pruned subtree and the regrafting position is at most d. PPN allows to begin the search for new topologies using global moves, reducing progressively d until this distance is equal to 1, which represents an NNI local move. This proposal has achieved promising results in real data sets, and allows to compete with state-of-the-art maximum parsimony approaches. In this work, we will consider the use of topological searches based on NNI, PPN and SPR neighbourhoods to generate phylogenetic topologies.

2.2 Maximum Likelihood Criterion

This approach is based on a statistical measure that assesses the probability that the evolutionary hypothesis suggested by a phylogenetic tree could give rise to the observed data [17]. Maximum likelihood approaches aim to reconstruct the most likely evolutionary history of the organisms. Likelihood in Phylogenetics is highly related to the topology of the tree to be evaluated, evolutionary times among related species (defined by the branch length values) and the molecular evolutionary model. Evolutionary models try to approximate the reality of the evolutionary process that gave rise to the species in the input of the procedure [7]. They describe the probabilities of change from a given state to other one on the molecular sequences of related species, so selecting the most accurate model for the input dataset will determine the success of the inference process.

Let τ be a phylogenetic tree, D the set of N-site sequences in input data, D_i the state of the ith site on the sequences and m the evolutionary model. The likelihood score for τ is given by [2]:

$$L[D, \tau, m] = \Pr[D|\tau, m] = \prod_{i=1}^{N} \prod_{j=1}^{B} (r_i t_j)^{n_{ij}} \tag{2}$$

where B is the set of branches among related species in τ, r_i the probability of change for the site i given by the evolutionary model m, t_j the period of time given by the branch j and n_{ij} the number of state changes between the nodes connected by j for the site i.

Likelihood formulation can be extended if we consider different occurrence frequencies on the patterns of nucleotide changes, which include *transitions*, substitutions between similar nucleotides, e.g. A–G (purines) or C–T (pyrimidines), and *transversions*, purine–pyrimidine substitution or vice versa. We can also bear in mind heterogeneity in substitution rates among sites, which can alter the probability of substitutions on the nucleotide level. This fact (known as among-site rate variation) can be modelled by gamma distributions [7].

The likelihood is an objective to be *maximized*. We will prefer those trees which maximize the likelihood because they would suggest the most likely evolutionary hypotheses. In order to calculate the likelihood we can use the Felsenstein algorithm [2]. Optimizing the previously mentioned parameters will allow us to improve the likelihood score for a phylogenetic tree. New topologies can be generated by using local and global topological operators. Also, we can apply optimization algorithms (such as the method of gradient descent) to improve branch lengths. Finally, the evolutionary model must be chosen in accordance with the dataset to be processed. In this work, we will study five different evolutionary models, considering among-site rate variation: Jukes-Cantor69 ($JC69 + \Gamma$), Kimura80 ($K80 + \Gamma$), Hasegawa-Kishino-Yano85 ($HKY85 + \Gamma$), Tamura-Nei93 ($TN93 + \Gamma$) and the General Time Reversible model ($GTR + \Gamma$) [2].

3   Multiobjective Artificial Bee Colony

In 2005, D. Karaboga proposed an algorithm to resolve optimization problems inspired by the behaviour of the honey bees [13]. The ABC is one of the most representative examples of swarm intelligence, a family of bioinspired algorithms which define a set of individuals with a specific role in the swarm and rules that allow them to interactuate each other with the aim of modelling a collective behaviour. The ABC considers three groups of bees, each one with a role and a collection of tasks to be performed: employed bees, onlooker bees and scout bees. Interactions among bees allow to interchange information about the quality of the food sources, in order to exploit the most promising sources and explore the environment for new ones. In literature, we can find the success of the ABC when tackling different single and multiobjective optimization problems [19].

Our proposal tries to extend the ABC original design applying multiobjective optimization techniques, which allow to consider simultaneously two or more criteria to resolve an optimization problem. The MOABC will be focused on addressing the phylogenetic reconstruction of tree topologies according to the maximum parsimony and maximum likelihood criteria, NP-hard problems whose resolution requires the selection of those operators and models that lead to quality evolutionary hypotheses. When we must evaluate solutions from a multiobjective perspective, we must bear in mind the *dominance* concept. Given two solutions a and b to the problem, we will say that a dominates b if and only if a has better or equal values than b in all considered objectives and, at least, a is better in one of them. By selecting the most promising configuration of models and topological search techniques, we aim to generate those multiobjective evolutionary hypotheses which are closer to the set of Pareto-optimal solutions to the problem. The MOABC algorithm will generate as output a collection of Pareto solutions which represent a consensus among different objectives. By representing these solutions in the value space of the n objective functions we have considered for the optimization process, we get an n-dimensional curve which is known as Pareto front.

3.1   MOABC Design

As well as other bioinspired approaches, the MOABC algorithm takes as input a variety of parameters which guide the optimization process:

- swarmSize. Bee population size.
- maxIterations. Number of iterations of the main loop to be performed.
- limit. Specific control parameter defined to avoid population stagnation.
- mutation. Mutation rate to apply over trees to generate new topologies.

Initially, the first half of the population will be composed by employed bees, and the remaining half by onlooker bees. To initialize these bees we will perform the following steps:

1. Initial topology selection. Starter trees are selected from an initial repository of 1000 bootstrap phylogenetic trees [2], 500 of them generated by maximum parsimony analysis, and the remaining 500 by maximum likelihood techniques. Internal encoding of phylogenetic trees is carried out by using the TreeTemplate class from the bioinformatics libraries BIO++ [20].

2. Evolutionary model configuration. As we remarked in Section 2, we will evaluate five evolutionary models: **JC69, K80, HKY85, TN93 and GTR**. We have considered the values suggested by PhyML [21] to configure the model parameters and the gamma shape value for each dataset.

We can differentiate three main sections in this algorithm: exploitation step by employed bees, selection and exploitation step by onlooker bees and exploration step by scout bees (a detailed explanation and pseudocode for this algorithm can be found in [16]).

Firstly, *employed bees* aim to find food sources for the hive, checking the neighbourhood of the currently exploited source for promising new ones. In this step, neighbour phylogenetic trees are computed by applying a mutation process on the starter topologies. NNI local moves are applied on randomly selected nodes according to the mutation rate parameter and random branch lengths are modified according to the gamma shape parameter of the distribution. We use the NNI operator in this step because local moves can be computed and evaluated faster than global arrangements. These new phylogenetic topologies will compete with the original trees using a multiobjective fitness (MOFitness), which takes into account the number of solutions dominated by the current tree and the number of solutions that dominate it [16]. Solutions that minimize MOFitness will be preferred and assigned to employed bees.

Once employed bees have finished their tasks, they return to the hive and interactuate with *onlooker bees*, performing dances to show them the quality of the food sources they have found. In accordance with these dances, onlooker bees select the most promising sources to exploit them. To model this behaviour, solutions found by employed bees are sorted using two operators proposed by Deb et al. [22]: fast non dominated sort and crowding distance. Following this, we compute a vector to define selection probabilities for each sorted solution. The most promising solutions will be associated to higher selection probabilities, so onlooker bees will check this vector and decide which solution must be exploited. Once again, we apply the mutation process to generate new neighbour phylogenetic trees, which will compete with the selected solutions by using MOFitness. In order to promote different topologies in the population, an onlooker bee will save the neighbour tree if it scores a better or equal MOFitness value in comparison with the selected tree.

In the third step, *scout bees* perform random searches for new undiscovered solutions. These bees are defined to avoid the algorithm to be trapped on local optima, one of the possible situations we must deal with when using metaheuristics. When the solution associated to a bee in MOABC is not improved in *limit* iterations, this bee is replaced by a scout bee. Scout bee conversion begins with the assignation of a new starter phylogenetic tree from the initial repository. After that, we introduce an optimization step which will allow the new trees to be able to compete with the solutions found by the algorithm. In this optimization step, we consider the following neighbourhood strategies:

- **NNI Neighbourhood.** Topology optimization is carried out by checking, for each node, random possible NNI moves. In each step, parsimony and likelihood scores are computed and the NNI neighbour tree will be saved if it dominates the current topology.

- **SPR Neighbourhood.** For each node in the phylogenetic tree, we define a set of candidate SPR moves according to the total number of nodes in the topology and the mutation rate parameter. New SPR neighbour topologies are generated and compared using the dominance concept to decide which topology must be saved. If several SPR topologies dominate the remaining neighbours and are not dominated by each other, we apply MOFitness to decide the most promising topology.
- **PPN Neighbourhood.** Random nodes are selected according to the mutation rate parameter. For each one, we calculate the parametric distance $d = v_{max} - 1$, where v_{max} is the longest distance between the selected node and the tree leaves [18]. Neighbour topologies are generated according to the progressive neighbourhood principle. Firstly, we check the neighbour topologies generated by pruning and regrafting the selected subtrees on branches at d distance. Neighbour topologies are saved according to the dominance concept and MOFitness. In further steps, we check for the $d - 1$ neighbour trees and so on. In the final step, $d = 1$ (NNI) neighbours will be computed.

Additionally, we apply a gradient descent search to improve branch length values of the current topology. These strategies allow us to explore undiscovered regions of the tree search space, generating quality trees that will be refined afterwards by other groups of bees.

4   Experimental Methodology and Results

In this section we show and explain our experimental methodology and results. Parameter configuration is based on the proposal we showed in our previous research [16]. MOABC execution will require 100 generations and a swarm size of 100 bees, using a 5% mutation rate and a limit parameter up to 15 iterations. These parameters were defined according to other authors' proposals [12] and our own experimentation [16]. Experiments have been carried out on four nucleotide data sets proposed in other multiobjective studies [12]: $rbcL\_55$, 55 sequences (1314 nucleotides per sequence) of the rbcL gene from different species of green plants. $mtDNA\_186$, 186 sequences (16608 nucleotides per sequence) of human mitochondrial DNA. $RDPII\_218$, 218 sequences (4182 nucleotides per sequence) of prokaryotic RNA. And $ZILLA\_500$, 500 sequences (759 nucleotides per sequence) from rbcL plastid gene.

Experimentation on Neighbourhood Methods. In order to evaluate the multiobjective performance of our proposal by using different neighbourhood approaches, we have carried out 10 runs of the algorithm for each dataset, using the $GTR + \Gamma$ evolutionary model. Pareto fronts have been evaluated from a multiobjective perspective by using the hypervolume metrics, a useful indicator which defines the percentage of the search space dominated by our Pareto solutions. We have also taken the execution times required by each configuration (using 8 OpenMP-threads). Table 1 shows mean hypervolumes, standard deviation values and processing times required by the proposal according to the neighbourhood strategy. According to this table, as we increase the complexity of the dataset, the hypervolume values achieved by PPN and SPR overcome the values obtained by NNI. The SPR neighbourhood achieves the best hypervolume values for all the data sets. However, a major drawback arises when using this neighbourhood due to the fact that execution time increases with the complexity of the instance. On the other hand, the PPN proposal allows to get significant hypervolume values without dramatic times in comparison with SPR. We can suggest that PPN approach supposes a consensus between NNI and SPR, improving the multiobjective results in reasonable times. Reference points used to compute hypervolume for each dataset are given by Table 2.

Table 1. Experimental results (neighbourhood methods)

Neighbourhood	Hypervolume metrics		
	Mean	Std. deviation	Time(s)
rbcL_55			
NNI	71.506%	0.0024	1611.0
PPN	71.620%	0.0020	1770.7
SPR	71.631%	0.0016	1918.5
mtDNA_186			
NNI	69.888%	0.0004	12798.9
PPN	69.994%	0.0002	17223.9
SPR	69.998%	0.0002	43369.9
RDPII_218			
NNI	73.147%	0.0335	18462.2
PPN	74.022%	0.0209	27622.0
SPR	74.063%	0.0290	54573.6
ZILLA_500			
NNI	71.250%	0.0024	20595.4
PPN	72.345%	0.0019	37499.4
SPR	72.566%	0.0018	104539.0

Table 2. Reference points for hypervolume

Dataset	Minimal Reference Point		Maximum Reference Point	
	Parsimony	Likelihood	Parsimony	Likelihood
rbcL_55	4774	-21569.69	5279	-23551.42
mtDNA_186	2376	-39272.20	2656	-43923.99
RDPII_218	40658	-132739.90	45841	-147224.59
ZILLA_500	15893	-79798.03	17588	-87876.39

Experimentation on Evolutionary Models. The impact of the evolutionary model in the inference process has been checked running a new series of experiments. We have performed 10 complete runs of the algorithm for each model and dataset, using the PPN neighbourhood for the scout bee step. Once again, Pareto fronts have been evaluated using the hypervolume metrics. Also, the statistical evaluation of models is carried out according to the Akaike Information Criterion (AIC) and Bayesian Information Criterion (BIC) [7]. Meanwhile the AIC defines the amount of information lost when an specific model is used to approximate the reality of the evolutionary process, the BIC evaluates models according to Bayesian estimation. Given a phylogenetic tree with likelihood L, an evolutionary model with K parameters and a dataset consisting of N-site sequences, we formulate AIC as $AIC = -2L + 2K$, and BIC as $BIC = -2L + K \log N$. We will prefer those models that minimize both criteria.

Table 3 presents experimental results for the execution that scored the hypervolume value closer to the mean hypervolume obtained by the overall experiments. As we can see, the models $HKY85 + \Gamma$, $TN93 + \Gamma$ and $GTR + \Gamma$ achieve the best likelihood scores and hypervolume values for each dataset (over 68% of the space defined by the reference points). The AIC and BIC select $GTR + \Gamma$ and $TN93 + \Gamma$ as the models which allow to generate the best extreme solutions for all the instances. According to these results, we can suggest that the $HKY85 + \Gamma$, $TN93 + \Gamma$ and, specially, $GTR + \Gamma$ evolutionary models allow to obtain a significant improvement in likelihood values. Figure 1 shows Pareto fronts for each dataset using the $HKY85 + \Gamma$, $TN93 + \Gamma$ and $GTR + \Gamma$ models.

Table 3. Experimental results (evolutionary models)

Evolutionary Model	Pareto Trees	Best parsimony tree				Best likelihood tree				Hypervolume	
		Pars.	Likelihood	AIC	BIC	Pars.	Likelihood	AIC	BIC	Mean	Std. dev.
rbcL_55											
$JC69 + \Gamma$ (K=109)	2	4874	-23041.19	46300.39	46865.10	4876	-23038.39	46294.46	46859.17	20.76%	0.0074
$K80 + \Gamma$ (K=110)	3	4874	-21986.32	44192.64	44762.53	4879	-21982.18	44184.37	44754.26	63.47%	0.0023
$HKY85 + \Gamma$ (K=113)	4	4874	-21834.78	43895.57	44481.00	4887	-21815.49	43856.99	44442.42	70.09%	0.0052
$TN93 + \Gamma$ (K=114)	4	4874	-21833.93	43895.87	44486.48	4891	-21811.82	43851.65	44442.26	70.17%	0.0035
$GTR + \Gamma$ (K=117)	5	4874	-21813.31	**43860.63**	**44466.79**	4891	-21781.12	**43796.25**	**44402.41**	**71.62%**	0.0020
mtDNA_186											
$JC69 + \Gamma$ (K=371)		2431	-42628.87	85999.75	88862.99	2444	-42557.45	85856.90	88720.14	23.52%	0.0003
$K80 + \Gamma$ (K=372)	11	2431	-40845.17	82434.34	85305.30	2445	-40779.31	82302.63	85173.60	53.88%	0.0003
$HKY85 + \Gamma$ (K=375)	13	2431	-39973.19	80696.38	83590.49	2450	-39888.73	80527.47	83421.58	69.66%	0.0004
$TN93 + \Gamma$ (K=376)	13	2431	-39953.90	80659.81	83561.65	2451	-39872.79	80497.58	**83399.42**	69.93%	0.0003
$GTR + \Gamma$ (K=379)	10	2431	-39930.90	**80619.80**	**83544.79**	2453	-39869.59	**80497.19**	83422.18	**69.99%**	0.0002
RDPII_218											
$JC69 + \Gamma$ (K=435)	40	41488	-143728.09	288326.18	291083.45	42985	-137096.72	275063.45	277820.72	54.66%	0.0957
$K80 + \Gamma$ (K=436)	41	41488	-141514.84	283955.69	286719.29	42928	-134667.44	270206.88	272970.49	68.73%	0.0849
$HKY85 + \Gamma$ (K=439)	35	41488	-136412.38	273702.77	276485.39	42837	-134146.85	269171.71	271954.33	73.53%	0.0468
$TN93 + \Gamma$ (K=440)	35	41488	-136404.56	273689.13	276478.09	42892	-134126.47	269132.94	271921.90	73.75%	0.0327
$GTR + \Gamma$ (K=443)	30	41488	-136319.82	**273525.65**	**276333.62**	42824	-134078.65	**269043.31**	271851.29	**74.02%**	0.0209
ZILLA_500											
$JC69 + \Gamma$ (K=999)	16	16218	-84650.84	171299.68	175927.05	16291	-84232.71	170463.43	175090.80	36.34%	0.0047
$K80 + \Gamma$ (K=1000)	24	16218	-81660.08	165320.17	169952.17	16311	-81099.15	164198.31	168830.31	67.62%	0.0007
$HKY85 + \Gamma$ (K=1003)	17	16218	-81569.03	165144.06	169789.96	16311	-80965.83	163937.66	168583.56	68.98%	0.0032
$TN93 + \Gamma$ (K=1004)	17	16218	-81568.02	165144.04	169794.57	16318	-80965.68	163939.37	168589.90	68.94%	0.0013
$GTR + \Gamma$ (K=1007)	24	16218	-81407.38	**164828.76**	**169493.18**	16317	-80599.40	**163212.81**	167877.24	72.34%	0.0019

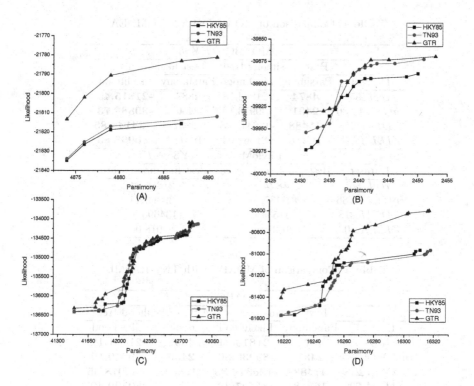

Fig. 1. Pareto fronts for the data sets $rbcL\_55$ (A), $mtDNA\_186$ (B), $RDPII\_218$ (C) and $ZILLA\_500$ (D)

Comparisons with Other Authors. To show the relevance of this approach, we compare the MOABC with other popular state-of-the-art approaches to phylogenetic inference. Firstly, Table 4 shows a comparison with PhyloMOEA, a multiobjective algorithm for phylogenetic inference proposed by Cancino and Delbem [12] which uses the $HKY85 + \Gamma$ evolutionary model. In this table we can find that our proposal improves the best parsimony and likelihood scores found by PhyloMOEA. For the $rbcL\_55$ dataset, the most parsimonious trees found by both algorithms score the same parsimony value, but our parsimonious solution improves the likelihood of their most likelihood tree. This fact shows that our solutions dominate the topologies reported by PhyloMOEA.

Additionally, in Table 5 we present a comparison with two widely-used single-criterion proposals: TNT (maximum parsimony) [23] and RAxML (maximum likelihood) [24], using the $GTR + \Gamma$ model. We have used BIO++ to configure the parameters of the evolutionary model, as well as to estimate branch lengths for TNT. According to this comparison, our solutions overcome the phylogenetic topologies generated by TNT and RAxML. As an exception, we can observe that the phylogenetic tree inferred by using RAxML scores a lower parsimony than our most likelihood topology for the $ZILLA\_500$ dataset. However, if we examine our Pareto front, we can find solutions that dominate this topology (e.g. Parsimony=16303 and Likelihood=-80621.28).

Table 4. Comparison of MOABC with PhyloMOEA

	MOABC $HKY85 + \Gamma$			
	Best parsimony tree		Best likelihood tree	
Dataset	Parsimony	Likelihood	Parsimony	Likelihood
*rbcL*_55	**4874**	-21834.78	4887	**-21815.49**
*mtDNA*_186	**2431**	-39973.19	2450	**-39888.73**
*RDPII*_218	**41488**	-136412.38	42837	**-134146.85**
*ZILLA*_500	**16218**	-81569.03	16311	**-80965.83**
	PhyloMOEA $HKY85 + \Gamma$			
Dataset	Best parsimony score		Best likelihood score	
*rbcL*_55	**4874**		-21889.84	
*mtDNA*_186	2437		-39896.44	
*RDPII*_218	41534		-134696.53	
*ZILLA*_500	16219		-81018.06	

Table 5. Comparison of MOABC with TNT-RAxML

	MOABC $GTR + \Gamma$			
	Best parsimony tree		Best likelihood tree	
Dataset	Parsimony	Likelihood	Parsimony	Likelihood
*rbcL*_55	**4874**	**-21813.31**	4891	**-21781.12**
*mtDNA*_186	**2431**	**-39930.90**	2453	**-39869.59**
*RDPII*_218	**41488**	**-136319.83**	42824	**-134078.65**
*ZILLA*_500	**16218**	**-81407.38**	16317	**-80599.40**
	TNT-BIO++ $GTR + \Gamma$		RAxML $GTR + \Gamma$	
Dataset	Parsimony	Likelihood	Parsimony	Likelihood
*rbcL*_55	**4874**	-21854.35	4893	-21791.98
*mtDNA*_186	**2431**	-39970.99	2453	-39869.63
*RDPII*_218	**41488**	-136726.89	42894	-134079.42
*ZILLA*_500	**16218**	-81571.77	**16305**	-80623.50

5   Conclusions and Future Research Lines

We have reported in this paper a study on different neighbourhood-based topological search proposals and evolutionary models to improve a multiobjective swarm intelligence approach to phylogenetic inference. Different sets of experiments have been performed on four real nucleotide data sets and Pareto solutions have been evaluated by using the hypervolume metrics and the AIC and BIC tests. According to these results, we can conclude that the use of PPN neighbourhood and evolutionary models like $GTR + \Gamma$ allows to obtain high-quality phylogenetic solutions in reasonable times under the maximum parsimony and maximum likelihood criteria. The comparison with approaches developed by other authors shows that MOABC can generate promising phylogenetic topologies, improving the results reported by previous multiobjective proposals.

As future research work, we will study the use of high performance computing to reduce the execution times required by the proposal, applying fine and coarse-grained parallelism on hybrid architectures. Also, other multiobjective bioinspired algorithms will be applied to resolve the phylogenetic inference problem, using new data sets and comparing multiobjective performance for each approach with different metrics (such as set coverage and attainment surface).

Acknowledgment. The authors would like to thank the Gobierno de Extremadura (Spain) for the GR10025 grant provided to the research group TIC015. Also, thanks to the Fundación Valhondo for the economic support offered to Sergio Santander-Jiménez.

References

1. Swofford, D., Olsen, G., Waddell, P., Hillis, D.: Phylogenetic Inference. Molecular Systematics 2, 407–514 (1996)
2. Felsenstein, J.: Inferring phylogenies. Sinauer Associates, Sunderland (2004) ISBN: 0-87893-177-5
3. Matsuda, H.: Construction of phylogenetic trees from amino acid sequences using a genetic algorithm. In: Proceedings of Genome Informatics Workshop, pp. 19–28. Universal Academy Press (1995)
4. Lewis, P.O.: A Genetic Algorithm for Maximum-Likelihood Phylogeny Inference Using Nucleotide Sequence Data. Molecular Biology and Evolution 15(3), 277–283 (1998)
5. Congdon, C.: GAPHYL: An evolutionary algorithms approach for the study of natural evolution. In: Genetic and Evolutionary Computation Conference, pp. 1057–1064 (2002)
6. Cotta, C., Moscato, P.: Inferring Phylogenetic Trees Using Evolutionary Algorithms. In: Guervós, J.J.M., Adamidis, P.A., Beyer, H.-G., Fernández-Villacañas, J.-L., Schwefel, H.-P. (eds.) PPSN VII. LNCS, vol. 2439, pp. 720–729. Springer, Heidelberg (2002)
7. Bos, D.H., Posada, D.: Using models of nucleotide evolution to build phylogenetic trees. Developmental and Comparative Immunology 29, 211–227 (2005)
8. Rokas, A., Williams, B.L., King, N., Carroll, S.B.: Genome-scale approaches to resolving incongruence in molecular phylogenies. Nature 425(6960), 798–804 (2003)
9. Deb, K.: Multi-objective Optimization Using Evolutionary Algorithms. Wiley-Interscience Series in Systems and Optimization. John Wiley & Sons, Chichester (2001) ISBN: 978-0-471-87339-6
10. Poladian, L., Jermiin, L.: Multi-Objective Evolutionary Algorithms and Phylogenetic Inference with Multiple Data Sets. Soft Computing 10(4), 359–368 (2006)
11. Coelho, G.P., da Silva, A.E.A., Von Zuben, F.J.: Evolving Phylogenetic Trees: A Multiobjective Approach. In: Sagot, M.-F., Walter, M.E.M.T. (eds.) BSB 2007. LNCS (LNBI), vol. 4643, pp. 113–125. Springer, Heidelberg (2007)
12. Cancino, W., Delbem, A.C.B.: A Multi-Criterion Evolutionary Approach Applied to Phylogenetic Reconstruction. In: Korosec, P. (ed.) New Achievements in Evolutionary Computation, pp. 135–156. InTech (2010) ISBN: 978-953-307-053-7
13. Karaboga, D.: An idea based on honey bee swarm for numerical optimization. Tech. Rep. TR06, Erciyes University, Engineering Faculty, Computer Engineering Department (2005)

14. Schmidt, O., Drake, H.L., Horn, M.A.: Hitherto Unknown [Fe-Fe]-Hydrogenase Gene Diversity in Anaerobes and Anoxic Enrichments from a Moderately Acidic Fen. Applied and Environmental Microbiology 76(6), 2027–2031 (2010)
15. Pol, D., Siddall, M.E.: Biases in Maximum Likelihood and Parsimony: A Simulation Approach to a 10-Taxon Case. Cladistics 17(3), 266–281 (2001)
16. Santander-Jiménez, S., Vega-Rodríguez, M.A., Gómez-Pulido, J.A., Sánchez-Pérez, J.M.: Inferring Phylogenetic Trees Using a Multiobjective Artificial Bee Colony Algorithm. In: Giacobini, M., Vanneschi, L., Bush, W.S. (eds.) EvoBIO 2012. LNCS, vol. 7246, pp. 144–155. Springer, Heidelberg (2012)
17. Snell, Q., Whiting, M., Clement, M., McLaughlin, D.: Parallel Phylogenetic Inference. In: Proceedings of the 2000 ACM/IEEE conference on Supercomputing, Article 35. IEEE Computer Society (2000)
18. Goëffon, A., Richer, J.M., Hao, J.K.: Progressive Tree Neighborhood Applied to the Maximum Parsimony Problem. IEEE/ACM Transactions on Computational Biology and Bioinformatics 5, 136–145 (2008)
19. Karaboga, D., Gorkemli, B., Ozturk, C., Karaboga, N.: A comprehensive survey: Artificial Bee Colony (ABC) algorithm and applications. Artificial Intelligence Review, 1–37 (2012), doi:10.1007/s10462-012-9328-0
20. Dutheil, J., Gaillard, S., Bazin, E., Glémin, S., Ranwez, V., Galtier, N., Belkhir, K.: Bio++: a set of C++ libraries for sequence analysis, phylogenetics, molecular evolution and population genetics. BMC Bioinformatics 7, 188–193 (2006)
21. Guindon, S., Dufayard, J.F., Lefort, V., Anisimova, M., Hordijk, W., Gascuel, O.: New Algorithms and Methods to Estimate Maximum-Likelihood Phylogenies: Assessing the Performance of PhyML 3.0. Systematic Biology 59(3), 307–321 (2010)
22. Deb, K., Pratap, A., Agarwal, S., Meyarivan, T.: A fast and elitist multi-objective genetic algorithm: NSGA-II. IEEE Transactions on Evolutionary Computation 6, 182–197 (2002)
23. Goloboff, P.A., Farris, J.S., Nixon, K.C.: TNT, a free program for phylogenetic analysis. Cladistics 24, 774–786 (2008)
24. Stamatakis, A.: RAxML-VI-HPC: Maximum Likelihood-based Phylogenetic Analyses with Thousands of Taxa and Mixed Models. Bioinformatics 22(21), 2688–2690 (2006)

Tissue P Systems with Cell Separation: Upper Bound by PSPACE

Petr Sosík[1,2] and Luděk Cienciala[2]

[1] Departamento de Inteligencia Artificial, Facultad de Informática,
Universidad Politécnica de Madrid, Campus de Montegancedo s/n,
Boadilla del Monte, 28660 Madrid, Spain
[2] Research Institute of the IT4Innovations Centre of Excellence,
Faculty of Philosophy and Science, Silesian University in Opava,
74601 Opava, Czech Republic
{petr.sosik,ludek.cienciala}@fpf.slu.cz

Abstract. Tissue P systems are a class of bio-inspired computing models motivated by biochemical interactions between cells in a tissue-like arrangement. This organization is formally described by an interaction graph with membranes at its vertices. Membranes communicate by exchanging objects from a finite set. This basic model was enhanced with the operation of cell separation, resulting in tissue P systems with cell separation. Uniform families of tissue P systems were recently studied. Their computational power was shown to range between **P** and **NP** $\cup$ **co** $-$ **NP**, characterizing borderlines between tractability and intractability by length of rules and some other features. Here we show that the computational power of these uniform families in polynomial time is limited from above by the class **PSPACE**. In this way we relate the information-processing potential of bio-inspired tissue-like systems to classical parallel computing models as PRAM or alternating Turing machine.

Keywords: Tissue P system, membrane computing, membrane separation, PSPACE.

1 Introduction

Tissue P system is a bio-inspired computing model introduced first in [8]. Biological justification of the model (see [9]) is the intercellular communication and cooperation between neurons and, generally, between tissue cells. The original motivation of the model can be seen as (1) to construct a distributed bio-inspired computing model *in-silico* based on interaction of simple finite-state components, and (2) to characterize the information-processing potential of biological systems based on cell-to-cell interaction bound with a fixed interaction graph. As another goal, the model might also provide a theoretical background for engineered cell-based systems harnessing the power of biological information processing. Such systems are recently being developed within the framework of

A.-H. Dediu, C. Martín-Vide, and B. Truthe (Eds.): TPNC 2012, LNCS 7505, pp. 201–215, 2012.

European FP7 research projects under the Bio-Chem IT (Biochemistry Based Information Technology) objective.

Cells in the model are able to communicate simple atomic objects. Instead of considering a hierarchical arrangement of membranes usual in classical models of membrane systems (called also P systems, see [12] for an overview and many examples), the underlying structure of tissue P systems is defined as an arbitrary interaction graph with membranes/cells in the nodes. The communication among cells alongside the edges of the virtual graph is based on symport/antiport rules which were introduced to P systems in [14]. Symport rules move objects across a membrane together in one direction, whereas antiport rules move objects across a membrane in opposite directions. In tissue P systems these two variants were unified as a unique type of rule. From the original definitions of tissue P systems [8, 9], several research lines have been developed and other variants have arisen (see, for example, [1–4, 6, 7]).

This paper deals with the variant of tissue P systems presented first in [11] and called *tissue P systems with cell separation*. Its computational efficiency was investigated and the following results were obtained: (a) only tractable problems can be efficiently solved when the length of communication rules is restricted to at most 2, and (b) an efficient (uniform) solution to the SAT problem by using communication rules with length at most 8 (and, of course, separation rules). These results have been achieved thanks to the strategy of trading space for time, none of which, of course, being an unlimited resource in physical computing systems. However, in the framework of recognizer tissue P systems with cell separation, the length of communication rules provides an borderline between efficiency and non-efficiency [11]. These results have been recently improved (the borderline between tractability and intractability was found between the length of rules 2 and 3) and more results of this kind have been presented in the Brainstorming Week on Membrane Computing, Seville, 2012.

In this paper we impose an upper bound on the power of tissue P systems with cell separation. Specifically, we show that tissue systems with cell separation can be simulated with Turing machine in polynomial space. As a consequence, the class of problems solvable by uniform families of these systems in polynomial time is limited from above by the class PSPACE, which characterizes the power of many classical models of parallel computing machines as PRAM or alternating Turing machine, relating thus classical and bio-inspired parallel computing devices. The rest of the paper is organized as follows: after introducing preliminary notation, definitions of tissue P systems with cell separation are given. Next, recognizer tissue P systems and computational complexity classes in this framework are described. In Section 3 we demonstrate that any such tissue P system can be simulated with a classical computer (and, hence, also with Turing machine) in a polynomial space. A short discussion concludes the paper.

2   Tissue P Systems with Cell Separation

A *multiset m* over an underlying set A is a pair (A, f) where $f : A \to \mathbb{N}$ is a mapping. If $m = (A, f)$ is a multiset then its *support* is defined as $supp(m) = \{x \in$

$A \mid f(x) > 0\}$. The total number of elements in a multiset, including repeated memberships, is the *cardinality* of the multiset. A multiset is empty (resp. finite) if its support is the empty set (resp. a finite set). If $m = (A, f)$ is a finite multiset over A, and $supp(m) = \{a_1, \ldots, a_k\}$ then it can also be represented by the string $a_1^{f(a_1)} \ldots a_k^{f(a_k)}$ over the alphabet $\{a_1, \ldots, a_k\}$. Nevertheless, all permutations of this string precisely identify the same multiset m. Throughout this paper, we speak about "the finite multiset m" where m is a string, and meaning "the finite multiset represented by the string m".

If $m_1 = (A, f_1)$, $m_2 = (A, f_2)$ are multisets over A, then we define the union of m_1 and m_2 as $m_1 + m_2 = (A, g)$, where $g = f_1 + f_2$.

For any sets A and B the *relative complement* $A \setminus B$ of B in A is defined as follows:

$$A \setminus B = \{x \in A \mid x \notin B\}$$

In what follows, we assume the reader is already familiar with the basic notions and the terminology of P systems. For details, see [12], for actual information please visit [18].

2.1 Basic Definition

The model is inspired by the cell-like model of P systems with membranes separation [10]. The biological inspiration is the following: alive tissues are not static network of cells but new cells are produced by membrane separation in a natural way. In this model, the cells are not polarized; the two cells obtained by separation have the same labels as the original cell, and if a cell is separated, its interaction with other cells or with the environment is blocked during the separation process.

Definition 1 ([11]). *A tissue P system with cell separation of degree $q \geq 1$ is a tuple*

$$\Pi = (\Gamma, \Gamma_1, \Gamma_2, \mathcal{E}, \mathcal{M}_1, \ldots, \mathcal{M}_q, \mathcal{R}, i_{out}),$$

where:

1. *Γ is a finite alphabet whose elements are called* objects;
2. *$\{\Gamma_1, \Gamma_2\}$ is a partition of Γ, that is, $\Gamma = \Gamma_1 \cup \Gamma_2$, $\Gamma_1, \Gamma_2 \neq \emptyset$, $\Gamma_1 \cap \Gamma_2 = \emptyset$;*
3. *$\mathcal{E} \subseteq \Gamma$ is a finite alphabet representing the set of objects initially in the environment of the system, and 0 is the label of the environment (the environment is not properly a cell of the system); let us assume that objects in the environment appear in arbitrary copies each;*
4. *$\mathcal{M}_1, \ldots, \mathcal{M}_q$ are strings over Γ, representing the finite multisets of objects placed in the q cells of the system at the beginning of the computation; $1, 2, \cdots, q$ are labels which identify the cells of the system;*
5. *$\mathcal{R}$ is a finite set of rules of the following forms:*
   (a) *Communication rules: $(i, u/v, j)$, for $i, j \in \{0, 1, 2, \ldots, q\}, i \neq j$, $u, v \in \Gamma^*$, $|uv| > 0$;*

    (b) Separation rules: $[a]_i \rightarrow [\Gamma_1]_i[\Gamma_2]_i$, where $i \in \{1, 2, \ldots, q\}$ and $a \in \Gamma$, and $i \neq i_{out}$. In reaction with an object a, the cell i is separated into two cells with the same label; at the same time, object a is consumed; the objects from Γ_1 are placed in the first cell, those from Γ_2 are placed in the second cell; the output cell i_{out} cannot be separated;

6. $i_{out} \in \{0, 1, 2, \ldots, q\}$ is the output cell.

A communication rule $(i, u/v, j)$ is called a *symport rule* if $u = \lambda$ or $v = \lambda$. A symport rule $(i, u/\lambda, j)$, with $i \neq 0, j \neq 0$, provides a virtual arc from cell i to cell j. A communication rule $(i, u/v, j)$ is called an *antiport rule* if $u \neq \lambda$ and $v \neq \lambda$. An antiport rule $(i, u/v, j)$ provides two arcs: one from cell i to cell j and another one from cell j to cell i. Thus, every tissue P systems has an underlying directed graph whose nodes are the cells of the system and the arcs are obtained from communication rules. In this context, the environment can be considered as a virtual node of the graph such that their connections are defined by antiport rules of the form $(i, u/v, j)$, with $i = 0$ or $j = 0$. The length of the communication rule $(i, u/v, j)$ is defined as $|u| + |v|$.

The object a triggers rule $[a]_i \rightarrow [\Gamma_1]_i [\Gamma_2]_i$ and it is consumed. Nevertheless, this rule does not produce any new object in new cells. The remaining objects in cell i are distributed between the new cells, according to sets Γ_1 and Γ_2. If there are n objects in the cell i where the rule is applied, the total number of objects in the cells created is $n - 1$. If the rules are consecutively applied during k transition steps in a cell i which contains n objects 2^k new cells are created, and the total number of objects is $n - k$.

The rules of a system like the above one are used in the non-deterministic maximally parallel manner as customary in Membrane Computing. At each step, all cells which can evolve must evolve in a maximally parallel way (at each step we apply a multiset of rules which is maximal, no further rule can be added being applicable). There is one important restriction: when a cell is separated, the separation rule is the only one which is applied for that cell at that step; thus, the objects inside that cell do not evolve by means of communication rules. The label of a cell precisely identify the rules which can be applied to it.

A *configuration* of a tissue P system with cell separation at any instant is described by all multisets of objects over Γ associated with all the cells present in the system, and the multiset of objects over $\Gamma - \mathcal{E}$ associated with the environment at that moment. Bearing in mind the objects from $\mathcal{E}$ have infinite copies in the environment, they are not properly changed along the computation. The *initial configuration* is $(\mathcal{M}_1, \cdots, \mathcal{M}_q; \emptyset)$. A configuration is a *halting configuration* if no rule of the system is applicable to it.

We say that configuration C_1 yields configuration C_2 in one *transition step*, denoted $C_1 \Rightarrow_\Pi C_2$, if we can pass from C_1 to C_2 by applying the rules from $\mathcal{R}$ as specified above. A *computation* of Π is a (finite or infinite) sequence of configurations such that:

1. the first term of the sequence is the initial configuration of the system;
2. each non-initial configuration of the sequence is obtained from the previous configuration by applying rules of the system in a maximally parallel manner with the restrictions previously mentioned; and
3. if the sequence is finite (called *halting computation*) then the last term of the sequence is a halting configuration.

Halting computations give a result which is encoded by the objects present in the output cell i_{out} in the halting configuration.

2.2 Recognizer Tissue P Systems with Cell Separation

Let us denote a *decision problem* as a pair (I_X, θ_X) where I_X is a language over a finite alphabet (whose elements are called *instances*) and θ_X is a total boolean function over I_X. A natural correspondence between decision problems and languages over a finite alphabet can be established as follows. Given a decision problem $X = (I_X, \theta_X)$, its associated language is $L_X = \{w \in I_X : \theta_X(w) = 1\}$. Conversely, given a language L over an alphabet Σ, its associated decision problem is $X_L = (I_{X_L}, \theta_{X_L})$, where $I_{X_L} = \Sigma^*$, and $\theta_{X_L} = \{(x, 1) : x \in L\} \cup \{(x, 0) : x \notin L\}$. The solvability of decision problems is defined through the recognition of the languages associated with them, by using languages recognizer devices.

In order to study the computational efficiency of membrane systems, the notions from classical *computational complexity theory* are adapted for Membrane Computing, and a special class of cell-like P systems is introduced in [13]: *recognizer P systems*. For tissue P systems, with the same idea as recognizer cell-like P systems, *recognizer tissue P systems* is introduced in [15].

Definition 2 ([11]). *A recognizer tissue P system with cell separation of degree $q \geq 1$ is a tuple*

$$\Pi = (\Gamma, \Gamma_1, \Gamma_2, \Sigma, \mathcal{E}, \mathcal{M}_1, \ldots, \mathcal{M}_q, \mathcal{R}, i_{in}, i_{out})$$

where:

1. *$(\Gamma, \Gamma_1, \Gamma_2, \mathcal{E}, \mathcal{M}_1, \ldots, \mathcal{M}_q, \mathcal{R}, i_{out})$ is a tissue P system with cell separation of degree $q \geq 1$ (as defined in the previous section).*
2. *The working alphabet Γ has two distinguished objects* **yes** *and* **no** *being, at least, one copy of them present in some initial multisets $\mathcal{M}_1, \ldots, \mathcal{M}_q$, but none of them are present in $\mathcal{E}$.*
3. *Σ is an (input) alphabet strictly contained in Γ, and $\mathcal{E} \subseteq \Gamma \setminus \Sigma$.*
4. *$\mathcal{M}_1, \ldots, \mathcal{M}_q$ are strings over $\Gamma \setminus \Sigma$;*
5. *$i_{in} \in \{1, \ldots, q\}$ is the input cell.*
6. *The output region i_{out} is the environment.*
7. *All computations halt.*
8. *If $\mathcal{C}$ is a computation of Π, then either object* **yes** *or object* **no** *(but not both) must have been released into the environment, and only at the last step of the computation.*

For each $w \in \Sigma^*$, the *computation of the system Π with input* $w \in \Sigma^*$ starts from the configuration of the form $(\mathcal{M}_1, \mathcal{M}_2, \ldots, \mathcal{M}_{i_{in}} + w, \ldots, \mathcal{M}_q; \emptyset)$, that is, the input multiset w has been added to the contents of the input cell i_{in}. Therefore, we have an initial configuration associated with each input multiset w (over the input alphabet Σ) in this kind of systems.

Given a recognizer tissue P system with cell separation, we say that a computation $\mathcal{C}$ is an *accepting computation* (respectively, *rejecting computation*) if object **yes** (respectively, object **no**) appears in the environment associated with the corresponding halting configuration of $\mathcal{C}$, and neither object **yes** nor **no** appears in the environment associated with any non-halting configuration of $\mathcal{C}$.

For each natural number $k \geq 1$, we denote by $\mathbf{TSC}(k)$ the class of recognizer tissue P systems with cell separation and communication rules of length at most k. We denote by $\mathbf{TSC}$ the class of recognizer tissue P systems with cell separation and without restriction on the length of communication rules. Obviously, $\mathbf{TSC}(k) \subseteq \mathbf{TSC}$ for all $k \geq 1$.

2.3   Polynomial Complexity Classes of Tissue P Systems

Next, we define what means solving a decision problem in the framework of tissue P systems efficiently and in a uniform way. Bearing in mind that they provide devices with a finite description, a numerable family of tissue P systems will be necessary in order to solve a decision problem.

Definition 3 ([11]). *We say that a decision problem $X = (I_X, \theta_X)$ is solvable in a uniform way and polynomial time by a family $\mathbf{\Pi} = \{\Pi(n) \mid n \in \mathbb{N}\}$ of recognizer tissue P systems (with cell separation) if the following holds:*

1. *The family $\mathbf{\Pi}$ is polynomially uniform by Turing machines, that is, there exists a deterministic Turing machine working in polynomial time which constructs the system $\Pi(n)$ from $n \in \mathbb{N}$.*
2. *There exists a pair (cod, s) of polynomial-time computable functions over I_X such that:*
   (a) *for each instance $u \in I_X$, $s(u)$ is a natural number and $cod(u)$ is an input multiset of the system $\Pi(s(u))$;*
   (b) *for each $n \in \mathbb{N}$, $s^{-1}(n)$ is a finite set;*
   (c) *the family $\mathbf{\Pi}$ is polynomially bounded with regard to (X, cod, s), that is, there exists a polynomial function p, such that for each $u \in I_X$ every computation of $\Pi(s(u))$ with input $cod(u)$ is halting and it performs at most $p(|u|)$ steps;*
   (d) *the family $\mathbf{\Pi}$ is sound with regard to (X, cod, s), that is, for each $u \in I_X$, if there exists an accepting computation of $\Pi(s(u))$ with input $cod(u)$, then $\theta_X(u) = 1$;*
   (e) *the family $\mathbf{\Pi}$ is complete with regard to (X, cod, s), that is, for each $u \in I_X$, if $\theta_X(u) = 1$, then every computation of $\Pi(s(u))$ with input $cod(u)$ is an accepting one.*

From the soundness and completeness conditions above we deduce that every P system $\Pi(n)$ is *confluent*, in the following sense: every computation of a system with the *same* input multiset must always give the *same* answer.

Let **R** be a class of recognizer tissue P systems. We denote by $\mathbf{PMC_R}$ the set of all decision problems which can be solved in a uniform way and polynomial time by means of families of systems from **R**.

Theorem 4 ([5]). $\mathbf{P} = \mathbf{PMC}_{TSC(1)}$.

Theorem 5 ([11]). $\mathbf{NP} \cup \mathbf{co} - \mathbf{NP} \subseteq \mathbf{PMC}_{TSC(8)}$.

3 Simulation of Tissue P Systems with Cell Separation in Polynomial Space

In this section we demonstrate that any computation of a recognizer tissue P system with cell separation can be simulated in space polynomial to its initial size and the number of steps. Instead of simulating a computation of a P system from its initial configuration onwards (which would require exponential space for storing configurations), we create a recursive function which computes content of any cell h after a given number of steps. The recursive calls evaluate contents of the cells interacting with h in a reverse time order (towards the initial configuration). Thus we do not need to store content of any cell but we calculate it recursively whenever needed.

Simulated P systems are confluent, hence possibly nondeterministic, but the simulation will be performed in a deterministic way: only one possible sequence of configurations of the P system is traced. This corresponds to a weak priority relation between rules:

(i) separation rules are always applied prior to communication rules,
(ii) priority between communication rules given by the order in which they are listed,
(iii) priority between cells to which the rules are applied.

However, the confluency condition ensures that such a simulation is correct as all computations starting from the same initial configuration must lead to the same result.

Each cell of Π is assigned a unique label in the initial configuration. But cells may be separated during computation of Π, producing thus more membranes with the same label. To identify membranes uniquely, we add to each label a *compound index*. Each index is an empty string in the initial configuration. If a membrane is not separated in a computational step, digit 1 is attached to its index. If a separation rule is applied, the first resulting membrane has attached 1 and the second membrane 2 to its index. Hence, index of each membrane is an n-tuple of digits from $\{1, 2\}$ after n steps of computation. Notice that some n-tuples may denote non-existing membranes as membranes need not separate at each step. The situation is illustrated in Fig. 1: membrane h is separated at

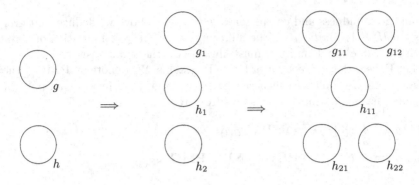

Fig. 1. An example of indexing of cells during first two computational steps

first step, membranes g_1 and h_2 are separated at second step. Membrane h_{12} does not exist, for instance.

Consider a confluent recognizer tissue P system with cell separation of degree $q \geq 1$, described formally as

$$\Pi = (\Gamma, \Gamma_1, \Gamma_2, \Sigma, \mathcal{E}, \mathcal{M}_1, \dots, \mathcal{M}_q, \mathcal{R}, i_{in}, i_{out}).$$

For any cell of Π we denote the multiset of objects contained in it at any instant simply as its *content*. We construct function **Content** which computes recursively the content of any cell h (with a particular compound index) of Π after $n \geq 0$ steps of computation. The function is described in an informal way but it could be processed by a Turing machine working in (asymptotically) the same space. Its basic scheme is:

1. verify whether the ancestor of cell h existed at previous computational step; if not, the cell does not exist;
2. for all rules in a fixed order: for all copies of cells affected by that rule:
   (a) subsequently and recursively calculate contents of these cells in previous step;
   (b) calculate the number of applications of the rule in the maximally parallel way;
   (c) if one of the affected cells is h, record the multiset of rules applied to it;
3. Re-calculate content of cell h in previous step of computation and apply the recorded rules to obtain new content of the cell.

When applying a rule to a particular cell in phase 2, one must start with the multiset of objects remaining in that cell after rules already applied in the same step n. Fortunately enough, it is not necessary to store contents of all cells or all multisets of rules applied to each cell in step n. Recall that the order of application of rules in $\mathcal{R}$ is fixed and so is the order of cells to which these rules are applied in a maximally parallel way. Then the multiset of rules already applied to a particular cell in step n can be always re-calculated when the cell is affected by another rule in the same step. The only value which must be stored is the total multiset of rules already applied in step n. Assume for simplicity that an input multiset of objects w is already included in the initial multiset $\mathcal{M}_{i_{in}}$.

function content

Parameters: $\ell \in \{1, \ldots, q\}$ – label of a cell
        $i_1 i_2 \ldots i_n$ – a compound index
        n – a number of step

Returns: the content of cell labeled ℓ with compound index $i_1 i_2 \ldots i_n$
        after n steps of computation, or null if such a cell does not exist.

Auxiliary variables:
`rulesAppliedTo`ℓ`, rulesAppliedTotal, rulesForCell1, rulesForCell2;`
(Multisets of applicable or applied rules with underlying set $\mathcal{R}$)

`contentCell1, contentCell2, contentFinal;`
(Multisets storing contents of cells)

if $n = 0$ then return $\mathcal{M}_\ell$; *(return the initial multiset of cell ℓ)*
`set multiplicity of all elements in rulesAppliedTotal to 0;`
`set multiplicity of all elements in rulesAppliedTo`ℓ` to 0;`

`for each communication rule` $(j, u/v, k)$ `in` $\mathcal{R}$ `do begin`
  (Now we scan all existing copies of cells labeled j and k affected by the rule.)

  `rulesForCell1 := rulesAppliedTotal;`

  `for each possible compound index` $j_1 j_2 \ldots j_{n-1}$ `do begin`
    `contentCell1 = content(`j`,` $j_1 j_2 \ldots j_{n-1}$`,` $n-1$`);`
    (Calculate the content of cell j with index $j_1 j_2 \ldots j_{n-1}$ in previous step)

    `if (contentCell1 = null) or (cell can apply a separation rule)`
      `then skip the rest of the cycle;`

    `calculate the maximal multiset of rules in rulesForCell1`
      `applicable to cell` j `with objects contentCell1;`
    `remove these rules from multiset rulesForCell1;`
    `remove the corresponding objects from contentCell1;`

    `rulesForCell2 := rulesAppliedTotal;`

    `for each possible compound index` $k_1 k_2 \ldots k_{n-1}$ `do begin`
      `contentCell2 = content(`k`,` $k_1 k_2 \ldots k_{n-1}$`,` $n-1$`);`

(Calculate the content of cell k with index $k_1 k_2 \ldots k_{n-1}$ in previous step)

```
if contentCell2 = null or cell can apply a separation rule
   then skip the rest of the cycle;

calculate the maximal multiset of rules in rulesForCell2
   applicable to cell k with contentCell2;
remove these rules from multiset rulesForCell2;
remove the corresponding objects from contentCell2;
```

(Now contentCell1 and ContentCell2 contain objects remaining in cell j with index $j_1 j_2 \ldots j_{n-1}$ and in cell k with index $k_1 k_2 \ldots k_{n-1}$, respectively, after application of previously scanned rules in step n.)

```
let x = maximum copies of rule (j, u/v, k) applicable to cells
   j, k with contentCell1 and contentCell2, respectively;

remove x copies of u from contentCell1;
add x copies of rule (j, u/v, k) to rulesAppliedTotal;

if one of the cells j or k is identical with cell ℓ
   with index i₁i₂...iₙ₋₁ then
      add x occurrences of rule (j, u/v, k) to rulesAppliedToℓ;
```

```
   end cycle; (cell k with index k₁k₂...kₙ₋₁)
  end cycle; (cell j with index j₁j₂...jₙ₋₁)
end cycle; (rule (j, u/v, k))
```

(At this moment, variable **rulesAppliedToℓ** *contains the complete multiset of rules applied in step n to cell ℓ with indices $i_1 i_2 \ldots i_{n-1}$.)*

```
contentFinal = content(ℓ, i₁i₂...iₙ₋₁, n − 1);
```
(Calculate the content of cell ℓ with index $i_1 i_2 \ldots i_{n-1}$ in previous step)

```
if contentFinal = null then return null and exit;

if a separation rule [a]ℓ → [Γ₁]ℓ[Γ₂]ℓ exists such that
contentFinal contains a then
   if iₙ = 1 then
     remove a and all objects not in Γ₁ from contentFinal;
   else
     remove a and all objects not in Γ₂ from contentFinal;
```
(Cell ℓ with index $i_1 i_2 \ldots i_{n-1}$ separates in step n)

```
else
```

```
if i_n = 2 then
    return null and exit;
```
*(The last element i_n of compound index corresponds to a copy of cell ℓ
dividing in step n which is not the case, hence this copy does not exist.)*

```
else
    apply all rules in rulesAppliedToℓ to contentFinal, i.e.,
        add/remove multisets of objects corresponding to cell ℓ
        in rules to/from contentFinal;
```

```
return contentFinal;
```

We defined explicitly internal variables with largest memory demands in function
`content` in its preamble. Other variables are used implicitly. This is necessary
for the following result.

Theorem 6. *A result of any n steps long computation of a confluent tissue
P system with cell separation can be computed with Turing machine in space
polynomial to n.*

Proof. A result of any computation of a confluent tissue P system

$$\Pi = (\Gamma, \Gamma_1, \Gamma_2, \Sigma, \mathcal{E}, \mathcal{M}_1, \ldots, \mathcal{M}_q, \mathcal{R}, i_{in}, i_{out})$$

with cell separation can be calculated with the aid of function `content` described
above. Observe that while this function evaluates the content of a particular cell
after n steps, an application of all possible rules during n-th step in all cells is
also simulated. Hence, it is very easy to check whether any rule is applied or, on
the contrary, whether the computation stops (the multiset `rulesAppliedTotal`
is empty). The result of computation of Π with an input w is obtained as follows:

1. Prepare the initial configuration of Π, add w to $\mathcal{M}_{i_{in}}$.
2. Subsequently compute `content`$(i_{out}, 11\ldots1, n)$ for $n = 0, 1, 2, \ldots$ until no
   rule is applicable. Note that the output membrane never separates and hence
   its index contains only 1's. Record in each step the presence of objects **yes**
   or **no**.
3. If one of objects **yes** or **no** appeared in the output membrane and only in
   the last step, return the result of computation.

Space complexity of the function `content`$(\ell, index, n)$ is determined by variables
storing multisets of objects and applicable rules. The first type represents a
multiset of objects contained in a particular cell. Its cardinality is limited from
above by the total number of objects in the system after n steps. Denote this
number by o_n. Therefore,

$$o_0 = \sum_{i=1}^{q} card(\mathcal{M}_i) + |w|. \tag{1}$$

At each step each cell can separate (which does not increase the number of its objects) or it can introduce new object to the system from the environment via antiport rules. Denote $\mathcal{R}_a$ the set of antiport rules in $\mathcal{R}$. Hence, we can write that $o_n \leq c o_{n-1}$ for $n \geq 1$ and a constant c, where

$$c = \max\{ \max_{(i,u/v,j) \in \mathcal{R}_a} \{|u|/|v|\}, \max_{(i,u/v,j) \in \mathcal{R}_a} \{|v|/|u|\}\}. \tag{2}$$

After n step we have

$$o_n \leq o_0 c^n \tag{3}$$

which is a value representable by dn bits for a constant

$$d \leq \log o_0 + \log c. \tag{4}$$

Finally, $|\Gamma| dn$ bits are necessary to describe any multiset with cardinality dn and with the underlying set Γ. This is also the maximum size of any variable of this type.

The situation is similar for multisets of applicable rules. The cardinality of each such multiset at n-th computational step is limited by the number o_n of objects in the system. Hence the size of each such variable is at most $|\mathcal{R}| dn$.

Finally, let us analyze the space complexity of function **content** and auxiliary functions it uses. None of these auxiliary functions creates large variables nor performs recursive calls. Function **content** with parameter n performs recursive calls of itself with parameter $n - 1$. It uses three variables storing multisets of objects and four variables with multisets of rules. For its space complexity $C(n)$ we can therefore write:

$$C(0) = \log o_0 \tag{5}$$
$$C(n) \leq C(n - 1) + 3|\Gamma| dn + 4|\mathcal{R}| dn, \qquad n \geq 1. \tag{6}$$

The solution to this recurrence is

$$C(n) = \mathcal{O}((|\Gamma| + |\mathcal{R}|) dn^2 + \log o_0). \tag{7}$$

Hence, with the aid of the function **content** described above, a conventional computer can simulate n steps of computation of the systems Π in space polynomial to n, and as the space necessary for Turing machine performing the same computation is asymptotically the same, the statement follows.   □

If we defined a descriptional complexity (i.e., a size of description) of any tissue P system with cell separation, Theorem 6 could be rephrased as follows: any computation of such a P systems can be simulated in space polynomial to the size of description of that P system and to the number of steps of its computation.

Theorem 7. $\mathbf{PMC}_{TSC} \subseteq \mathbf{PSPACE}$

Proof. Consider a family $\mathbf{\Pi} = \{\Pi(n) \mid n \in \mathbb{N}\}$ of recognizer tissue P systems with cell separation satisfying conditions of Definition 3, which solves in a uniform way and polynomial time a decision problem $X = (I_X, \theta_X)$. For each instance $u \in I_X$, denote

$$\Pi(s(u)) = (\Gamma, \Gamma_1, \Gamma_2, \Sigma, \mathcal{E}, \mathcal{M}_1, \ldots, \mathcal{M}_q, \mathcal{R}, i_{in}, i_{out})$$

and let $w = cod(u)$ be the corresponding input multiset. By Definition 3, paragraphs 1 and 2(a), the values of $card(w)$, $card(\mathcal{M}_1), \ldots, card(\mathcal{M}_q)$, and lengths of rules in $\mathcal{R}$ are exponential with respect to $|u|$ (they must be constructed by a deterministic Turing machine in polynomial time). Furthermore, values of $|\Gamma|$ and $|\mathcal{R}|$ are polynomial to $|u|$. (Actually, the alphabet Γ could possibly have exponentially many elements but only polynomially many of them can appear in the system $\Pi(s(u))$ during its computation and the rest can be ignored.).

By Definition 3, paragraph 2(c), also the number of steps n of any computation of system $\Pi(s(u))$ is polynomial to $|u|$. Then by (1)–(4) the value of d is polynomial to $|u|$ and, by (7), so is the space complexity of function content. Therefore, each instance $u \in I_X$ can be solved with a Turing machine in space polynomial to $|u|$. $\square$

4 Discussion

We have dealt with a bio-inspired computational model – tissue P system with cell separation. A sequence of research papers appeared recently, demonstrating interesting properties of the model and, besides its biological background, relating it to some classical topic in computer science, e.g., the **P** and **NP** separation problem. In this paper we have imposed an upper bound on the information-processing power of tissue P systems with cell separation. Particularly, we have shown that the class of problems solvable by the se systems "reasonably" (i.e., in a uniform way and polynomial time by means of families of tissue P systems with cell separation) lies between **NP** $\cup$ **co** − **NP** and **PSPACE**. The P systems used in the proof need not be deterministic but must be confluent, i.e., all computations from a fixed initial configuration must produce the same result. It remains as a research topic to investigate the power of non-confluent (hence non-deterministic) tissue P systems with cell separation. The presented proof cannot be simply adapted to this case by using a non-deterministic Turing (or other) machine for simulation. Observe that in our recursive algorithm the same configuration of a P system is typically re-calculated many times during one simulation run. If the simulation was non-deterministic, we could obtain different results for the same configuration which would make the simulation non-consistent.

The presented result is related to some previously or recently achieved ones dealing with other models of membrane systems. We mention two of them: firstly, it is shown in [17] that the class of problems solvable by uniform families of P systems with active membranes in polynomial time coincides with **PSPACE**. The principles of the proof in [17] are similar to those used here but there are significant differences. On the one hand, P systems with active membranes use many types of rules, including membrane dissolution rules, which makes their simulation more complex. On the other hand, their communication graph forms always an acyclic tree, hence it is rather straightforward to order and simulate sequentially their cell-to-cell interactions. In tissue P systems the interaction graphs are arbitrary with possible cycles and this complicates the simulation as the record of all interactions in one simulation step requires an exponential space. We solved the problem here by (a) scanning first rules and then cells to which the rules are applied, both in a fixed order, and (b) by observing that the content of a particular cell after application of certain subset of rules can be also re-calculated recursively.

Secondly, the conference paper [16] presents a result closely related to the one given here: also the computational power of another variant of tissue P systems with operation of cell division is limited by **PSPACE**.

Acknowledgements. This work was supported by the European Regional Development Fund in the IT4Innovations Centre of Excellence project (CZ.1.05/1.1.00/02.0070), by the Silesian University in Opava under the Student Funding Scheme, project no SGS/7/2011, and by the Ministerio de Ciencia e Innovación (MICINN), Spain, under project Tin2009-14421.

References

1. Alhazov, A., Martín-Vide, C., Pan, L.: Solving a PSPACE-complete problem by P systems with restricted active membranes. Fundamenta Informaticae 58(2), 67–77 (2003)
2. Alhazov, A., Freund, R., Oswald, M.: Tissue P Systems with Antiport Rules and Small Numbers of Symbols and Cells. In: De Felice, C., Restivo, A. (eds.) DLT 2005. LNCS, vol. 3572, pp. 100–111. Springer, Heidelberg (2005)
3. Bernardini, F., Gheorghe, M.: Cell communication in tissue P systems and cell division in population P systems. Soft Computing 9(9), 640–649 (2005)
4. Freund, R., Păun, G., Pérez-Jiménez, M.: Tissue P systems with channel states. Theoretical Computer Science 330, 101–116 (2005)
5. Gutiérrez–Escudero, R., Pérez–Jiménez, M.J., Rius–Font, M.: Characterizing Tractability by Tissue-Like P Systems. In: Păun, G., Pérez-Jiménez, M.J., Riscos-Núñez, A., Rozenberg, G., Salomaa, A. (eds.) WMC 2009. LNCS, vol. 5957, pp. 289–300. Springer, Heidelberg (2010)
6. Krishna, S., Lakshmanan, K., Rama, R.: Tissue P Systems with Contextual and Rewriting Rules. In: Păun, G., Rozenberg, G., Salomaa, A., Zandron, C. (eds.) WMC 2002. LNCS, vol. 2597, pp. 339–351. Springer, Heidelberg (2003)
7. Lakshmanan, K., Rama, R.: The computational efficiency of insertion deletion tissue P systems. In: Subramanian, K., Rangarajan, K., Mukund, M. (eds.) Formal Models, Languages and Applications, pp. 235–245. World Scientific (2006)
8. Martín-Vide, C., Pazos, J., Păun, G., Rodríguez-Patón, A.: A New Class of Symbolic Abstract Neural Nets: Tissue P Systems. In: Ibarra, O.H., Zhang, L. (eds.) COCOON 2002. LNCS, vol. 2387, pp. 290–299. Springer, Heidelberg (2002)
9. Martín Vide, C., Pazos, J., Păun, G., Rodríguez Patón, A.: Tissue P systems. Theoretical Computer Science 296, 295–326 (2003)

10. Pan, L., Ishdorj, T.O.: P systems with active membranes and separation rules. Journal of Universal Computer Science 10(5), 630–649 (2004)
11. Pan, L., Pérez-Jiménez, M.: Computational complexity of tissue–like P systems. Journal of Complexity 26(3), 296–315 (2010)
12. Păun, G., Rozenberg, G., Salomaa, A. (eds.): The Oxford Handbook of Membrane Computing. Oxford University Press, Oxford (2010)
13. Pérez-Jiménez, M., Romero-Jiménez, A., Sancho-Caparrini, F.: A polynomial complexity class in P systems using membrane division. Journal of Automata, Languages and Combinatorics 11(4), 423–434 (2006)
14. Păun, A., Păun, G.: The power of communication: P systems with symport/antiport. New Generation Comput. 20(3), 295–306 (2002)
15. Păun, G., Pérez-Jiménez, M., Riscos-Núñez, A.: Tissue P systems with cell division. Int. J. of Computers, Communications and Control 3(3), 295–303 (2008)
16. Sosík, P.: Limits of the power of tissue P systems with cell division. In: Proceedings of the Thirteenth International Conference on Membrane Computing (to appear, 2012)
17. Sosík, P., Rodríguez-Patón, A.: Membrane computing and complexity theory: A characterization of PSPACE. J. Comput. System Sci. 73(1), 137–152 (2007)
18. The P Systems Web Page, http://ppage.psystems.eu/ (cit. May 29, 2012)

Maze Exploration with Molecular-Scale Walkers

Darko Stefanovic[1,2]

[1] Department of Computer Science, University of New Mexico
[2] Center for Biomedical Engineering, University of New Mexico
Albuquerque, NM 87131, USA

Abstract. Molecular spiders are nanoscale walkers made with catalytic DNA legs attached to a rigid body. They move in a matrix of DNA substrates, cleaving them and leaving behind product DNA strands. Unlike a self-avoiding walker, a spider is able to revisit the products. However, the legs cleave and detach from substrates more slowly than they detach from products. This difference in residence time and the presence of multiple legs make a spider move differently from an ordinary random walker. The number of legs, and their lengths, can be varied, and this defines the spider's local gait, which affects its behavior in global tasks. In this work we define an abstract model of molecular spiders, and within it we study the efficiency of maze exploration as a function of the spider structure. For a fixed geometry, there is an optimal setting of chemical kinetics parameters that minimizes the mean time to traverse a maze.

Keywords: molecular walkers, maze search, DNA computing.

1 Introduction

The tasks of spatial search and exploration are among the hallmarks of intelligent behavior. Among such tasks, exploring mazes or labyrinths has a glorious history, from the myth of Theseus to the recent maze explorations by physarum [1] and fungi [2]. But, is it possible for even simpler, not quite living agents, also to explore mazes?

The agents we will use are synthetic nanoscale walkers called molecular spiders [3, 4], which move using a mechanism of multivalent chemical interactions of their multiple legs with the environment (Section 2), in which the legs catalytically convert substrates to products, thereby extracting chemical energy from the environment. Molecular spiders may find use in biomedical applications, such as searching for clinically relevant targets on the surface of a cell; exploring mazes is an abstraction of such walks in unknown environments with obstacles. Ahead of constructing mazes in the laboratory, here we present simulation-based results on the speed of maze exploration by molecular spiders. Spiders and their targets are simulated on a two-dimensional grid of chemical sites (Section 3), corresponding to the DNA origami [5, 6] on which our mazes will be self-assembled.

Previous studies have shown that, at a sufficiently high level of abstraction, the main kinetic parameter governing the walking behavior of a molecular spider is the ratio r between the residence time of a spider's leg on a previously visited site (i.e., a spent product) and the residence time on a new site (i.e., a fresh substrate) [7–10]. When $r = 1$,

A.-H. Dediu, C. Martín-Vide, and B. Truthe (Eds.): TPNC 2012, LNCS 7505, pp. 216–226, 2012.

ordinary diffusion ensues; when $r < 1$, the motion exhibits an increasingly strong superdiffusive transient as r decreases. Here we find that the chemical kinetics influences the efficiency of maze exploration as well. The dependence is strong: for two-legged walkers in our test maze, a clear optimum r value emerges at around 1:100 product-to-substrate residence time ratio (Section 4). This behavior is a consequence of the interplay between the multivalency and the kinetic bias (Section 5): if catalysis is absent ($r = 1$), two-legged walkers are slower than one-legged spiders (ordinary random walkers); with catalysis, one-legged spiders are only ever slowed down by the longer residence time on substrates, whereas two-legged spiders are faster for a range of values $r < 1$ thanks to the emergent bias towards substrates [8, 9]. This bias may be useful in a maze: a spider emerging for the first time from a dead end faces a T-junction, at which it will be biased towards the unexplored path rather than the path whence it originally came.

2 Molecular Spiders

Translational molecular motors, made of proteins, are nature's solution to the problem of efficient molecular cargo transport across the large diameter of a cell. They walk directionally along self-assembled, directional filaments and microtubules [11–17]. Recent advances in single-molecule chemistry have led to the development of *synthetic* molecular motors [18, 19], including molecular assemblies that walk over surfaces, following fabricated or self-assembled tracks [4, 20–27]. Among them are *molecular spiders*, autonomous synthetic molecular motors based on catalytic DNA [3, 4].

Fig. 1. Molecular spider walking across a substrate-laden surface: "blue" substrates are transformed into "red" products

A molecular spider has a rigid inert body and several flexible enzymatic legs (Figure 1). We have made spiders with up to six legs, using a streptavidin or streptavidin dimer scaffold for the body [3]. Each leg is a deoxyribozyme—an enzymatic sequence of single-stranded DNA that can bind to and cleave a complementary strand of a DNA substrate [28]. The hip joint between the body and a leg is a flexible biotin linkage. When a molecular spider is placed on a surface coated with the single-stranded DNA substrate, its legs bind to the substrate. A bound leg can either detach from the substrate without modifying it, or it can catalyze the cleavage of the substrate, creating two product strands. Upon cleavage the two product strands eventually dissociate from the enzyme leg. The lower product remains bound to the surface. Because the lower product is complementary to the lower part of the spider's leg, there is a residual binding of the leg to the product, i.e., it is possible for a spider's legs to visit products; however, this binding is typically much weaker than the leg-substrate binding and thus much shorter-lived.

The small scale of the spiders makes their direct observation difficult and necessitates detailed modelling work, which several groups have undertaken through mathematical analysis and computer-based simulations [7–10, 29–31]. The motion of a spiders can be described as a special type of random walk. Their asymptotic behavior is diffusive, just as with ordinary random walkers. Surprisingly, however, superdiffusive behavior is observed in the transient, and it lasts for significant amounts of time, over which a spider covers significant distances. This has profound implications for practical applications, including for maze exploration. We showed [9] that the residence-time bias between substrates and products causes this behavior through a micromechanism of the spider's switching between two states—being on the boundary of the area of fresh substrates, and being in the area of already cleaved products. A spider on the boundary extracts chemical energy from the landscape, moves preferentially towards fresh substrates, and thus carries the boundary along. A spider that has left the boundary and stepped back into the products simply diffuses. Eventually this behavior dominates.

By varying the spiders' geometry and chemical characteristics, we can optimize how they walk. The next question is what they can do—for instance, they may transport molecular cargo, search and capture targets, or follow predesigned tracks. Here we look at spiders following complex branching tracks, i.e., mazes. We describe models of future experiments in which spiders released at one end of a maze (self-assembled using DNA origami techniques) race to the goal at the opposite end. We are interested in the end-to-end time. Alternatively, we could ask how much time it takes to explore the entire maze—we defer this question to future work.

3   Abstract Model of Molecular Spider Motion for Maze Exploration

Spider Motion. In our model, a k-legged spider walks on a square lattice of chemical sites. At all times, all legs are attached to sites, i.e., the reattachment process is complete and infinitely fast—this is expedient, but a gross simplification that ignores the kinetics of reattachment, which we treat elsewhere [10]. No more than one leg can be attached to a site at a time (complete exclusion). A leg detaches from a site according to a Poisson process, i.e., according to first-order chemical kinetics that describe the dissociation of the leg DNA strand and the product DNA strand. For a leg visiting a substrate, we also fold the kinetics of catalysis into a single detachment rate. Thus, a leg detaches at rate 1 from a product, and at rate r from a substrate. When a leg detaches from a substrate, that substrate is transformed into a product. Once detached, the leg immediately attaches to another site. The new site is chosen at random from among a set of feasible locations, and all of those are taken as equally probable.

Fig. 2. The maze used for the exploration task. Black walls are areas on the DNA origami tile without exposed single-stranded DNA, and assumed inaccessible to the spider. Each blue dot is a chemical site, initially a substrate. The spider starts in the top right corner with its two legs at the two purple sites. Its goal is the bottom left corner, where it can be trapped by uncleavable substrates, shown in green. The shortest path to the goal is of length 197 maze tiles, or 591 inter-substrate spaces.

The model admits a variety of options for the set of feasible new locations. When a physical spider's leg moves, it remains attached to the body, and while the body can move, it can only do so within the constraints imposed by the remaining legs, still attached to the surface. This can be expressed in the model as a constraint that the new locations must be within a certain distance S from each remaining leg's position. Furthermore, either the kinetics of binding to a new site or the diffusion needed to reach it can be the limiting factor for reattachment, and to express the latter case the model can restrict the feasible new sites to be within a certain distance R from the old site (the site from which the leg detached). A physical spider's leg can always reattach to the site it just left, but in a model such unproductive steps can be ruled out to expedite simulations. In this paper we take $k = 2$, $S = 2$, and $R = 1$, measuring distances using the Euclidean metric. In other words, we consider two-legged spiders with nearest-neighbor hopping.

Maze Exploration. Onto a grid of chemical substrates we superimpose a maze grid with a pitch of three, i.e., the tracks in the maze are three substrates wide, and the walls of the maze are also three sites wide, but empty. We generate random, tile-based (with walls of finite thickness), perfect (loop-free) mazes. All results below pertain to one particular randomly generated maze, shown in Figure 2. The size of this maze is chosen to correspond to realistic mazes we can build in the future. We will use the new generation of DNA origami,[1] which can measure 200 nm by 300 nm. With three-substrate-wide walking tracks and walls, the maze grid can be 21 by 31, large enough for non-trivial mazes.

4 Simulation Results

Together the spider state and the state of the entire surface represent the state of the continuous-time Markov process for our model. We use the Kinetic Monte Carlo method (see [32]) to simulate multiple trajectories of this Markov process. The simulation stops when the spider is trapped at the goal, and we record the simulated time as an observation of a first-passage-time random variable, viz., the time it took the spider to cross the maze from the start corner to the goal corner. The results below will show the mean first passage time, as well as the probability distribution of first passage times, estimated from our traces.

The space of possible spider configurations is large. Here we only use the canonical two-legged spider with nearest-neighbor hopping, i.e., $k = 2, S = 2, R = 1$, and a one-legged walker (normally we do not call such walkers spiders).

Before we examine the statistics, we illustrate one random trajectory of a two-legged spider on the test maze. Figure 3 shows how many times each chemical site was visited. The start and the large, branched dead end in the middle of the maze were the most heavily visited areas.

Fig. 3. A typical exploration trajectory. The number of visits to a site is shown by shading: darker sites were visited more times. Some unvisited substrates remain (blue dots).

---

[1] Thomas LaBean, personal communication, 2012.

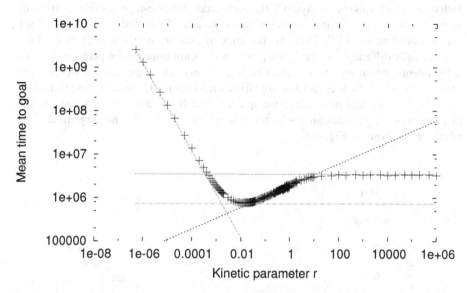

Fig. 4. Mean first passage time to the goal: two-legged spiders ($k = 2$). Note the log-log scale. The lines drawn in are visually estimated asymptotes (for < 0.001, $1200 \times r^{-1}$; for $0.05 < r < 10$, $1.9 \times 10^6 \times r^{0.25}$; and for $r \to \infty$, 3.5×10^6) and the minimum mean first passage time of 7.3×10^5, obtained at $r = 0.01$.

In Figure 4 we show the mean time to the goal for two-legged spiders as a function of the kinetic rate r. We vary the kinetic parameter r over 12 orders of magnitude. At $r = 1$ there is no distinction between substrates and products, and the motion degenerates into a bipedal random walk [7]. Reducing r, we introduce catalysis and make substrates "stickier", so a leg spends more time visiting a substrate. Although this may at first seem counterintuitive, this improves the overall performance, up to a critical value of $r \approx 0.01$. This is in agreement with our previous observations of the superdiffusive transient in 1D spiders [9]. At $r \approx 0.01$, the shortest mean time is obtained: if we are free to design the chemical kinetics of the legs for a fixed two-legged geometry, we should aim for this ratio. Below 0.01, the time is dominated by new substrate visits and the mean time to the goal scales as $1/x$. Usually it is assumed that $r \leqslant 1$, but it is possible (for spiders, or other walkers with different chemical structure) to have the products be stickier than substrates, $r > 1$. We simulated this case as well. Performance worsens as r is increased above 1, but it approaches an asymptote; as $r \to \infty$, substrates are immediately converted to products, and this has the effect of repelling the walker backwards. In the range $0.01 < r < 10$, we empirically estimate that the mean time to the goal scales as $r^{1/4}$; this dependence calls for further analytical studies.

To explore the utility of spiders as multivalent random walkers, we compare them with one-legged walkers. In Figure 5, the performance of one-legged spiders uniformly improves as r increases; this is similar to the results of the study of one-legged spiders in one dimension [8]. Thus, the presence of memory on the surface in the form of kinetically differing substrates and products does not improve the performance of a monovalent random walker. The plots answer a likely design question: if we have perfected a design for the legs and therefore fixed their chemical kinetics r, how should we decide how many legs to attach to the spider body? If the choice is between one and two legs, a two-legged design is advantageous whenever $r \lesssim 0.1$. The magnitude of the advantage is shown in Figure 6.

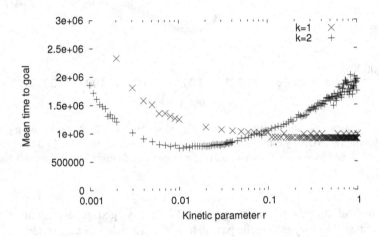

Fig. 5. Mean first passage time to the goal for one- and two-legged spiders, focusing on the (chemically most plausible) range of r values between 0.001 and 1

4.1 Search Time Distribution

The mean first passage times to the goal tell only one part of the story. The complete probability distribution of first passage times displays high variance. For two-legged spiders, and one particular value $r = 0.01$, we show a histogram of the distribution in Figure 7. The mode of the distribution is well below its mean. Similar fairly long tails obtain for other parameters. This will be important to keep in mind in the design of applications and laboratory experiments using molecular walkers, whenever the task is of a first-passage-time flavor.

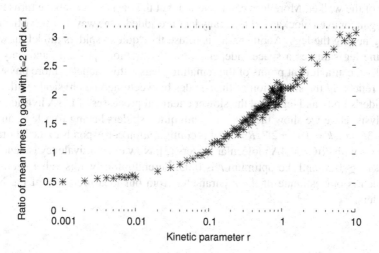

Fig. 6. Advantage of multivalency. Shown is the ratio of mean first passage time for two- and for one-legged spiders.

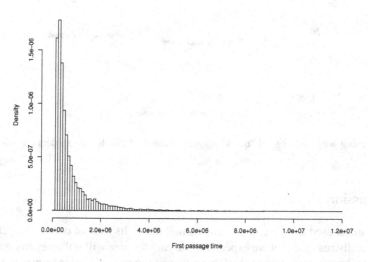

Fig. 7. Probability distribution of first passage times for $k = 2$ and $r = 0.01$. Histogram based on 14395 sample trajectories.

4.2   The Effect of the Gait

Note added in print. It is possible to improve search times further by changing the structure of the walker. More legs can be added, but the basic model above turns into a shuffling gait, or even blockage, if too many legs are added. One way to resolve the issue is by lengthening the legs. Another way is to use the "quick" spiders model, in which the moving leg samples a space independent of its previous position, and only constrained by the attachment points of the remaining legs—this model is more physically realistic, reflecting the separation of time-scales between the fast physical equilibrium of the spider's body and legs, and the slower chemical processes of DNA hybridization and catalysis. Here we show the outcome with quick spiders having four legs, and leg lengths 1.35, i.e., $k = 4, S = 2.7, R = \infty$; this configuration corresponds to the laboratory experiments with NICK 4.4A molecular spiders [3]. Now the multivalency is beneficial as soon as $r \lesssim 0.5$, and the optimum r is 0.05. Serendipitously, this value is close to 0.04, which is our estimate of the r parameter from our measurements of the NICK 4.4A spiders.

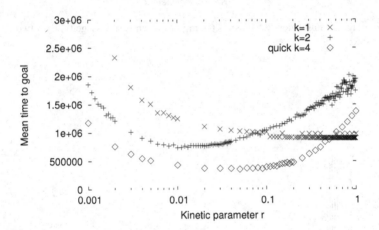

Fig. 8. Searching with four-legged "quick" spiders. (One- and two-legged spiders are left in for comparison.)

5   Discussion

The simulations used a fixed and relatively small maze. Its size, of course, was chosen to be physically realistic, but we expect that varying the size will influence the optimizing r values, because a larger or smaller portion of the superdiffusive transient will be exploited. It remains to be seen if, under laboratory conditions, it will be possible to exploit the superdiffusive transient or if, at the scale dictated by such conditions, the motion will be dominated by the diffusive asymptotics. Even in the latter case, however, the effective diffusion coefficient will be governed by the details of the gait; therefore, it will be useful to explore a variety of randomly generated mazes, including non-perfect ones (with loops), and differing track widths, to understand the interplay between maze geometry and the spider kinematic constraints such as k, S, and R.

Elsewhere we have studied the behavior of multiple molecular spiders released at a point source on an infinite 1D lattice [30]. Multiple spiders injected at the start and absorbed at the goal may search more efficiently than a single spider, and we intend to study this scenario as well.

A number of assumptions had to made to reduce the complex interactions of physical molecular spiders on DNA origami tiles, which have not yet been fully experimentally characterized and understood, to a tractable mathematical model amenable to efficient computer simulation and parameter space exploration. We will use finer-grain models [10] to refine these initial results.

Acknowledgments. I am grateful to Paul Krapivsky, Mark Olah, Oleg Semenov, and Milan Stojanovic for many inspirational conversations, and to Steven Taylor for the detailed kinetic characterization of molecular spiders' legs. I thank the conference reviewers for their incisive comments. This material is based upon work supported by the National Science Foundation under grants 0829896 and 1028238.

References

1. Nakagaki, T., Yamada, H., Tóth, A.: Maze-solving by an amoeboid organism. Nature 407, 470 (2000)
2. Nicolau, D.V., Nicolau Jr., D.V., Solana, G., Hanson, K.L., Filipponi, L., Wang, L., Lee, A.P.: Molecular motors-based micro- and nano-biocomputation devices. Microelectronic Engineering 83(4-9), 1582–1588 (2006)
3. Pei, R., Taylor, S.K., Stefanovic, D., Rudchenko, S., Mitchell, T.E., Stojanovic, M.N.: Behavior of polycatalytic assemblies in a substrate-displaying matrix. Journal of the American Chemical Society 128(39), 12693–12699 (2006)
4. Lund, K., Manzo, A.J., Dabby, N., Michelotti, N., Johnson-Buck, A., Nangreave, J., Taylor, S., Pei, R., Stojanovic, M.N., Walter, N.G., Winfree, E., Yan, H.: Molecular robots guided by prescriptive landscapes. Nature 465, 206–210 (2010)
5. Rothemund, P.W.K.: Folding DNA to create nanoscale shapes and patterns. Nature 440, 297–302 (2006)
6. Pinheiro, A.V., Han, D., Shih, W.M., Yan, H.: Challenges and opportunities for structural DNA nanotechnology. Nature Nanotechnology 6, 763–772 (2011)
7. Antal, T., Krapivsky, P.L., Mallick, K.: Molecular spiders in one dimension. Journal of Statistical Mechanics: Theory and Experiment 2007(08), P08027 (2007)
8. Antal, T., Krapivsky, P.L.: Molecular spiders with memory. Physical Review E 76(2), 021121 (2007)
9. Semenov, O., Olah, M.J., Stefanovic, D.: Mechanism of diffusive transport in molecular spider models. Physical Review E 83(2), 021117 (2011)
10. Olah, M.J., Stefanovic, D.: Multivalent Random Walkers — A Model for Deoxyribozyme Walkers. In: Cardelli, L., Shih, W. (eds.) DNA 17 2011. LNCS, vol. 6937, pp. 160–174. Springer, Heidelberg (2011)
11. Alberts, B., Johnson, A., Lewis, J., Raff, M., Roberts, K., Walter, P.: Molecular Biology of the Cell, 4th edn. Garland Science (2002)
12. Kolomeisky, A.B., Fisher, M.E.: Molecular motors: A theorist's perspective. Annual Review of Physical Chemistry 58, 675–695 (2007)

13. Bier, M.: The energetics, chemistry, and mechanics of a processive motor protein. BioSystems 93, 23–28 (2008)

14. Astumian, R.D.: Thermodynamics and kinetics of molecular motors. Biophysical Journal 98, 2401–2409 (2010)

15. Jamison, D.K., Driver, J.W., Rogers, A.R., Constantinou, P.E., Diehl, M.R.: Two kinesins transport cargo primarily via the action of one motor: Implications for intracellular transport. Biophysical Journal 99, 2967–2977 (2010)

16. Lipowsky, R., Beeg, J., Dimova, R., Klumpp, S., Müller, M.K.I.: Cooperative behavior of molecular motors: Cargo transport and traffic phenomena. Physica E 42, 649–661 (2010)

17. Driver, J.W., Jamison, D.K., Uppulury, K., Rogers, A.R., Kolomeisky, A.B., Diehl, M.R.: Productive cooperation among processive motors depends inversely on their mechanochemical efficiency. Biophysical Journal 101, 386–395 (2011)

18. Kay, E.R., Leigh, D.A., Zerbetto, F.: Synthetic molecular motors and mechanical machines. Angew. Chem. Int. Ed. 46, 72–191 (2007)

19. Hugel, T., Lumme, C.: Bio-inspired novel design principles for artificial molecular motors. Current Opinion in Biotechnology 21(5), 683–689 (2010)

20. Yurke, B., Turberfield, A.J., Mills Jr., A.P., Simmel, F.C., Neumann, J.L.: A DNA-fuelled molecular machine made of DNA. Nature 406, 605–608 (2000)

21. Shirai, Y., Osgood, A.J., Zhao, Y., Kelly, K.F., Tour, J.M.: Directional control in thermally driven single-molecule nanocars. Nano Letters 5(11), 2330–2334 (2005)

22. Tian, Y., He, Y., Chen, Y., Yin, P., Mao, C.: A DNAzyme that walks processively and autonomously along a one-dimensional track. Angew. Chem. Int. Ed. 44, 4355–4358 (2005)

23. Venkataraman, S., Dirks, R.M., Rothemund, P.W.K., Winfree, E., Pierce, N.A.: An autonomous polymerization motor powered by DNA hybridization. Nature Nanotechnology 2, 490–494 (2007)

24. Green, S.J., Bath, J., Turberfield, A.J.: Coordinated chemomechanical cycles: A mechanism for autonomous molecular motion. Physical Review Letters 101, 238101–+ (2008)

25. Omabegho, T., Sha, R., Seeman, N.C.: A bipedal DNA brownian motor with coordinated legs. Science 324, 67–71 (2009)

26. Bath, J., Green, S.J., Allen, K.E., Turberfield, A.J.: Mechanism for a directional, processive, and reversible DNA motor. Small 5(13), 1513–1516 (2009)

27. Gu, H., Chao, J., Xiao, S.J., Seeman, N.C.: A proximity-based programmable DNA nanoscale assembly line. Nature 465, 202–206 (2010)

28. Santoro, S.W., Joyce, G.F.: A general purpose RNA-cleaving DNA enzyme. Proceedings of the National Academy of Sciences of the USA (PNAS) 94, 4262–4266 (1997)

29. Samii, L., Linke, H., Zuckermann, M.J., Forde, N.R.: Biased motion and molecular motor properties of bipedal spiders. Physical Review E 81(2), 021106–+ (2010)

30. Semenov, O., Olah, M.J., Stefanovic, D.: Multiple Molecular Spiders with a Single Localized Source—The One-Dimensional Case. In: Cardelli, L., Shih, W. (eds.) DNA 17. LNCS, vol. 6937, pp. 204–216. Springer, Heidelberg (2011)

31. Samii, L., Blab, G.A., Bromley, E.H.C., Linke, H., Curmi, P.M.G., Zuckermann, M.J., Forde, N.R.: Time-dependent motor properties of multipedal molecular spiders. Phys. Rev. E 84, 031111 (2011)

32. Bortz, A.B., Kalos, M.H., Lebowitz, J.L.: A new algorithm for Monte Carlo simulation of Ising spin systems. Journal of Computational Physics 17(1), 10–18 (1975)

Author Index